"Modern New Testament scholars have sometimes missed or even denied what seemed obvious to the early fathers of the church—namely that the figure of Adam, and not merely the shadow of Israel, serves as the ultimate background to the Gospel narratives. In *The Last Adam* Brandon Crowe helps to right this wrong in a scholarly, comprehensive, readable, and indeed theologically thrilling way. Here is a work of carefully argued biblical scholarship that also makes a significant contribution to the work of systematic theologians. In addition it satisfies a great *desideratum* for ministers of the gospel and teachers: a resource book filled with a cornucopia of good things that will stimulate their thinking and enrich their preaching and teaching."

—**Sinclair B. Ferguson**, Redeemer Seminary

"Brandon Crowe continues to produce clearly written and thoughtful biblical scholarship that is consciously rooted in the Reformed theological tradition. This book is no exception, and I heartily agree with its goal—to show that Jesus's obedient *life* (not just his death) as explicated in the Gospels matters. Crowe's emphasis on Jesus as the last Adam is an important contribution to a theological reading of the Gospels."

—**Jonathan Pennington**, Southern Baptist Theological Seminary

The Last Adam

A THEOLOGY of the OBEDIENT LIFE of JESUS in the GOSPELS

BRANDON D. CROWE

B
Baker Academic
a division of Baker Publishing Group
Grand Rapids, Michigan

© 2017 by Brandon D. Crowe

Published by Baker Academic
a division of Baker Publishing Group
P.O. Box 6287, Grand Rapids, MI 49516-6287
www.bakeracademic.com

Printed in the United States of America

Library of Congress Cataloging-in-Publication Data
Names: Crowe, Brandon D., author.
Title: The last Adam : a theology of the obedient life of Jesus in the Gospels / Brandon D. Crowe.
Description: Grand Rapids, MI : Baker Academic, 2017. | Includes bibliographical references and
    index.
Identifiers: LCCN 2016032073 | ISBN 9780801096266 (pbk.)
Subjects: LCSH: Jesus Christ—Person and offices—Biblical teaching. | Bible. Gospels—Theology. |
    Bible. Gospels—Criticism, interpretation, etc. | Adam (Biblical figure) | Typology (Theology)
Classification: LCC BT203 .C77 2017 | DDC 232—dc23
LC record available at https://lccn.loc.gov/2016032073

Unless otherwise indicated, all translations of Scripture are those of the author.

In keeping with biblical principles of creation stewardship, Baker Publishing Group advocates the responsible use of our natural resources. As a member of the Green Press Initiative, our company uses recycled paper when possible. The text paper of this book is composed in part of post-consumer waste.

For Simeon Christopher

καὶ [Συμεὼν] ἐδέξατο αὐτὸ εἰς τὰς ἀγκάλας καὶ
εὐλόγησεν τὸν θεὸν καὶ εἶπεν . . .
εἶδον οἱ ὀφθαλμοί μου τὸ σωτήριόν σου,
ὃ ἡτοίμασας κατὰ πρόσωπον πάντων τῶν λαῶν,
φῶς εἰς ἀποκάλυψιν ἐθνῶν
καὶ δόξαν λαοῦ σου Ἰσραήλ.

And Simeon took [Jesus] in his arms and blessed God and said . . .
"My eyes have seen your salvation,
Which you have prepared in the presence of all peoples;
A light for revelation to the gentiles
And the glory of your people, Israel."
Luke 2:28, 30–32

May you be borne up by Christ, that you may bear him to others.

How has Christ abolished sin, banished the separation between us and God, and acquired righteousness to render God favorable and kindly toward us? . . . He has achieved this for us by the whole course of his obedience.

—John Calvin, *Institutes of the Christian Religion* 2.16.5

Contents

Preface

My aim in this volume is to set forth the soteriological significance of the life of Jesus in the Gospels. I have written the kind of book that I would like to read, in answer to the question that I have often asked: what is Jesus doing in the Gospels? This is primarily an exegetical study, but I have not shied away from engaging with and gleaning from historical and systematic theology where relevant. Though I have written this book largely to answer my own questions, I hope it will also be helpful and accessible to anyone interested in the Jesus of the Gospels. It is particularly my desire that professors, pastors, students, and all interested exegetes will be stimulated by this study to reflect further on the life of Jesus for their various contexts. What follows is by no means the final word but is my effort to make a contribution to ongoing discussions relating to the theology and Christology of the Gospel narratives.

Writing this book has been a labor of love and is the result of a number of years of reflection, conversation, and learning from many sources. It is not possible to thank everyone who has helped my own understanding or who has provided feedback in some form. Nevertheless, it seems appropriate to thank the following people specifically. First, thanks to the board of trustees, faculty, administration, and staff (especially the tireless efforts of the Montgomery Library staff) of Westminster Theological Seminary for the resources, assistance, and support that have aided in the completion of this project. Special thanks to the board of trustees and faculty for granting a Professional Advancement Leave for the first half of 2015, which allowed me to complete the bulk of this manuscript. My colleagues in the New Testament Department, Greg Beale and Vern Poythress, are continually sources of wisdom and encouragement, and I am grateful for their collegiality. Second, thanks to all those who have taken the time to provide more formal feedback on early drafts of the manuscript, and those who have contributed by way of conversation, including Andrew Abernethy, Bill Fullilove, Richard Gaffin, Josh Leim, Jonathan Pennington, Stephen Presley, Scott Swain, Lane Tipton, and Carlton Wynne. Any shortcomings remain my own. Thanks also to faculty assistants Dylan Bailey, David Barry, Charles Williams, and Jason Yuh for research and assistance of various sorts. Third, thanks to James Ernest, who first helped get this project off the ground at Baker Academic, along with Bryan Dyer and the entire professional team at Baker Academic for capably shepherding this volume through to completion.

Finally, singular thanks goes to my family. My wife Cheryl is a source of constant encouragement and is the crown of her husband (Prov. 12:4), and our four children manifest the joie de vivre in all sorts of creative ways. Additionally, the continued love and support of my parents and parents-in-law is a great blessing. I dedicate this volume to our second child, Simeon Christopher, whose name is inspired by the speaker of the Nunc Dimittis in Luke 2. For Simeon, to hold Jesus was to behold and embrace salvation, which is a father's highest prayer for his children.

Abbreviations

| 1–3 John | 1–3 John | | Rev. | Revelation |
| Jude | Jude | | | |

General

b.	Babylonian Talmud		frag.	fragment
B	Codex Vaticanus		LXX	Septuagint
ca.	circa		m.	Mishnah
cf.	*confer*, compare		MT	Masoretic Text
chap(s).	chapter(s)		NT	New Testament
esp.	especially		OT	Old Testament
ET	English translation		par(r).	parallel(s)
EVV	English versions		v(v).	verse(s)
fl.	*floruit*, flourished		y.	Jerusalem Talmud

Bible Versions

CEB	Common English Bible		MT	Masoretic Text
ESV	English Standard Version		NASB	New American Standard Bible
HCSB	Holman Christian Standard Bible		NIV	New International Version
			NRSV	New Revised Standard Version
KJV	King James Version		OG	Old Greek
LXX	Septuagint			

Apocrypha and Septuagint

| 2 Esd. | 2 Esdras | | Wis. | Wisdom of Solomon |
| Sir. | Sirach/Ecclesiasticus | | | |

Dead Sea Scrolls and Related Literature

1QH[a]	Thanksgiving Hymns		4Q504	Words of the Luminaries
1QM	War Scroll		4Q521	Messianic Apocalypse
1QS	Rule of the Community		4QDeut[q]	4QDeuteronomy[q]
4Q167	4QpHos[b]		11Q13	Melchizedek
4Q246	Apocryphon of Daniel		11QT[a]	Temple Scroll[a]
4Q285	Sefer Hamilḥamah		CD	Damascus Document

Old Testament Pseudepigrapha

Apoc. Adam	*Apocalypse of Adam*		*Jub.*	*Jubilees*
Apoc. Mos.	*Apocalypse of Moses*		*LAE*	*Life of Adam and Eve*
2 Bar.	*2 Baruch*		*Pss. Sol.*	*Psalms of Solomon*
Cav. Tr.	*Cave of Treasures*		*Ques. Ezra*	*Questions of Ezra*
1 En.	*1 Enoch*		*Sib. Or.*	*Sibylline Oracles*
2 En.	*2 Enoch*		*T. Ab.*	*Testament of Abraham*
4 Ezra	*4 Ezra*		*T. Levi*	*Testament of Levi*
6 Ezra	*6 Ezra*		*T. Mos.*	*Testament of Moses*

| T. Naph. | Testament of Naphtali | T. Sol. | Testament of Solomon |
| T. Sim. | Testament of Simeon | | |

Mishnah and Talmud Tractates

Ḥag.	Ḥagigah	Nid.	Niddah
Mak.	Makkot	Qidd.	Qiddušin
Neg.	Nega'im	Zabim	Zabim

Other Rabbinic Works

Deut. Rab.	Deuteronomy Rabbah	Pesiq. Rab.	Pesiqta Rabbati
Gen. Rab.	Genesis Rabbah	Pirqe R. El.	Pirqe Rabbi Eliezer
Mek. Exod.	Mekilta Exodus	Sipre	Sipre
Num. Rab.	Numbers Rabbah		

Apostolic Fathers

| Diogn. | Epistle to Diognetus | Ign. Magn. | Ignatius, To the |
| Ign. Eph. | Ignatius, To the Ephesians | | Magnesians |

Other Greek and Latin Works

Athanasius of Alexandria

C. Ar.	Orationes contra Arianos
Ep. Aeg. Lib.	Epistula ad episcopos Aegypti et Libyae
Inc.	De incarnatione

Augustus (Roman emperor)

| Res gest. divi Aug. | Res gestae divi Augusti |

John Calvin

| Inst. | Institutio christianae religionis |

Eusebius of Caesarea

| Hist. eccl. | Historia ecclesiastica |

Homer

| Il. | Ilias |

Irenaeus

| Epid. | Epideixis tou apostolikou kērygmatos (Demonstration of the Apostolic Preaching) |
| Haer. | Adversus haereses (Against Heresies) |

Jerome

| Comm. Matt. | Commentariorum in Matthaeum libri IV |
| Epist. | Epistulae |

John Chrysostom

| Hom. Jo. | Homiliae in Joannem |

Josephus

| Ant. | Jewish Antiquities |
| J.W. | Jewish War |

Justin

| Dial. | Dialogus cum Tryphone |

Philo

Leg.	Legum allegoriae
Opif.	De opificio mundi
QG	Quaestiones et solutiones in Genesin
Virt.	De virtutibus

Tertullian		*Francis Turretin*	
Carn. Chr.	*De carne Christi*	*Inst.*	*Institutio theologiae elencticae*

Modern Works

AB	Anchor Bible
ABRL	Anchor Bible Reference Library
ACCS	Ancient Christian Commentary on Scripture
ACT	Ancient Christian Texts
ANF	*The Ante-Nicene Fathers.* Edited by Alexander Roberts and James Donaldson. 1885–1887. 10 vols. Reprint, Peabody, MA: Hendrickson, 1994
ANZK	Archiv für neutestamentliche Zeitgeschichte und Kulturkunde
ArBib	The Aramaic Bible
ASBT	Acadia Studies in Bible and Theology
ATANT	Abhandlungen zur Theologie des Alten und Neuen Testaments
AYB	Anchor Yale Bible
BBET	Beiträge zur biblischen Exegese und Theologie
BBR	*Bulletin for Biblical Research*
BDAG	W. Bauer, F. W. Danker, W. F. Arndt, and F. W. Gingrich. *Greek-English Lexicon of the New Testament and Other Early Christian Literature.* 3rd ed. Chicago: University of Chicago Press, 1999
BDF	Friedrich Blass, Albert Debrunner, and Robert W. Funk. *A Greek Grammar of the New Testament and Other Early Christian Literature.* Chicago: University of Chicago Press, 1961
BECNT	Baker Exegetical Commentary on the New Testament
BGBE	Beiträge zur Geschichte der biblischen Exegese
BHQ	*Biblia Hebraica Quinta.* Edited by Adrian Schenker et al. Stuttgart: Deutsche Bibelgesellschaft, 2004–
Bib	*Biblica*
BibAnChr	Bible in Ancient Christianity
BMSEC	Baylor–Mohr Siebeck Studies in Early Christianity
BRS	Biblical Resource Series
BST	The Bible Speaks Today
BTB	*Biblical Theology Bulletin*
BTNT	Biblical Theology of the New Testament
BZ	*Biblische Zeitschrift*
BZNW	Beihefte zur Zeitschrift für die neutestamentliche Wissenschaft
CAHQ	Christian Answers to Hard Questions
CBQ	*Catholic Biblical Quarterly*
CC	Cascade Companions
CCT	Contours of Christian Theology
CGTC	Cambridge Greek Testament Commentary
CM	Christianity in the Making
CNT	Commentaire du Nouveau Testament
COQG	Christian Origins and the Question of God
CSS	Cistercian Studies Series
CTQ	*Concordia Theological Quarterly*

CurTM	Currents in Theology and Mission
DCH	Dictionary of Classical Hebrew. Edited by David J. A. Clines. 9 vols. Sheffield: Sheffield Phoenix, 1993–2014
DCLS	Deuterocanonical and Cognate Literature Studies
DJD	Discoveries in the Judaean Desert
DJG	Dictionary of Jesus and the Gospels. Edited by Joel B. Green and Scot McKnight. Downers Grove, IL: InterVarsity, 1992
EHS.T	Europäische Hochschulschriften: Reihe 23, Theologie
EKKNT	Evangelisch-katholischer Kommentar zum Neuen Testament
EuroJTh	European Journal of Theology
ExpTim	Expository Times
FRLANT	Forschungen zur Religion und Literatur des Alten und Neuen Testaments
FTS	Freiburger theologische Studien
GBSNT	Guides to Biblical Scholarship: New Testament Series
GH	Gorgias Handbooks
HALOT	The Hebrew and Aramaic Lexicon of the Old Testament. Ludwig Koehler, Walter Baumgartner, and Johann J. Stamm. Translated and edited under the supervision of Mervyn E. J. Richardson. 4 vols. Leiden: Brill, 1994–1999
HBT	Horizons in Biblical Theology
HThKNT	Herders Theologischer Kommentar zum Neuen Testament
HTR	Harvard Theological Review
HvTSt	Hervormde teologiese studies
IBHS	An Introduction to Biblical Hebrew Syntax. Bruce K. Waltke and Michael O'Connor. Winona Lake, IN: Eisenbrauns, 1990
ICC	International Critical Commentary
JBL	Journal of Biblical Literature
JETS	Journal of the Evangelical Theological Society
JSJSup	Supplements to the Journal for the Study of Judaism
JSNT	Journal for the Study of the New Testament
JSNTSup	Journal for the Study of the New Testament Supplement Series
JSOTSup	Journal for the Study of the Old Testament Supplement Series
JSP	Journal for the Study of the Pseudepigrapha
JSPSup	Journal for the Study of the Pseudepigrapha Supplement Series
JTISup	Journal of Theological Interpretation, Supplements
JTS	Journal of Theological Studies
K&D	Carl Friedrich Keil and Franz Delitzsch. Biblical Commentary on the Old Testament. Translated by James Martin et al. 25 vols. Edinburgh, 1857–1878. Repr., 10 vols., Peabody, MA: Hendrickson, 1996
KBOST	Koinonia: Beiträge zur ökumenischen Spiritualität und Theologie
LCC	Library of Christian Classics
LHBOTS	The Library of Hebrew Bible/Old Testament Studies
LNTS	The Library of New Testament Studies
LTP	Laval théologique et philosophique
MdB	Le Monde de la Bible
MST	Mediaeval Sources in Translation
NAC	New American Commentary

NACSBT	New American Commentary Studies in Bible & Theology
NIBCNT	New International Biblical Commentary on the New Testament
NIBCOT	New International Biblical Commentary on the Old Testament
NICNT	New International Commentary on the New Testament
NICOT	New International Commentary on the Old Testament
NIGTC	New International Greek Testament Commentary
NIVAC	NIV Application Commentary
NovT	*Novum Testamentum*
NovTSup	Supplements to Novum Testamentum
NPNF[1]	*The Nicene and Post-Nicene Fathers*, Series 1. Edited by Philip Schaff. 1886–89. 14 vols. Reprint, Peabody, MA: Hendrickson, 1994
NPNF[2]	*The Nicene and Post-Nicene Fathers*, Series 2. Edited by Philip Schaff and Henry Wace. 1890–1900. 14 vols. Reprint, Peabody, MA: Hendrickson, 1994
NSBT	New Studies in Biblical Theology
NTL	New Testament Library
NTS	*New Testament Studies*
NTTSD	New Testament Tools, Studies, and Documents
OTL	Old Testament Library
OTP	*Old Testament Pseudepigrapha*. Edited by James H. Charlesworth. 2 vols. Anchor Bible Reference Library. Garden City, NY: Doubleday, 1983, 1985
PC	Proclamation Commentaries
PNTC	Pillar New Testament Commentary
PPS	Popular Patristics Series
Presb	*Presbyterion*
ProEccl	*Pro Ecclesia*
PRR	*Presbyterian and Reformed Review*
PRSt	*Perspectives in Religious Studies*
RB	*Revue biblique*
REC	Reformed Expository Commentary
RHT	Reformed Historical Theology
SBET	*Scottish Bulletin of Evangelical Theology*
SBT	Studies in Biblical Theology
ScRel	*Sciences religieuses*
SNTSMS	Society for New Testament Studies Monograph Series
SNTW	Studies of the New Testament and Its World
ST	*Studia Theologica*
StPatr	Studia Patristica
Str-B	Hermann L. Strack and Paul Billerbeck. *Kommentar zum Neuen Testament aus Talmud und Midrasch*. 6 vols. Munich, 1922–1961
TBC	Torch Bible Commentaries
TBT	*The Bible Today*
TDNT	*Theological Dictionary of the New Testament*. Edited by Gerhard Kittel and Gerhard Friedrich. Translated by Geoffrey W. Bromiley. 10 vols. Grand Rapids: Eerdmans, 1964–1976
TEG	Traditio Exegetica Graeca
TL	A Theology of Lordship

TNTC	Tyndale New Testament Commentaries
TOTC	Tyndale Old Testament Commentaries
TS	*Theological Studies*
TWOT	*Theological Wordbook of the Old Testament*. Edited by R. Laird Harris, Gleason L. Archer Jr., and Bruce K. Waltke. 2 vols. Chicago: Moody Press, 1980
TynBul	*Tyndale Bulletin*
VC	*Vigiliae Christianae*
VSI	A Very Short Introduction
VTSup	Supplements to Vetus Testamentum
WBC	Word Biblical Commentary
WTJ	*Westminster Theological Journal*
WUNT	Wissenschaftliche Untersuchungen zum Neuen Testament
WW	*Word and World*
ZAW	*Zeitschrift für die alttestamentliche Wissenschaft*
ZECNT	Zondervan Exegetical Commentary on the New Testament
ZNW	*Zeitschrift für die neutestamentliche Wissenschaft und die Kunde der älteren Kirche*

A Tale of Two Adams in the History
of Interpretation

A Crucial Question

What is the purpose and significance of the life and ministry of Jesus in the Gospels? At one level, this may seem like an obvious question. The Gospels[1] are all about Jesus. Moreover, given the structure of each of the four Gospels, it is difficult to miss the central role played by the Passion Narratives. And yet there is much more in the Gospels beyond the Passion Narratives. Jesus is amazingly active. He preaches, heals, exorcises, prays, rebukes, forgives, calls, authorizes, confounds, challenges, rejoices, weeps, blesses, curses, prophesies, and more. In addition, he consistently draws attention to himself as he does these things.

And then there are the Christmas stories (that is, the infancy narratives). These are among the more familiar parts of the Gospels in today's culture. But what is the relationship between the infancy narratives and salvation?[2] Jesus

---

1. I will be working from the four canonical Gospels. This is not the place to argue for the legitimacy of the four canonical Gospels, but these Gospels have the greatest claim to being the earliest and most widely used Gospels in the early church. See further Charles E. Hill, *Who Chose the Gospels? Probing the Great Gospel Conspiracy* (Oxford: Oxford University Press, 2010).

2. *Salvation* is difficult to define concisely, since it is richly multifaceted, entailing at once various dimensions, which would take many hundreds of pages to tease out sufficiently. However,

1

appears to be quite passive lying in the manger as he is adored by shepherds, and we do not find him to be very active when the magi come and prostrate themselves before him in Matthew 2. But can we look even to the infancy of Jesus and say that Jesus was somehow already beginning to *accomplish* something of significance? To ask this question is to lead us back to the driving question of this volume, since Jesus did not bypass infancy, childhood, adolescence, or adulthood on his way to the cross. Why? What was it about the life of Jesus that was necessary for salvation—from the manger to the cross and everything in between?[3] Do the Evangelists themselves give us any indications that this is a question they have in view as they write their Gospels? I will argue that they do.

In this volume I will argue that we find a shared perspective among the diversity of the four Gospels that the obedient life of Jesus—in its entirety—is vicarious and salvific in character.[4] More specifically, I will argue that Jesus is portrayed in the Gospels as the last Adam whose obedience is necessary for God's people to experience the blessings of salvation. In pursuit of this thesis, I will consider what the Gospels themselves say about the lifelong obedience of Jesus, which concomitantly involves considering how Jesus's life and ministry are related to his passion. By concentrating on the Gospels I do not intend to imply that these are the only documents in the New Testament that speak to this issue. I do believe, however, that a focus on the Gospels qua Gospels is important because of the way they narrate the life of Jesus, and because their testimony to the significance of Jesus's life for salvation has often not been given sufficient attention. Thus a sub-aim of this book is to help us read and interpret the Gospels theologically.

I will explain more of my method and limitations below. At this juncture I would like to linger over the need to identify the theological significance of the life of Jesus *from the Gospels*. In recent years many have emphasized the importance of the Gospels' theological contributions, along with the need to articulate more fully the task and mission of Jesus in accord with how we approach the Gospels. This concern is evident in Jürgen Moltmann's *The Way of Jesus Christ*, where Moltmann traces the messianic mission of Christ in the Gospels and suggests that the standard creeds, such as the Apostles' Creed

---

by way of shorthand I will consider salvation to be deliverance from sin unto everlasting life in fellowship with the Triune God. For fuller studies, see John Murray, *Redemption Accomplished and Applied* (Grand Rapids: Eerdmans, 1955); Herman Bavinck, *Reformed Dogmatics*, ed. John Bolt, trans. John Vriend, 4 vols. (Grand Rapids: Baker Academic, 2003–8), esp. vols. 3–4.

3. N. T. Wright asks a similar question in *How God Became King: The Forgotten Story of the Gospels* (San Francisco: HarperOne, 2012), 3, 8.

4. See similarly, among others, Robert Letham, *The Work of Christ*, CCT (Downers Grove, IL: IVP Academic, 1993), 113–17; Bavinck, *Reformed Dogmatics*, 3:378–80, 405.

and Nicene Creed, would have done well to fill in the details between "born of the Virgin Mary / was made man" and "suffered under Pontius Pilate."[5]

An even more relevant volume is N. T. Wright's *Jesus and the Victory of God*. Wright in his typically provocative way suggests that the Reformers have never had a great answer to the question "Why did Jesus live?" and "orthodoxy, represented by much popular preaching and writing, has had no clear idea of the purpose of Jesus' ministry."[6] Wright proceeds with his answer to the perceived dilemma, arguing for a prophetic, suffering-servant role for Jesus the Messiah, who announces, enacts, and embodies the end of exile, the defeat of evil, and Yahweh's returning to Zion.[7]

Wright's assessment of the task of Jesus places Jesus firmly within the context of Israel's history. His approach has been influential, and he continues to popularize it. In the more recent *How God Became King* he refers to the question of "Why did Jesus live?" as the "puzzle of a lifetime" and warns us against lopping off *de facto* the four Gospels from the front of the New Testament canon.[8] I concur with the question Wright is asking, and I have been stimulated by his writings. Yet I believe there is more to be said.

Another example is the recent work of Scot McKnight, who wants to show us that the *gospel* is in *the Gospels*.[9] McKnight, much like Wright, emphasizes that the story of Israel is resolved in the person of Jesus in a saving way.[10] Further, we find the gospel in the Gospels because "the gospel is the saving Story of Jesus completing Israel's Story, and Jesus clearly set himself at the center of God's saving plan for Israel."[11] McKnight correctly observes that the good news has a clear focus on Jesus.[12] Not only in his more popular work but also in a recent essay, McKnight explores the story of Jesus's life in the context of Israel and affirms that the story of Jesus is a *saving* story. For McKnight, the Gospel of Matthew is gospel because Jesus releases his people from the burden of sin in the inner conscience *and* because he liberates in a more comprehensive manner (i.e., from oppressing burdens).[13] But can we still say

---

5. Jürgen Moltmann, *The Way of Jesus Christ: Christology in Messianic Dimensions*, trans. Margaret Kohl (Minneapolis: Fortress, 1993), 69–70, 73–150.

6. Wright, *Jesus and the Victory of God*, COQG 2 (Minneapolis: Fortress, 1996), 14.

7. Ibid., 481, 593.

8. See Wright, *How God Became King*, 9.

9. Scot McKnight, *The King Jesus Gospel: The Original Good News Revisited* (Grand Rapids: Zondervan, 2011).

10. Ibid., 79, 82–83. McKnight also cites Martin Hengel and I. H. Marshall to this end (ibid., 83).

11. Ibid., 111.

12. Ibid., 92–93.

13. Scot McKnight, "Matthew as 'Gospel,'" in *Jesus, Matthew's Gospel and Early Christianity: Studies in Memory of Graham N. Stanton*, ed. Daniel M. Gurtner, Joel Willitts, and Richard A. Burridge, LNTS 435 (London: T&T Clark, 2011), 59–75.

more about how the holistic story of Jesus's life is a *saving* story? McKnight rightly points to the movement toward the cross in the Gospels,[14] along with the more integrated means by which Jesus bears our burdens in accord with Isaiah 53 in Matthew 8:16–17.[15] Even still, I believe there are further connections between the saving character of Jesus's life and his death to be explored.

Close to the time McKnight's *King Jesus Gospel* appeared, Darrell Bock released *Recovering the Real Lost Gospel*, in which he argues that to understand the New Testament gospel we must recognize that Jesus "brought the good news that God's promised rule of deliverance had arrived."[16] Further, Bock notes that Jesus's dying for sin is not the whole gospel, but the cross (at least as we find it in 1 Cor.) "functions as a hub and a synecdoche for all that Jesus' work brings."[17] Although neither Bock's *Recovering the Real Lost Gospel* nor McKnight's *King Jesus Gospel* is concerned exclusively with the message of the Gospels, both acknowledge the need to understand the message pertaining to the work of Christ more holistically, in a way that considers more than just the cross, and these holistic approaches have implications for how we read the Gospels.

A more sustained focus on the Gospels is found in Jonathan Pennington's *Reading the Gospels Wisely*. As he considers the meaning of *euangelion* in the Gospels, Pennington first observes that the gospel originated as an oral message about Jesus Christ, including especially who he was and what he accomplished in his life, death, and resurrection.[18] It is instructive that Pennington includes much more than just the death of Christ in this introductory definition. As he considers the definition of *euangelion* in the Gospels, Pennington observes the connection between the gospel and the kingdom and focuses on the good news of the return of God's restorative reign.[19] Thus kingship is front and center in the good news that "your God reigns" (Isa. 52:7). Additionally, Pennington helpfully observes that the message of the forgiveness of sins cannot be separated from the kingdom message of Jesus.[20] There is, in other words, an intricate connection between the good news of God's kingly reign and the good news of forgiveness of sins, which must be related to the Gospels as thoroughly christological documents. Pennington

14. McKnight, *King Jesus Gospel*, 85.

15. McKnight, "Matthew as 'Gospel,'" 71.

16. Darrell L. Bock, *Recovering the Real Lost Gospel: Reclaiming the Gospel as Good News* (Nashville: B&H, 2010), 1.

17. Ibid., 3–4.

18. Jonathan T. Pennington, *Reading the Gospels Wisely: A Narrative and Theological Introduction* (Grand Rapids: Baker Academic, 2012), 5.

19. Ibid., 10–16.

20. Ibid., 16 and 16n39.

brings into sharp focus the need to define the good news of the life of Jesus from the Gospels in light of the current scholarly conversation about the role of Israel and also the realization that the Gospels are centrally important *narratives* about Jesus.[21] These are important observations, and we will consider the narrative Christology of the Gospels throughout this study.

One final recent example is Michael Bird's *Evangelical Theology*. A distinctive aspect of this volume is the thoroughgoing focus on the evangel, which leads Bird to focus significantly on the life and ministry of Jesus. In Bird's estimation, the life of Jesus does not figure prominently in evangelical theology; many are content with Jesus being born of a virgin and dying as a sinless sacrifice for sin.[22] In this Bird echoes Wright's sentiment that a number of standard doctrinal formulations do not sufficiently reference the life and teaching of Jesus. Bird poses an important question: "what is the theological significance of [Jesus's] life and teaching?"[23] He proceeds to consider the significance of these in accord with such topics as Jesus's messianic anointing, miracles, parables, fulfillment of Old Testament hopes for Israel, and especially the inauguration of the kingdom of God.[24] Bird's desire to focus on the work of Jesus on these points is to be commended. His articulation of the purpose of Jesus's ministry as God becoming king of Israel in Jesus's work stands in clear continuity with the view of Wright noted above. Although I agree that due attention needs to be given to the life of Jesus, I am not convinced that Christian theology (or Reformed theology, more specifically) has been quite as silent on this point as Bird suggests. Nor does the history of exegesis lack the categories to deal with the life of Jesus in the Gospels. I do think Bird, Moltmann, Wright, McKnight, and others are correct that the life of Jesus is not always emphasized in theological discourse. Nevertheless, we can find wisdom from previous generations that will help us today understand and articulate the saving significance of Jesus's life and ministry in the Gospels.

I am therefore encouraged by the conversation that is under way. Some points of fairly wide consensus seem to be developing. Israel's story as we find it in Scripture must provide our framework for understanding Jesus's actions, and those actions must be understood in the context of each Gospel's narrative structure. In the Gospels we find Jesus coming in the fullness of time as Israel's messianic king, bringing the already/not-yet kingdom of God, and fulfilling the eschatological hopes of the prophets. Wright even avers that

21. Ibid., 35.
22. Michael F. Bird, *Evangelical Theology: A Biblical and Systematic Introduction* (Grand Rapids: Zondervan, 2013), 357.
23. Ibid.
24. Ibid., 375–82.

Jesus's whole life is gospel.[25] These are important advancements over some of the more fragmented approaches of form criticism from the first half of the twentieth century. Yet more needs to be said about what we mean. *How* and *why* is the life of Jesus significant as narrated in the Gospels and for the gospel? Why is there such a strong focus on the *obedience* of Jesus throughout all four Gospels?[26] How does the *life* of Jesus relate to the kingdom of God? Why does Jesus so often speak of himself? Is there something about the obedience of the king that lends efficacy to his death on the cross?

In this book I desire to give more attention to questions relating to the saving significance of the life of Jesus in the Gospels, and I will do so through the lens of Christ as the last Adam. By so doing, I hope to help answer the question, how does Jesus's lifelong obedience in the Gospels relate to the salvation of his people?

A Practical Question

As the authors canvassed above have often argued, this debate is not merely academic; it has important implications for the church. By arguing for Jesus as the obedient last Adam in the Gospels, I hope also to illuminate the role of the non–Passion Narrative portions of the Gospels in order to support the preaching of the Gospels. Martin Kähler (in)famously referred to the Gospels as Passion Narratives with extended introductions.[27] This identification is debatable, but his comments point us to a legitimate question: how do pastors preach from the so-called extended introductions in a way that does justice to the Passion Narratives yet also recognizes that earlier portions of the Gospels have something vitally important to say about how Jesus saves? Historically, too many have seen Jesus as merely providing an inspiring example or an encouragement for humanity to reach its highest potential.[28] Such readings vastly underestimate the significance of Jesus in the Gospels.[29] For others, perhaps following in the spirit of Kähler's statement, the beginning chapters

---

25. Wright, *Jesus*, xiv.

26. I will defend this view in following chapters.

27. Martin Kähler, *The So-Called Historical Jesus and the Historic, Biblical Christ*, trans. Carl E. Braaten (Philadelphia: Fortress, 1964), 80n11.

28. See the critique of the "moral lives of Jesus" in Albert Schweitzer, *The Quest of the Historical Jesus: A Critical Study of Its Progress from Reimarus to Wrede*, trans. W. Montgomery (New York: MacMillan, 1968). See also James D. G. Dunn, *Jesus Remembered*, CM 1 (Grand Rapids: Eerdmans, 2003), 34–39.

29. However, I do not deny there is a place for imitation, when understood rightly. See Jason B. Hood, *Imitating God in Christ: Recapturing a Biblical Pattern* (Downers Grove, IL: IVP Academic, 2013); Pennington, *Reading the Gospels Wisely*, 161–62; C. D. "Jimmy" Agan III, *The*

of the (Synoptic) Gospels—featuring various sayings, miracles, narratives, and so forth—demonstrate the authority of Jesus but are secondary to the core message of the cross.[30] Yet if most Gospel passages should be considered merely as extended introductions, we must admit that these are richly nuanced and wide-ranging introductions. Indeed, we must admit that these "introductions" are actually more extensive than the Passion Narratives themselves.[31]

There must be a way to navigate between the Scylla of the merely exemplary, moralistic life of Jesus and the Charybdis of Jesus's life as only a preparatory "warm-up" for the Passion Narratives. To this end, focusing on Christ as the last Adam in the Gospels offers a viable way forward. This approach is able to take into account what recent scholarship has been saying about the centrality of the kingdom of God, while also recognizing the clear importance of the Passion Narratives. Understanding Christ as the last Adam need not discount the model of righteousness that Christ provides, but first recognizes the obedience of Jesus as a *representative* figure. Further supporting this approach are the rich and varied Christian exegetical and theological traditions relating Adam to Christ.

Two Adams in the History of Interpretation

We turn now to consider some voices from previous generations, specifically related to the pervasive Adam-Christ parallel.[32] Though the following examples are not all from the Gospels, many are, and these approaches may prove insightful for reading the Gospels today. Among the earliest church fathers, Irenaeus (ca. 130–ca. 202) is well known for having a theology of recapitulation in which Jesus's obedience overcomes the disobedience of Adam.[33] Irenaeus

---

Imitation of Christ in the Gospel of Luke: Growing in Christlike Love for God and Neighbor (Phillipsburg, NJ: P&R, 2014).

30. E.g., Rudolf Bultmann, *Theology of the New Testament*, trans. Kendrick Grobel, 2 vols. (New York: Scribner, 1951–55), 1:86.

31. Kähler himself recognized he was putting the matter "somewhat provocatively," as he distanced himself from those who focused on the supposed development of Jesus's consciousness before the passion (*So-Called Historical Jesus*, 80n11). Yet I do not agree with Kähler when he suggests that the emphasis in the "extended introductions" is not so much on *what* happened as the *who* and *how* of his actions (ibid., 81). Instead, the *what* of the so-called extended introductions is crucially important.

32. See also Letham, *Work of Christ*, 24–37. I use the term "Adam-Christ parallel" as a collective term to refer to an array of comparisons between Adam and Christ, recognizing the diversity of views among those who make such comparisons. Yet the singular "parallel" is intended to denote the relative consistency of such an approach in the history of Christian interpretation.

33. See, e.g., *Haer.* 3.18.1; 3.18.7; 3.21.10; 3.23.1; 4.4.2; 5.1.2; 5.16.3; 5.21.1. It has been noted in recent years that recapitulation may not be the center of Irenaeus's theology, yet it is

seems to derive this teaching in large measure from Paul's statements,[34] but, as I will argue at the conclusion of this chapter, he does not derive his Adam Christology *only* from Paul. Irenaeus also gleans from the Gospels to explain Christ's work in Adamic terms.

The *Epistle to Diognetus*, though difficult to date with certainty, is probably also from the second century. Here one finds echoes of Romans 5:18–19 in the climactic soteriological section: "O the sweet exchange, O the incomprehensible work of God, O the unexpected blessings, that the sinfulness of many should be hidden in one righteous person, while the righteousness of one should justify many sinners!" (9:5).[35] While not mentioning Adam explicitly, *Diognetus* 9 views the work of Christ in the incarnation as the means of undoing the sinfulness that had befallen humanity (9:2–4). If we connect this passage to Romans 5:18–19, which is a reasonable conclusion given the verbal parallels between the two passages, then Adamic imagery is likely in view.[36]

Athanasius of Alexandria (ca. 296–373) has much to say about the work of Christ in the incarnation, including the relationship between Adam and Christ. We read in *On the Incarnation*: "For since from man it was that death prevailed over men, for this cause conversely, by the Word of God being made man has come about the destruction of death and the resurrection of life."[37] Similarly, in his *Homily on Matthew 11:27*: "[God] delivered to [the Son] man, that the Word himself might be made Flesh, and by taking the Flesh, restore it wholly."[38] Likewise, in his *Expositio fidei* Athanasius compares the paradise opened by Christ with the paradise forfeited by Adam.[39]

---

clearly an important organizing principle for him. See Eric Osborn, *Irenaeus of Lyons* (Cambridge: Cambridge University Press, 2001), 110–11; Thomas Holsinger-Friesen, *Irenaeus and Genesis: A Study of Competition in Early Christian Hermeneutics*, JTISup 1 (Winona Lake, IN: Eisenbrauns, 2009), 1–26; Ronald E. Heine, *Classical Christian Doctrine: Introducing the Essentials of the Ancient Faith* (Grand Rapids: Baker Academic, 2013), 116–21. Recapitulation in Irenaeus is a complex concept, on which see the conclusion of this chapter.

34. J. T. Nielsen, *Adam and Christ in the Theology of Irenaeus of Lyons: An Examination of the Function of the Adam-Christ Typology in the "Adversus Haereses" of Irenaeus, against the Background of the Gnosticism of His Time* (Assen, Netherlands: Van Gorcum, 1968), 68–82; Ben C. Blackwell, *Christosis: Pauline Soteriology in Light of Deification in Irenaeus and Cyril of Alexandria*, WUNT 2/314 (Tübingen: Mohr Siebeck, 2011), 41–43.

35. Translation from Michael W. Holmes, ed. and trans., *The Apostolic Fathers: Greek Texts and English Translations*, 3rd ed. (Grand Rapids: Baker Academic, 2007), 711.

36. See further Brandon D. Crowe, "Oh Sweet Exchange! The Soteriological Significance of the Incarnation in the *Epistle to Diognetus*," ZNW 102 (2011): 108–9.

37. Athanasius, *Inc.* 10.2 (NPNF[2] 4:41).

38. Translation from NPNF[2] 4:87.

39. NPNF[2] 4:84–85. See also *Ep. Aeg. Lib.* 2; *C. Ar.* 1.44, 51, 59; 2.51, 61, 65, 68; 3.33, 38.

The Adam-Christ parallel is a major organizing feature in Cyril of Alexandria's (ca. 375–444) exegesis. Indeed, Christ as the second Adam[40] is perhaps the center of Cyril's theological synthesis and is a key to the overall *skopos* (aim, goal) of Scripture.[41] The descent of the Spirit on Jesus in John 1, for example, provides an opportunity for Cyril to explain Christ as hospitable to the Holy Spirit using new Adam terminology: "He knew no sin at all so that, just as through the disobedience of the first we came under God's wrath, so through the obedience of the second, we might escape the curse and its evils might come to nothing. . . . The Spirit flew away because of sin, but the one who knew no sin became one of us so that the Spirit might become accustomed to remain in us."[42]

Moving ahead to the seventh century, Maximus the Confessor (ca. 580–662) sees in Christ's life the overcoming of Adam's sin. In *Ad Thalassium* 21 Maximus contrasts the passions that overtook Adam with the victory Christ gained in his temptation, and then again at the cross, in which he overcame the passions that overtook humanity since the days of Adam.[43]

Likely from somewhere near the same time as Maximus, the Christian pseudepigraphical work *Cave of Treasures* makes extensive comparisons between Christ and Adam.[44] *Cave of Treasures* even gives hour-by-hour comparisons of Jesus's experience on the cross to Adam's experience in the garden, concluding that "Christ resembled Adam in everything" (*Cav. Tr.* 48–49). This interpretive grid illustrates the extent to which an early Christian author (or authors) compared Adam and Christ.

The present volume is not the place for an extended survey of the Adam-Christ parallel in the ancient church. Indeed, time would fail me to speak of

40. The New Testament does not refer to Christ explicitly as second Adam but rather as last (*eschatos*) Adam (1 Cor. 15:45). Nevertheless, "second Adam" is common terminology among exegetes and theologians, and is also implied in the second man language (*ho deuteros anthrōpos*) of 1 Cor. 15:47. Throughout this study I will prefer the terminology "last Adam."

41. Robert Louis Wilken, "St. Cyril of Alexandria: The Mystery of Christ in the Bible," *ProEccl* 4 (1995): 454–78.

42. Cyril of Alexandria, *Commentary on John* 184, in *Commentary on John*, trans. David R. Maxwell, ed. Joel C. Elowsky, 2 vols., ACT (Downers Grove, IL: IVP Academic, 2013–15), 1:82. One notes how naturally Cyril moves between Gospel texts and Paul at this point (cf. Rom. 5:18–19). See also Daniel Keating, "The Baptism of Jesus in Cyril of Alexandria: The Re-Creation of the Human Race," *ProEccl* 8 (1999): 210–22; Kilian McDonnell, "Jesus' Baptism in the Jordan," *TS* 56 (1995): 222.

43. Maximus the Confessor, *On the Cosmic Mystery of Jesus Christ*, trans. Paul Blowers and Robert Louis Wilken, PPS 25 (Crestwood, NY: St. Vladimir's Seminary Press, 2003), 109–13, cf. 13–43. See also *Ambiguum* 42; *Quaestiones ad Thalassium* 42 in ibid.

44. Alexander Toepel, "The Cave of Treasures: A New Translation and Introduction," in *Old Testament Pseudepigrapha: More Noncanonical Scriptures*, ed. Richard Bauckham, James R. Davila, and Alexander Panayotov, vol. 1 (Grand Rapids: Eerdmans, 2013), 531–84.

Justin, Tertullian, Hilary, Cyril of Jerusalem, Gregory of Nyssa, Theodore, Theodoret, and Ambrose.[45] In other words, one is not hard pressed to find any number of ancient interpreters seizing upon a perceived two-Adam structure within Scripture. Significantly, this structure is often paired with an emphasis on the obedience of the second Adam unto salvation in contrast to the disobedience of the first Adam.

A comparative approach to the two Adams is found not only in the ancient church. Similar features are seen in later interpreters as diverse as Anselm (ca. 1033–1109), Peter Lombard (ca. 1100–ca. 1160), Thomas Aquinas (ca. 1225–1274), Martin Luther (1483–1546), Menno Simons (1496–1561), John Calvin (1509–1564), Thomas Goodwin (1600–1680), and John Owen (1616–1683).[46] By way of illustration, Calvin states: "Accordingly, our Lord came in order to take Adam's place in obeying the Father, to present our flesh as the price of satisfaction to God's righteous judgment, and, in the same flesh, to pay the penalty that we had deserved."[47] And again, "Truly, Christ was sanctified from earliest infancy in order that he might sanctify in himself his elect from every age without distinction. For, to wipe out the guilt of the disobedience which had been committed in our flesh, he took that very flesh that in it, for our sake, and in our stead, he might achieve perfect obedience."[48] Similarly, in Thomas Goodwin's exposition, "[Paul] speaks of [Adam and

45. E.g., Justin, *Dial.* 88, 100, 103; Tertullian, *Carn. Chr.* 16–17. See other examples in Douglas F. Kelly, *Systematic Theology: Grounded in Holy Scripture and Understood in the Light of the Church*, vol. 2, *The Beauty of Christ: A Trinitarian Vision* (Fearn, UK: Mentor, 2014), 313; J. N. D. Kelly, *Early Christian Doctrines*, 5th rev. ed. (Peabody, MA: Prince Press, 2007), 297, 312, 380–81, 385, 388–89, 395; Jean Daniélou, SJ, *From Shadows to Reality: Studies in the Biblical Typology of the Fathers*, trans. Dom Wulstan Hibberd (London: Burns and Oates, 1960), 11–65 (thanks to Laura Leon for bringing Daniélou's work to my attention).

46. See variously Anselm, *Cur deus homo* 8–9; Lombard, *Sentences* 3.15–20; Thomas Aquinas, *Summa Theologiae* 3.39.1; 3.41.2; 3.46.4, 10; 3.51.2; Martin Luther, *Sermons on the Gospel of St. John Chapters 1–4*, vol. 22 of *Luther's Works*, ed. Jaroslav Pelikan (St. Louis: Concordia, 1957), 88, 119–23, 131, 286, 359, 382, 491; Martin Luther, *Sermons on the Gospel of St. John Chapters 14–16*, vol. 24 of *Luther's Works*, ed. Jaroslav Pelikan (St. Louis: Concordia, 1957), 344; Lydia Harder, "Power and Authority in Mennonite Theological Development," in *Power, Authority, and the Anabaptist Tradition*, ed. Benjamin W. Redekop and Calvin W. Redekop (Baltimore: Johns Hopkins University Press, 2001), 77; Calvin, *Inst.* 2.12.1, 3; 2.16.5; Mark Jones, *Why Heaven Kissed Earth: The Christology of the Puritan Reformed Orthodox Theologian, Thomas Goodwin (1600–1680)*, RHT 13 (Göttingen: Vandenhoeck & Ruprecht, 2010), 77–86, 173–95; John Owen, *The Glory of Christ*, vol. 1 of *The Works of John Owen*, ed. William H. Goold (Edinburgh: Banner of Truth, 1965), 338–42; Sinclair B. Ferguson, *John Owen on the Christian Life* (Edinburgh: Banner of Truth, 1987), 87.

47. Calvin, *Inst.* 2.12.3, in John Calvin, *Institutes of the Christian Religion*, ed. John T. McNeill, trans. Ford Lewis Battles, 2 vols., LCC 20 (Louisville: Westminster John Knox, 1960), 1:466.

48. Calvin, *Inst.* 4.16.18 (Battles).

Christ] as if there had never been any more men in the world . . . because these two between them had all the rest of the sons of men hanging at their girdle."[49]

If we fast-forward to the twentieth century, we can find many similar features among theologians and biblical scholars articulating the significance of the work of Jesus. Reformed dogmatician Herman Bavinck has much to say regarding the Adam-Christ parallel,[50] as does Karl Barth.[51] Likewise T. F. Torrance—Barth's onetime student who drew heavily upon the church fathers—in places emphasizes the obedience of Christ in contrast to Adam.[52]

Two more points are to be noted before moving on. First, an Adam-Christ parallel is explicit in Paul's letters (esp. Rom. 5; 1 Cor. 15). It is thus quite common to find discussions of Adam and Christ in treatments of Paul's Christology.[53] However, this structure is less often expanded upon in discussions of the Gospel accounts, Luke's genealogy notwithstanding.[54] Second, even though many may demur at an Adam-Christ parallel in the Gospels, it is common to recognize Scripture's emphasis on the obedience of Jesus in his incarnate state, especially in the Gospels. However, this has not always been true in Gospel studies, which brings us to our next section.

Questing for the Life of Jesus?

As we consider the significance of the life of Jesus in the Gospels, it is instructive to pay heed to the ebbs and flows of New Testament scholarship from

49. Thomas Goodwin, *Christ Set Forth*, vol. 4 of *The Works of Thomas Goodwin* (Edinburgh: James Nichol, 1862), 31. Cf. F. F. Bruce, *Romans*, 2nd ed., TNTC (Grand Rapids: Eerdmans, 1985), 120. Thanks to Jonathan Gibson for first alerting me to this pithy quote, and to Sinclair Ferguson for pointing me to its source.

50. Bavinck, *Reformed Dogmatics*, 3:226–31, 377–81, 394–95.

51. Karl Barth, *Church Dogmatics* IV/1, ed. T. F. Torrance, trans. Geoffrey W. Bromiley (Edinburgh: T&T Clark, 1956), 257–58, 512–13; cf. Peter Lengsfeld, *Die Adam-Christus-Typologie im Neuen Testament und ihre dogmatische Verwendung bei M. J. Scheeben und K. Barth*, KBOST 9 (Essen: Ludgerus, 1965), 162–216.

52. E.g., T. F. Torrance, *Incarnation: The Person and Life of Christ*, ed. Robert T. Walker (Downers Grove, IL: IVP Academic, 2008), 73; cf. Kevin Chiarot, *The Unassumed Is the Unhealed: The Humanity of Christ in the Theology of T. F. Torrance* (Eugene, OR: Pickwick, 2013).

53. See Felipe de Jésus Legaretta-Castillo, *The Figure of Adam in Romans 5 and 1 Corinthians 15: The New Creation and Its Ethical and Social Reconfiguration* (Minneapolis: Fortress, 2014); James D. G. Dunn, *Christology in the Making: A New Testament Inquiry into the Origins of the Doctrine of the Incarnation*, 2nd ed. (Grand Rapids: Eerdmans, 1989), 98–128; N. T. Wright, *The Climax of the Covenant: Christ and the Law in Pauline Theology* (Minneapolis: Fortress, 1992), 18–40; Gordon D. Fee, *Pauline Christology: An Exegetical-Theological Study* (Peabody, MA: Hendrickson, 2007), 513–29.

54. McKnight (*King Jesus Gospel*, 35) does note Adam in relation to the story of Jesus in the Gospels, though he expands it more in relation to Paul (ibid., 136–42). Luke's Christology will be considered in greater detail in following chapters.

the past three hundred years, since the degree to which the Gospels focus on the *life* of Jesus has often been debated. We begin this 30,000-foot overview with Albert Schweitzer's watershed appraisal that traced the development of the quest of the historical Jesus from H. S. Reimarus to William Wrede.[55] Schweitzer's critiques are well known, particularly his critique of the movement of the German and French authors in the eighteenth and nineteenth centuries who attempted to write something like modern biographies of Jesus. These inevitably ended up being what Schweitzer's English translator dubbed "imaginative" or "fictitious lives"[56] of Jesus that were, in Schweitzer's estimation, unsatisfactory and far-fetched.

Another significant voice in these discussions, which Schweitzer did not canvass in his work, is that of Martin Kähler. I have already mentioned that Kähler referred to the Gospels as Passion Narratives with extended introductions. To understand this statement, it is necessary to place Kähler in his historical context, since he was responding to what he perceived to be the trend of historical criticism to make pronouncements on theological issues beyond its capabilities.[57] He too, in other words, was reacting against the psychologized, reconstructed lives-of-Jesus movement from the eighteenth and nineteenth centuries. Kähler downplayed the significance of the life of Jesus in the Gospels and posited a distinction between the *historische* Jesus and the *geschichtliche* Jesus. Precise translations of these two German terms is difficult, but the distinction amounts to a difference between the so-called *historical* Jesus, which is reconstructed using the tools of historical criticism, and the *historic* Christ of the church who is the object of faith.[58]

Schweitzer's deconstruction of the lives-of-Jesus movement, along with Kähler's critique of the reconstructed lives of Jesus that employed what we might today call Troeltschian principles of historical criticism,[59] helped clear the deck for the following era of Gospels and Jesus studies that was dominated by form criticism. As is well known, form criticism was generally more interested in the *Sitze im Leben* of the early Christian communities that lay behind the Gospels than in the Gospels as integrated wholes. Each pericope was evaluated in a way that gave comparatively little consideration to the overall structure of the relevant Gospel. Thus the focus was on the

---

55. Schweitzer, *Quest of the Historical Jesus.*
56. Ibid., v.
57. Kähler, *So-Called Historical Jesus*, 52–55, 62–63, 69.
58. See discussions in Robert B. Strimple, *The Modern Search for the Real Jesus: An Introductory Survey of the Historical Roots of Gospels Criticism* (Phillipsburg, NJ: P&R, 1995), 89–101; J. P. Meier, *A Marginal Jew: Rethinking the Historical Jesus*, 5 vols., ABRL (New York: Doubleday, 1991–2016), 1:27–30, 35–36n19; Pennington, *Reading the Gospels Wisely*, 81–82.
59. See also Pennington, *Reading the Gospels Wisely*, 82.

forms of individual units and the situation that gave rise to that literary form rather than on the overall narrative or coherence of the Gospels.[60] This was a decided step away from the biographical impulse in interpreting the Gospels and led (at least in Rudolf Bultmann's formulation) to the elevation of the *kērygma* and the experience thereof above a synthetic appeal to events or to a historical figure from the past.[61] Thus, for example, Bultmann wrote a book that focused on the message of Jesus and not on his life, since in Bultmann's estimation "we can know almost nothing concerning the life and personality of Jesus."[62] This too was part of Bultmann's response, much like Schweitzer's and Kähler's, to the psychologizing *Tendenz* of the lives-of-Jesus movement.[63]

However, not all scholars studying the Gospels in the early twentieth century imbibed deeply from the well of form criticism. One notable example is C. H. Dodd, who argues in an article titled "The Framework of the Gospel Narrative" that the pericopae in Mark "originally and intrinsically" belonged to certain stages of Jesus's ministry and that part of the *kērygma* is the order of the events (whether chronological or topical), which is often preserved in Mark.[64] Indeed, for Dodd the Markan summaries "fall naturally into something very much like a continuous narrative."[65] Dodd sees more inherent continuity and order among the Markan pericopae than do form critics such as K. L. Schmidt. One can see continuity in this article with Dodd's fuller treatment in *The Apostolic Preaching and Its Developments*.[66] Dodd argues that the early apostolic preaching (diverse as he sees it to be) consistently made reference to the person and character of Jesus. He notes, for example, Jesus's Davidic descent, his miracles, the role of the servant, and the character of Jesus in his trial. As central as the Passion Narratives surely are, Dodd also draws attention to the importance of the ministry of Jesus. He concludes that "the history of Jesus . . . was of decisive importance for the tradition, just because in the Preaching the life, death, and resurrection

60. See the classic treatment in Rudolf Bultmann, *The History of the Synoptic Tradition*, trans. John Marsh, rev. ed. (New York: Harper & Row, 1968).

61. Jens Schröter sees the anticipation of this in Adolf von Harnack's focus on the proclamation of Jesus. See Schröter, *From Jesus to the New Testament*, trans. Wayne Coppins, BMSEC (Waco: Baylor University Press, 2013), 17.

62. Rudolf Bultmann, *Jesus and the Word*, trans. Louise Pettibone Smith and Erminie Huntress Lantero (New York: Scribner, 1958), 8, 12 (quote from p. 8).

63. See Meier, *Marginal Jew*, 1:37–38n24.

64. C. H. Dodd, "The Framework of the Gospel Narrative," *ExpTim* 43 (1931–32): 396–400 (quote from 397).

65. Ibid., 399.

66. C. H. Dodd, *The Apostolic Preaching and Its Developments* (New York: Harper & Row, 1936).

of Jesus were held to be the climax of all history, the coming of the Kingdom of God."[67] Dodd was in many ways a voice in the wilderness in the early twentieth century, as he brought attention to the importance of the narrative structures of the Gospels and concomitantly to the character of Jesus as the founder of Christianity.[68] Dodd's approach proved to be prescient for the direction much of Gospels studies would move toward the end of the twentieth century.[69]

More extensive focus on the life of Jesus in conversation with form criticism can be found in Vincent Taylor's *The Life and Ministry of Jesus* (1955)[70] and especially Graham Stanton's 1974 volume *Jesus of Nazareth in New Testament Preaching*, in which Stanton argues that the early Christian message reveals a deep interest in the life and character of Jesus of Nazareth.[71] Stanton sees a dual perspective in the Gospels—they are interested both in the *kērygma* and in the life of Jesus.[72] Significantly for the present volume, Stanton concludes: "If the early church was uninterested in the past of Jesus, the emergence of the gospels becomes a puzzle. For, in spite of all possible qualification, the gospels . . . look very much like lives of Jesus."[73] Stanton thus distinguished his own position from much of form criticism, yet in this early work he is reluctant to identify the Gospels as biographies.

67. Ibid., 56. See also p. 49: "Not only in His death, Mark seems to say, but in His ministry, Jesus overcame the principalities and powers."

68. C. H. Dodd, *The Founder of Christianity* (London: Collins, 1971), though in this volume Dodd underscores the centrality of the Passion Narratives (33–36).

69. Dodd (*Apostolic Preaching*, 55) also points to the Muratorian Fragment as a witness to the interest in the saving facts of Jesus's life in the Gospels in the late second century, since the Muratorian Fragment mentions Jesus's nativity, passion, resurrection, conversations with his disciples, and second coming (lines 20–26). Dodd is by no means alone in dating the Muratorian Fragment to the second century. This date is still to be preferred. See variously Bruce M. Metzger, *The Canon of the New Testament: Its Origin, Development, and Significance* (Oxford: Clarendon, 1987), 194; Eckhard Schnabel, "The Muratorian Fragment: The State of Research," *JETS* 57 (2014): 231–64; Joseph Verheyden, "The Canon Muratori: A Matter of Dispute," in *The Biblical Canons*, ed. J.-M. Auwers and H. J. de Jonge (Leuven: Leuven University Press, 2003), 487–556; Michael J. Kruger, *The Question of Canon: Challenging the Status Quo in the New Testament Debate* (Downers Grove, IL: IVP Academic, 2013), 162–64. For an alternative view, see Geoffrey Mark Hahneman, *The Muratorian Fragment and the Development of the Canon* (Oxford: Clarendon, 1992), where one can also find a transcription of the fragment (pp. 6–7). For the argument that the fragment is from the third century, see Jonathan J. Armstrong, "Victorinus of Pettau as the Author of the Canon Muratori," *VC* 62 (2008): 1–34.

70. Vincent Taylor, *The Life and Ministry of Jesus* (Nashville: Abingdon, 1955).

71. Graham N. Stanton, *Jesus of Nazareth in New Testament Preaching*, SNTSMS 27 (Cambridge: Cambridge University Press, 1974), 1. McKnight ("Matthew as 'Gospel'") also reflects on the significance of Stanton's work for understanding the significance of Jesus's life in the Gospels.

72. Stanton, *Jesus of Nazareth*, 172.

73. Ibid., 186.

Stanton later argued, however, that the Gospels are a form of ancient biography, and he acknowledged his appreciation for the work of Richard Burridge, who argues persuasively in *What Are the Gospels?* that the genre of the Gospels falls within the broad category of Greco-Roman *bios* (i.e., biography).[74] Burridge's work was originally published in 1992 as the fruition of his graduate work and is one of those rare PhD theses that has helped to shape the current state of discussion. Although Burridge's articulation of the Gospels as a form of Greco-Roman *bios* stands open to refinement,[75] his overarching thesis, built on an impressive comparison with ancient literature, has been generally convincing, and now the starting point for discussion of the genre of the Gospels is Greco-Roman *bios*. This is a significant departure from the form-critical paradigm of the early twentieth century that saw the Gospels as a unique genre (*sui generis*) of low-brow literature (*Kleinliteratur*).

The upshot of these moves away from form criticism (including the advent of redaction criticism and more recently narrative criticism) is that more scholars today recognize the need to read the Gospels as theologically integrated documents. Reading the Gospels "vertically," that is, beginning-to-end as holistic narratives, allows one to see the development and unfolding of the narratives in a way that appreciates the depth and richness of the theological contribution of each Gospel. Form criticism's focus on isolated, individual pericopae still casts a shadow on the study of the Gospels, but its influence has begun to wane in recent decades. The work of scholars such as Stanton and Burridge has laid the groundwork to understand that the Gospels are not just Passion Narratives but are, in Burridge's words, "Christology in narrative form."[76] It therefore behooves the reader to heed the christological contours of each Gospel in a way that neglects neither the life and ministry of Jesus (which, in Burridge's estimation, accounts for roughly 80 percent of the Gospels![77]) nor Jesus's sacrificial death. Although in various ways Schweitzer, Kähler, and form critics cautioned against reconstructed lives of Jesus, in many respects the discussion has come full circle, and today it is widely recognized that the Gospels stand close to Greco-Roman *bioi* and therefore are thoroughly about Jesus from beginning to end. This is, of course, not the same thing as trying to reconstruct a modern, psychological biography, but genre considerations do

74. Graham N. Stanton, foreword to *What Are the Gospels? A Comparison with Graeco-Roman Biography* by Richard A. Burridge, 2nd ed., BRS (Grand Rapids: Eerdmans, 2004), viii–ix; Stanton, *A Gospel for a New People: Studies in Matthew* (Edinburgh: T&T Clark, 1992), 63–64.

75. One aspect is the need to focus more on the Old Testament precedent for the Gospels. See further Burridge, *What Are the Gospels?*, chap. 11; Pennington, *Reading the Gospels Wisely*, 25–31.

76. Burridge, *What Are the Gospels?*, 289.

77. Ibid., 195. This percentage may be a bit high, but the point is valid.

help us recognize the significance accorded to the words and deeds of Christ throughout the entirety of the Gospels (i.e., not just in the Passion Narratives).

In addition to this renewed interest in the life of Jesus, we can also observe the consistent emphasis on the obedience of Jesus among those who have addressed the Christology of the Gospels. This is true even among those who might view the Gospels as Passion Narratives with extended introductions. Two brief examples will suffice here. On the Synoptic Gospels, Oscar Cullmann noted that Jesus was fully obedient as Son of God and in some sense had to "live atonement."[78] On the theology of John's Gospel, no less than Rudolf Bultmann emphasizes that the *works* of Jesus "are ultimately one single work."[79] That is, the work of Jesus in his life and death is a unified whole such that his death is the completion of his incarnate obedience.[80] Indeed, for Bultmann the sacrifice of Jesus in John is not only in Jesus's death, but it involves his whole ministry.[81] In sum, the obedience of Jesus has consistently been recognized as central to the Gospels' presentations of Jesus. These observations provide fertile soil for the present study.

Toward a Solution: Vicarious Obedience

The thoroughgoing emphasis on Jesus Christ and his obedience in the Gospels, combined with the historically recognized two-Adam structure in the New Testament, provides fuel for the present volume. In what follows I will argue for a pervasive Adam Christology in the Gospels, by which I also aim to show that Christ is a *representative* figure. Moreover, Adam is also foundational for understanding Israel in the biblical narrative, so considering Christ as the last Adam will also lead us to consider how Christ relates to the nation of Israel. In both cases I will argue that Christ is portrayed in covenantal terms: as the last Adam, Christ is the covenantal (or *federal*)[82] head of his people, the mediator of the new covenant.[83]

I will further seek to show that the lifelong obedience of Jesus must not be dichotomized from his death, nor should his death be separated from his life.

78. Oscar Cullmann, *The Christology of the New Testament*, trans. Shirley C. Guthrie and Charles A. M. Hall, rev. ed. (Philadelphia: Westminster, 1963), 61, 277, 283.

79. Bultmann, *Theology of the New Testament*, 2:52 (§47.2).

80. Ibid.

81. Ibid., 2:53–54.

82. I use *federal* here deriving from the Latin *foedus*, denoting *covenant*.

83. One can also speak of Christ as the head and mediator of the covenant of grace, which refers to the entire plan of redemption after the fall. Cf. Bavinck, *Reformed Dogmatics*, 3:195, 225–32.

Instead, the work of Christ in the Gospels is a *unified* obedience that entails both his life and his death. This is more than saying the Gospels teach the sinlessness of Jesus, but it is surely not saying less than that. It is to say that Jesus was accomplishing salvation throughout his life. This makes sense of the Gospels' overarching focus on the obedience of Jesus outside the Passion Narratives, and it aligns with the focus of the early church on the life of Jesus as having a *saving* character.[84]

Limits and Method

The focus of this study will be on the four canonical Gospels.[85] My focus will be not on the communities behind the Gospels, or on the sources underlying the Gospels, but on the text of the Gospels as we have them.[86] That is to say, my primary focus will be not on form or source criticism but on the Gospels as unified wholes.[87] I will also not attempt to reconstruct a historical Jesus; rather, my task is primarily exegetical: to consider relevant texts from the Gospels that speak to the vicarious obedience of Jesus.

Identifying shared theological perspectives among all the canonical Gospels can be a tricky enterprise. My aim is not to downplay the distinctive aspects of any of the Gospels. Yet from the earliest days of the church these four Gospels were viewed as one gospel.[88] Nor indeed do we find a sharp distinction between the theology of the Gospels and the rest of the New Testament. As Adolf Schlatter observed of New Testament theology: "Each individual formation is worthy of individual attention. At the same time, one must take care to observe that all these free and personally believing men [New Testament authors] still constitute a unity."[89] So it is important to recognize the diversity as well as the unity within the canonical witness. Yet among the diversity of

84. Cf. Dodd, *Apostolic Preaching*, 42–45.

85. I will also consider what Acts has to say about the life and ministry of Jesus in places, but my focus will be predominantly on the Gospels.

86. To be sure, one cannot shirk text-critical questions, and I will engage them where necessary.

87. My approach is closely akin to what is often called composition criticism.

88. Cf. Martin Hengel, *The Four Gospels and the One Gospel of Jesus Christ: An Investigation of the Collection and Origin of the Canonical Gospels*, trans. John Bowden (Harrisburg, PA: Trinity Press International, 2000); Graham N. Stanton, "The Fourfold Gospel," *NTS* 43 (1997): 317–46.

89. Adolf Schlatter, "The Theology of the New Testament and Dogmatics," in *The Nature of New Testament Theology: The Contribution of William Wrede and Adolf Schlatter*, ed. and trans. Robert Morgan, SBT 2/25 (Naperville, IL: Allenson, 1973), 140. Similarly, Bavinck (*Reformed Dogmatics*, 3:252) concludes that the "Synoptics already contain in principle all of the things that the apostles and the Christian church later taught about the person of Christ."

the Fourfold Gospel we find a common perspective that the obedience of Jesus is vicarious in character. Thus, one way we see the fundamental unity of the Gospel witnesses is in the shared conviction that Jesus's life was accomplishing what was necessary for salvation. The present volume is not designed to be the last word on the subject, but I do hope to advance the conversation in ways that will be beneficial.

I will also be considering the Scriptures as a whole, attempting to engage in a biblical-theological understanding of the obedience of Jesus. My approach generally follows that of Geerhardus Vos,[90] which has more recently been appropriated by G. K. Beale.[91] In sum, my aim will be to read the Gospels sensitively in their own contexts and in light of the primary corpus of documents quoted in the Gospels—the Old Testament. Taking a biblical-theological approach also means that I will devote more attention to canonical texts than noncanonical texts, and I will not hesitate to use other biblical texts as corroborating and potentially enlightening witnesses where relevant. However, I am also eager to consider the obedience of Jesus in light of various Jewish perspectives and the history of Christian interpretation. Therefore, I will also interact with an array of noncanonical writings where possible.

Organization of Argument

My argument is structured as follows. In chapter 2, I argue that Jesus is portrayed in the Gospels as the last Adam, and I will relate this to Jesus's identity as the Son of Man. In chapter 3, I consider the Old Testament background of Adam and Israel as sons of God and correlate these with Jesus as the obedient Son of God. Here I will give particular emphasis to Jesus's obedience in the baptism and temptation episodes. In chapter 4, I consider in more detail the divine constraints on Jesus's obedience, namely, how the divine will and Scripture pertain to the obedience of Jesus and the accomplishment of salvation. In chapter 5, I give attention to the unique contours of John's Gospel and argue that the works of Jesus in John are ultimately one work, and the Fourth Gospel narrates the climactic moments of this unified work in Adamic terms. In chapter 6, I investigate the kingdom of God and how Jesus's life, deeds, and teaching relate to the binding of the strong man and the inauguration of the kingdom, which are also laced with Adamic imagery. In chapter 7, I look

---

90. E.g., Geerhardus Vos, *Biblical Theology: Old and New Testaments* (1948; repr., Edinburgh: Banner of Truth, 1975).

91. G. K. Beale, *A New Testament Biblical Theology: The Unfolding of the Old Testament in the New* (Grand Rapids: Baker Academic, 2011).

to the contours of the new covenant in the Gospels and seek to relate the life of Jesus more explicitly to his death. Again Adamic imagery looms large in the mercy that Jesus shows and in his glorious resurrection life. Finally, in chapter 8, I offer a synthesis and some theological conclusions resulting from the identification of Jesus as the last Adam in the Gospels.

Retrospect and Prospect: Irenaeus on Jesus, Adam, and the Fourfold Gospel

As we prepare to embark on the study before us, I would like to till the ex-egetical ground by returning briefly to Irenaeus, one of the most well-known early developers of the Adam-Christ parallel, in order to consider some ways he may serve as a bridge between the apostolic age and the postapostolic age. Irenaeus claims to have known Polycarp, the purported disciple of the apostle John, and thereby assures the reader that his knowledge (especially of the Gospels!) is trustworthy. In light of this, a couple of features of Irenaeus's thought are relevant for the present study. In the first place, Irenaeus is explicit in his theology of recapitulation that the second Adam undoes the sin of the first Adam. Second, Irenaeus manifests a deep interest in the Fourfold Gospel. Might these two features be held together in Irenaeus in a way that provides some guidance for how we are to read the Gospels today? Let us consider each of these points a bit further.

First, Irenaeus focuses on the obedience of Jesus through the lens of the second Adam who corrects and perfects humankind and also inaugurates and consummates a new humanity.[92] For Irenaeus recapitulation is a multifaceted concept, but in précis one can say that the obedience of Christ, the second Adam, overcomes the disobedience of the first Adam.[93] In the words of J. N. D. Kelly, "since the essence of Adam's sin was disobedience, the obedience of Christ was indispensable; it is obedience that God requires, and in which man's glory consists."[94] Irenaeus seems to draw much of this from Paul's Adam-Christ parallel in Romans 5 and 1 Corinthians 15.[95] Yet significantly, Irenaeus elaborates upon many aspects of this parallel beyond the details Paul himself

92. Osborn, *Irenaeus*, 97.
93. *Haer.* 3.18.7. Osborn (*Irenaeus*, 97) notes the complexity of recapitulation in Irenaeus. I recognize the complexities of this concept, but for this brief discussion I am using recapitulation as a shorthand to encapsulate the Adam-Christ parallel in Irenaeus. See also Holsinger-Friesen, *Irenaeus and Genesis*, 18–26.
94. Kelly, *Early Christian Doctrines*, 174. On Irenaeus's understanding of atonement, see ibid., 173; D. Kelly, *Systematic Theology*, 2:439.
95. Nielsen, *Adam and Christ*, 68–82.

provides. For Irenaeus, then, recapitulation is closely tied to the two-Adam schema, and various details for his schema seem to derive from the Gospels. For example, not only does Jesus recapitulate Adam, but Mary in some way recapitulates and overcomes the disobedience of Eve.[96]

Second, and perhaps related to the breadth of the two-Adam schema, Irenaeus is well known for his deep interest in the Fourfold Gospel.[97] In book 3 of *Against Heresies*, Irenaeus shifts to discuss the scriptural proofs for orthodox doctrine in contrast to the heretics and heresies he canvasses in books 1–2. Key here for Irenaeus is the role of the apostles, as noted in *Against Heresies* 3.1. For Irenaeus the gospel has come down to those in his own day in the Scriptures, which can be traced back to the apostles. In this context he mentions not only Peter and Paul as apostles, but also gives his understanding that the four Gospels all derive from apostles or apostolic spokesmen: Matthew (the disciple of Jesus), Mark (the disciple and interpreter of Peter), Luke (the companion of Paul), and John (for Irenaeus, one of the Twelve). The unity of the gospel among all the apostolic witnesses is fundamental to Irenaeus's thought; there is no dichotomy for him between Paul or Peter or Matthew or John. All are unified and testify to the recapitulation in Christ (cf. Eph. 1:10).

For Irenaeus, then, Jesus's recapitulation of Adam is not simply a Pauline doctrine; it is found throughout the New Testament.[98] As one peruses book 3 where Irenaeus articulates this correspondence, it is clear that much comes from Paul (*Haer.* 3.18.7), and yet in the preceding paragraph we find that Jesus as the Son of Man "fought and conquered . . . and through obedience [did] away with disobedience completely: for he bound the strong man and set free the weak."[99] Here the binding of the strong man is a clear allusion to Jesus's statements of binding the strong man in the Gospels (Matt. 12:29 // Mark 3:27; cf. Luke 11:21–22), which Irenaeus understands to refer to the wide-ranging work of Jesus.[100] And the presupposition for this is the coming of the Holy Spirit upon Jesus Christ, which enabled him to renew humanity[101]—an episode that Irenaeus most likely derives more from the baptism in the Gospels than from Paul. Additionally, it has recently been argued that the key chiasm

---

96. *Haer.* 5.19.1: "As the human race fell into bondage to death by means of a virgin, so is it rescued by a virgin; virginal disobedience having been balanced in the opposite scale by virginal obedience" (*ANF* 1:547). See also, e.g., 3.18.7; 3.21.10; 3.22.4; 5.21.1; D. Jeffrey Bingham, *Irenaeus' Use of Matthew's Gospel in "Adversus Haereses,"* TEG 7 (Leuven: Peeters, 1998), 164–68.

97. See C. E. Hill, *Who Chose the Gospels?*, 33–68; Stanton, "Fourfold Gospel," 317–46.

98. On Irenaeus and the New Testament, see Metzger, *Canon of the New Testament*, 153–56; *Haer.* 4.15.2; 4.17.5; 4.28.1–2; 5.34.1.

99. *Haer.* 3.18.6 (*ANF* 1:447–48).

100. See Heine, *Classical Christian Doctrine*, 119–21.

101. *Haer.* 3.17. See Osborn, *Irenaeus*, 133.

in book 3 comes in 3.23.1–8, which deals with the reversal of Adam's sin in humanity that was recapitulated in Jesus Christ.[102] Significantly, it appears that this section is framed around the contrast between Adam's disobedience and Christ's obedience, and the imagery for this section comes in large part from Luke's Gospel (10:19; 15:4–7; 19:10; cf. Matt. 12:29 // Mark 3:27).[103]

Earlier, Irenaeus observes the way Luke's genealogy relates Jesus all the way back to Adam, thereby "connecting the end to the beginning, and implying that it is he who has summed up in Himself all nations dispersed from Adam downwards."[104] Thus, in Irenaeus's exposition, the Gospel of Luke provides scriptural foundation for showing us that Jesus recapitulates Adam,[105] and this is followed immediately by a discussion of how the obedience of Jesus leads to life, in contrast to Adam (3.22.4). Significantly, in 3.22.4 Irenaeus explicitly connects Luke's portrayal of Jesus as second Adam with Paul's understanding of Adam as a type of Christ.

There is, then, a unity of the teaching of the Gospels and Paul in Irenaeus's theology of Christ's obedience as that which rectifies the disobedience of Adam. Irenaeus, especially in *Against Heresies* 3, relies heavily on both the Gospels and Paul to make his point that the obedience of Christ undoes the disobedience of Adam.[106] Given Irenaeus's contention that he is not an innovator but stands in continuity with tradition, we can likely also posit that his hermeneutic highlighting Christ's obedience as second Adam—including its foundation in *both* Paul and the Gospels—stands in continuity with earlier tradition.[107] Stated more boldly, we seem to find in Irenaeus an exegetical trail that leads back to the four Gospels themselves.[108]

A detailed discussion of Irenaeus and the early church fathers is beyond the scope of this volume. But by highlighting the theme of Christ as second Adam in Irenaeus in conjunction with his emphasis on the Fourfold Gospel, I hope to show the legitimacy of looking deeper into the significance of Jesus's life in light of Adam; Irenaeus and others have asked similar questions. I also hope to show that the answer Irenaeus gives not only adumbrates later tradition but may itself be an offshoot of something rooted in the earliest Gospel traditions. If indeed this is a viable option, then it behooves

102. Stephen O. Presley, "The Lost Sheep Who Is Found: Irenaeus' Intertextual Reading of Genesis 3 in *Adversus Haereses* III 23.1–8," StPatr 52 (2010): 47–59.

103. Ibid., 49–58; cf. Stephen O. Presley, *The Intertextual Reception of Genesis 1–3 in Irenaeus of Lyons*, BibAnChr 8 (Leiden: Brill, 2015), 88–133.

104. *Haer.* 3.22.3 (ANF 1:455).

105. Thanks to Stephen Presley for sparking my own reflections on this point.

106. Irenaeus also interweaves the Gospels and Paul in *Epid.* 31–42.

107. See, e.g., Justin, *Dial.* 88, 94.

108. This is also related to the *regula fidei* (rule of faith), which I discuss in chap. 8.

present-day interpreters to keep this two-Adam structure in mind as we ask what is not only an appropriate question but a crucial question of the Gospels: how was Jesus accomplishing salvation in his life and ministry? In pursuit of this answer I turn now to exegesis, beginning with the Adam Christology of the Gospels.

The Last Adam and the Son of Man
in the Gospels

The purpose of this chapter is to establish that the Gospel writers consistently use Adam language and imagery for Jesus, and that Jesus's identity as the obedient Son of Man is part of this Adamic topos. In the Gospels Jesus is presented as a representative man who corresponds to the first man in Scripture. In this light, Jesus's obedience as the last Adam realizes the obedience originally required of the first Adam. This chapter is necessary to highlight the framework of the Gospels' eschatology that assumes and builds upon—indeed, portrays Jesus in light of—an Adamic protology. In what follows I will outline the rationale for viewing Jesus as the last Adam in the Gospels. In subsequent chapters I will provide more sustained discussions of the contours of Jesus's obedience within this Adamic framework.

Adam Christology in the Gospels

The Lay of the Land: A Sparse Adam Topography

As noted in chapter 1, it is widely acknowledged that Paul articulates an Adam-Christ parallel.[1] However, it is not as common to find extensive

1. See Rom. 5:12–21; 1 Cor. 15:42–49.

discussions of Adam Christology in the Gospels. To be sure, in a few texts scholars do often identify comparisons between Adam and Christ, but these are generally the exception rather than the rule. One of the comparatively rare texts from the Synoptics that has often been invoked in favor of an Adam typology is Mark's temptation account (1:12–13). Jesus's encounters with Satan and the wild animals in the Markan temptation (along with, as we will see, Mark's emphasis on Jesus as Son of Man) provide ample reasons for positing an Adam Christology in Mark. Thus, for example, whereas Adam failed the temptation in the *garden* and was cast out, Jesus is led by the Spirit to the *wilderness*—a setting redolent of both the place of Israel's testing and the desolation resulting from the fall[2]—where Jesus does not succumb to the temptation of Satan.[3] And in both cases—in Adam's expulsion from the garden, and Jesus's being thrust into the wilderness—the strong term *ekballō* is employed.[4] Additionally, Jesus is with the perennially hostile wild animals in the wilderness and is not harmed, which is unusual in the postlapsarian world. Jesus's peaceful coexistence with the wild animals signifies his authority over them and recalls Adam's original dominion over the animals in the garden (cf. Gen. 1:26; 2:19–20). As Joel Marcus has suggested of Mark's temptation narrative: "Like Adam . . . [Jesus] has been granted worldwide dominion, thereby becoming the instrument through whom God's own dominion over the earth may be realized (cf. Gen. 1:26–28)."[5]

Although the Adamic view of Mark 1:12–13 is by no means a consensus, Richard Bauckham observed a little over twenty years ago that the interpretation of Jesus as new Adam in Mark 1 probably enjoyed the support of most exegetes at that time.[6] To be sure, plenty of interpreters demur at the proposed

2. The wilderness is also the place from which redemption comes.

3. For more on the wilderness theme, see Ulrich Mauser, *Christ in the Wilderness: The Wilderness Theme in the Second Gospel and Its Basis in the Biblical Tradition*, SBT 39 (London: SCM, 1963). William L. Lane points out that the wilderness is a place to test one's obedience (*The Gospel according to Mark*, NICNT [Grand Rapids: Eerdmans, 1974], 60).

4. See Gen. 3:24. Thanks to Iain Duguid for first alerting me to the use of *ekballō* in Genesis.

5. Joel Marcus, *Mark 1–8: A New Translation with Introduction and Commentary*, AB 27 (New York: Doubleday, 2000), 170–71; cf. *Apoc. Mos.* 39:1–3.

6. Richard Bauckham, "Jesus and the Wild Animals," in *Jesus of Nazareth: Lord and Christ; Essays on the Historical Jesus and New Testament Christology*, ed. Joel B. Green and Max Turner (Grand Rapids: Eerdmans, 1994), 7. See also, e.g., Hermann Mahnke, *Die Versuchungsgeschichte im Rahmen der synoptischen Evangelien: Ein Beitrag zur frühen Christologie*, BBET 9 (Frankfurt: Peter Lang, 1978), 28–38; Rudolf Pesch, *Das Markusevangelium*, 2 vols., HThKNT 2 (Freiburg: Herder, 1976–77), 1:94–96; Joachim Gnilka, *Das Evangelium nach Markus*, 2 vols., EKKNT 2 (Zürich: Benziger; Neukirchen-Vluyn: Neukirchener, 1978–79), 1:56–60; Robert A. Guelich, *Mark 1–8:26*, WBC 34A (Waco: Word, 1989), 39; Eric Grässer, "ΚΑΙ ΗΝ ΜΕΤΑ ΤΩΝ ΘΗΡΙΩΝ (Mk 1,13b): Ansätze einer theologischen Tierschutzethik," in *Studien zum Text und zur Ethik des Neuen Testaments: Festschrift zum 80. Geburtstag von Heinrich Greeven*, ed.

parallels between Adam and Christ in Mark 1. Indeed, when surveying the literature since Bauckham's essay, one encounters a bevy of alternative proposals.[7] Bauckham himself is skeptical that we encounter Adam Christology in Mark 1, in large measure because he finds no Adam Christology elsewhere in Mark.[8] Nor are recent commentators James Edwards,[9] R. T. France,[10] or Robert Stein convinced, the latter of whom summarizes: "We should not interpret 1:12–13 as an Adam-Christ typology where Jesus is undoing Adam's temptation and fall. . . . Such a typology plays no real part in Mark's Christology elsewhere in his Gospel."[11] Instead, commentators often point to 1 Kings 19:4–8, which speaks of Elijah's sojourn in the wilderness in which he is served by an angel and then goes for forty days to Horeb.

However, without discounting parallels to Elijah, we should not overlook the Adamic resonances of Jesus's testing by Satan,[12] since this aspect is not explicit in the proposed Elijah parallel from 1 Kings 19.[13] Likewise, Jesus's peaceful

---

Wolfgang Schrage, BZNW 47 (Berlin: Walter de Gruyter, 1986), 150–54; Joel William Parkman, "Adam Christological Motifs in the Synoptic Traditions" (PhD diss., Baylor University, 1994), 105–22; Harald Sahlin, "Adam-Christologie im Neuen Testament," *ST* 41 (1987): 11–32 (who sees Adam Christology in Mark 1 as *unbestreitbar*, or "indisputable"); W. D. Davies and Dale C. Allison Jr., *A Critical and Exegetical Commentary on the Gospel according to St. Matthew*, 3 vols., ICC (Edinburgh: T&T Clark, 1988–97), 1:356. More recently, see Marcus, *Mark 1–8*, 169; Christian Schramm, "Paradiesische Reminiszenz(en) in Mk 1,13?! Der Streit um die Adam-Christus-Typologie auf dem hermeneutischen Prüfstand," in *Theologies of Creation in Early Judaism and Ancient Judaism: In Honour of Hans Klein*, ed. Tobias Nicklas and Korinna Zamfir, DCLS 6 (Berlin: Walter de Gruyter, 2010), 267–98; Joseph Ratzinger [Pope Benedict XVI], *Jesus of Nazareth: From the Baptism in the Jordan to the Transfiguration*, trans. Adrian J. Walker (London: Bloomsbury, 2007), 26–27.

7. Some include John Paul Heil, "Jesus with the Wild Animals in Mark 1:13," *CBQ* 68 (2006): 63–78; Charles A. Gieschen, "Why Was Jesus with the Wild Beasts (Mark 1:13)?," *CTQ* 73 (2009): 77–80; Jeffrey B. Gibson, "Jesus' Wilderness Temptation according to Mark," *JSNT* 53 (1994): 3–34; Ardel B. Caneday, "Mark's Provocative Use of Scripture in Narration: 'He Was with the Wild Animals and Angels Ministered to Him,'" *BBR* 9 (1999): 19–36. Caneday does allow for some echoes of Adamic imagery in Mark.

8. Bauckham, "Jesus and the Wild Animals," 19.

9. James R. Edwards, *The Gospel according to Mark*, PNTC (Grand Rapids: Eerdmans, 2002), 40–41.

10. R. T. France, *The Gospel of Mark*, NIGTC (Grand Rapids: Eerdmans, 2002), 85–87.

11. Robert H. Stein, *Mark*, BECNT (Grand Rapids: Baker Academic, 2008), 65. For a more extensive assessment that is also skeptical of Adam Christology in Mark, see Hans-Günter Leder, "Sündenfallerzählung und Versuchungsgeschichte: Zur Interpretation von Mc 1,12f," *ZNW* 54 (1963): 188–216.

12. A standard interpretation of Gen. 3 in the first century was that the serpent was Satan. See Marcus, *Mark 1–8*, 169.

13. In contrast to the other Synoptic Gospels, Mark does not give the details of Jesus's temptations but mentions the temptations by means of a participle (*peirazomenos*). Though it is possible that this participle with the previous *ēn* could be a periphrastic construction that highlights the imperfective or durative aspect of Jesus's temptation, C. E. B. Cranfield is probably

presence with the wild animals likely also evokes prophetic imagery of the peaceful messianic age in which the animals do not attack (Isa. 11:6–9; 65:25; Ezek. 34:25–29; Hosea 2:18; cf. Lev. 26:6, 22; 2 Bar. 73:6), and the wilderness is transformed into a paradisal, edenic state (Isa. 43:20; 65:22 LXX).[14] If so, this imagery would provide additional dimensions to the Adamic resonances of Mark 1. Thus, even though Bauckham does not lean toward Adam Christology in Mark 1, he does observe verbal parallels between Isaiah 65:25 and Genesis 3:14, suggesting that the original harmony between humans and animals will be restored.[15] Isaiah's new-creational imagery therefore recalls Adam's position in God's original created order, and Mark's portrayal of Jesus inaugurating the anticipated latter days (or *Endzeit*, cf. Mark 1:15) seems to portray Jesus as the last Adam who marks the beginning of new creation.[16]

Further reinforcing the likelihood that Mark 1 conveys Adamic imagery is its consistency with some Jewish eschatological expectations[17] along with early Christian theology.[18] Thus in *Testament of Levi* 18:10–14 the work of the Messiah on whom rests the spirit of holiness will undo the sword that has lingered since Adam.[19] We also encounter animals rebelling against Eve and Seth because of human sinfulness in *Apocalypse of Moses* 10–11 and *Life of Adam and Eve* 37–38.[20] In addition to Adam's ruling over the animals in the

---

correct to express caution against this being a periphrastic construction (*The Gospel according to St. Mark: An Introduction and Commentary*, CGTC [Cambridge: Cambridge University Press, 1959], 57). See also C. F. D. Moule, *An Idiom Book of New Testament Greek*, 2nd ed. (Cambridge: Cambridge University Press, 1959), 17–18.

14. See Bauckham, "Jesus and the Wild Animals," 6–7; Pesch, *Markusevangelium*, 1:95–96; so Herman N. Ridderbos, *The Coming of the Kingdom*, trans. H. de Jongste, ed. Raymond O. Zorn (Philadelphia: P&R, 1962), 116; G. K. Beale, *A New Testament Biblical Theology: The Unfolding of the Old Testament in the New* (Grand Rapids: Baker Academic, 2011), 418–20.

15. Bauckham, "Jesus and the Wild Animals," 16; cf. Parkman, "Adam Christological Motifs," 118.

16. See also Schramm, "Paradiesische Reminiszenz(en)?," 294–95.

17. However, one should note the diversity of views of Adam in ancient Jewish literature, as has been shown by John R. Levison, *Portraits of Adam in Early Judaism: From Sirach to 2 Baruch*, JSPSup 1 (Sheffield: JSOT Press, 1988).

18. The prominence of the Adam-Christ parallel in Christian tradition is also noted by Ernest Best, *The Temptation and the Passion: The Markan Soteriology*, 2nd ed., SNTSMS 2 (Cambridge: Cambridge University Press, 1990), 6.

19. The *Testaments of the Twelve Patriarchs* have often been interpreted as Jewish documents, though they also show evidence of some Christian influences. Whether they are predominantly Jewish or Christian, they are relevant for the present discussion. See variously David A. deSilva, "The *Testaments of the Twelve Patriarchs* as Witnesses to Pre-Christian Judaism: A Re-Assessment," *JSP* 23 (2013): 21–68; James R. Davila, *The Provenance of the Pseudepigrapha: Jewish, Christian, or Other?*, JSJSup 105 (Leiden: Brill, 2005), 232–33; H. C. Kee, introduction to "*Testaments of the Twelve Patriarchs*," in OTP, 1:775–80.

20. See further John L. Sharpe III, "The Second Adam in the Apocalypse of Moses," *CBQ* 35 (1973): 35–46.

garden, we find interpretive traditions that associate Adam with forty days of fasting in *Life of Adam and Eve* 6. Similarly, in *Jubilees* 3:9 Adam is brought into the garden forty days after he was created.[21] Other traditions suggest that angels served Adam in the garden.[22] Despite variations among these extracanonical sources, they reveal a consistent interest in the protological role of Adam in early Jewish sources and serve as corroboratory witnesses for understanding Jesus's obedient victory over Satan in Mark in Adamic terms.

Likewise, I observed in the previous chapter the prevalence of the Adam-Christ parallel among early Christian theologians. To this we can add that many early church fathers compared and contrasted Adam's temptation in the garden with Christ's victory over temptation in the wilderness, though we often find less interaction of the early church fathers with Mark's temptation narrative.[23] Nevertheless, one study concludes that "among the synoptic traditions the Markan temptation narrative, with the possible exception of Luke 3:38, is the most direct comparison and contrast between Adam and Jesus."[24]

However, even though some recognize Adamic resonances in Mark's temptation account, finding scholars who advocate a thoroughgoing Adam Christology in Mark is remarkably rare.[25] Nor is it common to posit pervasive Adam Christology in the other Gospels. To be sure, there are some welcome exceptions, such as the unpublished dissertation of Joel William Parkman,[26] the articles and commentary of Joel Marcus,[27] and the recent synthesis of

21. For these texts see Marcus, *Mark 1–8*, 169; Joel Marcus, "Son of Man as Son of Adam," *RB* 110 (2003): 55; Pesch, *Markusevangelium*, 1:95. See also Ulrich Mell, "Jesu Taufe durch Johannes (Markus 1,9–15)—zur narrativen Christologie vom neuen Adam," *BZ* 40 (1996): 176–77.

22. *Apoc. Mos.* 7, 13; *LAE* 33–39. Additionally, *T. Naph.* 8.4 anticipates the last day when angels would serve the righteous. See Mahnke, *Versuchungsgeschichte*, 30; Grässer, "ΚΑΙ ΗΝ ΜΕΤΑ ΤΩΝ ΘΗΡΙΩΝ," 147.

23. On which see Klaus-Peter Köppen, *Die Auslegung der Versuchungsgeschichte unter besonderer Berücksichtigung der Alten Kirche*, BGBE 4 (Tübingen: Mohr Siebeck, 1961), esp. 74–93. He notes Justin, *Dial.* 103, as one example of the parallel (and Justin explicitly notes that the account is recorded in the *memoirs of the apostles*). Justin also observes that Adam and Christ shared a common enemy, and Jesus's response is what Adam's should have been. Cf. Martin Steiner, *La tentation de Jésus dans l'interprétation patristique de Saint Justin a Origène* (Paris: Librairie Lecoffre, 1962), 12–22; Oskar Skarsaune, *The Proof from Prophecy: A Study in Justin Martyr's Proof Text Tradition: Text-Type, Provenance, Theological Profile*, NovTSup 56 (Leiden: Brill, 1987), 383–84.

24. Parkman, "Adam Christological Motifs," 121.

25. Thus even Joachim Jeremias ("Ἀδάμ," *TDNT*, 1:141–43), whose article is foundational for many who see Adamic parallels in Mark 1:13, sees this text as one of only three clear examples of Adam Christology in the New Testament.

26. Parkman, "Adam Christological Motifs."

27. Marcus, *Mark 1–8*; Marcus, *Mark 8–16: A New Translation with Introduction and Commentary*, AYB 27A (New Haven: Yale University Press, 2009); Marcus, "Son of Man as Son of Adam," 38–61; Marcus, "Son of Man as Son of Adam. Part II: Exegesis," *RB* 110 (2003): 370–86.

G. K. Beale.[28] By way of illustration, in chapter 13 of his *New Testament Biblical Theology*, Beale traces what he labels the "end-time restoration of God's image" in the Synoptic Gospels, focusing largely on the Gospel of Matthew. He identifies several features of the creational task given to Adam that are echoed in the Gospels, including ruling, multiplying, and resting. Beale sees in Jesus the complete and perfect reflection of God's image, the absolutely righteous last Adam who obtained the eschatological blessings and glory. Thus, not only did Jesus recapitulate what Adam did, "but also he went beyond that in his faithfulness and obedience to succeed in the task at which Adam had failed."[29] Beale admits that this may be one of the most controversial chapters of his tome, yet he has mounted an impressive argument that highlights many connections between Adam and Christ in the Gospels.

In the remainder of this chapter, I will highlight some other textual features that reveal a more extensive Adam Christology in the Gospels than is sometimes recognized. To this end, I will focus largely on the genealogies of Jesus and on the implications of Jesus as Son of Man. In chapter 3, I will say more about Jesus's baptism and wilderness testing.

Jesus, Adam, and Luke's Genealogy (and Beyond)

Luke's genealogy traces Jesus all the way back to Adam (3:38), which provides warrant for considering whether Adam Christology may be found elsewhere in Luke. Commentators generally agree that by tracing Jesus's ancestry to Adam, Luke is emphasizing Jesus's universal relevance—Jesus is the Redeemer not only for Israel but for all humanity descended from Adam.[30] Yet it is highly likely that Luke also intends to identify Jesus as the last Adam.[31] This can be seen in the structure of Luke's narrative, which places Jesus's temptation directly after the genealogy that concludes with "son of Adam,

---

28. Beale, *New Testament Biblical Theology*.

29. Ibid., 386.

30. Darrell L. Bock, *Luke*, 2 vols., BECNT (Grand Rapids: Baker Academic, 1994–96), 1:360; Norval Geldenhuys, *Commentary on the Gospel of Luke*, NICNT (Grand Rapids: Eerdmans, 1951), 153; Joel B. Green, *The Gospel of Luke*, NICNT (Grand Rapids: Eerdmans, 1997), 189.

31. See also Geldenhuys, *Gospel of Luke*, 153; Bock, *Luke*, 1:125; I. H. Marshall, *The Gospel of Luke*, NIGTC (Grand Rapids: Eerdmans, 1978), 161; Adolf Schlatter, *Das Evangelium des Lukas: Aus seinen Quellen erklärt*, 2nd ed. (Stuttgart: Calwer, 1960), 218; Peter J. Scaer, "Lukan Christology: Jesus as Beautiful Savior," *CTQ* 69 (2005): 63–74; James R. Edwards, *The Gospel according to Luke*, PNTC (Grand Rapids: Eerdmans, 2015), 124; Craig A. Evans and James A. Sanders, *Luke and Scripture: The Function of Sacred Tradition in Luke-Acts* (Minneapolis: Fortress, 1994), 36–42; Jerome Neyrey, *The Passion according to Luke: A Redaction Study of Luke's Soteriology* (New York: Paulist, 1985), 165–84.

son of God" (3:38). Thus Jesus not only is descended from Adam but also overcomes temptation in contrast to Adam.[32] This is precisely the point of Irenaeus we noted in chapter 1, as Luke shows how Jesus recapitulates Adam and overcomes his disobedience.[33]

Second, the testings of Jesus's sonship in the temptation narrative (4:3, 9) reinforce the Adamic imagery of 3:38, since the manner of obedience required of God's son originates with Adam. We will look in more detail at the obedience of God's son in the next chapter,[34] but at this point I would like to underscore the interrelationship of Adamic and filial themes in the biblical witness. The correlation of Adam and divine sonship is found not only in Luke 3:38 but already in the genealogy of Genesis 5. We read in Genesis 5:1 that God created Adam in his own likeness (Hebrew: *dəmût*; Greek: *eikōn*), and in 5:3 we read that Adam begat a son in his likeness (*dəmût*) and image (*ṣelem*; see also Gen. 1:26). The implication is that, in a way analogous to Adam's fatherhood of Seth (and on down the line), God is Father to Adam, and therefore Adam should be understood as son of God.[35] This also seems to be a clear implication of the conclusion to Luke's genealogy in 3:38 ("son of Adam, son of God").

The Adamic-filial precedent of Genesis also makes sense of the identification of the nation of Israel as son of God (Exod. 4:22–23; Deut. 1:31; 8:5; 14:1–2; 32:4–6, 18–20, 43; Isa. 1:2; Jer. 3–4, and others), and it provides the foundation for the sonship of the king (2 Sam. 7:14; Ps. 2:7, and others). Just as Israel as son was a royal nation since God was Israel's great King, so the Davidic king as the representative of the nation is identified as God's royal son. Later we will explore how Jesus as Son of Man is also Adamic imagery, and how this relates to Jesus as Son of God. At this point it will suffice to note that, since the Old Testament provides the primary literary background for

---

32. Beale, *New Testament Biblical Theology*, 418; David E. Garland, *Luke*, ZECNT (Grand Rapids: Zondervan, 2011), 173–74; cf. the suggestive comments of Marshall, *Gospel of Luke*, 161. Schlatter (*Evangelium des Lukas*, 219) demurs on this point, stating that the notion that Jesus restores what was lost through Adam is foreign to the context of the genealogy. However, he does not comment on the genealogy's narrative relationship to the temptation account, which he discusses later in his commentary.

33. *Haer.* 3.22.3–4.

34. On the obedience of the Son of God, see Oscar Cullmann, *The Christology of the New Testament*, trans. Shirley C. Guthrie and Charles A. M. Hall, rev. ed. (Philadelphia: Westminster, 1963), 283; Scaer, "Lukan Christology," 71.

35. See further Beale, *New Testament Biblical Theology*, 401–6; Stephen G. Dempster, *Dominion and Dynasty: A Theology of the Hebrew Bible*, NSBT 15 (Downers Grove, IL: IVP Academic, 2003), 58; Parkman, "Adam Christological Motifs," 162–63. In accord with common custom and for sake of clarity, I will capitalize "Son of God" when it refers to Jesus but not when "son" refers to someone else.

the New Testament, we should most likely understand Son of God to have an Adamic foundation in Luke's Gospel.

A third Adamic theme in Luke's temptation narrative, which I also mentioned in connection with Mark's narrative, is the more difficult circumstances facing the last Adam than faced the first Adam. Jesus had to overcome temptation in the desolate wilderness, whereas Adam was tested in the paradisal garden. Additionally, Jesus had to overcome temptation in the wake of thousands of years of rebellion, whereas Adam's failure came in the prelapsarian world.[36] Thus, John Nolland observes: "Luke would have us see that Jesus takes his place in the human family and thus in its (since Adam's disobedience) flawed sonship; however, in his own person, in virtue of his unique origin (Luke 1:35) but also as worked out in his active obedience (4:1–13), he marks a new beginning to sonship."[37]

Beyond Luke's genealogy and temptation narrative, we have good reason to identify Jesus as the last Adam more extensively in Luke. One way we see this is through the temptations Jesus encounters later in Luke. If Jesus is viewed as the last Adam when he overcomes temptation in Luke 4, then Adamic imagery is most likely also operative in other Lukan passages in which Jesus faces temptation. From a narrative perspective, this is likely because the framework for how we understand Jesus has been established in the opening chapters of Luke's Gospel, so the implied reader is to understand later events in light of the earlier framework provided by Luke.[38]

We indeed find other examples of Jesus facing and overcoming temptation beyond Luke 4. After the encounter between Jesus and the devil in the wilderness, Luke 4:13 indicates that the devil left Jesus until the appropriate time (*achri kairou*).[39] This suggestive phrase has been taken various ways, but we should note two aspects of it here. First, Jesus's obedience in response to Satan's temptations is a singularly epochal event in the history of redemption. The departure of Satan indicates that we should view this as a decisive battle won by Jesus. Jesus's obedience in the temptation narrative is quite plausibly Jesus's initial victory over the strong man that he mentions later in his ministry (cf. Luke 11:22).[40] If so, then Jesus's temptations are not just three

36. Neyrey (*Passion*, 173–74) suggests that Jesus's temptations in Luke are modeled after three temptations given to Adam.

37. John Nolland, *Luke*, 3 vols., WBC 35A–C (Dallas: Word, 1989–93), 1:173; cf. Philo, *Virt.* 204–5.

38. For a similar point in relation to Matthew's Gospel, see Jack Dean Kingsbury, "The Figure of Jesus in Matthew's Story: A Literary-Critical Probe," *JSNT* 21 (1984): 3–36.

39. On *kairos*, see BDAG, "καιρός," 497–98.

40. See Sinclair B. Ferguson, *The Holy Spirit*, CCT (Downers Grove, IL: InterVarsity, 1996), 48; Geerhardus Vos, *Biblical Theology: Old and New Testaments* (1948; repr., Edinburgh: Banner

temptations illustrative of everyone's temptations (though they are instructive in that way) but a threefold messianic victory.

The location of the temptation in Luke's narrative structure further supports this messianic interpretation. In Luke 3:15–17 John the Baptist testifies of one who would be mightier than he, who would baptize with the Holy Spirit and fire, which is John's response to the question of whether John might be the Messiah. Immediately following, Jesus is baptized by John, identifying himself with the people and John's ministry, and is anointed as Messiah by the Holy Spirit. Moreover, immediately following the temptation, Jesus invokes messianic language from Isaiah 61 for his Spirit-anointed ministry in the synagogue at Nazareth (4:17–22), and at the end of Luke Jesus twice explains that all that happened to him was necessary for the Christ (24:25–27, 44–47). In Luke's second volume, Peter gives clear confirmation that Jesus is the Christ (Acts 2:36), was anointed with the power of the Holy Spirit (10:36–38), and possesses the resurrected authority to bestow the Spirit (2:31–35). Jesus's temptations are therefore presented to the reader within this messianic framework as he begins his ministry of word and deed in the power of the messianic Holy Spirit.[41] And the location of Luke's genealogy in the midst of this opening act of Jesus's ministry strongly suggests that the Messiah—who is son of Adam and Son of God—is portrayed in Adamic terms.

Second, in addition to the messianic nature of the temptations, we also must not assume that the departure of the devil recounted in Luke 4:13 means that Jesus encountered no spiritual opposition during his ministry. In Luke 22:3–6 we do read that Satan, through Judas, finds an opportune time (*eukairia*) to return with a vengeance at the conclusion of Jesus's ministry,[42] and Jesus is again tempted to forego his task of obedient suffering on the cross (Luke 22:3, 35–39; cf. 22:28, 31, 53). Yet Jesus's spiritual battle is not limited to the events immediately associated with his death but extends throughout his ministry. Spiritual opposition to Jesus is evident in his encounters with the demon possessed[43] and in his various comments about Satan's activity during his ministry (10:18; 11:18; 13:16). Indeed, from one perspective, Jesus's entire ministry can be described as "testings" or "temptations" (*peirasmois* [22:28]).[44]

---

of Truth, 1975), 330–31; Geldenhuys, *Gospel of Luke*, 163, 302. I will discuss the binding of the strong man in chap. 6.

41. For other texts associating the Spirit with the Messiah, see Isa. 11:1–5; 32:15; 42:1; 48:16; 59:21; Zech. 4:6.

42. Evans and Sanders, *Luke and Scripture*, 37–38.

43. See Bock, *Luke*, 1:382.

44. Green, *Luke*, 196; cf. C. D. "Jimmy" Agan III, *The Imitation of Christ in the Gospel of Luke: Growing in Christlike Love for God and Neighbor* (Phillipsburg, NJ: P&R, 2014), 30.

Nevertheless, though temptations in one sense extend throughout the ministry of Jesus, the temptation narrative in Luke 4:1–13 should be viewed as a decisive moment in the conflict between the Messiah and the devil.

The upshot of Jesus's testing throughout his ministry in Luke is that, if Jesus's temptations are to be seen in Adamic terms, and if Jesus is in some sense tested throughout his ministry, then Luke's Adam Christology is operative more extensively throughout Luke. We should therefore interpret Jesus's obedience in the face of temptation throughout Luke in Adamic terms. This is particularly evident at the end of the Gospel, as Jerome Neyrey has argued at length. We find, for example, a possible repetition of the third wilderness temptation (Luke 4:9–12) in the temptation for Jesus to be guarded from death (22:39–46).[45] In this light it is not surprising to find Jesus speaking in Adamic terms on the cross, when he promises the repentant thief that "today" he would be with Jesus in paradise (*paradeisos* [23:43]), echoing language used for the garden of Eden in the LXX (cf. Gen. 2:8–10, 15; 3:1, 8, 10, 23–34; Isa. 51:3; Ezek. 28:13; 31:8–9; 36:35).[46]

Jesus is, then, the last Adam not only at the beginning of the Gospel but also on the cross. Whereas Adam was exiled from paradise because of his sin, Jesus as the obedient, last Adam has the authority to reopen paradise for those who believe—even the brigand on the cross next to him. As the obedient last Adam in the face of temptation, Jesus brings the beginning of new creation, the eschatological *Endzeit* that marks the turn of the ages, in contrast to the first age that came with the first Adam.[47]

A few other aspects of Luke's presentation of Jesus may bespeak Adamic parallels, including the role of the Holy Spirit. We have seen the role of the Holy Spirit in the messianic task of Jesus, but Jesus was also conceived by the power of the Holy Spirit (Luke 1:35). Particularly intriguing is the filial connection in 1:35: Jesus's identity as the Son of God is related to the holiness of God's Spirit who overshadowed Mary. Jesus's conception has often been identified as Adamic imagery, especially in light of the breath of God that imparted life to Adam in Genesis 2:7 (*nišmat ḥayyîm*). Though the term *rûaḥ* is not used in Genesis 2:7, we have good reason for relating the breath of God to the work of the Holy Spirit.[48] In light of this, Craig Evans suggests a

45. Neyrey, *Passion*, 177–79.

46. See similarly Agan, *Imitation*, 30.

47. Neyrey, *Passion*, 167–68.

48. Historically, see Herman Bavinck, *Reformed Dogmatics*, ed. John Bolt, trans. John Vriend, 4 vols. (Grand Rapids: Baker Academic, 2003–8), 2:277, 558; Geerhardus Vos, *Reformed Dogmatics*, 5 vols., ed. and trans. Richard B. Gaffin Jr. (Bellingham, WA: Lexham Press, 2012–16), 1:68; Louis Berkhof, *Systematic Theology*, 4th ed. (Grand Rapids: Eerdmans, 1941), 192; John M. Frame, *Systematic Theology: An Introduction to Christian Belief* (Phillipsburg,

plausible parallel: "If it was by virtue of his Spirit-generation that Jesus was regarded as the 'Son of God,' then Luke likewise must have regarded Adam as 'son of God' by virtue of his generation by the Spirit (or breath) of God."[49] In sum, if the parallels between Luke 1:35 and Genesis 2:7 are valid, then the Holy Spirit is an additional connection between Christ as the last Adam in comparison and contrast to the first Adam.[50]

In addition, Jesus's obedience, for Luke, is empowered by the Holy Spirit (cf. Luke 4:1–13; Acts 10:36–38), and Jesus's relationship to the Spirit is unhindered. In Paul's exposition, Adam was not able to impart the Spirit (1 Cor. 15:49; cf. Gen. 5:1, 3), but the last Adam has become life-giving Spirit (1 Cor. 15:45).[51] For Luke, "Jesus' continued obedience to the will of his Father, in the power of the Holy Spirit, preserves his righteous character and safeguards his claim to divine sonship."[52] Luke narrates Jesus as the fully righteous one (cf. Luke 23:47) who has been exalted as Lord and Christ, and therefore possesses full authority to pour out the Spirit (Acts 2:33–36).

A third additional Adamic feature of Luke's Christology—Jesus as the Son of Man—is worthy of extended discussion and will be discussed in greater detail below.

In sum, Luke describes Jesus as the last Adam by means of his genealogy and wilderness testing, but also through the descriptions of Jesus as Son of God and, as I have introduced but not yet discussed, as Son of Man. Significantly, Luke's emphasis on Jesus as the last Adam is related to his universalizing message in which Jesus is the Savior for the whole world (Luke 2:31–32). Christ as the last Adam stands at the head of a new humanity. To be sure, the theological argument for this is given more fully by Paul (Rom. 5:12–21; 1 Cor. 15:45–49), but Luke communicates similar concepts through his narrative.[53] It should not be surprising that Luke's theology resembles Paul's given Luke's

---

NJ: P&R, 2013), 472; Charles Hodge, *Systematic Theology*, 3 vols. (repr., Peabody, MA: Hendrickson, 2008), 1:530; cf. Gen. 1:2; Prov. 1:23; Ezek. 37:9. The various Hebrew terms used in these contexts—*nešamah* (Greek: *pnoē*), *rûaḥ* (Greek: *pneuma*), and the verb *nāpaḥ* (Greek: *emphysa*)—are in many ways interchangeable. See also Yongbom Lee, *The Son of Man as the Last Adam: The Early Church Tradition as a Source of Paul's Adam Christology* (Eugene, OR: Pickwick, 2012), 130–31.

49. Evans and Sanders, *Luke and Scripture*, 39.

50. See similarly Sahlin, "Adam-Christologie," 13.

51. See Benjamin L. Gladd, "The Last Adam as the 'Life-Giving Spirit' Revisited: A Possible Old Testament Background of One of Paul's Most Perplexing Phrases," *WTJ* 71 (2009): 297–309; cf. Richard B. Gaffin Jr., *Resurrection and Redemption: A Study in Paul's Soteriology*, 2nd ed. (Phillipsburg, NJ: P&R, 1987), 87.

52. Evans and Sanders, *Luke and Scripture*, 39–40. Note also the breathing out of Jesus in John 20:22, and his words to his disciples: "Receive the Holy Spirit."

53. See also Scaer, "Lukan Christology," 72; cf. Parkman, "Adam Christological Motifs," 195.

own testimony that he and Paul were traveling companions.[54] Regardless of one's assessment of the presentation of Paul in Acts (and I am convinced it is an accurate portrait), unless one has good reason to think otherwise, the most likely prima facie option is to understand the views of Paul and Luke to be complementary on issues, such as Adam, where they seem to be speaking in similar ways.[55] This approach also makes sense of the prominence of the Adam-Christ parallel in the early church.[56] In other words, the Adam-Christ parallel is not only a Pauline idea.

In addition, if we allow Paul's understanding of Jesus as the last Adam to be in accord with our understanding of Luke's view of Jesus as the last Adam, then we can see how the obedience of Jesus as the last Adam can in some sense be done on behalf of those who trust in him. If the disobedience of Adam had negative consequences for all who are "in him," so will the obedience of the last Adam, himself a representative figure, have positive consequences for all those "in him" (cf. Rom. 5:12–21). At the same time, one need not rely wholly on Pauline texts to see that Jesus represents his people; this is also prominent in the Gospels. I will provide additional rationale for this view throughout the remainder of this study.

To summarize Luke's view of Jesus as the last Adam, Neyrey's articulation is apropos: "It is, then, suggested by the genealogy that Jesus is an Adam-like figure whose obedience will have saving significance for his tribe or nation."[57]

Jesus, Adam, and Matthew's Genealogy (and Beyond)

We turn now to Matthew's genealogy. Although Matthew does not explicitly include Adam in Jesus's genealogy, probable allusions to Genesis 5 and new creation do seem to indicate Adamic imagery in Matthew 1. The first two words of Matthew's Gospel (*biblos geneseōs*)—whether they refer to the entire

---

54. I am referring here to the famous "we" passages (Acts 16:10–17; 20:5–15; 21:1–18; 27:1–28:16). See also Col. 4:14; Philem. 24; 2 Tim. 4:11; Eusebius, *Hist. eccl.* 2.22; 3.4; Irenaeus, *Haer.* 3.1.1; 3.14.1. Though some deny that the "we" passages derive from Luke's personal journeys with Paul, they most likely do. See further Brandon D. Crowe, "The Sources for Luke-Acts: Where Did Luke Get His Material (And Why Does It Matter)?," in *Issues in Luke-Acts: Selected Essays*, ed. Sean A. Adams and Michael W. Pahl, GH (Piscataway, NJ: Gorgias, 2012), 91. For the argument that Luke's Gospel was known to Paul, see Michael J. Kruger, *Canon Revisited: Establishing the Origins and Authority of the New Testament Books* (Wheaton: Crossway, 2012), 205–6.

55. On Luke's presentation of Paul in Acts, see Craig S. Keener, *Acts: An Exegetical Commentary*, 4 vols. (Grand Rapids: Baker Academic, 2012–15), 1:221–57. On Paul's knowledge of the Adam-Christ parallel in early Christian tradition, see Lee, *Son of Man*, 96–123.

56. Especially in the temptation accounts, on which see Köppen, *Auslegung*.

57. Neyrey, *Passion*, 172.

Gospel, the genealogy only, or something in between[58]—are found elsewhere in Scripture only in Genesis 2:4 and 5:1.[59] As we saw with Luke, this is significant because Genesis 5:1–3, along with Genesis 1:26, provides a framework for understanding Adam as Son of God. What Luke communicates by the phrase "son of Adam, son of God" (Luke 3:38), Matthew communicates by means of verbal parallels to Genesis 5:1, along with new-creational imagery. This includes the role of the Holy Spirit in the conception of Jesus (Matt. 1:18, 20) and at his baptism (Matt. 3:16; cf. Gen. 1:2),[60] echoes to Genesis elsewhere in Matthew, and Matthew's explicit "new creation" language (e.g., *palingenesia* [Matt. 19:28]).[61]

Beyond the Adamic possibilities in Matthew 1, Matthew's genealogy presents Jesus as a covenant representative, particularly in Matthew's identification of Jesus as son of David and son of Abraham (1:1). God's covenantal relationship to Israel was particularized in the royal covenant made with David (2 Sam. 7:14; Pss. 89; 132), who summed up the people in himself as the leader and the "epitome" of his people.[62] One way to summarize this relationship is "as the king goes, so goes the people." Thus, if the king walked in righteousness, it would lead to blessings for the people (Ps. 72). If the king went astray, it would lead to curses. As the son of Abraham, Jesus is the promised seed of Abraham—the father of Israel, the one with whom God made a covenant and promised through his family to bless all the nations of the earth (Gen. 12:1–3).[63] This Abrahamic connection correlates well with Matthew's emphasis on Jesus as the recapitulation of Israel—he sums up the history of the nation in himself.[64] As son of David and son of Abraham,

---

58. Dale C. Allison Jr., "Matthew's First Two Words (Matt. 1:1)," in *Studies in Matthew: Interpretation Past and Present* (Grand Rapids: Baker Academic, 2005), 157–62.

59. Beale, *New Testament Biblical Theology*, 388–89.

60. See Brandon D. Crowe, "The Song of Moses and Divine Begetting in Matt 1,20," *Bib* 90 (2009): 47–58.

61. Jonathan T. Pennington, "Heaven, Earth, and a New Genesis," in *Cosmology and New Testament Theology*, ed. Jonathan T. Pennington and Sean M. McDonough, LNTS 355 (London: T&T Clark, 2008), 28–44.

62. Joachim Bieneck, *Sohn Gottes als Christusbezeichnung der Synoptiker*, ATANT 21 (Zürich: Zwingli, 1951), 22; Geralde Cooke, "The Israelite King as Son of God," *ZAW* 73 (1961): 202–25.

63. A commonly used definition for covenant is "an elected, as opposed to natural, relationship of obligation established under divine sanction" (Gordon Paul Hugenberger, *Marriage as Covenant: A Study of Biblical Law and Ethics Governing Marriage Developed from the Perspective of Malachi*, VTSup 52 [Leiden: Brill, 1994], 171; cf. Brandon D. Crowe, *The Obedient Son: Deuteronomy and Christology in the Gospel of Matthew*, BZNW [Berlin: de Gruyter, 2012], 91; Beale, *New Testament Biblical Theology*, 42n39).

64. See Joel Kennedy, *The Recapitulation of Israel: Use of Israel's History in Matthew 1:1–4:11*, WUNT 2/257 (Tübingen: Mohr Siebeck, 2008), 23. Kennedy notes four elements of recapitulation: repetition, summing up, representation, embodiment.

Jesus is presented in covenantal and representative categories that correlate to his role as the last Adam, head of a new covenant people. In Luke Jesus is the Messiah of Israel who is also the son of Adam, and therefore his mission is relevant for all humanity; in Matthew Jesus fulfills the covenant promises to Israel, but these promises prominently include gentiles as well (Tamar, Rahab, Ruth, Uriah).[65] Though Matthew's genealogy does not relate Jesus to Adam as prominently as Luke's, his tracing of the Genesis storyline through the genealogy, which begins with the Adamic language *biblos geneseōs*, arguably frames Jesus's work as son of David and son of Abraham in Matthew in relation to the first man.

At this point we can consider three other features of Jesus's ministry in Matthew (and the other Synoptic Gospels) that seem to reflect an interest in Adamic themes.[66] First, Jesus's promise in Matthew to provide rest from heavy labors (Matt. 11:28–30) provides an answer to the curse of Adam's toil (Gen. 3:16–19). In the same context Jesus identifies himself as gentle and humble in heart, which may be contrasted with Adam's prideful sin leading to the curse (cf. Lam. 1:14). It is also possible, if one posits Sirach 51:23–27 as a background source for Matthew 11:28–30, that Christ may fulfill the role of wisdom, which was often associated with the creation of Adam (Gen. 2:18–20; Wis. 10:1–2; *2 Bar.* 51:3; Philo, *Opif.* 148, 150; Philo, *QG* 1.20–21; *Pesiq. Rab.* 14:10).[67] However, it is by no means clear that Matthew 11 is an allusion to Sirach 51.[68]

Second, Jesus on several occasions appeals to God's original created order. For example, when Jesus responds to questions concerning marriage and divorce (Matt. 19:3–12 // Mark 10:2–12), his answer invokes creation and clearly alludes to Adam and Eve (Matt. 19:4 // Mark 10:6). By framing the issue in this way, Jesus not only speaks to the nature and permanency of marriage but also indicates that the messianic age has arrived, in which the ethics of the latter days (*Endzeit*) correspond to God's original created order (*Urzeit*).[69] Similarly, Jesus also appeals to God's created order in Sabbath controversies. In Mark 2:27 Jesus affirms God's original intent for the Sabbath, and Jesus's

---

65. Matthew mentions Uriah's name explicitly (and not Bathsheba) in 1:6.

66. For the following three features, I am drawing upon Parkman, "Adam Christological Motifs," 95–132.

67. See Robin Scroggs, *The Last Adam: A Study in Pauline Anthropology* (Philadelphia: Fortress, 1966), 4, 121–22; Levison, *Portraits of Adam*, 54–62, 141–44, 153, 159.

68. So, e.g., Davies and Allison, *Matthew*, 2:292–93; Grant Macaskill, *Union with Christ in the New Testament* (Oxford: Oxford University Press, 2013), 293.

69. Parkman, "Adam Christological Motifs," 98–99, drawing upon W. D. Davies, *Paul and Rabbinic Judaism: Some Rabbinic Elements in Pauline Theology* (London: SPCK, 1948), 39. See also *2 Bar.* 4:1–7; 51:1–16; 56:6; 73:6–74:1, noted in Levison, *Portraits of Adam*, 143–44.

focus on the Sabbath and life in Mark 3:4 also draws upon the created order. This latter text may also evince Jesus's (divine) ability to give life (cf. John 5:21, 26), which, in light of the creation imagery, can be viewed in contrast to Adam who begot death (1 Cor. 15:45–49).[70]

Third, and more briefly, Jesus's miracles recall the original creative power of God.[71] Thus, Jesus's authority over the natural realm through his words (Matt. 8:23–27 // Mark 4:35–41 // Luke 8:22–25) reflects the role of God's words in the Genesis account of creation. God's created order also seems to be in view in many contexts where Jesus is described as Son of Man, to which our study now turns.

Jesus, Adam, and the Son of Man

Thus far I have alluded to the pertinence of Jesus as Son of Man for under-standing Jesus as the last Adam in the Gospels, but I have not argued for this position.[72] In what follows I will articulate in brief scope what I understand to be the Old Testament background to the Son of Man statements in the Gospels and the implications this has for understanding Jesus's vicarious obedience as the last Adam. An important caveat is necessary at this point: anyone familiar with the state of investigation on the Son of Man will know how varied and voluminous are the discussions. If Morna Hooker could claim in 1967 that "the material has continued to pour from the Press at an ever-increasing rate,"[73] one could echo that statement (with compound inter-est) today. I will therefore not be able to enter into all the debates. Instead, my aim is to sketch where I fall in the current discussions, which have been debated at length in other contexts.[74] In what follows I discuss how Jesus's identity as Son of Man aids in the portrayal of Jesus as the obedient last Adam in the Gospels.

70. See similarly Parkman, "Adam Christological Motifs," 105.
71. I discuss miracles further in chap. 6.
72. For others who identify Son of Man as a last Adam figure in the Gospels, see, e.g., Morna D. Hooker, *The Son of Man in Mark: A Study of the Background of the Term "Son of Man" and Its Use in St. Mark's Gospel* (London: SPCK, 1967), 189–90; Lee, *Son of Man*, 96–123; Marcus, "Son of Man as Son of Adam," 38–61; Marcus, "Son of Man as Son of Adam. Part II," 370–86; Beale, *New Testament Biblical Theology*, 400; Dan G. McCartney, "*Ecce Homo:* The Coming of the Kingdom as the Restoration of Human Viceregency," *WTJ* 56 (1994): 12.
73. Hooker, *Son of Man*, 3.
74. See recently Larry W. Hurtado and Paul L. Owen, eds., *"Who Is This Son of Man?" The Latest Scholarship on a Puzzling Expression of the Historical Jesus*, LNTS 390 (London: T&T Clark, 2011).

Son of Man and the Old Testament

One of the most debated questions of Christology is how we should understand the Son of Man sayings attributed to Jesus in the Gospels. Is "Son of Man" a title? Or is it perhaps only a self-referential, even obfuscatory way for Jesus to speak of "a man like me"? The issues are myriad.

To offer some assessment, it does seem apparent that Son of Man is a way to speak of oneself, which perhaps explains why this phrase is not generally used by others for Jesus in the Gospels (John 12:34 is an exception, but this appears to be a question posed to Jesus about his identity). It is difficult to speak of any kind of consensus when engaging with the Son of Man question, but we do seem to be able to categorize Jesus's Son of Man statements in at least three ways: (1) sayings that refer to the work of the Son of Man on earth; (2) sayings that refer to the suffering of the Son of Man; (3) sayings about the future glory of the Son of Man.[75]

One aspect of the Son of Man question is the origin of the term. It is prudent to consider texts such as the *Similitudes of Enoch* (*1 En.* 37–71) when discussing the Son of Man in the Gospels, since *1 Enoch* might provide evidence of a pre-Christian usage of the Son of Man phrase (in conjunction with Dan. 7) similar to that of the Gospels.[76] However, for sake of brevity I will mainly leave this discussion to the side, in light of what I believe to be a more likely background. In my view the strongest possibility is that Jesus, by invoking this title (or perhaps coining the title)[77] in the Gospels, is alluding to the son of man figure(s?) in Daniel 7:13–14.[78] This is significant for the Gospels because Daniel 7 contrasts the kingdom of the son of man to the beastly kingdoms in a way that builds, from a canonical perspective, on the royal, Adamic imagery of Genesis 1–2 and Psalm 8.

In Daniel 7:13–14 we read of one like a son of man (Aramaic: *bar 'enāš*; Greek: *huios anthrōpou*) who comes with the clouds of heaven in the presence

75. See the discussions in Thomas R. Schreiner, *New Testament Theology: Magnifying God in Christ* (Grand Rapids: Baker Academic, 2008), 219–22; I. H. Marshall, "Son of Man," *DJG*, 775–81; Rudolf Bultmann, *Theology of the New Testament*, trans. Kendrick Grobel, 2 vols. (New York: Scribner, 1951–55), 1:30.

76. See, e.g., the discussions in James D. G. Dunn, *Jesus Remembered*, CM 1 (Grand Rapids: Eerdmans, 2003), 730–33; Bock, "Use of Daniel 7," 86n19; Davies and Allison, *Matthew*, 2:45–46. Of course, even if a pre-Christian usage could be established, it would not necessarily mean that "Son of Man" was a stock messianic phrase in the days of Jesus.

77. R. T. France, *The Gospel of Matthew*, NICNT (Grand Rapids: Eerdmans, 2007), 327.

78. See similarly Schreiner, *New Testament Theology*, 213–26; Ridderbos, *Coming of the Kingdom*, 32–33; Bock, "Use of Daniel 7"; Beale, *New Testament Biblical Theology*, 396–401; N. T. Wright, *Jesus and the Victory of God*, COQG 2 (Minneapolis: Fortress, 1996), 510–19; France, *Matthew*, 326–28; Davies and Allison, *Matthew*, 2:43–52.

of the Ancient of Days and is given an everlasting kingdom. Additionally, in Daniel 7:18 it is the saints of the most high who collectively receive the kingdom and the dominion forever. A plausible explanation for this interplay between the individual and the corporate is that the son of man is an individual figure who represents God's people corporately.[79] This is consistent with the biblical paradigm in which the king represents his people.[80] If this is correct, then the son of man in Daniel 7 is described both as an individual and as those whom this individual represents.

Consistent with this view is the observation that the son of man in Daniel 7, from a canonical perspective, builds upon the royal imagery for humanity originally given to Adam; the son of man in Daniel is the fulfiller of the Adamic task of ruling in God's image. Adam in Genesis 1–2 is portrayed in kingly terms—he is to be God's vice-regent exercising dominion in the world.[81] This royal imagery for humanity is further developed in Psalm 8, where the son of man (Hebrew: *ben 'ādām*) is crowned with glory and honor, exercising dominion over all the works of God—including the fauna—which forms part of the canonical background for the son of man's dominion over the beastly kingdoms in Daniel 7 (cf. Ps. 80:17).[82]

Additionally, the language in Psalm 8 not only is spoken of humankind in general, echoing language of Genesis 1 but can preeminently be applied to a royal representative who embodies the kingly role originally given to Adam. If we view Psalms 1–2 as a prelude to the entire Psalter, then we have warrant for understanding the psalms in an extensively royal manner. This means that we often find particular relevance for the king of Israel in the psalms (e.g., Pss. 2; 22; 41; 45; 72; 89; 132).[83] Thus, what is true of Adam in the garden

---

79. So, e.g., Beale, *New Testament Biblical Theology*, 395; Cullmann, *Christology*, 140.

80. Joyce G. Baldwin, *Daniel: An Introduction and Commentary*, TOTC (Downers Grove, IL: InterVarsity, 1978), 151; cf. Alfons Deissler, "Der 'Menschensohn' und 'das Volk der Heiligen des Höchsten' in Dan 7," in *Jesus und der Menschensohn: Für Anton Vögtle*, ed. Rudolf Pesch and Rudolf Schnackenburg (Freiburg: Herder, 1975), 81–91.

81. See Dempster, *Dominion and Dynasty*, 59; Richard L. Pratt Jr., *He Gave Us Stories: The Bible Student's Guide to Interpreting Old Testament Narrative* (Phillipsburg, NJ: P&R, 1990), 327; Bruce K. Waltke with Cathi J. Fredricks, *Genesis: A Commentary* (Grand Rapids: Zondervan, 2001), 65–66; Bavinck, *Reformed Dogmatics*, 2:246, 533, 560; McCartney, "Ecce Homo," 3–4; D. J. A. Clines, "The Image of God in Man," *TynBul* 19 (1968): 53–103; Gerhard von Rad, *Genesis: A Commentary*, trans. John H. Marks, rev. ed., OTL (Philadelphia: Westminster, 1972), 59–60. See also Wis. 9:1–4; 10:1–2; Sir. 17:2–4; *T. Ab.* 13:3–6; *Cav. Tr.* 2:17–25.

82. See also Beale, *New Testament Biblical Theology*, 83–84, 401; Dempster, *Dominion and Dynasty*, 217.

83. Bruce K. Waltke with Charles Yu, *An Old Testament Theology: An Exegetical, Canonical, and Thematic Approach* (Grand Rapids: Zondervan, 2007), 873–74, 884; O. Palmer Robertson, *The Flow of the Psalms: Discovering Their Structure and Theology* (Phillipsburg, NJ: P&R, 2015), 13–15, 54–61.

(being made in the royal image of God) is later seen with particular clarity in the anointed king who models the royal image of God representatively (cf. Ps. 21:5).[84]

This all-too-brief overview of the son of man in Old Testament context strongly suggests that Daniel 7, in light of Genesis 1–2 and Psalm 8 in particular, should be understood in terms of the creation of Adam in the image of God to rule over the created world as a vice-regent. This image-bearing task is in one sense subsequently entrusted to all humanity made in the image of God, but the Old Testament also maintains a royal, representative focus on the king of Israel. Yet, it must be emphasized, the institution of the monarchy has a precedent in the royal role of humanity that is present already in the creation of Adam and Eve. Thus the kingship dovetails with the royal realities that have been part of humankind having been made in the image of God from the beginning. Additionally, it should be stressed that the son of man, as a royal figure, is a *representative* individual,[85] and therefore what is true of the representative will in some sense be true of those whom he represents. Thus, the son of man is heir to Adam's task, which must be remembered when we interpret Jesus's Son of Man sayings. However, as likely as I perceive the references to Daniel 7 to be for the Son of Man sayings in the Gospels, Adam typology is not necessarily dependent on this connection; Adamic imagery could be in the background even if Daniel 7 is not in view.

To summarize, Jesus's Son of Man sayings—especially in light of Daniel 7—lend additional exegetical warrant for construing Jesus as the last Adam in the Gospels.

Son of Man and Adam in the Synoptic Gospels

The task remains to explain in more detail why Daniel 7 should be viewed as the most likely background to the Son of Man sayings in the Gospels. To this end, it is helpful to begin at the end of Jesus's ministry, where Jesus appears most explicitly to invoke Daniel 7 in connection with his role as Son of Man. In Matthew 26:64 // Mark 14:62 // Luke 22:69 we have the three Synoptic accounts of Jesus's answer to the high priest's question of whether he was (in Mark's language) the Christ, the Son of the Blessed One. Although neither Matthew, Mark, nor Luke records precisely the same language for Jesus's response to the question (nor indeed is the question posed precisely

---

84. The relevance of Ps. 21, esp. in relation to Ps. 8, was first brought to my attention by Jonathan Gibson.

85. See Schreiner, *New Testament Theology*, 225; Beale, *New Testament Biblical Theology*, 398.

the same way in any of the accounts), Jesus's responses in Matthew and Mark include verbal parallels to Daniel 7:13 (along with Ps. 110:1) as part of Jesus's explanation of the glory of the Son of Man. Additionally, Luke, though he does not mention "coming on/with the clouds of heaven," nevertheless does mention the Son of Man, which, in light of Luke's Gospel more broadly, likely also evokes Daniel 7:[86]

Daniel 7:13	Matthew 26:64	Mark 14:62	Luke 22:69
epi tōn nephelōn tou ouranou hōs huios anthrōpou ērcheto	*opsesthe ton huion tou anthrōpou kathēmenon ek dexiōn tēs dynameōs kai erchomenon epi tōn nephelōn tou ouranou*	*opsesthe ton huion tou anthrōpou ek dexiōn kathēmenon tēs dynameōs kai erchomenon meta tōn nephelōn tou ouranou*	*estai ho huios tou anthrōpou kathēmenos ek dexiōn tēs dynameōs tou theou*
on the clouds of heaven was com-ing [one] like a son of man	you will see the Son of Man seated at the right hand of power and coming on the clouds of heaven	you will see the Son of Man seated at the right hand of power and com-ing with the clouds of heaven	the Son of Man will be seated at the right hand of the power of God

In Mark 14:62 and Matthew 26:64 Jesus clearly articulates his role as the glorious Son of Man in the language of Daniel 7:13–14. Even if one grants these allusions, it is not self-evident that an allusion to Daniel 7 here would neces-sitate a Daniel 7 background to *all* of Jesus's Son of Man sayings. However, a good case can be made that Jesus's trial, as a key moment in the Gospels, provides the occasion for the fullest articulation of the significance of the Son of Man sayings that are peppered throughout the Gospels. When Jesus speaks openly about his identity, declaring that he would sit at the right hand of God (Ps. 110:1) and come with the clouds of glory (Dan. 7:13), Caiaphas views his words as blasphemy (Matt. 26:65 // Mark 14:63–64 // Luke 22:71). Coming with the clouds is language of theophany, and the language Jesus uses from Daniel 7 would further evoke the dominion of the Son of Man in the presence of the Ancient of Days. By this collocation of imagery, Jesus appears to be claiming that the Son of Man is a man in contrast to the beasts and is given a divine dominion, associating him closely with the glory of the Ancient of Days.

It is therefore exceedingly plausible that Jesus announces with greatest clarity at the end of the Gospels his identity and authority as the Son of Man that he has been progressively revealing throughout his ministry.[87] Were

86. Bock, "Use of Daniel 7," 95.
87. See similarly Bock, *Luke*, 1:927–30.

Jesus to have spoken so explicitly about the Son of Man's divine prerogatives in relation to his own task earlier in his public ministry, it seems not at all unlikely that the Jewish leadership would have had clear reason to seize him earlier than they did. It is further likely that Jesus avoided the use of the term *messiah* to describe his task for this very reason—it was widely understood in a revolutionary or militaristic sense that did not helpfully communicate the view Jesus had of his own mission (not to mention the concomitant risks of identifying oneself openly as "messiah").[88] Though I do believe that Jesus is clearly identified in the Gospels as the Messiah, the Son of Man was a more prudent phrase for Jesus to describe his mission since it appears not to have been used prominently before its use by Jesus, and therefore had less interpretive and cultural baggage to be overcome.[89]

Jesus as Son of Man in relationship to Daniel 7 is probably most clearly articulated during his trial, but this stands in continuity with the Son of Man sayings elsewhere in the Gospels. Working our way backward through the Gospels (which is prudent if the identity of the Son of Man becomes clearer as the Gospel progresses), in the Olivet Discourse Jesus also describes the authority of the Son of Man in the language of Daniel 7—he will come with clouds and power and great glory (Matt. 24:30 // Mark 13:26 // Luke 21:27).[90] Another rather clear collocation of Daniel 7 and the Son of Man is found in Matthew 16:27 // Mark 8:38 // Luke 9:26.[91] Here again we find mention of the Son of Man coming (*erchomai*), in this case coming with the glory of his Father.[92] Similarly, in Matthew the transfiguration is explicitly linked to Jesus's glorious coming in his kingdom as the Son of Man (16:28), though only Peter, James, and John actually see the transfiguration. This occasion also marks a turning point in the Gospel narratives. After the messianic confession of Peter at Caesarea Philippi, Jesus announces with greater clarity the necessity of the Son of Man's suffering and vindication, though the disciples remain slow to understand. Indeed, although the Son of Man is to endure humiliation and suffering, the authority that Jesus claims as the Son of Man is remarkable.

88. See variously Wright, *Jesus*, 481–86; Dunn, *Jesus Remembered*, 653; Richard N. Longenecker, *The Christology of Early Jewish Christianity*, SBT 2/17 (London: SCM, 1970), 63–74; Cullmann, *Christology*, 111–33; J. R. Edwards, *Mark*, 79; briefly Richard Bauckham, *Jesus: A Very Short Introduction*, VSI 275 (Oxford: Oxford University Press, 2011), 87–88.

89. See also Schreiner, *New Testament Theology*, 225.

90. Davies and Allison, *Matthew*, 2:48.

91. Ibid., 2:674; Marcus, *Way*, 166; Bock, *Luke*, 1:856–57; Green, *Luke*, 375.

92. In this instance Jesus makes similar claims to what he later makes before the high priest. In Mark and Luke the crowds are apparently privy to this statement (Matthew mentions only the disciples [16:24]), but Jesus's speech appears to be obfuscated sufficiently to avoid any immediate charge of blasphemy.

Daniel 7 is relevant for understanding the theological significance of Jesus's life in the Gospels because, if Daniel 7 provides part of the background for the Son of Man sayings in the Gospels (or at least many of them), then we should also view Jesus as Son of Man in Adamic terms. As Son of Man, Jesus fulfills the intended destiny of the royal dominion of humanity.[93] In what follows I provide a brief survey of select Son of Man themes and indicate how these seem to fit within a Son of Man = last Adam schema. It will be helpful to categorize these Son of Man statements according to the three categories of usage we noted above: (1) the work of the Son of Man on earth; (2) the suffering of the Son of Man; (3) the coming glory of the Son of Man.

The Work of the Son of Man on Earth

The first category of texts to consider includes those that speak of Jesus's earthly work as Son of Man. Here we see the authority the Son of Man exercises as God's representative man. We begin with the two Son of Man sayings among the five controversies of Mark 2:1–3:6, in which Jesus demonstrates his authority and articulates his mission, thereby precipitating the increasing conflict between himself and the religious leaders (cf. Mark 3:6). In the first encounter—which entails a climactic, apothegmatic statement (in addition to bearing earmarks of a miracle story)—we read that the Son of Man has authority to forgive sins (2:10). Viewed in light of the overall Adamic background to the Son of Man argued above, it is not unlikely that a thematic allusion may be found that contrasts the first Adam's fall into sin with the authority of the Son of Man as the last Adam to forgive sins. Additionally, Marcus has argued that the *lectio difficilior*, and therefore the preferred reading of 2:10, is *epi tēs gēs aphienai hamartias* (instead of *aphienai hamartias epi tēs gēs*).[94] By fronting "on the earth," this reading would emphasize the earthly location of the Son of Man's authority, possibly recalling the authority originally invested to Adam. Though Marcus's preferred reading has impressive external evidence, it does not resist harmonization (Matt. 9:6 // Luke 5:24) and is not to be preferred from a text-critical perspective. Nevertheless, even if one did not follow Marcus's reading for Mark 2:10, both Matthew and Luke do front the phrase *epi tēs gēs*, which could constitute an Adamic resonance, though this phrase may just as well indicate the timing, extent, or relationship vis-à-vis

---

93. As Son of Man, "Christ is revealed as the true Adam who has come to restore Paradise" (Jean Daniélou, SJ, *From Shadows to Reality: Studies in the Biblical Typology of the Fathers*, trans. Dom Wulstan Hibberd [London: Burns and Oates, 1960], 17).

94. Marcus, *Mark 1–8*, 218.

heaven of the Son of Man's authority.[95] Further in accord with this possible Adamic imagery, one should not neglect to reflect upon the implied relationship between the sinlessness of the Son of Man and the authority to forgive sins—how could one who is himself a sinner forgive the sins of others? This may be part of what underlies the question of the leaders who ask, "Who can forgive sins but God alone?" This question is often debated in relation to Jesus's divinity,[96] but concomitant with that question is the issue of God's perfection and sinlessness that the Son of Man is by implication claiming at this juncture, in contrast to the entrance of sin into the world through Adam.[97] Consistent with this, we find in the larger context surrounding the parallel texts (Matt. 9:1–8 // Luke 5:17–26) rather clear interests in the sinlessness of Jesus (Matt. 3:14–15; Luke 4:34; cf. Acts 3:14). In sum, the authority of Jesus as Son of Man reflects the authority originally entrusted to Adam in his created state of sinlessness (cf. Eccles. 7:29).

In the second Markan controversy story to mention the Son of Man, Jesus claims authority over the Sabbath day (2:28). Discussions of the Christology of this passage are lively, with some maintaining that Jesus is using Son of Man in a titular sense for himself, and others claiming that Jesus is stating only that the Sabbath was made for humankind more generally. In my view the former option is much more likely given the consistency of "Son of Man" as a title throughout Mark and the other Gospels (note, e.g., the articular use of the phrase), although the latter view rightly acknowledges the emphasis on the humanity of the Son of Man. Particularly relevant for possible Adamic parallels is the Sabbath's role in the created order. Although the Sabbath command first appears in the Decalogue, the narrative of Genesis 1–2 portrays a world in which the Creator rested on the seventh day, and this pattern provides the rationale for humanity's need to keep the Sabbath (Exod. 20:11). For the New Testament writers, the Sabbath would likely have been closely associated with the creation account and the creation of the first man.[98] Although the Sabbath was God's day (Gen. 2:3), given that humanity is the pinnacle of God's creation,[99] one can also legitimately say that the

95. See Davies and Allison, *Matthew*, 2:93; John Nolland, *The Gospel of Matthew*, NIGTC (Grand Rapids: Eerdmans, 2005), 382.

96. See Daniel Johansson, "'Who Can Forgive Sins but God Alone?' Human and Angelic Agents, and Divine Forgiveness in Early Judaism," *JSNT* 33 (2011): 351–74.

97. On Jesus's sinlessness, see Adolf Schlatter, *The History of the Christ: The Foundation for New Testament Theology*, trans. Andreas J. Köstenberger (Grand Rapids: Baker, 1997), 75, 120. However, Schlatter himself does not understand Son of Man as Adamic imagery (ibid., 136).

98. So, e.g., Mark 2:27.

99. Three ways we see this are as follows: (1) only humanity is created in the image of God; (2) only after the creation of humanity does God declare it was *very* good; and (3) more space

Sabbath was made for humanity.[100] And yet the claim of Jesus exceeds beyond simply identifying the blessing of the Sabbath for humanity—Jesus is in fact claiming divine prerogative over the divine day of rest even as he points to the Sabbath's benefit for humanity.[101]

Finally, among the first category of sayings are Jesus's words on discipleship, which indicate that not even the Son of Man has a place to lay his head (Matt. 8:20 // Luke 9:58). This is surprising in light of the Son of Man's authority. In contrast to the birds and the foxes, the one who will come with the clouds and be given all authority in accord with Daniel 7:13–14 (cf. Matt. 24:30; 28:18) has not even a place to lay his head.[102] This is likely another Adamic allusion: whereas Adam was the pinnacle of God's creation, possessing authority over the animals, in Jesus's state of humiliation on earth he had not even a place to lay his head; he was worse off, in that sense, than the animals. However, the Son of Man's humble work on earth was not a cul-de-sac but the path of blessing by which he realized, through his resurrection, the dignity designed for all humanity.[103] Thus we find an Adamic accent in the contrast between the restlessness of the Son of Man and the respite of the fauna.

THE SUFFERING OF THE SON OF MAN

For the second category of texts, which focus even more explicitly on the suffering of the Son of Man, the ransom logion found in Matthew 20:28 // Mark 10:45 provides a suitable entrée. I will say more about the ransom logion in chapter 7, but here I mention a few aspects of this text that bespeak Adamic imagery. First, if we grant the Danielic background to the "Son of Man" title, then we have here another ironic allusion to the glorious figure from Daniel 7:14 who in that context is to be served by all peoples.[104] As argued above, this authoritative Son of Man in Daniel 7 is modeled after the protological vice-regency of Adam. The ransom logion thus flips the expectations—instead of the Son of Man receiving service and worship, in Matthew and Mark (see also

---

is devoted to the creation of humanity. Indeed, we have two complementary accounts of the creation of humanity in Gen. 1 and 2.

100. See also *Mek. Exod.* 31:13, cited by (among others) J. R. Edwards, *Mark*, 96; Marcus, "Son of Man as Son of Adam. Part II," 374–75. Marcus even suggests that the articular "the man" in Mark 2:27–28 refers to Adam as the progenitor of all humanity (ibid., 375–76; Marcus, *Mark 1–8*, 245–46).

101. See also J. R. Edwards, *Mark*, 97; McCartney, "*Ecce Homo*," 12–13. Note also the parallel passage in Matthew, in which Jesus claims to be not only Lord of the Sabbath (Matt. 12:8) but also even greater than the temple (12:6).

102. Davies and Allison, *Matthew*, 2:52, 3:99; France, *Matthew*, 327.

103. This also accords with the quotation of Ps. 8:4–6 in Heb. 2:4–9.

104. Marcus, "Son of Man as Son of Adam. Part II," 376.

Luke 22:27) the Son of Man comes to serve others. This is counterintuitive in light of the Danielic background to the Son of Man, in which "the dominion of Adam is restored to the rightful owner . . . in contrast to those whose sin and rebellion has reduced them to the level of beasts."[105]

Yet—and here is a second Adamic feature of the ransom logion—the Son of Man's service extends even to giving his life as a ransom for many (*dounai tēn psychēn autou lytron anti pollōn*). This language is noticeably similar to Paul's Adam-Christ parallel in Romans 5:15, 19, where he speaks of the effects of Adam's sin for "the many" (*polloi*), compared and contrasted with the benefits of Christ's obedience for the many (cf. Isa. 53:10–12).[106] However, the victorious vision of Daniel 7 is by no means abrogated, because the Son of Man's death is overcome in the resurrection and ascension; all nations will indeed worship and serve Jesus (cf. Matt. 28:18–20; Acts 2:29–36). Thus, the vision of Daniel is realized through the suffering of the Son of Man, who, in contrast to Adam, "is obedient to God's law . . . [and] reverses the transgression of Adam."[107]

A third Adamic parallel is the principle of representation in the ransom logion: the Son of Man is a *representative* figure who gives his life on behalf of others. This is consistent with the individual-corporate interplay of the Son of Man in Daniel 7 highlighted above, and with the covenantal *Weltanschauung* (worldview) of Scripture in which an anointed individual represents others. Thus, to choose a few examples among many, in the account of David and Goliath, the warrior from Gath challenges an Israelite champion to fight on behalf of the army (1 Sam. 17:8–10).[108] It is therefore fitting that David has already been anointed as king (1 Sam. 16:13) when he slays the gentile (1 Sam. 17:43–50). Similar features of representation are seen in the priesthood. For example, the names of the twelve tribes were emblazoned upon the breastpiece of the high priest (Exod. 28:17–21), which illustrates the high priest's representation of all twelve tribes by means of his anointed office.[109] Similarly, on the Day of Atonement the high priest had to undergo a thorough cleansing and atonement for his household before he could appear in the Holy of Holies to represent Israel (Lev. 16:1–6; cf. Zech. 3:1–4). Negatively, Achan's sin had consequences for all of Israel (Josh. 7),

---

105. Hooker, *Son of Man*, 29.

106. Marcus, "Son of Man as Son of Adam. Part II," 377; Lee, *Son of Man*, 99–102.

107. Hooker, *Son of Man*, 141.

108. See also the representative battle between Paris and Menelaus in *Il.* 3, which is of particular interest if one were to associate the Philistines with the descendants of the Sea Peoples who migrated south after the supposed Trojan War.

109. See similarly Robert Letham, *Union with Christ: In Scripture, History, and Theology* (Phillipsburg, NJ: P&R, 2011), 62.

and the rebellion of Korah led not only to his own destruction but also to the destruction of his family (Num. 16).[110]

These examples could be multiplied many dozens of times over. I mention them here because the principle of representation can ultimately be traced back to Adam. Indeed, Matthew 20:28 // Mark 10:45 appear to reflect upon the Adamic principle of representation as the Son of Man obediently gives his life on behalf of the many unrighteous sons of Adam. As Marcus concludes: the Son of Man "has reversed the effect of Adam's sin, the death which he passed on to his offspring; the one Son of Adam has given his life as a ransom for the many children of Adam who were deprived of life by their forebear's transgression."[111] We therefore must not miss the obedience of the Son of Man in the ransom logion, which enables his ability to give himself representatively and, indeed, as a substitute.

We further see the obedience of the Son of Man in his suffering unto the point of death. On at least three occasions in the Gospels, Jesus clearly predicts his death (and resurrection) as the Son of Man (Mark 8:31–33; 9:30–32; 10:32–34; and parr.). Therefore, we should most likely view the Passion Narratives in light of Jesus's Son of Man predictions, even where the phrase may not be used. This means we may expect to find Adamic resonances in events pertaining to the cross, as indeed we have noted already (cf. Luke 23:43). It has recently been argued that the darkness that covered the land at the time of Jesus's crucifixion is an allusion not only to the darkness of the plagues of Exodus 10 or the darkness of mourning in Amos 8, but even to the primordial chaos of Genesis 1:2–3. This makes sense of the extent of not only the darkness motif but also its location "over the whole land" (Mark 15:33). However, this same article argues that not only do we find judgment in Mark 15:33, but we also find the inauguration of eschatological new creation.[112] Among the various rationales given for the new creation theme here (along with, e.g., the association of darkness and light in the Bible and the statement in Mark 16:2) is the association of Jesus's death with last-Adam imagery as the one who inaugurates the new age of the eschaton.[113]

Further corroborating this Adamic interpretation are the parallels to the death of Christ and Adam in the reception history of the passion. Irenaeus

110. See further Joel S. Kaminsky, *Corporate Responsibility in the Hebrew Bible*, JSOTSup 196 (Sheffield: Sheffield Academic, 1995).
111. Marcus, "Son of Man as Son of Adam. Part II," 377.
112. G. K. Beale and Dane Ortlund, "Darkness over the Whole Land: A Biblical-Theological Reflection on Mark 15:33," *WTJ* 75 (2013): 221–38.
113. Similarly, darkness is associated with the sin of Adam in *LAE* 46:1. See Beale and Ortlund, "Darkness," 235.

speaks of the obedience of Jesus on the tree undoing the disobedience of Adam occasioned by the tree in the garden.[114] Additionally, early Christian interpreters consistently linked Golgotha, the Place of the Skull (Matt. 27:33 // Mark 15:22 // John 19:17), with the skull of Adam that was said to be buried beneath the hill.[115] Jerome explains: "Tradition has it that . . . on this very spot, Adam lived and died. The place where our Lord was crucified is called Calvary [Latin for *Golgotha*], because the skull of the primitive man was buried there. So it came to pass that the second Adam, that is the blood of Christ, as it dropped from the cross, washed away the sins of the buried protoplast, the first Adam."[116] Additionally, the early Christian writing *Cave of Treasures* includes an extensive account of how the creation and fall of Adam is recapitulated in the death of Christ.[117] Even though the historical value of this tradition is uncertain,[118] its pervasiveness in Christian tradition provides additional warrant for relating the death of Christ to Adam.

THE COMING GLORY OF THE SON OF MAN

The third category of texts, which deals with the coming glory of the Son of Man, is often set in contrast to the present suffering of the Son of Man. These texts seem to reflect the glory of Jesus as the realization of the glory that was not realized in Adam. We begin with the Olivet Discourse, where the coming glory of the Son of Man may be taken in an Adamic direction as seen through the lens of Daniel 7. In Matthew 24:30 // Mark 13:26 // Luke 21:27 Jesus speaks of the coming of the Son of Man upon/in/with (the) cloud(s) with (much) power and glory. Each Evangelist words it slightly differently, and exegetes differ as to when this will take place, but there is little question that the imagery is that of the son of man in Daniel 7: son of man, coming, clouds, glory, and even the universality of the mourning echo Daniel 7:13–14. This vision of the Son of Man demonstrates the cosmic scope of the Son of Man's authority in Adamic terms.[119]

---

114. *Epid.* 34; *Haer.* 5.16.3.

115. Joachim Jeremias, *Golgotha*, ANZK 1 (Leipzig: Eduard Pfeiffer, 1926), 34–40; Ulrich Luz, *Matthew*, trans. James E. Crouch, 3 vols., Hermeneia (Minneapolis: Fortress, 2001–7), 3:530–31.

116. *Epist.* 46 to Marcella (NPNF[2] 6:61). See also Chrysostom, *Hom. Jo.* 85 (NPNF[1] 14:317); Chromatius, in Manlio Simonetti, ed., *Matthew 14–28*, ACCS 1b (Downers Grove, IL: IVP Academic, 2002), 287–88; *Cav. Tr.* 49.

117. *Cav. Tr.* 48. Cf. Alexander Toepel, "The Cave of Treasures: A New Translation and Introduction," in *Old Testament Pseudepigrapha: More Noncanonical Scriptures*, ed. Richard Bauckham, James R. Davila, and Alexander Panayotov, vol. 1 (Grand Rapids: Eerdmans, 2013), 535–36, who dates it to the sixth or seventh century.

118. As noted already by Jerome, *Comm. Matt.* 27:33; see Marcus, *Mark 8–16*, 1042.

119. Marcus ("Son of Man as Son of Adam. Part II," 378 and 378n29) has even suggested that the lightning-like, cosmic vision of the coming of the Son of Man in Matt. 24:27 // Luke

We may also find Adamic imagery in the transfiguration of Jesus. In Matthew 17:2 // Mark 9:2–3 // Luke 9:29 Jesus's clothing becomes gloriously bright. Some have read this in light of Jewish and Christian traditions, in which Adam in his prelapsarian state was clothed in divine glory (Sir. 49:16; *LAE* 16:2; *Apoc. Mos.* 20:1–2; 21:2, 6; *2 En.* 30:11–14; *Gen. Rab.* 20:12; *Pirqe R. El.* 14; *Apoc. Adam* 1:2).[120] These texts commonly relate the created state of righteousness to the glory of Adam and note that when sin came, the glory was forfeited (*LAE* 16:2; *Gen. Rab.* 12:6; *Apoc. Mos.* 20:1–2; 21:2, 6; *Pesiq. Rab.* 14:10; cf. Ezek. 28:13–14). At Qumran we find expectations that the elect will receive the glory of Adam (CD III, 20–21; 1QS IV, 22–23), which is in other texts explicitly linked to the coming of the Messiah (*Gen. Rab.* 12:6). Other traditions describe the garments of *post*lapsarian Adam as being resplendent with glory, such as we find in *Targum Pseudo-Jonathan* on Genesis 3:21: "And the Lord God made *garments of glory* for Adam and his wife *from the skin which the serpent had cast off*."[121] This rendering is likely built upon a wordplay between "light" (*'ôr*) and "skin" (*'ôr*) in Hebrew, and is also reflected in *Genesis Rabbah* 20:12 and *Targum Neofiti* on Genesis 3:21.[122]

However, despite these various extrabiblical traditions, the biblical accounts do not ascribe resplendent glory to either the pre- or postlapsarian Adam.[123] The glory that Jesus manifests in the transfiguration may be better taken as the divine glory (Ps. 104:1; Dan. 7:9) or the glory of theophany (Exod. 19:16; 33:21–23; 40:34–35; Num. 16:19; Pss. 18:14; 97:4; 144:6). Yet Adamic resonances may also be present inasmuch as Jesus manifests this divine glory as the (Adamic) Son of Man.[124] Additionally, we do not find a uniform tradition

---

17:24 reflects Jewish traditions in which Adam was not only glorious but also enormous in size (e.g., *b. Ḥag.* 12a; *Gen. Rab.* 8:1; 12:3; cf. Irenaeus, *Haer.* 1.30.6). However, these interpretive traditions are later, and their interpretations of biblical texts such as Deut. 4:32 and Ps. 139:5 are not persuasive; there is little reason to see the coming of the Son of Man in the Gospels as echoing the legendary enormous size of Adam.

120. See also Parkman, "Adam Christological Motifs," 33–52; Nissan Rubin and Admiel Kossman, "The Clothing of the Primordial Adam as a Symbol of Apocalyptic Time in Midrashic Sources," *HTR* 90 (1997): 155–70; Marcus, *Mark 8–16*, 1113–14; Marcus, "Son of Man as Son of Adam," 57n77.

121. Translation from Michael Maher, *Targum Pseudo-Jonathan: Genesis*, ArBib 1B (Collegeville, MN: Liturgical Press, 1992), 29 (italics original).

122. Ibid., 29n43; Martin McNamara, *Targum Neofiti 1: Genesis*, ArBib 1A (Collegeville, MN: Liturgical Press, 1992), 62–63.

123. However, the king of Tyre's description in Ezek. 28:13–14, where he is adorned with precious jewels and described in Adamic terms, is suggestive. Cf. Beale, *New Testament Biblical Theology*, 74.

124. Macaskill (*Union with Christ*, 136) points to the *Exagōgē* of Ezekiel the Tragedian to show an early Jewish text in which human glory is derivative of the divine glory.

of a glorious Adam even in early Jewish sources.[125] Nevertheless, we can say that in his transfiguration the Son of Man excels the glory that was not realized by Adam.[126]

Canonical connections between Jesus's transfiguration and his resurrection and glorification enhance the plausibility that the glory of the Son of Man stands in contrast to Adam's lack of eschatological glory. Numerous texts relate the divine glory of Jesus to his role as the one entrusted with all dominion (e.g., 1 Cor. 2:8; Eph. 1:20–23; Phil. 2:6–11; Heb. 1:1–4; James 2:1; 1 Pet. 4:11; 2 Pet. 3:18)—excelling Adam's original dominion—and these emphases are sometimes associated with Adamic "image of God" language (e.g., 2 Cor. 4:4–6; Col. 1:15–20; cf. Gen. 1:27). In light of these texts and Daniel 7, we can conclude that the Son of Man's transfiguration anticipates his resurrection glory.[127] Similarly, Matthew's Great Commission (Matt. 28:18–20), though it does not employ the "Son of Man" title, clearly alludes to the authority of the Son of Man in Daniel 7. Common vocabulary and themes lead W. D. Davies and Dale Allison to conclude cogently: "The inference, that 28.16–20 should trigger recollection of Daniel, is hard to resist, and the common affirmation, that the resurrected Lord has fulfilled or proleptically realised the promise of the Son of man's vindication, commends itself."[128] As such, Jesus fulfills the (Adamic) task of ruling over all creation in his resurrected state, having been perfectly obedient to his Father, particularly through suffering.

In sum, Jesus is the mysterious and revealing, suffering and serving, but authoritative and glorious Son of Man spoken of in Daniel 7, and this explains both his divine authority and his role as representative ruler of humanity as the last Adam. "Son of Man" is thus an appropriate moniker for one who is truly man and who obediently brought a kingdom that will outlast all other kingdoms.[129]

The Son of Man in the Gospel of John

To this point I have focused almost exclusively on the Son of Man in the Synoptic Gospels. In chapter 5, I will give extended consideration to John's Gospel, but we can also include a few words at this point about the Adam Christology of the Fourth Gospel, primarily in terms of the Son of Man. Although we find different emphases in John, one should not too quickly

125. See Levison, *Portraits of Adam*; Macaskill, *Union with Christ*, 128.
126. See similarly Marcus, *Mark 8–16*, 1113.
127. See, e.g., Lane, *Gospel according to Mark*, 312–13; 2 Pet. 1:16–19.
128. Davies and Allison, *Matthew*, 3:683.
129. See also Hooker, *Son of Man*, 29.

dismiss the similarities between the Son of Man sayings in John and those in the Synoptics.[130] Even if one were to see more discontinuity, however, it should be rather uncontroversial that the Son of Man in John is an exalted figure, and is entrusted with the task of judging, as we would expect to find if the background is Daniel 7 (John 5:27).[131] Additionally, the apocalyptic references to angels ascending and descending on the Son of Man (John 1:51), and the Son of Man's ascent and descent (John 3:13), also make sense in light of the vision of Daniel 7:13–14. These references are further consistent with the parousia glory that characterizes the Son of Man sayings in the Synoptics, and the phrase "Son of Man" appears to have been enigmatic to at least some among Jesus's auditors (John 12:34). In view of these features, John's use of Son of Man most likely also draws upon Daniel 7. Therefore, we have exegetical warrant in John for understanding Jesus's task in terms of the exalted, Adamic Son of Man.

If so, it is not surprising that we encounter additional Adamic allusions in John. For example, Jesus is said to have all life in himself (John 5:21, 26). This is most certainly a divine claim, in light of the overall context of Jesus's speech in John 5. And yet, as we noted above in relation to Luke and Mark, the ability to impart life is antithetical to the death that sprang from Adam's line. Thus, we may have both divine and Adamic imagery in Jesus's claim to give life.[132] Additionally, Jesus's exhortation not to toil for food that is perishing may also recall the futility of work in the postlapsarian order, deriving from Adam's protological sin (John 6:27).[133] Indeed, this possibility is increased because John 6 speaks of Jesus as the Son of Man (cf. 6:53). The answer to the problem of the food that perishes is to partake of the bread of life, which comes by feasting upon Jesus (6:35, 51–56).[134] In chapter 5, I will also argue that Pilate's presentation of Jesus in John 19:5 ("behold the man") is an Adamic reference, and that Jesus's ability to dispense the Spirit in his resurrected state (John 20:22; cf. 15:26; 16:7) accords with Paul's teaching that Jesus—as resurrected last Adam—became life-giving Spirit (1 Cor. 15:45).

---

130. See further Schreiner, *New Testament Theology*, 226–29.

131. This usage in John 5:27 is anarthrous (*huios anthrōpou*), in distinction from the Synoptic sayings, but it is most likely to be taken in the titular sense as well. This usage may in fact reflect more precisely the language of Dan. 7:13. Cf. C. K. Barrett, *The Gospel according to St. John: An Introduction with Commentary and Notes on the Greek Text*, 2nd ed. (Philadelphia: Westminster, 1978), 262; cf. Sahlin, "Adam-Christologie," 23.

132. In John 5:22 Jesus is identified as the one who judges, which is a task associated with Adam in some early Jewish sources (e.g., *T. Ab.* 13:3–6).

133. See Parkman, "Adam Christological Motifs," 125–26.

134. Sahlin ("Adam-Christologie," 22–26) suggests some other possibilities, though not all are persuasive.

Implications: Son of Man, Adam, and Israel

I have by no means exhausted all of the Adam-Christ parallels in the Gospels, but I hope to have provided enough argument to establish that we do have sufficient exegetical warrant for identifying Jesus as the last Adam throughout the Gospels. It has been necessary to argue rather extensively for a pervasive Adam typology in the Gospels because of the dearth of attention this topic typically receives. Nevertheless, in spite of this relative lack of discussion, numerous parallels between Adam and Christ are present in the Gospels. Additionally, this is not an altogether new observation but is consistent with the sustained interest in Adam in the history of interpretation (Jewish and Christian).

Yet my main purpose is not simply to argue *that* we find an Adam Christology in the Gospels but to explore *why* it matters. I believe the implications are far-reaching. It will be helpful to enumerate three of the most significant observations from this chapter, after which I will discuss two implications of the parallels I have suggested. First, here are three observations:

1. We find Adam typology throughout the Gospels, including in the genealogies, in the temptation narratives, and the "Son of Man" title.
2. Adam was the head of the original creation; Jesus is the head of the new creation.
3. The first Adam was disobedient; the last Adam is fully obedient.

In light of these observations, I suggest two implications moving forward. First, Jesus is a representative person. Just as Adam was a representative person at the beginning of creation, so also is Jesus a representative person at the beginning of the new creation. Just as Adam's sin had consequences for others besides himself,[135] so too does Jesus's obedience have implications for others besides himself. In the rest of this study, I will investigate this claim in further detail. We will also consider in the next chapter how "Son of God" is a representative title and how Jesus as Son of God relates both to Adam and to the nation of Israel.

Second, an important question we have not yet addressed is how Jesus as Son of Man relates to Jesus as Messiah (*christos*). "Son of God" is perhaps more obviously a christological title, given the Davidic covenant applicable to God's son (2 Sam. 7:14; 1 Chron. 17:13; 22:10; Ps. 89:27). Perhaps it is not surprising that more debate has centered around whether "Son of Man" is a

---

135. See also 2 Esd. 7:118.

messianic title. Although the term was sufficiently ambiguous for Jesus to use it with comparatively less baggage during his ministry, it does seem to have messianic implications, not least because it can be a collective term for the saints of the Most High, while also being an individual. Interestingly, we find in 4Q246 the interplay between Son of God, Son of the Most High (cf. Luke 1:32, 35), and references to Daniel 7.[136] Moreover, in the first century "Son of Man" appears to have been taken as a messianic title. This has been argued from the *Similitudes of Enoch* and *4 Ezra*, along with some other nonbiblical texts,[137] and we also find in the New Testament the understanding that the Son of Man is the Messiah. Thus in John 12:34 the crowds appear to con-flate the titles "Christ" and "Son of Man." Even more explicitly in Matthew 26:63–64 // Mark 14:61–62 // Luke 22:67–69, when the high priest asks Jesus if he is the *Christ* (which is included in all three Synoptics), Jesus answers in the affirmative by invoking the authority of the *Son of Man*.

Additionally, Peter's confession in Matthew that Jesus is the *Christ* (Matt. 16:16) answers Jesus's question regarding the identity of the *Son of Man* (Matt. 16:13; cf. Mark 8:29–31; Luke 9:20–22). In contrast to the false mes-siahs Jesus predicted, his coming as the Son of Man will be gloriously known (Matt. 24:5, 23–31, and parr.). Likewise, the explanation of the scriptural necessity of Jesus's suffering and resurrection in Luke can be described in terms of either Son of Man (Luke 24:7) or Christ (Luke 24:26, 46). Thus, we have solid reasons for understanding the Son of Man in messianic and Adamic terms. And because Jesus is the Messiah, his actions have implications for the people he leads.

If these points are granted, then the reader will be able to anticipate the implications for the present argument: Jesus's obedience as the last Adam is representative in a way that is comparable to Adam's representative disobe-dience. We will spend the rest of this volume exploring this in more detail. We turn now to Jesus's sonship in relationship to Adam and Israel, where we will see how "Jesus' two roles as the last Adam and true Israel are two sides of one redemptive-historical coin."[138]

---

136. See the discussion in Beale, *New Testament Biblical Theology*, 404–5; cf. Bock, *Luke*, 1:113–14.

137. John J. Collins, "The Son of Man in First-Century Judaism," *NTS* 38 (1992): 465; Wil-liam Horbury, "The Messianic Associations of 'the Son of Man,'" *JTS* 36 (1985): 34–55. For Dan. 7:13–14 as a messianic text, see Matthew V. Novenson, *Christ among the Messiahs: Christ Language in Paul and Messiah Language in Ancient Judaism* (Oxford: Oxford University Press, 2012), 57–59.

138. Beale, *New Testament Biblical Theology*, 428.

The Last Adam as the Obedient
Son of God

In the previous chapter I sketched some of the exegetical warrant for understanding Jesus in Adamic terms in the Gospels. Moreover, I argued that the Adamic emphasis throughout the Gospels informs how we construe Jesus's obedience. Whereas Adam, the first man, failed in the garden, Jesus as the Son of Man remained perfectly obedient even in the face of suffering. In this chapter I will explore in more detail the relationship of Jesus as the last Adam to his sonship. This will provide opportunity to consider Jesus's obedience in greater detail, including how his obedience relates to his recapitulation of Israel's history.

In what follows I will argue that Jesus's identity as Son of God, which features prominently in the Gospels, operates on at least three levels. Jesus's sonship underscores his role (1) as the last Adam, (2) as the embodiment of true Israel, and (3) as the royal representative of his people. In this chapter I will focus primarily on the first two (chap. 6 focuses on the third): Jesus as the last Adam and as the *telos* (goal, purpose, end) of Israel's history. The obedience ascribed to Jesus must be understood in light of the typological role of Israel, but even more fundamentally, Jesus's obedience must also be understood in light of the obedience required of Adam.

Adam and Israel as Son of God

In chapter 1, I observed that it is now commonplace to emphasize the importance of Israel for understanding the words and actions of Jesus in the Gospels. This is indeed a crucial observation, and one that I have written about more extensively elsewhere, specifically in relation to Matthew.[1] To understand the obedience of Jesus, we must read the Gospels in light of the Old Testament, which is quoted, alluded to, and assumed throughout. It is particularly instructive that Jesus quotes from Deuteronomy more than any other Old Testament text,[2] a book in which the father-son relationship underscores the need for Israel's covenantal faithfulness.[3] However, the requirement for God's son to be covenantally obedient in Scripture is ultimately to be traced back to Adam. The sonship of Jesus—which is arguably the most important rubric in the Gospels to underscore Jesus's obedience—therefore has an Adamic foundation.

In light of this, my aim is to consider Jesus's obedience not only in relation to Israel's filial identity but also (and primarily) in respect to the necessity of Adam's filial obedience. To be clear, by focusing on Adam, my purpose is not to ignore or attempt to trump the view that Jesus comes as the fulfillment of Israel's hope. My aim is to add another layer to the discussion.

In the first half of this chapter, I will consider the identity of Adam as son of God and will relate Adam's sonship to Israel's sonship. Obedience is a requirement for both, though Adam's role was different from Israel's in some important ways. In the second half of this chapter, I will consider Jesus's obedience in relation to two key events centered around his sonship: Jesus's baptism and temptation.

Adam as (Covenantal) Son of God

We saw in the previous chapter that filial imagery is not distinct from Adamic imagery since Adam is identified as son of God in Genesis 5:1, 3. And as son of God, Adam was to be obedient. Adam and Eve were to be fruitful and multiply, fill the earth and subdue it (Gen. 1:28), but Adam was also entrusted with a unique, probationary task. Adam was given every tree

---

1. Brandon D. Crowe, *The Obedient Son: Deuteronomy and Christology in the Gospel of Matthew*, BZNW 188 (Berlin: Walter de Gruyter, 2012).

2. See Bruce K. Waltke with Charles Yu, *An Old Testament Theology: An Exegetical, Canonical, and Thematic Approach* (Grand Rapids: Zondervan, 2007), 480; cf. Daniel I. Block, *Deuteronomy*, NIVAC (Grand Rapids: Zondervan, 2012), 26.

3. See esp. Deut. 8:5–6; 14:1–2; 32:4–6, 18–20. For further explication see Crowe, *Obedient Son*, chap. 3.

of the garden but was forbidden to eat of the tree of the knowledge of good and evil, even under satanic pressure (2:16–17).[4] Tragically, Adam failed and was banished from the garden, and his actions resulted in the entrance of sin and death into the world (Gen. 3:22–24; cf. Rom. 5:12–14).[5] In sum, in Genesis 1–5 Adam is the son of God who was created in a sinless state but whose disobedience led to personal and cosmic consequences given his unique role at the head of humanity.

Before we trace more explicitly the interrelated themes of obedience and sonship as it pertains to Adam (and Israel), it will be helpful to identify which Old Testament texts may speak of Adam. Though Adam is not often mentioned by name in the Old Testament after Genesis, we have seen in previous chapters that in some Jewish traditions, and in the New Testament, Adam's unique position was often reflected upon. The events of Genesis 1–3 are echoed and alluded to already within the Old Testament. G. K. Beale has written extensively on the verbal parallels between some of the commands given to Adam and Eve in the prelapsarian state (Gen. 1:26–28) and the various restatements given to the patriarchs and Israel elsewhere in the Old Testament.[6] Thus we often find the command to be fruitful and multiply that was originally given to Adam repeated to Adam's descendants (e.g., Gen. 9:1, 7; 35:11–12; cf. 47:27). It is also significant that some of the commands given to Adam are in many later texts restated in the form of promises (e.g., Gen. 12:2–3; 17:2, 6, 8; 22:17–18; 26:3–4, 24; 28:13–14),[7] which implies the need for God's intervention to bring about the intended state of being fruitful and blessed since the entrance of sin into the world. Further recalling the early chapters of Genesis is the new-creational imagery used in the Old Testament to speak of Israel's promised land (Lev. 26:6–12) and restoration after exile (Jer. 3:16; 23:3; Ezek. 36:11).[8] Though the probationary command (Gen. 2:16–17) is not

4. See Meredith G. Kline, *Kingdom Prologue: Genesis Foundations for a Covenantal Worldview* (Overland Park, KS: Two Age Press, 2000), 103–7. Note that the command is given to Adam alone (Gen. 2:16).

5. Of course, Adam was not alone; Eve was with him. Nevertheless, the New Testament consistently identifies Adam as the one who was responsible, through whom sin entered the world (Rom. 5:12, 17–19; 1 Cor. 15:22; cf. Gen. 3:17).

6. G. K. Beale, *A New Testament Biblical Theology: The Unfolding of the Old Testament in the New* (Grand Rapids: Baker Academic, 2011), 46–52; Beale, *The Temple and the Church's Mission: A Biblical Theology of the Dwelling Place of God*, NSBT 17 (Downers Grove, IL: Intervarsity, 2004), 81–121.

7. See the fuller explanation in Beale, *New Testament Biblical Theology*, 54; cf. N. T. Wright, *The Climax of the Covenant: Christ and the Law in Pauline Theology* (Minneapolis: Fortress, 1992), 21–26.

8. Wright, *Climax of the Covenant*, 23; Beale, *Temple*, 110. On parallels between Ezekiel and Adam, see Iain M. Duguid, *Ezekiel*, NIVAC (Grand Rapids: Zondervan, 1999), 69–70.

repeated, the texts listed above nevertheless recall the original created order and commands given to Adam, enabling the attentive reader to identify points of continuity with Adam and his offspring.

Beyond these passages, the sin of the first man appears to be variously recalled in several texts. One possibility is found in Isaiah 43:27, which recalls the sin of Israel's first father. Though "first father" may more likely be a reference to Jacob or Abraham, it could plausibly be a reference to Adam, who is the original father of Israel as well as the perpetrator of the first sin.[9] Perhaps more explicit is Job 31:33. Though the reference to Adam is often obscured in English translations (and not apparent in the LXX), Job 31:33 speaks of concealing transgressions *like Adam (kə'ādām)*. Though *kə'ādām* could be taken generically, a specifically Adamic reference seems to fit best with apparent mentions of the first man elsewhere in Job (15:7–8; 20:4).[10] Finally, Adam is also listed in the Chronicler's genealogy (1 Chron. 1:1).

The parallels between Eve and Achan also illustrate the interest of other biblical authors in humanity's first sin.[11] In Genesis 3:6–8 we read that Eve *saw* and *desired* food from the tree, then *took* the fruit, and then after giving the fruit to Adam, she and Adam *hid themselves*.[12] This same language of *seeing (rā'āh)*, *taking (lāqaḥ)*, *desiring (ḥāmad)*, and similar language for *hiding* (Gen. 3:8: *ḥābā'*; Josh. 7:21: *ṭāman*) is found in Achan's explanation of his own sin (Josh. 7:21), and thus his actions may recall the tragic choices of the first couple. Further, just as Adam's sin in the garden had deathly implications for his offspring, so did Achan's actions have the consequence of death for his offspring.

What is more, Scripture identifies Achan's sin as transgressing the covenant (Josh. 7:11, 15), and one must consider the possibility that the first sin in the garden should also be construed in covenantal terms. At this point, we bring our discussion back to the interrelated themes of sonship and obedience,

9. See J. Alec Motyer, *The Prophecy of Isaiah: An Introduction and Commentary* (Downers Grove, IL: IVP Academic, 1993), 341; cf. John D. W. Watts, *Isaiah 34–66*, rev. ed., WBC 25 (Nashville: Thomas Nelson, 2005), 687; Brevard S. Childs, *Isaiah: A Commentary*, OTL (Louisville: Westminster John Knox, 2001), 341.

10. Cf. David J. A. Clines, *Job 21–37*, WBC 18A (Nashville: Thomas Nelson, 2006), 349–50, 484, 499 (though Clines does not interpret Job 15 as a reference to Adam).

11. I owe the following observations on the parallels to Achan to G. K. Beale, who first suggested them to me in personal correspondence. Cf. David M. Howard Jr., *Joshua*, NAC 5 (Nashville: Broadman & Holman, 1998), 197. For other Jewish and Christian texts associating death with Adam's (and/or Eve's) first sin, see Sir. 25:24; Wis. 2:24; *4 Ezra* 3:7; Rom. 5:12; 6:23. Cf. Dale C. Allison Jr., *A Critical and Exegetical Commentary on the Epistle of James*, ICC (London: Bloomsbury T&T Clark, 2013), 253n248.

12. As noted above, Eve surely plays a role in the first sin as well, though Adam is held responsible in light of the commands given to him in Gen. 2:16–17.

which are held together in the biblical worldview by the concept of covenant. Indeed, another Old Testament passage that may identify Adam by name is Hosea 6:7, which speaks of Ephraim's and Judah's transgressions of the Lord's covenant "like *'ādām.*" Historically this text has often been taken to refer to the person Adam,[13] though many modern exegetes lean toward a locative or perhaps collective identification of *'ādām.*[14] The Hebrew of Hosea 6:7 can be variously construed. Thus, *shām* in Hosea 6:7b seems naturally to draw the reader's attention to a place (cf. Hosea 6:10).[15] Yet *'ādām* is not a prominent biblical location (cf. Josh. 3:16), nor is it clear what sufficiently notorious event may have happened there that transgressed the covenant.[16] Further, though admittedly not likely, it is not out of the realm of possibility that *shām* could be rendered as a deictic adverb with a more temporal nuance ("then"),[17] though this does not appear to be the way Hosea uses the term elsewhere (Hosea 2:17; 6:10; 9:15; 10:9; 12:4; 13:8). Regardless of the force of the adverb, a significant factor that seems to belie taking *'ādām* as a location is the need sensed by many commentators to emend the text to read *bə'ādām* in place of *kə'ādām*. However, as it has recently been noted in *Biblia Hebraica Quinta*, there is no textual support for emending the Hebrew text in this way.[18] This does not, however, solve the exegetical question, since it is still possible to take *kaph* (*k*) affixed to *'ādām* in a locative sense.[19]

Nevertheless, the difficulties of rendering *'ādām* as a place remain, and on balance it seems best to take *'ādām* personally. Indeed, it is instructive that *'ādām* is construed personally (in the collective sense) in the Old Greek (*hōs anthrōpos*), in *Targum of the Prophets*, and *Leviticus Rabbah* 6:1, 5—and *'ādām* is understood as the person Adam in *Genesis Rabbah* 19:9. Likewise, Qumran (4Q167), the ancient versions, Jerome, and the later work of Rashi

13. K&D 10:66; A. A. Macintosh, *A Critical and Exegetical Commentary on Hosea*, ICC (Edinburgh: T&T Clark, 1997), 236.

14. See Francis I. Andersen and David Noel Freedman, *Hosea: A New Translation with Introduction and Commentary*, AB 24 (Garden City, NY: Doubleday, 1980), 436; Hans Walter Wolff, *Hosea: A Commentary on the Book of the Prophet Hosea*, trans. Gary Stansell, Hermeneia (Philadelphia: Fortress, 1974), 121.

15. See recently Stephen G. Dempster, "From Slight Peg to Cornerstone to Capstone: The Resurrection of Christ 'On the Third Day' according to the Scriptures," *WTJ* 76 (2014): 371–409.

16. Douglas J. Stuart (*Hosea–Jonah*, WBC 31 [Waco: Word, 1987], 99, 111) concurs with the obscurity of Adam as a location but suggests that *kə'ādām* should be translated "like dirt."

17. *IBHS*, §39.3.1g–h; cf. §17.2b. Stuart (*Hosea–Jonah*, 111) takes *shām* as "see."

18. Anthony Gelston, ed., *The Twelve Minor Prophets*, BHQ 13 (Stuttgart: Deutsche Bibelgesellschaft, 2010), 60*. Macintosh (*Hosea*, 236) notes that Codex 554, referenced in the edition of G. B. de Rossi, exhibits a *beth* prefix. However, the value of de Rossi's edition for determining the earliest text is minimal; see Ernst Würthwein, *The Text of the Old Testament: An Introduction to the Biblia Hebraica*, trans. Erroll F. Rhodes, 2nd ed. (Grand Rapids: Eerdmans, 1995), 40.

19. See *IBHS*, §11.2.9a. Cf. Isa. 28:21.

all seem to provide evidence for taking the phrase personally.[20] Consistent with a personal reference to Adam, Hosea often alludes to Genesis, including covenantal texts from Genesis (Hosea 1:9–10; 2:20 [2:18 EVV]; 2:25 [2:23 EVV]), and Hosea also alludes to the original created order in various places (e.g., birds of the air and beasts of the field [Hosea 2:20; 4:3], briars and thorns [9:6; 10:8]).[21] Additionally, Hosea echoes language from covenantal texts in the Pentateuch more broadly (Hosea 4:1; 8:1; 11:1; 13:4–6). Thus a reference to a covenant with Adam in Hosea 6:7 would fit contextually with Hosea's covenantal concerns elsewhere.[22] And if a covenant with Adam is in view in Hosea 6:7, this would be an additional reference to covenantal *sonship* that we find elsewhere in Hosea (Hosea 2:1 [1:10 EVV]; 11:1). Beyond these factors, the possibility that the person Adam is intended in Hosea 6:7 is strengthened in light of the probable parallel to Job 31:33, where *kəʾādām* appears to refer to Adam personally.

In sum, in spite of recent suggestions otherwise, the reading in which Hosea 6:7 refers to transgressing the divine covenant "like Adam" still has much to commend it.[23] At the very least, one can admit that a rendering that highlights the first man's transgression as a transgression of the covenant would fit well with the New Testament's emphasis on Jesus's obedience overcoming the disobedience of Adam, though this New Testament teaching does not depend on an Adamic rendering of Hosea 6:7. Even if one were to opt for a different interpretation of Hosea 6:7, the understanding of Paul—and, as I will further argue, the Gospel writers—of Jesus and Adam as covenantal, representative figures remains.

The covenant *concept* (the word *bərît* is not used in Gen. 1–3, and *diathēkē* is found sparingly in the Gospels) makes the best sense of what we saw in the last chapter, that Adam stands as the representative head of the original creation, with Jesus standing as representative head of the new creation. As

20. Macintosh, *Hosea*, 236.

21. See further Byron G. Curtis, "Hosea 6:7 and the Covenant-Breaking like/at Adam," in *The Law Is Not of Faith: Essays on Work and Grace in the Mosaic Covenant*, ed. Bryan D. Estelle, J. V. Fesko, and David VanDrunen (Phillipsburg, NJ: P&R, 2009), 170–209. Curtis suggests a double entendre, building on *shām*, whereby Hosea refers to both the person of Adam *and* the place of Adam.

22. Crowe, *Obedient Son*, 120–24.

23. For more rationale on Hosea 6:7 as Adamic covenant, see the lengthy footnote in Beale, *New Testament Biblical Theology*, 43n44; K&D 10:66; Derek Kidner, *Love to the Loveless: The Message of Hosea*, BST (Downers Grove, IL: InterVarsity, 1981), 69. See also the discussion of the various options in Herman Bavinck, *Reformed Dogmatics*, ed. John Bolt, trans. John Vriend, 4 vols. (Grand Rapids: Baker Academic, 2003–8), 2:565. Beale (*New Testament Biblical Theology*, 43n44) notes several other Jewish texts that speak of a covenant with Adam, including 2 En. [J] 31:1; *Apoc. Mos.* 8:1–2; Sir. 17:11–12; 1QS IV, 22–23; cf. Philo, *Leg.* 3.246.

the one who stands at the head of original humanity in Scripture, Adam was created to be God's son who would be faithful to God's (covenantal) commands. Adam was to reflect the image of God by ruling faithfully over creation. When Adam failed as the protological vice-regent, he acted contrary to his status as righteous son of God who was created in the glorious image of God. Sonship in Scripture is consistently paired with obedience,[24] and it is highly significant that the requisite relationship between sonship and obedience is properly traced scripturally back to Adam.

The blessings that appear to have been offered to Adam upon condition of his obedience further suggest a covenantal arrangement with Adam and may also illumine the blessings secured by Jesus's obedience in the Gospels. Key here is the offer of *life* given to Adam. On the one hand, the prospect of the curse of death was set before Adam if he disobeyed God's command in the garden. On the other hand, the positive prospect of the Adamic administration, though not stated explicitly, was the possibility of the continuation—or better, the increasing experience—of life in God's presence. In his created state Adam did not yet possess the fullness of eternal life (as the resulting curse of death makes clear), but the prospect of fullness of life was held out before him. Thus, the tree of life, which in some sense would have bestowed life,[25] was originally in the garden, but access to it was taken away as part of Adam's banishment from the garden. The divine verdict on Adam thus includes the inability for Adam to take from the tree of life lest he live forever (Gen. 3:22–24).

Further support for the prospect of the increasing experience of life held out to Adam may come from Daniel 7. The kingship envisioned in Daniel 7 is perfect and everlasting kingship portrayed in Adamic terms, and this may derive, at least in part, from the understanding that Adam's rule should have been forever.[26] Similarly, the commands for Adam to be fruitful and multiply and fill the earth and subdue it (Gen. 1:28) seem to indicate that a greater experience of blessings would come when Adam, made in the image of God, exercised dominion over the created realm. It even seems probable that Adam's successful passing of the probationary test would have led to an everlasting Sabbath rest. If we understand these blessings to be contingent upon Adam's obedience, we find further support for understanding the Adamic administration as a covenant.[27]

24. See Crowe, *Obedient Son*, esp. chaps. 3–4.
25. Cf. Geerhardus Vos, *Biblical Theology: Old and New Testaments* (1948; repr., Edinburgh: Banner of Truth, 1975), 28.
26. For the following points see Beale, *New Testament Biblical Theology*, 32–46.
27. Thus the historic language of the "covenant of life" made with Adam (cf. Westminster Shorter Catechism 12).

Israel as Covenantal Son of God

Adam's creation as God's son provides the canonical foundation for Israel's filial relationship to God, and this latter relationship of obligation is clearly construed in covenantal terms. The similarities between Adam and Israel in this regard provide corroboration that the Adamic administration should be construed in covenantal terms. When God condescended to Adam and gave him his law, Adam was expected to be obedient as son of God, made in the image of the great King of creation. After the Primeval History of Genesis 1–11, Adam recedes into the background, and Genesis shifts to focus on Abraham. Yet Adam remains the foundation for the reader of the Pentateuch to understand that the God who calls Abram is the God of all creation. Under the leadership of Joseph, the Israelites grew to a mighty people. This later caused alarm for the new pharaoh who did not know Joseph, leading to the Israelites' enslavement (Exod. 1:8–14). Nevertheless, the Israelites continued to grow and increase in accord with the covenantal promise given to Abraham (Gen. 12:2–3). When the Lord raised up Moses and instructed him to go to Pharaoh and demand that his people be freed, it is significant that this call is couched in *filial* terms—Israel was to be set free because Israel was God's firstborn son (Exod. 4:22–23).

Israel's sonship is thus proclaimed in conjunction with the exodus, and the nation is soon established in covenant with their divine King and charged with maintaining covenant obligations (Exod. 19–24).[28] Deuteronomy further expounds the father-son relationship between the Lord and Israel. Indeed, the father-son relationship between Israel and the Lord is among the central features of the entire book (Deut. 1:31; 8:5; 14:1–2; 32:1–20, 43).[29] Moreover, this father-son relationship is a relationship of covenantal *obligation*, so that as son of God, Israel must be obedient to their divine Father. Thus, in Deuteronomy 14:1–2 the logic is: *because* the sons of Israel are sons of the Lord their God, *therefore* they must be holy. A similar framework is likely for the logical relationship between Deuteronomy 8:5 and 8:6: *because* God disciplines Israel as a son, *therefore* Israel is to keep God's commandments. The interrelatedness of sonship and obedience is further emphasized in the climactic Song of Moses (Deut. 32), where the prophetic voice of Moses contrasts the faithfulness of God

---

28. In what follows I am summarizing Crowe, *Obedient Son*, chap. 3, where readers can find fuller discussions and bibliography. I use the plural pronoun to refer to Israel (1) to avoid the awkwardness that comes from using a feminine pronoun ("her") to refer to Israel as *son* of God, and (2) to avoid the more impersonal "its." The plural also helpfully underscores the collective nature of Israel as a people. See also Crowe, *Obedient Son*, 95n51.

29. For sonship in Deut. 32:43, the OG and 4QDeut^q most likely witness the more original reading. For further discussion of Deut. 32 in the context of Deuteronomy, see Crowe, *Obedient Son*, 106–11.

with the faithlessness of his sons and daughters (32:4–20), yet with the prospect that the Lord will eventually avenge the blood of his sons (32:43). Additionally, Deuteronomy's emphasis on the covenantal father-son relationship goes hand in hand with its emphasis on love. Love is tantamount to obedience in the context of the covenant (Deut. 7:1; 11:1, 13; cf. 6:5; 10:12; 13:3; 30:6), and this love is to characterize the devotion and fealty of Israel as son to its divine Father. Thus, when Jesus discusses love as the greatest commandment, this should be viewed in light of the Deuteronomic emphasis on love as obedient sonship.

In light of the need for obedient sonship in Deuteronomy, it is also striking that similar relationships between sonship and obedience can be observed throughout the Old Testament,[30] along with extracanonical and some later Jewish literature.[31] It is into such a context, almost certainly influenced by the Deuteronomic view of sonship, that the Gospels are written to explain the obedience of Jesus as Son of God. In light of these texts, it is perhaps not surprising that Deuteronomy has been considered the most important book for Old Testament theology and is one of the most important books for understanding the New Testament.[32] It is, of course, Deuteronomy that Jesus quotes in his three temptations that center around his own sonship.

Another aspect of the covenantal relationship of Israel to YHWH was the covenant consequences held out before Israel. Again we see this clearly in Deuteronomy, where the voice of Moses impels the Israelites to choose the way of blessing and life, not the way of cursing and death. This exhortation permeates Deuteronomy, but we find it most fully expounded in Deuteronomy 27–30. Here the reader encounters the prospect of tremendous blessings if Israel is faithful to the covenant stipulations, but devastating curses if Israel is unfaithful. Although, tragically, in the concluding chapters of Deuteronomy the curses appear to be inevitable, texts such as Deuteronomy 30:1–10 and the latter portions of Deuteronomy 32 (see 32:34–43) indicate the hope of restoration that would emerge on the other side of cursing.

Parallels between Israel and Adam

This background for Israel's need for obedience brings us to a point where we can consider more fully the relationship between Israel and Adam. First,

30. Isa. 1:2; 30:1; 63:7–64:12; Jer. 3–4; 31:1–20; Hosea 1–2; 11; cf. Prov. 4:3.

31. Wis. 2:13–18; *Jub.* 1:24–25; *Pss. Sol.* 13:4–9; *6 Ezra* 1:24–25; 11QT[a] XLVIII, 7–10; 4Q504 III, 4–7; 1QH[a] XVII, 35–36; *Sipre* Deut. §§32, 36, 48, 96–97, 308–9, 320; *y. Qidd.* 61c; *b. Qidd.* 36a; *Deut. Rab.* 7:9.

32. Waltke, *Old Testament Theology*, 479; Elizabeth Achtemeier, *Deuteronomy, Jeremiah*, PC (Philadelphia: Fortress, 1978), 9; Block, *Deuteronomy*, 25–33.

both Adam and Israel are sons of God, not physically, but in a covenantal (or created) sense. Second, in light of the covenantal contexts, both Adam and Israel as sons of God are called to be obedient to their covenantal Lord. Third, the charge given to Adam in the garden to be fruitful and multiply and exercise dominion on the earth and fill it (Gen. 1:28) is repeated to Israel.[33] This indicates some measure of continuity of covenant administration between Adam and Israel. Fourth, both Adam and Israel faced the possibilities of the curse of death for transgressing the covenant, whereas both Adam and Israel also stood to receive the divine blessings for persevering in faithfulness to the divinely instituted covenantal terms.

Fifth, the original dwelling place of Adam in the garden of Eden is recapitulated elsewhere in the Old Testament in the tabernacle and temple.[34] We see this, for example, because Eden was the place of the special presence of God, where God walked back and forth (Gen. 3:8), and the same language is used of God's presence in the tabernacle (Deut. 23:15 [23:14 EVV]). Additionally, the promised land itself was identified as the place of God's special dwelling (Lev. 26:12; Ps. 78:54), which is further redolent of Adam's communion with God in Eden. Additionally, Adam's task in the garden of serving (ʿābād) and guarding (šāmar) utilizes language later used of the priestly task in the temple (Num. 3:7–8; 8:25–26; 18:5–6; 1 Chron. 23:32; Ezek. 44:14). Furthermore, this language of serving and guarding is also used of the Israelites in their task of keeping the commandments of God (e.g., Deut. 11:16; 13:14; 16:12; Josh. 1:7; 22:5; 1 Kings 9:6; cf. 1 Kings 11:34, 38; 14:8), which increases the probability that the same terminology used for Adam's original state denoted continual obedience to God.

Beyond these parallels, both the tabernacle and the temple featured edenic imagery. For example, the lampstand may have been patterned on the tree of life, Solomon's temple was festooned with botanical and arboreal artistry (1 Kings 6:14–36; 7:13–51), and Solomon himself is identified in Adamic terms as an ideal gardener (1 Kings 5:13 [4:33 EVV]). Eden was a place of gold and precious stones, which are reflected in the gold and precious jewels of the tabernacle, temple, and the priestly garments (Gen. 2:12; Exod. 25:1–40; 28:1–43; 1 Kings 6:20–22; cf. Num. Rab. 4:8).[35] Further, in the biblical texts and for others in the ancient Near East, it was the king who built the temple.[36]

33. See Beale, New Testament Biblical Theology, 46–57; Beale, Temple, 93–121.
34. My discussion on this fifth point draws largely from Beale, Temple, 66–77; cf. Waltke, Old Testament Theology, 255–56, 460, 741.
35. See also N. T. Wright, The New Testament and the People of God, COQG 1 (Minneapolis: Fortress, 1992), 265.
36. In addition to David and Solomon, note the role of Cyrus (Ezra 1:2) and the role of Zerubbabel in Zech. 4:6–7. See further N. T. Wright, Jesus and the Victory of God, COQG 2 (Minneapolis: Fortress, 1996), 483.

Therefore Adam's service in the edenic temple dovetails with his presentation as a royal son of God. Indeed, Adam should be viewed as the first priest-king, which would later be anticipated of the Messiah (cf. Zech. 6:12–13).[37] Adam's expulsion from the garden of Eden was therefore tantamount to being cast out of God's sanctuary, and this foreshadows Israel's exile from the promised land, which is also portrayed in edenic terms (Exod. 23:29; Lev. 26:1–13; Deut. 7:22; cf. Lev. 26:22).

These five features—(1) sonship, (2) obedience, (3) continuity of commands, (4) blessings and curses, and (5) their relation to the place of God's covenantal presence—highlight some key parallels between Adam and Israel in Scripture.[38] Yet we also find some significant differences between Israel and Adam.

Differences between Israel and Adam

It is important to observe the similarities between Adam and Israel because of the clarity with which Jesus's obedience is portrayed in the Gospels in terms of Israel. At the same time, given the argument of the present volume that Jesus's obedience excels what was required of Israel, it is also necessary to observe some differences between Adam and Israel. I have introduced these above, but here I will focus on two significant differences between Adam and Israel.

First, in canonical context Adam as the head of humanity is the fountainhead and federal representative for all humanity descending from him. Paul makes much of this in Romans 5:12–21 and 1 Corinthians 15:20–29, 44–49, but one can already see the effects of Adam's sin in Genesis 3–5.[39] Adam, as the father of humanity, has only one ultimate peer in the mind of Paul and many other early Christian interpreters (noted in chap. 1)—Jesus Christ, the second and last Adam. The uniqueness of Adam stands parallel to the uniqueness of Christ. Adam was created without sin, without father or mother, while Jesus was supernaturally conceived and born of a virgin,[40] coinciding with his role as the head of a new humanity.

A second significant difference between Adam and Israel is the uniqueness of Adam's created state of uprightness. Adam was created without sin

37. Beale, *Temple*, 70; Bavinck, *Reformed Dogmatics*, 3:331.

38. See also the extended discussion of Seth D. Postell, *Adam as Israel: Genesis 1–3 as the Introduction to the Torah and the Tanakh* (Eugene, OR: Wipf & Stock, 2011).

39. In addition to the verdict of Gen. 3:14–19, note the intrusion of murder through Cain (4:8) and the ungodly Lamech (4:23–24), and the refrain of death in the Adamic genealogy of Gen. 5.

40. For a discussion of the virginal conception, see Brandon D. Crowe, *Was Jesus Really Born of a Virgin?*, CAHQ (Phillipsburg, NJ: P&R, 2013).

in a state of perfect harmony with God. Israel, on the other hand, was a nation chosen by God but which had inherited the effects of Adam's sin. The implications of this are far-reaching. Adam was created sinless, in no need of redemption, whereas in the covenant at Sinai the problems of sin are assumed and addressed (Exod. 19–23), and the nation had to be sprinkled with the blood of the covenant to be acceptable for communion with God (Exod. 24:8–11). Likewise, Deuteronomy makes it clear that God's electing love toward Israel was not due to any inherently virtuous characteristic in Israel, for they were a stiff-necked people (7:6–8; 9:4–21; cf. Deut. 10:16).[41] Israel's need for redemption (cf. Deut. 6:20–25), coupled with their persistent covenantal failures (and therefore the failure permanently to possess the land), underscores the biblical view that Israel was not created upright but inherited the consequences of Adam's sin. In the New Testament we read that the sin of the first Adam is overcome only by the obedience of the last Adam, which yields life for all who are in him. Though this is arguably clearest in Paul, the Gospel writers also portray the obedience of Jesus, in vicarious terms, as the answer to Adam's disobedience.

To anticipate the following discussion, to overturn the sin of Adam and realize God's design for humanity, someone would have to come from Abraham's family—since the promise of redemption was channeled through Abraham (cf. Gen. 12:7; 13:16; 15:5; 22:17)—whose obedience would somehow provide the answer to the sin that came through Adam.[42] The Old Testament illustrates in countless ways the deathly effects of sin in each generation. These include the necessity of sacrifice and the failures of even the greatest of Israel's leaders, none of whom was able to bring final deliverance.[43] Therefore, we must look to Abraham's family (and thus Israel as a nation) for final deliverance from Adam's sin, yet to start with Abraham would be to miss the beginning of the story. The promise of the seed (*zera'*) given to Abraham (Gen. 12:7; 13:16; 15:5; 22:17) is preceded by the promise of the woman's seed in Genesis 3:15.[44] The blessing that comes through Abraham therefore also assumes the deathly effects resulting from Adam's sin, which is assumed in the call of Abraham to sacrifice Isaac (Gen. 22:9–18). Thus, we must understand the work of Christ in the Gospels ultimately as the answer to Adam's sin. To be

41. See further R. E. Clements, *God's Chosen People: A Theological Interpretation of the Book of Deuteronomy* (London: SCM, 1968), 33.

42. Cf. N. T. Wright, *Paul and the Faithfulness of God*, COQG 4 (Minneapolis: Fortress, 2013), 889–90.

43. Even those figures who were models of piety (e.g., Daniel) were not able to bring the blessings of the eschaton (cf. Dan. 9).

44. See Jack P. Lewis, "The Woman's Seed (Gen. 3:15)," *JETS* 34 (1991): 299–319.

sure, Jesus is the true Israelite and son of Abraham, but he is also uniquely the second and last Adam. Therefore, in spite of whatever parallels we find between Adam and Israel in Scripture, the uniqueness of Adam and Jesus, and the uniqueness of their actions, must be maintained. It is best, in other words, to follow Paul in referring to Jesus (and not Israel) as the second and last Adam (cf. 1 Cor. 15:45, 47). In sum, we must take due note of the Israel-shaped contours of Jesus's obedience in the Gospels, but we also must not neglect to reflect upon the Adamic dimensions of Jesus's obedience. Indeed, it is Adam who provides the closest biblical foil for understanding the nature and implications of Jesus's vicarious obedience.

Summary: Adam and Israel

In conclusion, whether or not God's original interactions with Adam should be viewed as a covenant (and I believe this is the best option), it is clear that Adam was created to be an obedient son. The themes of sonship and obedience are further elaborated in relation to the nation of Israel, especially in the covenantal context of Deuteronomy. The covenant curses that befell the covenant people of God were due to their breaking of the covenant stipulations (Deut. 27–30), which is ultimately a result of Adam's failure in the first covenantal administration. The Adamic and the national are further intertwined with the promised seed (Gen. 3:15; 12:7; 15:5; 22:17) and the advent of the king and the hopes that arose alongside the royal anticipations of a coming kingdom. Surely the sense that one should have at the beginning of the New Testament era, on the basis of the history of Israel to that point, is the need for God to intervene supernaturally to bring lasting deliverance.

Jesus as Covenantally Obedient Son of God

We read in the Gospels of the kingdom that comes through the royal Son of God—building upon the sonship of Adam and Israel—on the coattails of his obedience. In the rest of this chapter we will consider the beginnings of Jesus's public ministry in the Gospels, particularly the baptism and tempta-tion narratives. These first stages of Jesus's public work provide much of the framework for understanding what Jesus does later in the Gospels, and as such bear a weighty hermeneutical load. Significantly, these opening accounts feature the declaration and confirmation of Jesus's sonship, his identification with Israel in various ways, and his singular obedience. Jesus is portrayed not only as the fulfillment of Israel but also as the representative leader of Israel who realizes the obedience required of God's son.[45] Jesus's obedience provides the ultimate answer to Adam's disobedience, which accomplishes salvation for those he represents.

Jesus's Baptism

We begin with the significance of Jesus's baptism, which highlights Jesus's role as a representative and begins to show how his obedience yields salvation for others. Three aspects of the baptism are particularly relevant.

ANOINTED AS REPRESENTATIVE MESSIAH

First, by participating in John's baptism Jesus identifies with God's people as their representative, which is part of the logic for why his obedience can be counted vicariously. Jesus's baptism is the occasion for the manifestation of his messiahship and his anointing by the Spirit, which set Jesus apart for the public task of leading and representing his people. More specifically, Jesus identifies with the need for God's people to repent and receive forgiveness for sins. John was prophetically calling God's people to repentance before the Lord returned to his temple (cf. Mal. 3:1; Mark 1:3). John's ministry anticipated the stronger one who was coming—the Messiah, who would baptize with the Holy Spirit and fire (Matt. 3:11–12 // Luke 3:15–18; cf. Mark 1:7–8). Before baptizing others with the Holy Spirit and fire, Jesus first undergoes the baptism of John, entering figuratively into the estate of sin on behalf of those he came to save. He did this even though he was the stronger one who had no need for forgiveness (Matt. 3:11–15 and parr.).[46] As Craig Keener has commented, "This baptism . . . represents Jesus' ultimate identification with Israel at the

---

45. On son of God as Israel's representative, see Wright, *Jesus*, 485–86.

46. See Markus Bockmuehl, "The Baptism of Jesus as 'Super-Sacrament' of Redemption," *Theology* 115 (2012): 89; Cullmann, *Christology*, 67; W. D. Davies and Dale C. Allison Jr., *A Critical and Exegetical Commentary on the Gospel according to St. Matthew*, 3 vols., ICC (Edinburgh: T&T Clark, 1988–97), 1:324; Adolf Schlatter, *The History of the Christ: The Foundation for New Testament Theology*, trans. Andreas J. Köstenberger (Grand Rapids: Baker, 1997), 75.

That Jesus was sinless is also the consistent view of many church fathers (see below) and is reflected in the so-called *Gospel of the Nazareans*: "Behold, the mother of the Lord and his brothers were saying to him, 'John the Baptist is baptizing for the remission of sins. Let us go and be baptized by him.' But [the Lord] replied to them, 'What sin have I committed that I should go to be baptized by him?'" Found in Jerome, *Against the Pelagians* 3.2, cited in Bart D. Ehrman and Zlatko Pleše, *The Apocryphal Gospels: Texts and Translations* (Oxford: Oxford University Press, 2013), 207. Additionally, "Jesus' righteousness [=perfect observance of the Law]" was also important in Ebionite Christology. Oskar Skarsaune, "The Ebionites," in *Jewish Believers in Jesus: The Early Centuries*, ed. Oskar Skarsaune and Reidar Hvalvik (Peabody, MA: Hendrickson, 2007), 435.

climactic stage in her history. . . . Jesus' baptism, like his impending death (cf. Mark 10:38–39 with Mark 14:23–24, 36) would be vicarious, embraced on behalf of others with whom the Father had called him to identify."[47]

In the comparable context in the Fourth Gospel, John the Baptist confesses Jesus as the Lamb of God who takes away the sin of the world (John 1:29; cf. 1:36), and the one who will baptize with the Holy Spirit (John 1:33). These proclamations are similarly predicated upon the obedience of Jesus. The lamb imagery of John 1:29, 36 has been much discussed, but it seems most feasible that it should be understood (at least in part) in accord with Old Testament sacrificial language, particularly in relation to the Passover lamb (Exod. 12:5; cf. Lev. 16),[48] along with lamb and sin-bearing imagery associated with the servant in Isaiah 53:6–7. If so, these Johannine texts likely indicate that Jesus's obedience in his baptism—as spotless Lamb of God—is *substitutionary* in nature, since the Passover lamb, and later the servant, are viewed in sin-bearing terms.[49] The Lamb of God takes away the sin of the world and baptizes with the Holy Spirit because he is God's eschatological servant who serves a substitutionary function.[50] These insights, which flow from the prophetic ministry of John the Baptist, imply the sinlessness of Jesus.[51]

John's baptism therefore points to the hope for and need of a divine, eschatological washing from sin.[52] As the Messiah, Jesus enters into the purification rite as a unique, representative individual who does not need the cleansing

---

47. Craig S. Keener, *The Gospel of Matthew: A Socio-Rhetorical Commentary* (Grand Rapids: Eerdmans, 2009), 132; see also Ridderbos, *Coming of the Kingdom*, 384–85; Norval Geldenhuys, *Commentary on the Gospel of Luke*, NICNT (Grand Rapids: Eerdmans, 1951), 146; Oscar Cullmann, *The Christology of the New Testament*, trans. Shirley C. Guthrie and Charles A. M. Hall, rev. ed. (Philadelphia: Westminster, 1963), 67; James R. Edwards, *The Gospel according to Luke*, PNTC (Grand Rapids: Eerdmans, 2015), 120; Schlatter, *History of the Christ*, 74.

48. Craig S. Keener, *The Gospel of John: A Commentary*, 2 vols. (Peabody, MA: Hendrickson, 2003), 1:454; for further discussion, see C. K. Barrett, *The Gospel according to St. John: An Introduction with Commentary and Notes on the Greek Text*, 2nd ed. (Philadelphia: Westminster, 1978), 176–77.

49. See also Vos, *Biblical Theology*, 324–26; Simon Gathercole, *Defending Substitution: An Essay on Atonement in Paul*, ASBT (Grand Rapids: Baker Academic, 2015), 68–70; Bernd Janowski, "He Bore Our Sins: Isaiah 53 and the Drama of Taking Another's Place," in *The Suffering Servant: Isaiah 53 in Jewish and Christian Sources*, ed. Bernd Janowski and Peter Stuhlmacher, trans. Daniel P. Bailey (Grand Rapids: Eerdmans, 2004), 48–74.

50. It is instructive that in Ps. 51 David's need for (the washing of) forgiveness of sins (51:7, 10) is linked to the prayer for God not to take the Holy Spirit from him (51:11).

51. For a brief comment on this view among early church fathers, see Bockmuehl, "Baptism of Jesus," 88–89.

52. Ps. 51:2–12; Isa. 1:16; 4:4; Jer. 2:22; 4:14; Ezek. 36:25–27; Zech. 13:1; cf. Exod. 3:19–21; 40:12; 1QS III, 7–9; cf. II, 25–III, 5; V, 13–15. Some of these come from Bockmuehl, "Baptism of Jesus," 84–85. Though the baptism of John and washings of the Qumran community are

for himself. All these factors point toward the vicarious nature of Jesus's baptism as an aspect of his entire, vicarious obedience,[53] which provides final cleansing from sin. Indeed, some church fathers, at least as early as Ignatius of Antioch, even suggested that Jesus's baptism cleansed the waters on behalf of the people.[54] Similarly, John Chrysostom memorably pronounced that Jesus did not need baptism, but baptism needed the power of Christ,[55] and Athanasius averred that when the Lord was washed in the Jordan, "it was we who were washed in Him and by Him."[56] Moreover, Jesus's baptism has often been viewed as the vicarious obedience of the last Adam who washes away the sin of the first Adam.[57] In light of these observations and the symbolism of John's baptism, the conclusion of Geerhardus Vos seems to be well grounded: "Jesus' identification with the people in their baptism had the proximate end of securing for them vicariously what the sacrament aimed at, the forgiveness of sin."[58]

The Father's Pleasure in the Son

Second, the content of the heavenly voice at the baptism also underscores the representative nature of Jesus's obedience. When the heavens are opened and the Spirit descends, the revelatory *bat qōl* declares the fatherly good pleasure in Jesus (Matt. 3:11 // Mark 1:11 // Luke 3:22). Significantly, the proclamation of this good pleasure is occasioned by Jesus's baptism, and the divine voice emphasizes Jesus's obedience in the context of his *sonship*. The contours of Jesus's sonship are multifaceted, at once communicating Jesus's ontological-filial relationship to his Father,[59] announcing Jesus's messiahship (Pss. 2:7; 89:27; 2 Sam. 7:14), evoking corporate Israel (Exod. 4:22–23), and recalling Adam's royal-filial sonship. As messianic Son, Jesus represents Israel, and

---

not exactly the same, it is quite feasible that both are laying claim to scriptural anticipations of eschatological cleansing.

53. Jesus's baptism is part of what was necessary for the fulfilling of all righteousness (Matt. 3:15). I will discuss Matt. 3:15 further in chap. 4.

54. Ign. *Eph*. 18:2; cf. Thomas Aquinas, *Summa Theologiae* 3.39.1. See also Hilary of Poitiers, *On Matthew* 2.5; Theodore of Mopsuestia, *Fragment* 14, in Manlio Simonetti, ed., *Matthew 1–13*, ACCS 1a (Downers Grove, IL: IVP Academic, 2001), 50–51.

55. *Hom. Jo*. 17.2 (*NPNF*[1] 14:59–60).

56. *C. Ar*. 1.47, cited in Kilian McDonnell, "Jesus' Baptism in the Jordan," *TS* 56 (1995): 213. See also Gregory of Nyssa, *On the Baptism of Christ*: "He is baptized by John that He might cleanse him who was defiled" (*NPNF*[2] 5:518).

57. E.g., Gregory Nazianzen, *Oration* 39 (*NPNF*[2] 7:352–59); Cyril of Alexandria, *Commentary on Luke 3:21–22*, as discussed in Daniel Keating, "The Baptism of Jesus in Cyril of Alexandria: The Re-Creation of the Human Race," *ProEccl* 8 (1999): 208–11.

58. Vos, *Biblical Theology*, 320.

59. See more fully, e.g., Matt. 11:25–27 // Luke 10:21–22.

sonship is also the primary rubric by which the Gospel writers communicate Jesus's obedience.[60] One can therefore concur with Ulrich Luz, who succinctly comments on Jesus's baptism, "The Son of God is the just man who is fully and representatively obedient to God's will."[61]

The heavenly voice further underscores Jesus's obedience by explaining Jesus's sonship in terms of servanthood (cf. Isa. 42:1).[62] This is significant because the servant leads and represents others (e.g., Isa. 42:1–4; 52:13; 53:4–6, 11–12). Though some doubt that we can speak positively of a recognizable servant figure in Jesus's day, these objections are not decisive, and the traditional option—that the heavenly voice recalls the work of the Isaianic servant figure(s) in a way that would be recognizable to an audience in Jesus's own milieu—remains the best option.[63] This makes the most sense of the numerous quotations (e.g., Isa. 42:1–4 in Matt. 12:17–21) and allusions to Isaianic servant texts in the Gospels, including the death of Jesus that is portrayed in various ways in servant language.[64] Significantly, the divine sonship of Jesus is recognized by a human character in Mark's narrative only when Jesus had finished the Isaianic servant's task of obedience unto death (Mark 15:39). Likewise, in Luke-Acts the royal sonship and servanthood of Jesus are emphasized in the Passion Narrative in a way that recalls the heavenly voice at his baptism. Thus, Jesus setting his face toward Jerusalem (Luke 9:51) may recall the work of the servant in Isaiah 50:7.[65] Further, Philip uses Isaiah 53 to explain the work of Christ to the Ethiopian eunuch (Acts 8:30–35), and

60. See, e.g., Schlatter, *History of the Christ*, 30.

61. Ulrich Luz, *The Theology of the Gospel of Matthew*, trans. J. Bradford Robinson (Cambridge: Cambridge University Press, 1995), 36.

62. Notice that "in whom I am well pleased" is syntactically subordinate to the declaration of Jesus's sonship. Cf. Richard C. Beaton, *Isaiah's Christ in Matthew's Gospel*, SNTSMS 123 (Cambridge: Cambridge University Press, 2002), 176.

63. For those who doubt the prominence of a servant figure, see Leroy Andrew Huizenga, "The Incarnation of the Servant: The 'Suffering Servant' and Matthean Christology," *HBT* 27 (2005): 25–58; Morna D. Hooker, *Jesus and the Servant: The Influence of the Servant Concept of Deutero-Isaiah in the New Testament* (London: SPCK, 1959). For those that affirm it, see, e.g., Walther Zimmerli and Joachim Jeremias, *The Servant of God*, rev. ed., SBT 20 (London: SCM, 1965); Martin Hengel and Daniel P. Bailey, "The Effective-History of Isaiah 53 in the Pre-Christian Period," in *The Suffering Servant: Isaiah 53 in Jewish and Christian Sources*, ed. Bernd Janowski and Peter Stuhlmacher, trans. Daniel P. Bailey (Grand Rapids: Eerdmans, 2004), 75–146; Childs, *Isaiah*, 420–23; Wright, *Jesus*, 588–90; Cullmann, *Christology*, 51–82.

64. Cf. Joel Marcus, *The Way of the Lord: Christological Exegesis of the Old Testament in the Gospel of Mark*, SNTW (Edinburgh: T&T Clark, 1992), 186–94; Matthew C. Easter, "'Certainly This Man Was Righteous': Highlighting a Messianic Reading of the Centurion's Confession in Luke 23:47," *TynBul* 63 (2012): 46.

65. Schreiner, *New Testament Theology*, 265–66; cf. Mark L. Strauss, *The Davidic Messiah in Luke-Acts: The Promise and Its Fulfillment in Lukan Christology*, JSNTSup 110 (Sheffield: Sheffield Academic, 1995), 317–36.

Luke's identification of Jesus as the righteous one (*dikaios* [Luke 23:47; Acts 3:14; 7:52; 22:14]) also recalls servant language (Isa. 53:11).[66] Indeed, it is significant that in the parallel passages to Luke 23:47 (Matt. 27:54 // Mark 15:39) Jesus's *sonship* is affirmed, whereas in Luke it is Jesus's *righteousness* in his death, like the servant. This also corroborates the view that sonship and servanthood are complementary concepts, both of which underscore the representative obedience of Jesus.[67]

In sum, an allusion to the Isaianic servant in the heavenly voice is consonant with the actions of Jesus in the baptism argued above, in which Jesus identifies with the people in a representative, sin-bearing capacity.[68]

Empowered by the Holy Spirit

This brings us to a third relevant point from Jesus's baptism, which may also underscore Jesus's vicarious obedience—the role of the Holy Spirit in consecrating and empowering Jesus for his messianic task. Luke's Gospel illustrates the point. In Luke the Holy Spirit descends on Jesus at his baptism, anointing Jesus for his messianic task (cf. Acts 10:37–38),[69] which is followed by the Adamic genealogy and the victory of Jesus as the last Adam over the diabolic temptations. Immediately following this obedience, the Holy Spirit powerfully fills Jesus as he returns to Galilee (Luke 4:14). In Nazareth Jesus explains that the power upon him is that of the Holy Spirit, in accord with the (likely) messianic language of Isaiah 61:1–4 (Luke 4:16–21).[70] Jesus is anointed by the Spirit as Messiah, the one who brings salvation to his people. Elsewhere, in Isaiah 42, the servant is anointed with the Spirit of God, and this is set in vibrant contrast to the immediately preceding passage in which the non-salvific idols are nothing but empty wind (*rûaḥ*), or perhaps devoid of God's Spirit (Isa. 41:28–29).[71]

As Messiah, Jesus is empowered by the Spirit for various purposes: for accomplishing miraculous deeds, for the preaching of good news, and for

66. Easter, "'Certainly This Man Was Righteous.'"

67. See also R. H. Fuller, *The Mission and Achievement of Jesus: An Examination of the Presuppositions of New Testament Theology*, SBT 12 (London: SCM, 1954), 85–86.

68. See also R. T. France, *The Gospel of Matthew*, NICNT (Grand Rapids: Eerdmans, 2007), 120; cf. Joel Kennedy, *The Recapitulation of Israel: Use of Israel's History in Matthew 1:1–4:11*, WUNT 2/257 (Tübingen: Mohr Siebeck, 2008), esp. 172–84. Cullmann (*Christology*, 55) argues that the most important imagery of the servant in Isaiah is the notion of vicarious representation through suffering.

69. See also Dunn, *Jesus Remembered*, 373.

70. See Childs, *Isaiah*, 505.

71. Following the MT. Thanks to Christopher Fantuzzo for first suggesting this possibility to me.

perseverance in obedience despite opposition. This accords with the structure of all three Synoptics in which, after Jesus's anointing by the Holy Spirit, the Spirit immediately leads Jesus into the wilderness to be tempted (Matt. 4:1 // Mark 1:12 // Luke 4:1). Thus, we should most likely conclude that the Holy Spirit empowered Jesus to overcome the temptations of the devil (cf. Luke 4:14). Because of his Spirit-empowered victory, Jesus is able to help all those who are oppressed by the devil (cf. Acts 10:38). This is also consistent with the view that Jesus's obedience in his wilderness temptation was the initial binding of the strong man, which we will discuss at greater length in chapter 6. At this point it is significant to observe that in all three of the comparable passages in the Synoptics (Matt. 12:22–32 // Mark 3:22–30 // Luke 11:14–23) the authority of Jesus as the stronger one to overcome the strong man (Satan) is associated explicitly with the power of the Holy Spirit working through Jesus (Matt. 12:28, 32 // Mark 3:29 // Luke 11:20).[72]

The Holy Spirit's descent on Jesus at his baptism is another reason that many historically have considered Jesus's obedience in the baptism to be Adamic imagery. One example here will suffice. Cyril of Alexandria, commenting on the Spirit's descent on Jesus in the Gospel of John, states,[73]

> Since the first Adam did not persevere in the grace given by God, God the Father planned to send us the second Adam from heaven. . . . The one who knew no sin received the Spirit as man in order to keep the Spirit in our nature and root in us once again the grace that had left us. . . . The Spirit flew away from us because of sin, but the one who knew no sin became one of us so that the Spirit might become accustomed to remain in us.[74]

While allowing for some rhetorical flourish from Cyril, his statements represent the view that Jesus's anointing with the Spirit at his baptism is new-creational, last-Adam imagery.[75]

As we conclude this discussion of Jesus's baptism, it will be helpful to recount a few features that are particularly significant. By participating in John's divinely authorized baptism, Jesus demonstrates obedience to the

72. For a recent study on Mark's Gospel arguing that the "strong man" is the devil, see Elizabeth E. Shively, *Apocalyptic Imagination in the Gospel of Mark: The Literary and Theological Role of Mark 3:22–30*, BZNW 189 (Berlin: Walter de Gruyter, 2012).

73. The Gospel of John does not explicitly include the baptism of Jesus, but Cyril nevertheless relates the descent of the dove in John to Jesus's baptism.

74. Cyril of Alexandria, *Commentary on John*, vol. 1, trans. David R. Maxwell, ed. Joel C. Elowsky, ACT (Downers Grove, IL: IVP Academic, 2013), 82; cf. Keating, "Baptism of Jesus," 203–7; Robert Louis Wilken, "St. Cyril of Alexandria: The Mystery of Christ in the Bible," *ProEccl* 4 (1995): 470–73.

75. See also Theodore of Mopsuestia, *Fragment* 14; Bockmuehl, "Baptism of Jesus," 89.

divine will and identifies with God's people in their estate of sin and need for forgiveness. This act of solidarity accords with the messianic nature of his actions,[76] whereby he represents his people. Jesus is also anointed and empowered by the Holy Spirit for his messianic task, including the task of persevering in obedience, as he leads the people in righteousness. As a representative and Adamic figure, Jesus's obedience can be counted vicariously for others. The representative, filial obedience of Jesus receives greater attention in the temptation narratives of Matthew, Mark, and Luke, to which we now turn.

Temptation Narratives

Since Jesus identifies with and represents his people through his baptism and messianic anointing, his obedience beyond the baptism also functions vicariously. It is axiomatic that the baptism of Jesus and his temptation are closely related accounts and should be read in light of one another. This close relationship is perhaps clearest in Matthew and Mark, but it is true for all three Synoptics. Thus, Matthew 3:1–17 and 4:1–11 are closely linked thematically and verbally, with arguably the strongest parallels centering upon the obedient sonship of Jesus in the wilderness in light of Israel's sonship.[77] In Mark's briefer temptation account, the Spirit descends on Jesus in 1:10, and just after Jesus's baptism in 1:12 the Spirit immediately (*euthys*) casts Jesus out (*ekballō*) into the wilderness.[78] A close relationship between the baptism and temptation is also apparent in Luke. The Adamic genealogy (3:23–38) bridges the baptism (3:21–22) and temptation narratives (4:1–13), linking the obedience of Jesus in the baptism and temptation to his role as obedient last Adam. The point is that the baptism and temptation narratives are carefully linked in all three Synoptic Gospels. I argued in the previous chapter that the temptation accounts in Mark and Luke are likely to be taken in Adamic terms. Building on that discussion, in what follows I will argue more extensively for a vicarious role for Jesus's obedience in the temptation, primarily in Matthew and Luke.

76. So, e.g., Longenecker, *Christology*, 70.

77. See Kennedy, *Recapitulation*, 162–65; Davies and Allison, *Matthew*, 1:351; Kenyn M. Cureton, "Jesus as Son and Servant: An Investigation of the Baptism and Testing Narratives and Their Significance for Cohesion, Plot, and Christology in Matthew" (PhD diss., Southern Baptist Theological Seminary, 1993), 202–10; Crowe, *Obedient Son*, 182–83; Jeffrey A. Gibbs, "Israel Standing with Israel: The Baptism of Jesus in Matthew's Gospel (Matt. 3:13–17)," *CBQ* 64 (2002): 525–26.

78. Recall the earlier argument that *ekballō* in Mark 1:12 recalls Adam's original banishment from the garden (Gen. 3:24).

FILIAL OBEDIENCE

The close relationship between the baptism and temptation narratives has several implications. First, Jesus's obedience is *filial* obedience. That is, the framework for contextualizing Jesus's obedience is that of the Son to the Father, which recalls the sonship of both Israel and Adam. The sonship of Jesus is the primary emphasis of the heavenly voice at the baptism that announces the divine good pleasure in Jesus, and it is the sonship of Jesus that is explicitly tested by the devil in the wilderness in Matthew and Luke. In Matthew the sonship of Jesus is the focus of the first two temptations, whereas in Luke Jesus's sonship is the focus of the first and third temptations. Additionally, the words of the tempter that focus on the sonship of Jesus (*ei huios ei tou theou*) should be taken as first-class conditionals that assume the truth of the statements.[79] Thus, one could translate the tempter's challenges: "*Since* you are the Son of God," which accords with the filial emphasis of the heavenly voice in the baptism. In other words, the devil is not testing the *fact* of Jesus's sonship but the *mode* of Jesus's sonship.[80] Though in Mark's temptation account the sonship of Jesus is not explicitly mentioned in the temptation itself, the declaration of Jesus's sonship immediately precedes his wilderness testing. Additionally, if Mark's temptation narrative conveys Adamic imagery (see chap. 2), then these factors would complement the more extended narratives of Matthew and Luke in which the sonship of Jesus is explicitly the focus of the temptations. In sum, the temptation accounts are some of the clearest texts in the Gospels that underscore the obedience of Jesus, and this obedience is narrated within a *filial* framework.

PERFECT FILIAL OBEDIENCE

Second, Jesus's filial obedience in the temptation is to be seen not only in light of but also in distinction from both Israel and Adam. If both Israel and Adam should be understood as covenantal sons of God who owed covenantal obedience to God, in the temptation Jesus demonstrates undefiled filial faithfulness that correlates to perfect filial love.[81] It is widely agreed that in the temptation accounts of Matthew and Luke, Jesus recapitulates Israel's experiences in the wilderness.[82] Jesus responds to the three temptations from

79. BDF §371; cf. Mark Allan Powell, "The Plots and Subplots of Matthew's Gospel," *NTS* 38 (1992): 187–204; Donald A. Hagner, *Matthew*, 2 vols., WBC 33A–B (Dallas: Word, 1993–95), 1:65.

80. Crowe, *Obedient Son*, 160.

81. Cf. Schlatter, *History of the Christ*, 44, 77.

82. This section draws significantly from Crowe, *Obedient Son*, 159–66.

Deuteronomy (Deut. 6:13, 16; 8:3), the book of the covenant, which presents the testing of Israel as God's covenantal son (Deut. 8:5; cf. 1:31; 14:1; 32:4–6, 18–20, 43).[83] However, Deuteronomy also makes it clear that Israel did not pass the tests of God with flying colors, and the dangers of covenantal curses remained before them (cf. Deut. 26–28). Thus, the context of Deuteronomy 6–8 is important for interpreting the temptations in Matthew and Luke. In both contexts God's son is tested before a watershed event—in Deuteronomy the Israelites were preparing to enter the promised land, whereas in Matthew and Luke Jesus prepares to embark upon his public ministry. In both contexts God's son suffers lack. However, whereas the Israelites grumbled during their forty-year wanderings, Jesus proves faithful for forty days and is sustained by God's word instead of physical bread. Additionally, the Israelites were tested so that God might know their hearts (Deut. 8:2, 16), but they were not to test the Lord (Deut. 6:16a). The Israelites failed (Deut. 6:16b); Jesus did not fail (Matt. 4:7 // Luke 4:12). Additionally, the Israelites fell into idolatry on numerous occasions (Exod. 32; Num. 25; cf. Deut. 4:3), whereas Jesus refused to worship any other gods (Matt. 4:10; Luke 4:8). Thus, in the temptation narratives, we see that Son of God has "to do in part with Jesus as the personification or embodiment of true, obedient Israel."[84] Just as Israel passed through the waters of baptism into the testing of the wilderness, so Jesus comes through the waters of baptism into the testing of the wilderness, though Jesus remains fully faithful as God's Son, in contrast to Israel.[85]

Yet we must not only observe the parallels to Israel's history in the temptation accounts of Jesus but also consider how Jesus is portrayed as overcoming the disobedience of Adam. I introduced this topic in the last chapter in relation to Mark and Luke, but more remains to be said, especially as it pertains to Matthew. To recap and synthesize, in Luke the temptation is connected to the baptism by means of the genealogy that terminates with Adam, the son of God (Luke 3:38). Thus, not only do we find in Luke the Deuteronomic context of Israel as son of God in the temptation narrative, but the Adamic emphasis of the genealogy leads directly to the testing of Jesus as God's Son. Jesus overcomes temptation in the postlapsarian wilderness, in contrast to Adam who failed in the garden.[86] Additionally, Luke 4:1 states that Jesus was

83. For Deuteronomy as a covenantal book, see Crowe, *Obedient Son*, 90n12.

84. Davies and Allison, *Matthew*, 1:263–64; cf. William L. Kynes, *A Christology of Solidarity: Jesus as the Representative of His People in Matthew* (New York: University Press of America, 1991), 28–32; Darrell L. Bock, *Luke*, 2 vols., BECNT (Grand Rapids: Baker Academic, 1994–96), 1:363.

85. Davies and Allison, *Matthew*, 1:344–45; Hagner, *Matthew*, 1:61–62; cf. 1 Cor. 10:2.

86. Geldenhuys, *Gospel of Luke*, 158; J. R. Edwards, *Luke*, 130.

filled with the Holy Spirit, which we have noted may also be Adamic imagery, especially in light of the obedience Jesus offers to his Father, in contrast to the consequential sin of Adam.[87] In Mark, Jesus's presence with the wild animals in the context of temptation recalls Adam's original created state with the animals in paradise and presents us with last-Adam imagery for Jesus as the one who brings eschatological peace.

Do we also find Adamic imagery in Matthew's temptation account (Matt. 4:1–11)? Certainly one would want to argue that the background of Israel's sonship is emphasized in Matthew 4, and yet we risk truncating Matthew's rich Old Testament tapestries if we do not consider possible Adamic imagery in Matthew's temptation account as well.[88] As we have seen, Son of God imagery is multifaceted, and Israel's sonship is built upon an Adamic foundation. Indeed, the interrelatedness of Adam and Israel as son of God seems to be the presupposition for Luke, who mingles imagery of Adam as son of God with Israel as son of God in his presentation of Jesus's temptation. In addition to the imagery of sonship, another correspondence between Jesus and Adam in Matthew (and the other temptation accounts) is the temptation to eat for selfish reasons: whereas Adam was tempted to eat the forbidden fruit, Jesus refused to turn stones into bread to satiate his own hunger.

Another textual echo of Adam may come from Psalm 91. In Matthew and Luke the devil cites Psalm 91:11–12 to test Jesus's sonship, urging Jesus to throw himself down from the temple (Matt. 4:5–6; Luke 4:9–10). It is significant that Psalm 91:13 speaks of trampling the serpent, which quite possibly alludes to the messianic seed of the woman prophesied in Genesis 3:15.[89] Thus, in light of the Old Testament context, Matthew's second temptation, and Luke's third, bespeak a fusing of Son of God and Adam imagery to communicate an Adamic Christology of obedience. As Beale comments, "Jesus's refusal to follow Satan's advice during the wilderness temptations was the beginning victory over Satan professed in [Psalm 91]."[90] Indeed, the presence of an explicit tempter in all three Synoptics parallels the testing of Adam more closely than Israel. Additional support for an Adamic aspect of Son of God

87. See Mikeal C. Parsons, *Luke*, Paideia (Grand Rapids: Baker Academic, 2015), 74–75. Parsons gives several examples of the Adam-Christ parallel in Luke's temptation account from the history of interpretation, including Ambrose, Ephrem the Syrian, Cyril of Alexandria, and Augustine.

88. See, e.g., the discussion of Matthew's temptation account in William Perkins, "The Combat between Christ and the Devil Displayed; or, A Commentary upon the Temptations of Christ," in vol. 1 of *The Works of William Perkins*, ed. J. Stephen Yuille (Grand Rapids: Reformation Heritage, 2014), 98, 158.

89. Beale, *New Testament Biblical Theology*, 420.

90. Ibid.

in Matthew and Luke comes from several other New Testament passages in which we find the intersection of Son of God and son of Adam Christology (Rom. 8:3; 1 Cor. 15:21–28; Gal. 4:4; Heb. 1:1–3; 2:16–18).[91] Thus, both Son of God and Adam Christology underscore the obedience of Jesus, which means that, even in Matthew, the temptations of Jesus are those of the last Adam.[92]

To summarize, in the temptation Jesus is portrayed as the Son of God in ways that evoke Israel and Adam, though Jesus's obedience in the face of temptation distinguishes him from both Israel and Adam.[93] The uniqueness of Jesus's obedience as covenantal son of God is a point at which we do well to linger and consider the implications more fully. By setting Jesus's obedience in contrast to the failures of both Adam and Israel, the Evangelists communicate that Jesus's obedience surpasses the failures of his covenantal predecessors. The victory of Jesus over Satan in the wilderness realizes the obedience required of Israel. But this is not the end of the matter because, more fundamentally, Jesus's obedience in the wilderness fulfills the filial fealty required of Adam.

Vicarious Filial Obedience

This brings us to a third major implication of the temptation narrative. In light of Jesus's filial obedience in comparison and contrast to Adam and Israel, we should understand the obedience of Jesus in the temptation as *vicarious* obedience. In his temptation Jesus, the messianic Son, demonstrates faithfulness to the mission laid out before him as he moves toward the outset of his public ministry and the inauguration of the kingdom of God (Matt. 4:17 // Mark 1:14–15). Thus when Jesus overcomes the disobedience of Israel and Adam, he does so not as an isolated individual but as an inclusive representative[94] whose obedience benefits those whom he represents.

Epochally Significant Filial Obedience

Fourth, Jesus's perfect obedience in the face of temptation as God's anointed should be considered an epochally significant event in the history of redemption.[95] Jesus's obedience marks a decisive turning point in covenantal history,

---

91. This list is modified from Joel William Parkman, "Adam Christological Motifs in the Synoptic Traditions" (PhD diss., Baylor University, 1994), 162–76.

92. Cf. Pierre Bonnard, *L'Évangile selon Saint Matthieu*, 2nd ed., CNT 1 (Neuchatel: Delachaux & Niestlé, 1963), 42.

93. See also Beale, *New Testament Biblical Theology*, 403.

94. See R. T. France, *Matthew: Evangelist and Teacher* (Exeter: Paternoster, 1989), 209, following C. H. Dodd, *The Founder of Christianity* (London: Collins, 1971), 106.

95. See Sinclair B. Ferguson, *The Holy Spirit*, CCT (Downers Grove, IL: InterVarsity, 1996), 48; Vos, *Biblical Theology*, 320–21.

when the Son of God refuses the allures of sin and clings to the Word of God by faith. The uniqueness of Jesus's perfect obedience—seen particularly in the intensely focused, threefold temptation[96]—underscores Jesus's perfect obedience as God's covenantal representative, which provides the logic for the vicarious nature of his obedience. Jesus's obedience not only *surpasses* that of Israel and Adam, but *overcomes* the disobedience of prior canonical sons of God.

Several features of the narrative suggest that Jesus's obedience in the temptation is a decisive event in the history of redemption. All three Synoptics open their accounts of Jesus's ministry with his baptism and his subsequent obedience in the face of temptation. Just as the first words of Jesus are programmatic for the narratives that follow (Matt. 3:15; Mark 1:14–15; Luke 2:49), so the first actions of Jesus after the baptism provide an interpretive lens for the remainder of the Gospel narratives. Additionally, in all three Synoptics Jesus is the stronger one who comes in accord with John's prophecy (Matt. 3:11 // Mark 1:7 // Luke 3:16), is baptized, overcomes temptation, and then begins to preach and inaugurate the kingdom. The initial testing of Jesus's messianic sonship catapults Jesus into his ministry of obedient sonship,[97] in which he overcomes all spiritual opposition to his task, even to the point of obediently facing the unjust death on the cross. By his obedience and full possession of the Spirit, Jesus possesses unrivaled spiritual authority on earth. Indeed, in chapter 6 we will see that Jesus's authority to bind the strong man is linked textually with Jesus's obedience in the temptation. The unique authority of Jesus as the stronger man is therefore possible because of Jesus's full obedience, including his opening (and indeed decisive) victory over Satan in the threefold temptation. To be sure, conflicts between Jesus and the devil's kingdom continue throughout the Gospels, but Jesus's obedience at the beginning of his ministry provides much of the framework for understanding his spiritual authority in all that follows.

Additionally, we may find an implicit reference in the Lord's Prayer, particularly in Matthew, to Jesus's decisive obedience in the temptation. Whereas Jesus is led by the Spirit of God into the wilderness to be tempted, the disciples, in contrast, are instructed to pray that they *not* be led into temptation (Matt. 6:13 // Luke 11:4; cf. Matt. 27:43). To be sure, much debate exists about the nature of the temptation (or perhaps *testing*) in view of the Lord's Prayer, but from a narrative perspective it seems that what was appropriate for Jesus

---

96. In his *Gnomon*, J. A. Bengel observes that in the temptation of Jesus, the devil "expended all his weapons of offence," cited in J. R. Edwards, *Luke*, 130.

97. See Longenecker, *Christology*, 96.

as the last Adam—being led into temptation as the representative man—is not appropriate for his disciples, who should instead follow the one who has already proven decisively obedient in the face of temptation. This is consistent with the identity of *tou ponērou* in Matthew 6:13b, which is best taken as a personal reference to the devil, whom Jesus overcame in the wilderness. If this correlation between Jesus's temptation and the prayer of the disciples is valid, it would be another indication that Jesus's obedience was viewed as vicarious on behalf of others.

In following chapters we will consider in further detail how the obedience of Jesus is manifested throughout his ministry, but at this point we can observe that the respective beginnings of the Synoptic Gospels narrate events of cosmic significance. Jesus is the perfect Son of God, whose obedience complies fully with the will of God in a way that had never been realized before. The contrasts of Jesus's obedience with the disobedience of Israel and Adam, along with the roles that the temptation narratives serve as prerequisites for Jesus's public ministry, underscore the uniqueness of Jesus's actions in the history of redemption. Indeed, Jesus's absolute obedience as the last Adam—seen acutely and decisively in his spiritual conflict with Satan—overcomes the sin of Adam and is absolutely necessary for salvation. To put it starkly, "If Jesus had [in the temptation] . . . lost in the conflict, God's whole plan of redemption in Him would have been defeated."[98]

Conclusion and Implications

In this diachronically wide-ranging chapter, we have considered the Old Testament context for Israel and Adam as sons of God and the covenantal requirements given to them. Tragically, both Adam and Israel failed to exhibit the requisite obedience required of each. Adam failed to continue in his estate of uprightness, and not surprisingly, given Adam's failure, Israel demonstrated a persistent proclivity toward unfaithfulness. Covenant history provides much of the context for Jesus's identification as Son of God in his baptism and temptation. Jesus is declared to be the beloved Son of God in the baptism and is set apart as the representative Messiah of his people. It is as a representative that Jesus remains obedient in the face of the devil's three temptations, showing definitively how God's son should be fully obedient and devoted to the Lord.

As we conclude this chapter, it should be emphasized that Jesus's identity as Son of God underscores his obedience. Significantly, the sonship of Jesus is

98. Geldenhuys, *Gospel of Luke*, 158.

not just one identification among many but is arguably the most fundamental identification of Jesus in all four Gospels.[99] Therefore, the obedience of Jesus is emphasized not only in texts such as the temptation account where the sonship of Jesus is the focus of explicit reflection, but is likely also in view in other texts that speak of Jesus's sonship. Recognizing that Jesus's sonship entails his obedience as a representative supports the view that the Gospel writers emphasize the vicarious nature of Jesus's obedience.

With the appearance of Jesus as the fully obedient Son of God, we encounter a new day in the history of redemption—a day of eschatological salvation secured by the Messiah. In the next chapter we will explore this obedience in more detail, giving attention to the contours of each Gospel, as we continue to consider the life of the last Adam in the Gospels.

99. For Matthew, see the classic work of Jack Dean Kingsbury, *Matthew: Structure, Christology, Kingdom* (Philadelphia: Fortress, 1975). Son of God is also central to Mark's Gospel, though the term is used less frequently (note, e.g., the likely *inclusio* of Mark 1:1 and 15:39). In Luke Jesus's sonship is proclaimed by Gabriel before Jesus's birth (Luke 1:35). John's Gospel also emphasizes the sonship of Jesus, which we will consider further in chap. 5.

The Last Adam and the Fulfillment
of Scripture

In previous chapters I have argued that Jesus is portrayed in the Gospels as a representative figure like Adam, and this accords with the history of Christian interpretation. As a representative, Jesus is obedient as Son of God and Son of Man in a recapitulatory way that overcomes the sin of Adam and realizes what was required of God's son. In the present chapter we will examine in more detail *how* Jesus is obedient beyond his baptism and temptation. We will consider how Jesus's life accords with Scripture, and what it means for Jesus to be described as righteous and the fulfiller of righteousness.

Tracing the ways that Jesus fulfills Scripture merits many volumes, so I will limit the following discussion of the Synoptic Gospels primarily to texts that speak of fulfillment, divine necessity (i.e., *dei* statements), and the purposes of Jesus's coming. Additionally, I will relate these statements to the righteousness of Jesus in his life and death. Many of these texts focus on the sonship of Jesus, so it will be important to remember the textual connections between Jesus's sonship and his status as the last Adam as argued in previous chapters. To anticipate what follows, I will argue that Jesus's entire obedience in the Synoptics is the answer to Adam's disobedience and realizes what is necessary for salvation.

Fulfillment in Matthew and Mark

Fulfillment Quotations in Matthew

We begin our survey of Jesus's fulfillment of Scripture in Matthew's Gospel, which emphasizes Jesus's fulfillment of the Old Testament Scriptures in various ways. For example, Matthew 1:1 identifies Jesus as the son of David, son of Abraham, linking Jesus back to two key figures from the Old Testament. Additionally, Matthew's genealogy shows that Jesus is to be understood in the context of the flow of Israel's history, moving from humble beginnings, to the new heights under David, to the tragedy of exile, to the hope of a new kingdom.[1]

One of the clearest ways we see Matthew's emphasis on Jesus's fulfillment of Scripture is in his ten fulfillment citations (Matt. 1:22–23; 2:15, 17–18, 23; 4:14–16; 8:17; 12:17–21; 13:35; 21:4–5; 27:9–10).[2] These citations, which are unique to Matthew, not only show that Jesus is the fulfillment of specific texts, but also situate Jesus in relation to Israel's history, showing how Jesus's full-fledged obedience is in each case the answer to Israel's perennial recalcitrance. In support of this view, it appears that most, if not all, of the prophetic texts utilized in Matthew's fulfillment citations are taken from contexts that speak to the covenantal infidelity of Israel. If so, then the Matthean formula quotations show how the problem of covenantal transgression finds its resolution in the life of Christ, who was faithful to Scripture in every way, even as a small child.

Thus, for example, in Matthew 2 Jesus as a child is taken to Egypt and is protected from the intrigues of King Herod. In the oft-discussed text "out of Egypt I called my son" (Matt. 2:15; cf. Hosea 11:1), Jesus's sonship is communicated in light of Israel's status as son of God. Moreover, though Jesus's *return from* Egypt is emphasized in connection with his *flight to* Egypt in Matthew 2:14–15, we should not miss that Hosea anticipates a day of blessing in which the son of God would *come out* of Egypt (Hosea 11:10–11).[3] Thus, Jesus's flight to Egypt is portrayed as the eschatological resolution to the quandary in Hosea in which God's son, who was treated tenderly (Hosea 11:3–4), was treacherously disobedient. Matthew masterfully shows how Jesus, as true Israel and obedient Son of God, will come out of Egypt in

---

1. On Matthew's genealogy, see Richard B. Hays, "The Gospel of Matthew: Reconfigured Torah," *HvTSt* 61 (2005): 165–90; Jason B. Hood, *The Messiah, His Brothers, and the Nations (Matthew 1.1–17)*, LNTS 441 (London: T&T Clark, 2011).

2. For a defense of these ten fulfillment citations and further bibliography, see Brandon D. Crowe, "Fulfillment in Matthew as Eschatological Reversal," *WTJ* 75 (2013): 111–27, esp. 111n1. The following discussion summarizes this article.

3. See G. K. Beale, "The Use of Hosea 11:1 in Matthew 2:15: One More Time," *JETS* 55 (2012): 697–715.

accord with God's design for salvation. The use of Hosea 11:1 in Matthew 2:15 is one example of the ways that Jesus's lifelong and vicarious obedience is emphasized in Matthew's fulfillment quotations. One might gloss Matthew's understanding of fulfillment as Jesus's representative reversal, through his vicarious obedience, of the negative trajectory of Israel's history that was necessary to secure eschatological blessings for God's people. Certainly Jesus's death and resurrection are of central importance in this regard, but equally indispensable is Jesus's lifelong obedience to the will of God set forth in Scripture.

We must also recognize that *fulfillment* entails eschatology. In other words, though Jesus in some sense recapitulates both Israel and Adam, *fulfill* for Matthew does not simply mean *repeat*. Instead, fulfillment marks a redemptive-historical advancement, as Jesus brings salvation history to its goal. The need for fulfillment in Jesus is necessary because of the desideratum of a fully obedient people before the coming of Christ. If the plot of Matthew's Gospel can be summed up in "he will save his people from their sins" (1:21), then a significant aspect of how this is accomplished is by means of Jesus's wide-ranging, representative obedience.

Fulfillment in Mark

An eschatological sense of *fulfill* is also present in Mark's Gospel. Jesus's first words in Mark (1:14–15) set the tone for his ministry. Immediately after his baptism and temptation, Jesus proclaims that the time is *fulfilled* and the kingdom of God is at hand. These statements signify that the realization of the kingdom hopes of the Old Testament were being inaugurated through Jesus, who had just proven victorious over temptation in a way that recapitulates and overcomes the sin of Adam (1:12–13). Following on the heels of his initial obedience, Jesus's kingdom announcement entails the need to repent from sins, which underscores that the kingdom Jesus brings is one of righteousness in conformity with Scripture.

Mark also speaks explicitly of fulfillment at the arrest of Jesus in 14:49. This use of *fulfill* corresponds quite closely to the nuance in Matthew's formula quotations, in which *fulfillment* denotes the full measure of sin that must be overcome for the kingdom to be inaugurated (see especially Matt. 26:54–56). Mark has much more to say about the work of Christ in relation to Scripture, but he does not utilize *fulfillment* terminology as extensively as Matthew or Luke. Instead, Mark's verbal parallels to key Old Testament texts alert the reader to ways in which Jesus is fulfilling the Old Testament, such as we see in the Isaianic servant texts that I will discuss below.

Fulfilling All Righteousness

We now return to Matthew's concept of fulfillment as it pertains to righteousness, a concept we have introduced but not yet considered in detail. Matthew relates fulfillment in Jesus to the concept of righteousness. Historically, an important text in this regard has been Matthew 3:15: "But Jesus answered [John], 'Permit it now, for thus it is fitting for us to fulfill all righteousness.'" Not surprisingly, suggested interpretations for this phrase are legion. An exhaustive survey is not possible here,[4] but I will offer my own reading of this text in the context of Matthew's Gospel, in light of the salvation accomplished by Jesus.

Before considering the import of the phrasing, we should observe that Matthew 3:15 conveys the first words spoken by Jesus in Matthew, which are programmatic for his ministry.[5] We have already noted Matthew's emphasis on the obedience of Jesus in the fulfillment quotations, which are especially frequent in Matthew 1–4. Half of Matthew's ten fulfillment quotations appear in these first four chapters, which set forth the christological foundation for understanding Jesus in Matthew's narrative.[6] In Matthew 1–4 we are introduced to Jesus as the representative Messiah of Israel who is preparing to bring the kingdom of heaven. When Jesus first speaks in Matthew 3:15 he says that "now" (*arti*) it is fitting to fulfill all righteousness, indicating that the eschatological "now" of salvation had arrived (cf. Matt. 11:12).[7]

Much ink has been spilled discussing the meaning of righteousness in Matthew. In my view righteousness in Matthew must refer to God's requirement for humanity.[8] Thus, in at least one text Matthew explicitly contrasts the *righteous* and *sinners* (9:13). Yet a careful reading of Matthew should

4. For discussions see W. D. Davies and Dale C. Allison Jr., *A Critical and Exegetical Commentary on the Gospel according to St. Matthew*, 3 vols., ICC (Edinburgh: T&T Clark, 1988–97), 1:325–27; Otto Eissfeldt, "Πληρῶσαι πᾶσαν δικαιοσύνην in Matthäus 3,15," *ZNW* 61 (1970): 209–15. I am also expanding upon Brandon D. Crowe, *The Obedient Son: Deuteronomy and Christology in the Gospel of Matthew*, BZNW 188 (Berlin: Walter de Gruyter, 2012), 183–86.

5. Roland Deines, *Der Gerechtigkeit der Tora im Reich des Messias. Mt 5,13–20 als Schlüsseltext der matthäischen Theologie*, WUNT 177 (Tübingen: Mohr Siebeck, 2004), 127; Heinz Giesen, *Christliches Handeln: Eine redaktionskritische Untersuchung zum δικαιοσύνη-Begriff im Matthäus-Evangelium*, EHS.T 181 (Frankfurt: Peter Lang, 1981), 27–28.

6. See also Thomas Söding, "Der Gehorsam des Gottessohne: Zur Christologie der matthäischen Versuchungserzählung (4,1–11)," in *Jesus Christus als die Mitte der Schrift*, ed. Christof Landmesser, Hans-Joachim Eckstein, and Hermann Lichtenberger, BZNW 86 (Berlin: Walter de Gruyter, 1997), 711, 720; see similarly John Nolland, *The Gospel of Matthew*, NIGTC (Grand Rapids: Eerdmans, 2005), 161.

7. At the same time, there is also a "not yet" to this eschatological "now" in Matthew (23:39; 26:29; 26:64). See also Joshua E. Leim, *Matthew's Theological Grammar: The Father and the Son*, WUNT 2/402 (Tübingen: Mohr Siebeck, 2015), 69–71.

8. Benno Przybylski, *Righteousness in Matthew and in His World of Thought*, SNTSMS 41 (Cambridge: Cambridge University Press, 1981), 91; Söding, "Gehorsam des Gottessohne,"

also caution us against neglecting the *gracious* aspects of righteousness in the context of Matthew's narrative.[9] Put simply, Jesus's baptism is one part of his fulfilling all righteousness, and fulfilling all righteousness is necessary for Jesus to save his people from their sins (1:21). Or, as it has been recently stated of *dikaiosynē* in Matthew, the "salvific implication arises less from the lexical concept of δικαιοσύνη itself than from the discourse concept that Jesus, as the representative of his people, is identifying with them in their situation of unrighteousness in order 'to fulfill all (ethical) righteousness on their behalf.'"[10] Admittedly, this way of reading Matthew 3:15 is not affirmed by all, but when viewed in context of the progressive unfolding of Matthew's Gospel, we have sufficient grounds for concluding that Matthew 3:15 entails Jesus's vicarious accomplishment of righteousness.

Therefore, Matthew 3:15 supports the present argument (i.e., that Jesus's obedience is necessary for salvation) in several ways. First, the *fulfill* language, in the midst of a portion of Matthew (Matt. 1–4) that includes a high density of fulfillment quotations linked to Old Testament texts, encourages the reader to associate Jesus's fulfillment of all *righteousness* with the fulfillment of *Scripture*. Throughout Matthew, *fulfill* is a key christological term,[11] and certainly Matthew 3:15 is drawing our attention to a christological reality.

Second, a closely related point is the need to recognize righteousness as a christological category as well.[12] The christological emphasis on righteousness goes hand in hand with the christological emphasis on fulfillment. This christological emphasis on righteousness is clarified in the Sermon on the Mount, which we will examine below. Moreover, if Matthew 3–4 is a key portion of the Gospel that highlights the representative, recapitulatory obedience of Jesus (see chap. 3 above), then it seems likely that the most consistent and contextual reading of Matthew 3:15 is to view the righteousness of Jesus as a uniquely *christological* fulfillment of righteousness.

Third, this uniquely christological accomplishment of God's demand of righteousness fits well with the likely import of *all* righteousness (*pasan*

730; Eissfeldt, "Πληρῶσαι," 214; R. T. France, *The Gospel of Matthew*, NICNT (Grand Rapids: Eerdmans, 2007), 119.

9. See BDAG, "δικαιοσύνη," 247–48.

10. Charles Lee Irons, *The Righteousness of God: A Lexical Examination of the Covenant-Faithfulness Interpretation*, WUNT 2/386 (Tübingen: Mohr Siebeck, 2015), 265.

11. See Roland Deines, "Not the Law but the Messiah: Law and Righteousness in the Gospel of Matthew—an Ongoing Debate," in *Built Upon the Rock: Studies in the Gospel of Matthew*, ed. Daniel M. Gurtner and John Nolland (Grand Rapids: Eerdmans, 2008), 53–84; cf. C. F. D. Moule, "Fulfillment Words in the New Testament: Use and Abuse," in *Essays in New Testament Interpretation*, ed. C. F. D. Moule (Cambridge: Cambridge University Press, 1982), 3–36.

12. See the discussion below, in relation to the Sermon on the Mount and Matt. 5:10–12.

dikaiosynēn): Jesus fulfilled every aspect of righteousness.[13] At this point the question might arise: if Jesus's fulfillment of all righteousness points to his fulfillment of Scripture, then what text(s) is he fulfilling in his baptism? Are there specific Old Testament texts that required baptism of the Messiah? To pose the question in this way, however, may cause us to miss the broader point. On the one hand, Jesus's baptism was the requirement for God's people through the prophetic voice of John at that time.[14] The divine necessity of John's ministry also explains why Jesus includes John in the "us" who are fulfilling all righteousness: John was not definitively accomplishing salvation (as the thrust of Matthew's Gospel makes clear), but John did have a role to play in the coming of the messianic kingdom (cf. Matt. 21:32). John's ministry accords with the voice crying out in the wilderness in anticipation of a new salvation (Isa. 40:3), with the coming of Elijah (Mal. 3–4 [EVV]), and John's baptism corresponds to the predicted eschatological cleansing of God's people (Ps. 51:7–12; Isa. 4:4; 44:3; Jer. 4:14; Ezek. 36:25; Zech. 13:1).

As I argued in the previous chapter, Jesus's baptism also points to his representative, messianic work as the vicariously obedient one—the righteous sin-bearer. Therefore, viewed in the light of Old Testament anticipations more broadly, Jesus may be seen to be fulfilling any number of texts that anticipate a new day of salvation. However, on the basis of the content of the heavenly voice at the baptism more specifically, we might particularly note those texts that entail royal, messianic expectations, as the king represented the nation and led them in righteousness (cf. Pss. 2; 72; Isa. 9:7 [9:6 EVV]; 11:1–5; 32:1; Jer. 23:5–6; 33:14–16; Zech. 9:9). This imagery, especially from Isaiah, dovetails well with the second half of the heavenly voice that emphasizes the role of the Isaianic servant in establishing righteousness (Isa. 42:1–6; 49:6; 53:11–14).[15]

Fourth, building upon the previous point and the eschatology inherent in *fulfill* noted earlier, we must relate Jesus's fulfilling of all righteousness to the accomplishment of salvation. In other words, righteousness in Matthew is at once God's requirement and God's eschatological gift of salvation.[16] Jesus's

---

13. Cf. Georg Strecker, *Der Weg Gerechtigkeit: Untersuchung zur Theologie des Matthäus*, FRLANT 82 (Göttingen: Vandenhoeck & Ruprecht, 1962), 141; Richard C. Beaton, *Isaiah's Christ in Matthew's Gospel*, SNTSMS 123 (Cambridge: Cambridge University Press, 2002), 176; BDF §275(3); Crowe, *Obedient Son*, 185; Irons, *Righteousness of God*, 265.

14. Geerhardus Vos, *Biblical Theology: Old and New Testaments* (1948; repr., Edinburgh: Banner of Truth, 1975), 319.

15. I will discuss the servant further in chaps. 6–7.

16. Here I am paraphrasing Mogens Müller, who says that righteousness in Matthew is "Forderung und eschatologisches Heilsgut zugleich" ("Bundesideologie im Matthäusevangelium. Die Vorstellung vom neuen Bund als Grundlage der matthäischen Gesetzesverkündigung," *NTS* 58 [2011]: 35).

fulfillment of *all righteousness* should be viewed in light of the coming day of eschatological salvation that entailed eschatological righteousness.[17] Indeed, reflections on God's righteousness and/or the coming state of God's people being righteous are often found in tandem with the anticipation of eschatological salvation.[18]

The approach I am taking to "fulfilling all righteousness," however, by no means finds universal assent. W. D. Davies and Dale Allison, for example, list seven options for the import of the relevant phrases in Matthew 3:15.[19] Therefore, to support further the reading I am suggesting—that Jesus fulfills God's requirements vicariously as part of the accomplishment of salvation— I would like to turn now to the development of the interrelated themes of righteousness and Christology later in Matthew, especially in the Sermon on the Mount.

Righteousness and Christology in the Sermon on the Mount

The way Jesus fulfills all righteousness gains clarity as Matthew progresses. Therefore, attention to the relationship between righteousness and Christology in the Sermon on the Mount will shed further light on the christological accomplishment of righteousness spoken by Jesus in Matthew 3:15. Specifically, in Matthew 5 we find further indication that righteousness is defined by Jesus as the one who fulfills the Law and the Prophets. One need not conclude that the Sermon on the Mount presents only unattainable ideals to recognize the relationship between the righteousness set forth in the Sermon and Jesus's own, consummate fulfillment of that righteousness.

We begin with the Beatitudes, where righteousness is set in parallel to Jesus himself. In Matthew 5:10, the last of the standard form beatitudes, Jesus's macarism states that those who are persecuted for righteousness' sake are blessed. In the next verse (5:11), as Jesus sums up the beatitudes (5:11–12), Jesus states that those who are persecuted for *his* sake are blessed. The implication is that being persecuted for righteousness' sake means being persecuted for Jesus's sake,[20] especially in light of Matthew 3:15, where Jesus defines his own mission to include fulfilling all righteousness.

---

17. Cf. Isa. 1:2, 26–27; 9:6 [9:7 EVV]; 11:1–5; 32:16–17; 45:8; 46:12; 51:5; 56:1; 59:16; 60:21; 61:10–11; 62:1–2; 63:1; Jer. 23:5–6; 31:23; 33:15–16; Zech. 8:8; 9:9.

18. On Isaiah, see John D. W. Watts, *Isaiah 34–66*, rev. ed., WBC 25 (Nashville: Thomas Nelson, 2005), 674.

19. Davies and Allison, *Matthew*, 1:325–27.

20. See Kenneth E. Bailey, *Jesus through Middle Eastern Eyes: Cultural Studies in the Gospels* (Downers Grove, IL: IVP Academic, 2008), 85–86; cf. Deines, "Not the Law," 74; John R. W. Stott, *The Message of the Sermon on the Mount*, BST (Downers Grove, IL: InterVarsity, 1978), 52.

In addition to the parallels between Matthew 5:10 and 5:11, Matthew 5:6 further identifies Jesus with righteousness.[21] Many plausible structures for the Beatitudes have been suggested, but one viable option views 5:6 ("Blessed are those who hunger and thirst for righteousness, for they will be filled") to be something like a fulcrum for the first eight beatitudes. The promise in 5:6 is that those who long for righteousness will be satisfied, as with food. Additionally, as we have seen, the eighth beatitude (5:10) also focuses on righteousness in a way that is closely tied to the person of Jesus in light of 5:11. We can also identify a progression of logic between the first four and the second four beatitudes in which the need for filling in the first four beatitudes is answered in the promises of the second four beatitudes. The first eight beatitudes form a literary unit, identified by the kingdom *inclusio* in 5:3 and 5:10.[22] Additionally, the fourth and eighth beatitudes serve as conclusions for the first four and second four beatitudes, respectively, and both feature the term *righteousness* (*dikaiosynē*). In this light, Matthew 5:11–12 serves as a christological summary for the Beatitudes as a whole, which have much to say about kingdom and righteousness. Below I have provided this option for the structure of the Beatitudes.

A. Poor in spirit . . . theirs is the *kingdom* (5:3)
   B. Mourn . . . will be comforted (5:4)
      C. Meek . . . will inherit the earth (5:5)
         D. KEY: Hunger and thirst for righteousness . . . will be filled (5:6)
A′ Merciful . . . will receive mercy (5:7)
   B′ Pure in heart . . . will see God (5:8)
      C′ Peacemakers . . . will be called sons of God (5:9)
         D′ KEY: Persecuted for righteousness . . . theirs is the *kingdom* (5:10)
Christological Summary: **Righteousness** and Jesus (5:11–12)

If this structure has merit, then it signifies further the indissoluble relationship between Jesus and righteousness. The christological term *righteousness* features in the fourth and eighth beatitudes, and the eighth beatitude (forming an *inclusio* with the first beatitude) speaks of both righteousness and

21. For the structure of the Beatitudes, I have found D. Martyn Lloyd-Jones helpful, though I have modified his structure. See his *Studies in the Sermon on the Mount*, 2nd ed., 2 vols. (Grand Rapids: Eerdmans, 1971), 1:106–9.

22. See also Charles L. Quarles, *Sermon on the Mount: Restoring Christ's Message to the Modern Church*, NACSBT 11 (Nashville: Broadman & Holman, 2011), 15–16.

the kingdom inaugurated by Jesus. Thus the Beatitudes are consistent with what we have already seen elsewhere in Matthew, namely, that righteousness must be understood in relation to Jesus, who defines and fulfills righteousness. Furthermore, it is quite suggestive, in light of the association of Jesus with righteousness, that 5:6 promises "being satisfied" (*chortasthēsontai*) with righteousness in a context that evokes eating and drinking. Perhaps we have here an indication that the disciples' need of righteousness is something that can only be filled by the one who is identified with righteousness and fulfills all righteousness. In this light Geerhardus Vos, reflecting on Jesus's words in Matthew 5:6, states that "the coming order of things, the new kingdom of God, brings with itself, chief of all blessings, a perfect righteousness, as truly and absolutely the gift of God to man as is the entire kingdom. What is true of the kingdom—that no human merit can deserve, that no human effort call it into being—applies with equal force to the righteousness that forms its center."[23]

To be clear, identifying righteousness with the work of Jesus does *not* mean that righteousness is not also God's requirement. Indeed, in Matthew 5:20 and 6:1 we find explicit statements about *practicing* righteousness. But identifying righteousness with Jesus does mean that the righteousness we must practice cannot be divorced from Jesus, who fulfills all righteousness. Stated differently, there is no dichotomy between Jesus's all-encompassing, vicarious fulfilling of all righteousness and the disciples' charge to practice righteousness. To paraphrase Dale Allison, Jesus not only requires *dikaiosynē*, but he also lives it.[24] The righteousness described by Jesus in the Sermon on the Mount was incarnate in Jesus himself.[25] In other words, there is a consistent correlation between the righteousness Jesus requires of his disciples in the Sermon on the Mount and the actions of Jesus throughout Matthew.[26]

This correlation between the actions of Jesus and the command to practice righteousness raises an interesting possibility: if Jesus fulfills all righteousness and defines righteousness, and if the righteousness that Jesus commands his disciples to enact also characterizes Jesus's life, then the persecution Jesus himself encounters apparently also corresponds to the persecution mentioned in 5:10–12 (cf. 27:19–26). In other words, Jesus is persecuted because of the righteousness that he himself defines and fulfills.

23. Geerhardus Vos, "Hungering and Thirsting After Righteousness: Matthew 5:6," in *Grace and Glory: Sermons Preached in the Chapel of Princeton Theological Seminary* (Edinburgh: Banner of Truth, 1994), 41.

24. Dale C. Allison Jr., "Structure, Biographical Impulse, and the *Imitatio Christi*," in *Studies in Matthew: Interpretation Past and Present* (Grand Rapids: Baker Academic, 2005), 152.

25. Vos, "Hungering and Thirsting," 42.

26. Allison, "Structure," 147–53; John P. Meier, *The Vision of Matthew: Christ, Church, and Morality in the First Gospel* (1991; repr., Eugene, OR: Wipf & Stock, 2004), 188.

Beyond the Beatitudes, the *crux interpretum* Matthew 5:17–20 further underscores the christological aspects of righteousness. In 5:17 we read that Jesus came not to abolish but to *fulfill* the Law and the Prophets. In 5:20 Jesus states that those who wish to enter the kingdom of heaven must manifest a *righteousness* that surpasses that of the scribes and Pharisees. Indeed, as Roland Deines has argued, these four verses are key for unlocking the theology of Matthew's Gospel.[27]

We should first consider 5:17–18, where Jesus explains that he fulfills the Law and the Prophets. These verses are further indication that *fulfill* is preeminently a christological concept for Matthew. Jesus speaks uniquely of his own role in 5:17–18.[28] The authoritative teaching of Jesus in the Sermon on the Mount and elsewhere in Matthew is one way in which the Law and the Prophets are fulfilled.[29] However, Deines is most likely correct that it is the entire mission of Jesus, and not only his teaching, that fulfills the Law and Prophets.[30] This sheds light on Matthew 5:18, where Jesus states that not one jot or tittle will pass away from the law until all things are accomplished (*heōs an panta genētai*).[31] This accomplishment again underscores the uniqueness of Christ's role in accomplishing eschatological salvation. Thus, 5:18 speaks of a salvation-historical necessity,[32] and, with 5:17, provides further evidence that Jesus's messianic *actions* are necessary for eschatological salvation.

To pursue this matter further, the "therefore" (*oun*) of Matthew 5:19–20 is the logical result of Matthew 5:17–18. As Deines again states, Matthew 5:19–20 marks the transition "from christological fulfillment" to the "disciples' obligation."[33] Key in this regard is the mention in Matthew 5:20 that one's righteousness must excel that of the scribes and Pharisees. This righteousness must refer in some way to the disciples' actions, which are to be deeper and more consistent than those of the scribes and Pharisees (note, e.g., the depth of the law-keeping outlined in 5:21–48 and throughout the Sermon on the Mount, along with the "weightier matters of the law" in Matt. 23:23). Yet we must also understand righteousness in 5:20 in light of the foundation given earlier in Matthew's narrative. By the time readers encounter 5:20, they have learned at least that (1) Jesus fulfills all righteousness (3:15); (2) being persecuted for righteousness is tantamount to being persecuted for Jesus (5:10–11); (3) those

27. Deines, *Gerechtigkeit*. For an English summary see Deines, "Not the Law," 53–84.
28. Cf. Irenaeus, *Epid.* 89.
29. See the helpful discussion in Ned B. Stonehouse, *The Witness of Matthew and Mark to Christ* (Grand Rapids: Eerdmans, 1958), 188–212.
30. Deines, "Not the Law," 75.
31. On this phrase, see Deines, *Gerechtigkeit*, 345–70; Nolland, *Gospel of Matthew*, 218–21.
32. Deines, "Not the Law," 77.
33. Ibid.

who hunger and thirst will be filled with righteousness that is identified with Jesus (5:6); and (4) Jesus fulfills the Law and Prophets (5:17–18).

Thus, the greater righteousness in 5:20 must be viewed in close relationship to the righteousness that is defined by the actions of Jesus. Whatever else Matthew 5:20 means, it must entail seeking after a righteousness that is thoroughly christological and eschatological in character (cf. 6:33).[34] Disciples of Jesus must not only seek to practice righteousness but must especially recognize the need to identify themselves with the representative Messiah who fulfills all righteousness, who fulfills the Scriptures, and who brings the entire will of God to fruition.

Fulfillment in Luke

Fulfillment in Luke's Prologue

Luke's Gospel also emphasizes fulfillment in Jesus, beginning already in the prologue (1:1–4), which one could translate this way:

> Inasmuch as many have set their hands to compile a narrative concerning the deeds (*pragmatōn*) that have been fulfilled (*peplērophorēmenōn*) among us, just as they were handed down to us by those who were eyewitnesses and became servants of the word, it seemed good also to me, having followed all things diligently from the beginning, to write an orderly account for you, most excellent Theophilus, in order that you might know with certainty the doctrines (*logōn*) you have been taught.

Particularly relevant for the present argument are the *deeds that have been fulfilled*. What works specifically was Luke speaking of? At the base level, these works must refer to the deeds of Jesus, many of which are recorded in Luke. However, we must say more about these works, specifically in relation to the certainty Luke wants his readers to have. Indeed, the certainty Luke has in view concerns the doctrines (*logōn*) that stem from the events that have been fulfilled. The term *logōn* is often translated rather generally in English translations as the "things" that have been taught.[35] Though "things" is a perfectly fine translation, it is appropriate to underscore more specifically the doctrinal aspects of *logōn*, especially since it is paired with teaching (*katēchēthēs*).[36]

---

34. See similarly ibid., 81.

35. E.g., ESV, NIV, NRSV, NASB, HCSB, KJV; cf. the Schlachter German translation (*Dinge*).

36. See also the Luther Bible (*Lehre*); *Edition de Genève* 1979 (*enseignements*); CEB; cf. Graham N. Stanton, *Jesus of Nazareth in New Testament Preaching*, SNTSMS 27 (Cambridge: Cambridge University Press, 1974), 29; Joseph A. Fitzmyer, *The Gospel according to Luke*,

The doctrines, in other words, are closely related to the *deeds* fulfilled by Jesus, which were handed down to those who were taught in Luke's day. Moreover, these deeds are the deeds of salvation history,[37] which must imply that these are also *saving* deeds.[38] What are these deeds more specifically? To answer this we must read Luke's Gospel carefully. Certainly we must note the key role of the travel narrative in which Jesus is on his way to Jerusalem (Luke 9:51–19:28), which leads to the culmination of Jesus's work in his death and resurrection (22:1–24:53). However, Luke recounts much more than just the death and resurrection of Jesus. Even if we begin our discussion of Jesus's work in Jerusalem with the beginning of the travel narrative (9:51), we must still account sufficiently for the richness of the first nine chapters of Luke.

Fulfillment Inclusio *in Luke*

In Jesus's own explanation of his task toward the end of Luke (24:44–49), he points out not only the necessity of his death and resurrection but also that all the things written about him in the Law, the Prophets, and the Psalms had to be fulfilled (24:44). These events prominently include the suffering of Christ and his rising from the dead, but also the message that would go forth in his name (24:46–47). Earlier on the road to Emmaus, Jesus explained that the Christ must suffer and then enter into glory, and beginning with Moses and from all the prophets, Jesus explained what the Scriptures said about his task (24:26–27). It has sometimes been lamented that Luke does not provide us with the details of which Scriptures Jesus fulfilled and how he fulfilled them, but we can ascertain numerous ways Jesus fulfills Scripture by considering the whole of Luke's Gospel, and especially by reflecting upon the apostolic explanations of Jesus's fulfillment of Scripture in Acts.

If we look back to the beginning of Luke's Gospel in light of the end of Luke, we can identify an *inclusio* emphasizing fulfillment. Thus, the deeds of salvation history that have been fulfilled in Luke 1:1–4 are set in parallel to Jesus's fulfillment of the Law, Prophets, and Psalms (24:44; cf. 24:27).[39] This

---

2 vols., AB 28–28A (Garden City, NY: Doubleday, 1981–85), 1:301; David E. Garland, *Luke*, ZECNT (Grand Rapids: Zondervan, 2011), 56–57; Darrell L. Bock, *Luke*, 2 vols., BECNT (Grand Rapids: Baker Academic, 1994–96), 1:65–66.

37. Fitzmyer, *Gospel according to Luke*, 1:292; Bock, *Luke*, 1:57; Garland, *Luke*, 52–53; cf. Acts 26:22–26.

38. Bock, *Luke*, 1:57; Garland, *Luke*, 52–53; Ned B. Stonehouse, *Origins of the Synoptic Gospels: Some Basic Questions* (London: Tyndale Press, 1964), 132–33.

39. Although Luke 1:2 utilizes the term *plērophoreō* and Luke 24:44 utilizes *plēroō*, the terminology and concepts are sufficiently similar to posit a recognizable *inclusio*. Additionally, an *inclusio* focusing on fulfillment need not negate a temple *inclusio* as well (Luke 1:9 [and elsewhere in chaps. 1–2]; 24:53).

inclusio invites us to consider how *all* that Jesus does in the Gospel of Luke is a fulfillment of salvation history. Indeed, we have seen that Luke quite clearly identifies Jesus as Son of God in ways that recapitulate both Adam's sonship and Israel's sonship, and a distinguishing mark of Jesus's sonship is his obedience as the last Adam, which overcomes and reverses the sinfulness of previous generations (Luke 3–4). Therefore, we can conclude that Jesus's lifelong obedience is a large part of how Luke portrays the fulfillment of salvation history.

Fulfillment in Luke's Infancy Narrative

Jesus's obedience in Luke is evident even before the beginning of his public ministry. As is true for all the Gospels, the first words that Jesus speaks in Luke set the tone for what follows. It is therefore significant that Jesus first speaks in Luke as a twelve-year-old in the temple (Luke 2:49), and Jesus's statement seems already to reveal an awareness of, and determination to be faithful to, his messianic task. This is apparent because the young Jesus states that it is necessary (*dei*) for him to be occupied with the affairs of his Father,[40] and elsewhere in Luke *dei* most often denotes the divine necessity of salvation that comes through the *actions* of Jesus. We will return to Luke's *dei* statements below.

Thus, from the beginning of Luke's Gospel, salvation is identified with the person and work of Jesus. By way of example, Simeon prophesied that to see the child Jesus was to see salvation (2:30), and Jesus was destined for the rising and falling of many in Israel (2:34). Simeon does not spell out all the details of how this would happen, but we see with Simeon an awareness that Jesus is a representative figure whose actions will affect others—whether for blessing or curse.

We may also see indications of Jesus's representative obedience in the way Luke narrates Jesus's presentation in the temple, which comes a few weeks after his circumcision, as being in full accord with the Torah (2:22–24, 39). Several texts and ceremonies appear to be in view in 2:21–24. First, before Jesus's presentation in the temple, we read in Luke 2:21 that Jesus was circumcised on the eighth day, in accord with the Abrahamic covenant (Gen. 17:9–14) and

---

40. As is well known, Luke's phrase *en tois tou patros mou dei einai me* is somewhat ambiguous, perhaps intentionally so. But "among the business of my Father" seems to capture the active sense of the context and is consistent with Luke's use of *dei* elsewhere. See further James R. Edwards, *The Gospel according to Luke*, PNTC (Grand Rapids: Eerdmans, 2015), 95; Norval Geldenhuys, *Commentary on the Gospel of Luke*, NICNT (Grand Rapids: Eerdmans, 1951), 128; Garland, *Luke*, 145.

Leviticus 12:3. The sign of circumcision marked Jesus as a member of God's covenant community in continuity with the promises given to Abraham. The cutting away of the foreskin was infused with religious significance and was likely indicative of the uncleanness of the subject due to the sinful human condition that needed rectification.[41] Thus circumcision pointed beyond the physical act to something more inward and spiritual (cf. Deut. 10:6; 30:6; Jer. 4:4; 9:25–26). As in his baptism, Jesus's participation in the rite of circumcision was not due to his own need for cleansing as the holy Son of God (Luke 1:35) but was an identification with the covenant people and their need for eschatological cleansing.[42]

A spiritual understanding of circumcision is already evident in the Old Testament, which emphasizes in various ways the need for the Israelites to circumcise the foreskins of their hearts (Deut. 10:16; Jer. 4:4). The problem with God's covenant people was so often not their lack of keeping the covenant rites, such as circumcision, but their failure to be fully committed to God in their hearts. This was a problem already in the first generation of Israelites in the wilderness (Deut. 8:2; cf. 6:5), and it continued to be a problem for future generations (Jer. 4:4; 9:25–26; Ezek. 44:7; cf. Lev. 26:41, 43). In Matthew's Gospel, as we will discuss in due course, Jesus seizes upon the problematic dichotomy between sacrifice and obedience in his critique of the Pharisees (Matt. 9:13; 12:7; cf. Isa. 29:13; Hosea 6:6). The promise of Moses and the prophets, however, was that a new circumcision of the heart would be executed by God himself (Deut. 30:6; cf. *Jub.* 1:23), and it is in light of this hope that Jesus's life, even from his circumcision, is to be understood.

If these observations are correct, then Jesus's circumcision, no less than his baptism, indicates his identification with his covenant people in their estate of sin.[43] Moreover, Jesus's circumcision also points to his vicarious work, since circumcision signified the need for full, heartfelt commitment to God. By identifying with his people in both circumcision and baptism, Jesus

---

41. Vos, *Biblical Theology*, 89–90; G. K. Beale, *A New Testament Biblical Theology: The Unfolding of the Old Testament in the New* (Grand Rapids: Baker Academic, 2011), 806; Herman Bavinck, *Reformed Dogmatics*, ed. John Bolt, trans. John Vriend, 4 vols. (Grand Rapids: Baker Academic, 2003–8), 3:408; cf. John Calvin, *Commentary on a Harmony of the Evangelists, Matthew, Mark, and Luke*, trans. and ed. William Pringle, 3 vols. (repr., Grand Rapids: Baker, 2003), 1:126; 1QS V, 5, noted in Peter T. O'Brien, *Colossians and Philemon*, WBC 44 (Waco: Word, 1982), 115.

42. The circumcision of Christ in Col. 2:11 likely refers to Jesus's crucifixion, which was anticipated in his circumcision. See Bavinck, *Reformed Dogmatics*, 4:526–27; O'Brien, *Colossians and Philemon*, 117.

43. This is consistent with Col. 2:11–12, where baptism is identified as the corollary of circumcision. See further Beale, *New Testament Biblical Theology*, 803–16; Robert Letham, *The Work of Christ*, CCT (Downers Grove, IL: IVP Academic, 1993), 113.

participates in the initiatory rites of both the old and new covenants, which signified the need for cleansing and true devotion to God. Jesus embodies the reality to which circumcision pointed: he not only received the sign but demonstrated true circumcision of heart throughout his life. In Jesus there is no disjunction between internal and external circumcision.

Second, another ceremony that is fulfilled in Luke 2:21–24 (specifically 2:22–23) is Jesus's consecration as the firstborn son in accord with Exodus 13. In Luke 2:23 we read that the firstborn son is holy (*hagion*) to the Lord, echoing the way the Israelites were commanded to set apart the firstborn in Exodus 13:2 (*hagiason . . . pan prōtotokon*; cf. Exod. 13:12, 15; 22:29). Throughout Luke holiness characterizes Jesus. From the announcement of his birth as Son of God (1:35), to his presentation in the temple (2:22–23), to his conflicts with the demonic (4:34; cf. Acts 2:27), to his identity as the Messiah, to his constant filling with and guidance by the Holy Spirit (3:16, 22; 4:1; 10:21), and even to his death (Luke 23:47 with Acts 3:14), Jesus is holy in every way. It is thus fitting for Luke to lean upon the language of holiness to describe Jesus's conformity to the law as a weeks-old child.[44]

Additionally, the holiness of Jesus in Luke 2:23 recalls the design for the holiness of God's firstborn son in the Old Testament (Exod. 13:2). It is not difficult to connect this call for the Hebrews to consecrate their firstborn sons with the need for Israel to be consecrated as God's firstborn son. We see this already in Exodus 4:22–23 where the sonship of Israel is proclaimed, and indeed the climactic plague of death for the firstborn sons in Egypt is based on the premise that Israel is God's firstborn son (Exod. 4:22–23; 11–12). Additionally, the call for Israel to be holy is emphasized further in Deuteronomy, as we saw in the previous chapter. One of the clearest texts in this regard is

44. In light of Luke's emphasis on Jesus's holiness, the possibility arises whether Luke has intentionally not recounted the *redemption* of Jesus as the firstborn (Exod. 13:15, along with Num. 18:15–16) because Jesus did not need to be redeemed. As François Bovon has argued, "As 'something holy,' Jesus belongs to God. He has no need to be redeemed. Thus he can fulfill the λύτρωσις ('redemption') of Israel" (Bovon, *Luke*, trans. Christine M. Thomas, Donald S. Deer, and James Crouch, 3 vols., Hermeneia [Minneapolis: Fortress, 2002–13], 1:107; cf. Garland, *Luke*, 135; see alternatively Joel B. Green, *The Gospel of Luke*, NICNT [Grand Rapids: Eerdmans, 1997], 141–42). If such an omission is intended by Luke to convey Jesus as, for example, the Redeemer (cf. Luke 1:68; 2:38; 21:28), it would be difficult to establish since it is an argument from silence. Moreover, Jesus does undergo a baptism of repentance, something for which he personally had no need. Therefore, it seems that Jesus could have participated in the rite of redemption on behalf of others as a representative without implying he needed the redemption himself. Nevertheless, elsewhere Luke does present Jesus as one who was not in need of redemption, given his virginal conception (1:34–35), possession of the Holy Spirit (3:16, 22; 4:1; 10:21; Acts 2:27), and unique holiness of character (Luke 1:35; 4:34; Acts 2:27; 3:14). Therefore Jesus was supremely and uniquely suited for the task of redemption.

Deuteronomy 14:1–2, which, like Exodus 13:2, utilizes the root *qdš* in parallel with sonship: as sons of the Lord, the Israelites were to be holy in all their actions. The consecration of the firstborn, then, is a related category to the recapitulation of the sonship of Israel in Christ, which Luke will make clearer as the Gospel progresses.

Third, we should also consider the relation of Jesus to the purification rite in Luke 2:24. Here Mary and Joseph offer the sacrifice of two turtledoves, which fulfills the offering commanded in Leviticus 12 for purification after childbirth.[45] However, some other texts may also be in the background. One possibility is 1 Samuel 1–2, which is undeniably an influence throughout Luke's infancy narrative.[46] But another text to consider is Leviticus 5:11 (LXX), which mentions the sin offering of two turtledoves. If the sin offering of Leviticus 5 is part of the background to Luke 2:24, it would help explain why the plural pronoun *autōn* is used in Luke 2:22: "*their* purification" most likely refers to that of Mary and *Joseph*; an offering for *Jesus's* purification does not seem to be in view.[47]

The fulfillment of Scripture, the ceremonies, and especially the sacrifice(s) of Luke 2:21–24 provide insight into the vicarious nature of Jesus's life and obedience. As we have noted, Luke explicitly identifies these events as being in accord with the Torah (the law is mentioned four times in 2:22–24, 39). Certainly we should emphasize the obedience of Jesus's parents in these verses, but if the Gospels are indeed Christology in narrative form,[48] then our attention must not stray too far from Jesus himself in these law-conforming events. In this light, we can see Jesus's humiliation in the way that he was born under the law (cf. Gal. 4:4), was subject to its regulations, and met those regulations completely. The conformity of Jesus's life to the law of Moses as a small child in Luke is similar to what we see in Matthew, where the infant Jesus is in full accord with God's scriptural design for salvation. Likewise, the incarnation in Luke entails Jesus's conformity to biblical precepts for the consecration of the firstborn son. Jesus's conformity to the law in Luke 2 further indicates that all of Jesus's life—even his infancy—must be understood in light of the fulfillment of Scripture. As David Pao and Eckhard Schnabel state, "In fulfilling

45. On the relationship of sin and impurity, see Jay Sklar, "Sin and Impurity: Atoned or Purified? Yes!," in *Perspectives on Purity and Purification in the Bible*, ed. Baruch J. Schwartz et al., LHBOTS 474 (New York: T&T Clark, 2008), 18–31.

46. David W. Pao and Eckhard J. Schnabel, "Luke," in *Commentary on the New Testament Use of the Old Testament*, ed. G. K. Beale and D. A. Carson (Grand Rapids: Baker Academic, 2007), 271.

47. Ibid., 270; Bock, *Luke*, 1:236–37.

48. Richard A. Burridge, *What Are the Gospels? A Comparison with Graeco-Roman Biography*, 2nd ed., BRS (Grand Rapids: Eerdmans, 2004), 289.

the requirements of the law, Jesus fulfills the past by bringing it to its climax."[49] Jesus is not only the firstborn of Mary but "the 'holy one' whose life fulfills those of all the firstborn of Israel in his dedication to the service and plan of God."[50] As the Holy One, Jesus will provide the final, righteous sacrifice for his people (cf. Luke 23:47), which is indissolubly tied to his lifelong obedience.

If Jesus is portrayed as obedient throughout his life in accord with Scripture, what is the relationship between Jesus's lifelong obedience and Jesus's words in Luke 24:26, 46 that the Christ must suffer? This suffering is most often identified with the death of Christ, and rightly so. However, I would like to suggest that we should broaden our understanding of Jesus's suffering, so that Jesus's whole life, from one perspective, is part of the requisite suffering of the Christ mentioned in 24:26, 46.[51] By his fulfillment of Scripture and recapitulation of Israel's sonship, Jesus denied his own privileges as Son of God, thereby overcoming the disobedience of Adam and Israel as Son of God. If this is the case, then in Luke 24:26–27, 44–47 Jesus is speaking not only about the necessity of suffering in the final events of his life but about the necessity of suffering in his *entire* obedience, throughout his life. The path of messianic obedience was for Christ the path of perpetual self-denial and suffering.

Several features of Luke's narrative suggest the virtual equation of lifelong obedience and lifelong suffering. First, in the temptation Jesus is tempted to put God to the test, to force his Father's hand to provide for him an alternate path to that of suffering messiahship. However, in the temptation Jesus proves obedient, and his obedience entails suffering in both his immediate circumstances and the days of his coming ministry. Thus, Jesus's obedience is manifested in denying himself the nourishment of bread, in not receiving immediately the kingdoms of the world apart from the cross, and in refusing to tempt his Father to intervene in a spectacular way to save him.[52]

Second, beyond the temptation narrative, Jesus is tempted throughout his ministry in Luke.[53] If temptation can be rightly understood as a form of suffering, then the ongoing temptations of Jesus are further indications that Jesus's entire ministry can be viewed as a ministry of suffering.

This brings us to a third indication that the obedience of Jesus is tantamount to his suffering—the call for Jesus's disciples to take up their cross and follow him (Luke 9:23; cf. Matt. 16:24 // Mark 8:34). In Luke's presentation of

49. Pao and Schnabel, "Luke," 271.
50. Ibid.
51. Cf. Heidelberg Catechism 37.
52. Cf. Geldenhuys, *Gospel of Luke*, 162.
53. See the discussion of Jesus's lifelong temptation in Luke in chap. 2 of this volume.

this saying, the call to take up one's cross is a *daily* task. If this cross-bearing is to be done in imitation of Christ's own suffering unto the cross, which is exceedingly likely, then it implies that Jesus's own cross-bearing was not only a onetime event but a daily, metaphorical cross-bearing (= suffering) as well. Indeed, such a correlation between cross-bearing and the imitation of Christ is quite clearly in view in Mark's Gospel, where Jesus predicts his impending death and resurrection three times after Peter's confession at Caesarea Philippi (8:31–33; 9:30–32; 10:32–34). These three predictions are followed by three calls to discipleship (8:34–38; 9:33–37; 10:35–45), one of which is the need to take up one's cross and follow Jesus.[54]

In light of Mark's Gospel, it is also instructive to consider similarities with 1 Peter.[55] As in Mark, in 1 Peter we find not only an emphasis on the unique death of Jesus (1 Pet. 3:18) but also the call for Christians to follow daily in the footsteps of Christ's suffering (1 Pet. 2:4–5, 21–24; 4:1–2, 12–17; cf. 1:19). Just as Jesus was rejected by many but remained obedient to his Father in all things, so must Christians follow the pattern of Christ that leads from suffering to glory (cf. 1 Pet. 1:10–11; 5:1).[56] In sum, the call to take up one's cross and follow Christ serves as a metonymy for one's whole life commitment, just as the cross serves as a metonymy for the suffering that characterized all of Jesus's life. Thus, we have other examples in the New Testament of identifying the obedience of Jesus as an obedience of self-denial, which provides further corroboration that Jesus's lifelong obedience in Luke is tantamount to Jesus's lifelong suffering.

Fourth, we can speak of the suffering of Jesus beyond only the final events on the cross in Luke because Jesus himself speaks of his own suffering in the midst of his ministry. In Luke 12:49–50 Jesus speaks of a fire he has come to cast, in association with a baptism he must undergo. As he reflects on this baptism of fire, which is yet to be kindled in the full sense, Jesus nevertheless laments that his distress is already great until it is finished. The implication is that Jesus's ongoing obedience to his messianic task—and in Luke 12 Jesus is on the road to Jerusalem (cf. 9:51)—is identified as a path of suffering, even before the climactic suffering of his death. Moreover, the

---

54. Joel Marcus, *Mark 1–8: A New Translation with Introduction and Commentary*, AB 27 (New York: Doubleday, 2000), 532; Mark L. Strauss, *Four Portraits, One Jesus: A Survey of Jesus and the Gospels* (Grand Rapids: Zondervan, 2007), 184–85.

55. Of course, early Christian tradition associates the apostle Peter with both 1 Peter and the Gospel of Mark (cf. 1 Pet. 1:1; 5:13; Papias in Eusebius, *Hist. eccl.* 3.39.15). Therefore, similarities between the two writings are not surprising.

56. See further Brandon D. Crowe, *The Message of the General Epistles in the History of Redemption: Wisdom from James, Peter, John, and Jude* (Phillipsburg, NJ: P&R, 2015), 3–52. Note also 1 Pet. 1:10–11 in light of Luke 24:44–47.

language of baptism in 12:49–50 is redolent of Jesus's water baptism at the beginning of his public ministry, in which he entered into the sinful situation of his people, bearing the "eschatological-forensic reality of God's wrath"[57] in order to redeem them. Though Jesus's wrath-bearing is most climactically seen at the cross, Jesus was also bearing the wrath of God throughout the entire course of his messianic obedience. Thus, as Richard Gaffin has argued, Luke 12:49–50 "warrants viewing the entirety of Jesus' ministry, from the Jordan to the cross, as a kind of baptism, one large submission to the baptism-ordeal of God's judicial wrath."[58] In sum, the suffering of the Christ spoken of in the Scriptures in Luke 24:26, 46 is not only his death on the cross, but it extends at least to his entire messianic obedience (and likely entails his *lifelong* obedience).

Fifth, to appreciate another reason Jesus's entire life can be viewed as one of suffering, we must not neglect to consider the earthly ministry of Jesus in light of the significance of the incarnation of the Son of God. This, of course, assumes Jesus's divinity and preexistence in Luke, which is not universally accepted. Nevertheless, we have good reason for positing a preexistence Christology in Luke. The supernatural conception of Jesus, and the angelic announcement to Mary that her child was from the Holy Spirit and would be called holy, the Son of God (1:35), is already an indication of the supernatural character of Jesus. Additionally, in the Benedictus, Zechariah prophesies of the coming salvation from the sunrise from on high (*anatolē ex hypsous* [1:78]), which is likely a reference to Jesus's heavenly origin.[59] Luke's usage of "Lord" (*kyrios*) is also instructive, as he binds together the identities of the Father and Son in a way that reveals the divine character of both as Lord (e.g., 1:6, 9, 25, 28 with 1:43; 2:10).[60] Beyond this, the divinity of Jesus is manifested in various ways in Luke, including Jesus's awareness of his unique sonship as a child (2:49), the heavenly voice affirming the sonship of Jesus at the baptism

---

57. Richard B. Gaffin Jr., "Justification in Luke-Acts," in *Right with God: Justification in the Bible and the World*, ed. D. A. Carson (Grand Rapids: Baker, 1992), 111.

58. Ibid.

59. See also Simon J. Gathercole, *The Preexistent Son: Recovering the Christologies of Matthew, Mark, and Luke* (Grand Rapids: Eerdmans, 2006), 248–52; Richard B. Hays, *Reading Backwards: Figural Christology and the Fourfold Gospel Witness* (Waco: Baylor University Press, 2014), 67–68; Alan J. Thompson, "The Trinity in Luke-Acts," in *The Essential Trinity: New Testament Foundations and Practical Relevance*, ed. Brandon D. Crowe and Carl R. Trueman (London: Apollos, 2016). For a different view, see James D. G. Dunn, *Christology in the Making: A New Testament Inquiry into the Origins of the Doctrine of the Incarnation*, 2nd ed. (Grand Rapids: Eerdmans, 1989).

60. C. Kavin Rowe, *Early Narrative Christology: The Lord in the Gospel of Luke*, BZNW 139 (2006; repr., Grand Rapids: Baker Academic, 2009). Rowe refers to this phenomenon with the coined term *Verbindungsidentität* (ibid., 27 and 27n94).

and transfiguration (3:22; 9:35), and Jesus's jubilant prayer to the Father that indicates the Son's divine prerogatives (10:21–23).

If Jesus is portrayed as the divinely preexistent Son of God in Luke, then it further underscores that his suffering was not limited to the cross. Instead, Jesus's whole life was one of suffering because his incarnation entailed self-denial and a humiliation from a preexistent, heavenly estate that involved being made subject to the law and subject to death. Not only did the Son of God leave the glories of heaven to be born to the less-than-wealthy (Luke 2:22–24), but he was in some ways even lower than the animals (9:58). Paul's statement that we should consider the one who, though he was rich, became poor that we might be rich in him (2 Cor. 8:9), captures well the self-denial of the Son of God in Luke. The greatness of the Son's preexistence underscores the wonders of the humiliation in the incarnation, which as a whole can be described as the suffering of the Christ.[61]

In sum, the point of this rather lengthy discussion on the lifelong suffering of Christ has been to show that the necessity of Jesus's suffering in accord with Scripture (Luke 24:26, 46) applies not only to the cross but to his entire obedience.[62] As such, the suffering of Christ is an additional way that we see the need for Jesus's lifelong obedience as part of the salvation he accomplished. And Jesus's obedient suffering as *the Christ* is also the suffering of the *representative* of God's people. Of course, the suffering in Luke 24:26, 46 is most naturally taken to refer to the death of Jesus on the cross. Nevertheless, in light of the emphasis on fulfillment in Luke 24, and the various ways Jesus fulfills Scripture and God's will throughout the Gospel of Luke (and Acts, see below), it is reasonable to conclude that the suffering of Christ in Luke 24:26, 46 is metonymic for Jesus's lifelong obedience and fulfillment of Scripture throughout his life. If so, then we have further indication that the obedience of Jesus is entailed in the summary of Jesus's mission at the end of Luke.

Fulfillment in Acts

I have said much about fulfillment in Luke 1–24, but we can also see how Jesus fulfills Scripture by looking beyond Luke to the book of Acts. What we find in Acts is consistent with our survey of Luke's view of fulfillment

---

61. Cf. Calvin, *Inst.* 2.16.5.

62. Scot McKnight ("Matthew as 'Gospel,'" in *Jesus, Matthew's Gospel and Early Christianity: Studies in Memory of Graham N. Stanton*, ed. Daniel M. Gurtner, Joel Willitts, and Richard A. Burridge, LNTS 435 [London: T&T Clark, 2011], 64) asks a similar question of Pauline summaries: could Paul's summary that Christ *died* (1 Cor. 15:3) imply "a life of enough consternation to lead to a crucifixion"? In other words, could Paul's summaries of Christ dying for our sins be shorthand to refer to all that led up to his crucifixion as well?

throughout Jesus's life, in close connection to Jesus's holiness and death. One way we see an emphasis on the life of Jesus in Acts is through the lens of Peter's sermons. When explaining the significance of the work of Jesus for salvation, Peter emphasizes much more than only Jesus's death. He emphasizes the whole of Jesus's work, including his life (Acts 2:22; 3:14; 10:36–39; cf. 2:27; 13:35), death (2:23, 36; 3:14; 10:39), resurrection (2:29–32; 3:15; 10:40), ascension (2:33, 36), and return (3:20; 10:42).[63] In Acts 10:37–39 part of the explanation of the salvation wrought by Christ includes his powerful filling with the Holy Spirit, doing good, and healing those oppressed by the devil. Thus Scot McKnight argues that the apostolic gospel, such as we find in Acts, was framed in such a way that the story centered on and revolved around Jesus, and this is placed in the context of how Jesus fulfilled the messianic hopes of Israel.[64] Therefore, even in the identification of Jesus as *Christ* (Acts 2:36), we have *in nuce* a reference to the work of Jesus as Messiah of Israel and all that it entails.[65]

Significantly, the apostolic preaching in Acts that focuses on the life of Jesus quite often also focuses on expositions of the Old Testament Scriptures (e.g., Deut. 18; Pss. 2; 16 [15 LXX]; 110 [109 LXX]; Joel 2 [3 LXX]). In light of Luke 24:26–27, 44–47, which summarize the mission of the Christ *in accord with Scripture*, and in light of the Gospel's emphasis on *fulfillment*, the christological expositions of the Old Testament in Acts should inform our understanding of Christ's sufferings in Luke. As noted above, these sermons focus on Jesus's life and work more broadly (beyond his death), which provides corroboration for understanding the sufferings of Christ in Luke 24:26, 46 to include more than only the events associated with the passion. In sum, Luke's writings indicate that the entire work of Jesus incarnate is necessary for salvation.

The Life of Jesus and Divine Necessity (*Dei*)

"It Is Necessary" in Luke

Closely related to the language of fulfillment in the Gospels are the "it is necessary" (*dei*) statements, which are particularly prominent in Luke. Luke 24:25–27, 44–47 indicate not only that the suffering, resurrection, and message

63. See Scot McKnight, *The King Jesus Gospel: The Original Good News Revisited* (Grand Rapids: Zondervan, 2011), 118–20, 182n66; cf. C. H. Dodd, *The Apostolic Preaching and Its Developments* (New York: Harper & Row, 1936), 21–25.

64. See, e.g., McKnight, *King Jesus Gospel*, 118.

65. Ibid., 122.

of the Christ were fulfillments of Scripture, but that these events were *neces-sary*. This *dei* language in Luke is best taken as the divine necessity of events that must take place to bring about eschatological salvation.[66] In accord with the holistic sense of fulfillment in Luke discussed earlier, the relevance of these *dei* statements for the present study is how they indicate that various aspects of the life of Jesus were necessary for salvation. The first *dei* statement in Luke is found in 2:49, which we discussed briefly above. In this verse Jesus states that he must be occupied with the things of his Father (*en tois tou patros mou*). Whether this suggestive phrase refers to the *house* of Jesus's Father or to some-thing more along the lines of *business* (as I suggested), it is the *actions* of Jesus that are emphasized in accord with the divine will. Thus, the first words of Jesus in Luke already indicate the salvation-historical need to serve his Father.

Beyond these first words of Jesus, several other statements speak of various aspects of the mission Jesus had to accomplish. To be sure, many of these statements refer in some degree to the death of Jesus (9:22; 13:33; 17:25; 22:37; 24:7, 26, 44–46; cf. 22:7) and others to his resurrection (24:7, 46), but some refer to aspects of his life and ministry (2:49; 4:43; 13:16, 33), and some to the message of Jesus that will go forth (12:12; 24:47). Thus, Jesus had to preach the gospel to other towns (4:43), heal on the Sabbath (13:16), and finish his mis-sion (13:32). In addition, Jesus had to go to Zacchaeus's house (19:5) because the Son of Man came to seek and save the lost (19:10). Moreover, as I have argued, the suffering of Jesus, which is necessary in Luke, includes more than only Jesus's death. Though some of Luke's *dei* statements apply to the life of Jesus more than others, taken together they emphasize the entire obedience of Jesus that is necessary for the accomplishment of eschatological salvation.

Two *dei* passages from Luke 13 (13:10–17, 31–35) deserve further consider-ation. In the first of these passages, Jesus declares that it was necessary for him to deliver a daughter of Abraham on the Sabbath who had been in bondage to Satan for eighteen years (13:16). We will consider in more detail the miracles and exorcisms of Jesus in chapter 6, but at this point it is significant to observe that the necessity of Jesus's saving deeds in the incarnation are particularly appropriate on the Sabbath, a day that recalls God's original created order. Additionally, the imagery in Luke 13:10–17 of being bent over may evoke the effects of sin from the opening chapters of Genesis, especially in light of the woman's bondage to Satan. Instead of humans ruling over the animals as was originally intended for Adam and Eve, the reign of Satan held this woman

---

66. Fitzmyer, *Gospel according to Luke*, 1:179–81; Herman N. Ridderbos, *The Coming of the Kingdom*, trans. H. de Jongste, ed. Raymond O. Zorn (Philadelphia: P&R, 1962), 158–59; M. Dennis Hamm, SJ, "The Freeing of the Bent Woman and the Restoration of Israel: Luke 13.10–17 as Narrative Theology," *JSNT* 31 (1987): 33.

captive with the result that she was stooped over low, like an animal.[67] If this is so, we may have an indication that Jesus's actions are necessary to overcome the curse of sin—including the bondage of the bent-over woman (13:11)—that was introduced by Adam. Though the woman was cursed, Jesus's actions on the Sabbath release her from bondage and impart what is tantamount to new creation. Put differently, Jesus not only reverses the curse of Adam, but by his work he brings about the blessings promised to Abraham (cf. 13:16). The straightening of the bent woman further fits with Luke's broader emphasis on the lowly being exalted with the coming of salvation (1:46–55).[68]

Jesus's statements in 13:31–35 are also relevant, since Jesus speaks of the divine necessity of the totality of his mission in conjunction with his death.[69] Though in 13:31 the Pharisees claim that Herod is trying to kill Jesus, Jesus's response in 13:32–33 ("Behold, I cast out demons and complete healing today and tomorrow, and the third day I complete my goal.[70] But it is necessary for me to continue today and tomorrow and the following day . . .") indicates that his mission was not yet complete; more remained to be done. The phrase referring to three days (*sēmeron kai aurion kai tē echomenē*) need not refer to three literal days but is an intentionally vague way to indicate a quick succession of events that will culminate with the completion of Jesus's task.[71] Moreover, these are events that have begun and will continue without interruption until the task is finished.[72] Specifically, in 13:32 Jesus speaks of casting out demons and healing those in need. As I will argue further in chapter 6, part of Jesus's saving activity entails the various ways he bears the burden of sin. This includes healing the sick but also restraining the power of Satan by freeing those in bondage from diabolic strongholds. Therefore, it was necessary for Jesus to complete his incarnate work "today and tomorrow" before he finished his task in Jerusalem.[73]

Further emphasizing that the necessity of Christ's work throughout his ministry, and not only his death, is in view in 13:31–35 are the parallels to Luke

---

67. J. Duncan M. Derrett, "The Manger: Ritual Law and Soteriology," *Theology* 74 (1971): 566–71; cf. David M. May, "The Straightened Woman (Luke 13:10–17): Paradise Lost and Regained," *PRSt* 24 (1997): 245–58.

68. Heidi Torgerson, "The Healing of the Bent Woman: A Narrative Interpretation of Luke 13:10–17," *CurTM* 32 (2005): 176–86.

69. Thanks to Charles Williams for bringing this passage to my attention.

70. For this translation see BDAG, "τελειόω," 996.

71. BDAG, "σήμερον," 921; Bock, *Luke*, 2:1247.

72. See similarly Green, *Luke*, 536.

73. One other aspect of *dei* language in the Gospels that I have not addressed is the necessity of the "messianic woes" that precede the end of the age (see Matt. 24:6 // Mark 13:7 // Luke 21:9). See also, e.g., Dan. 2:28–29; *Sib. Or.* 3:571–72.

12:49–53. One can identify a possible chiastic structure in Luke 12:49–13:35 that is bracketed on the outer edges by Jesus's statements regarding the need to finish (*teleō*, *teleioō*) his mission of suffering.[74] In 12:49–53 Jesus reflects on the baptism of fire he was enduring during his ministry, noting his ongoing anguish as he anticipates the culmination (*telesthē* [12:50]) of his suffering on the cross. In 13:31–35 Jesus states that he must finish his course "today and tomorrow" and on the third day complete his mission (*teleioumai* [13:32]). Taken together, these two passages (12:49–53; 13:31–35) underscore the need for Jesus to accomplish his mission on behalf of others "today and tomorrow," before finishing obedience to his task in Jerusalem (13:33).[75] In Luke 12–13 Jesus had already been completing things that were necessary for salvation, and he commits to continue his mission until the end.

One final "it is necessary" text to consider has often been identified as programmatic for Luke. In Luke 19:10 Jesus declares that the Son of Man came to seek and save (*sōsai*) the lost. Luke's Gospel does not contain the ransom logion of Matthew 20:28 // Mark 10:45, but Jesus's words to Zacchaeus in Luke 19 serve a similar role, as Jesus explains the salvation he brings to those in need. Furthermore, the emphasis on the salvation that has come to Zacchaeus's house (19:9) is of a piece with Luke's broader emphasis on salvation in Christ (Luke 1:69, 77; 2:11, 30; 3:6; Acts 4:12; 5:31; 13:23, 26, 47; 16:17; 28:28). Therefore, the incarnate task of Jesus as Son of Man, including his seeking out Zacchaeus as a son of Abraham, is necessary (19:5) for the accomplishment of eschatological salvation. Jesus is on his way to Jerusalem in Luke 19, but his task of bringing salvation extends beyond just the events in Jerusalem.

Before concluding the discussion of Luke's *dei* statements, I would like to suggest one other possibility that could speak to the necessity of Jesus's obedience for eschatological salvation. A glance at the (infrequent) usage of *dei* in Leviticus (LXX) indicates that sins are things that ought not to be done (*ou dei poiein* [Lev. 4:2; 5:17]).[76] If we read Luke's use of *dei* in light of Leviticus, it could imply that Jesus's accomplishment of salvation entails the sinlessness of his task. Such a connection is possibly in view in Luke 11:42, where Jesus rebukes the Pharisees, not for tithing per se,[77] but for tithing to the neglect of justice and the love of God. Jesus's rebuke thus entails the necessity

74. For a discussion of the chiasm, including the relevant verbal parallels, see Hamm, "Freeing of the Bent Woman," 30–31. It is also noteworthy that the pivot of the chiasm would be the *dei* passage relating to the loosing of the stooped-over woman in Luke 13:10–17.

75. The contrast between the present actions and the coming death of Jesus is emphasized in Allan H. Gilbert, "Σήμερον καὶ αὔριον, καὶ τῇ τρίτῃ (Luke 13:32)," *JBL* 35 (1916): 315–18, though he posits too sharp of a contrast.

76. Cf. BDAG, "δεῖ," 214, #1.b.

77. Indeed, Jesus affirms the rightness of tithing (Luke 11:42).

of following the Torah in the more ceremonial aspects (cf. Lev. 27:30; Deut. 12:6; 14:22–23; 26:12–15),[78] but also the necessity of following the Torah by loving God, which Deuteronomy clarifies is tantamount to obedience.[79] The dichotomy the Pharisees manifested in outward rites on the one hand, and lack of love for God and practice of his righteousness on the other hand, is the dichotomy that Jesus overcomes in his delight to do his Father's will, even to the point of death.

"It Is Necessary" in Matthew and Mark

Luke is not the only Evangelist to speak of the necessity of Jesus's incarnate works for the accomplishment of salvation. Though Matthew and Mark use *dei* much less frequently, they also connect the divine necessity to the fulfill-ment of Scripture, such as we see in Matthew 26:54, which specifically refers to events surrounding the passion. The betrayal, arrest, and crucifixion of Jesus were *necessary* for salvation. At Caesarea Philippi, Jesus likewise as-sociates the divine *necessity* with the task of suffering in Jerusalem (Matt. 16:21 // Mark 8:31), and later he is asked why it was *necessary* for Elijah to come first, to restore all things (Matt. 17:10 // Mark 9:11). Additionally, in Matthew 23:23 Jesus rebukes the Pharisees for things they *ought* to have done, which may reflect the need for the true fulfillment of God's law suggested above in Luke 11:42.

All told, the *dei* statements in the Gospels, especially in Luke, emphasize the incarnate works of Jesus as necessary for the realization of eschatological salvation. These necessary works prominently include the events that took place in Jerusalem at the end of Jesus's life, but we also see that Jesus's entire obedience, throughout his life, is necessary for salvation.

The Purposes of Jesus's Coming

Jesus's Ministry of Preaching and Teaching

Closely related to the *dei* statements are the passages in the Synoptic Gos-pels that speak of the reasons for Jesus's coming. These statements, especially

78. See John Nolland, *Luke*, 3 vols., WBC 35A–C (Dallas: Word, 1989–93), 2:666.

79. It is noteworthy that in Deut. 26 the practice of tithing is associated with *justice* (Jesus critiques the Pharisees for rending these asunder), in a book that emphasizes the need for Israel to *love* the Lord (Deut. 6:5; 7:9; 10:12; 10:18–19; 11:1, 13, 22; 13:3; 19:9; 30:16, 19–20; cf. 30:6). On love and obedience in Deuteronomy, see Crowe, *Obedient Son*, 113–15 and bibliography there; cf. Adolf Schlatter, *Das Evangelium des Lukas: Aus seinen Quellen erklärt*, 2nd ed. (Stuttgart: Calwer, 1960), 519.

when viewed in tandem with the *dei* passages, also speak of the mission of Jesus holistically, which means they are *necessary* for salvation.[80] Much could be said about the statements in which Jesus speaks of the purposes of his coming, but the present study asks how the coming of Jesus relates to his overall mission and the accomplishment of salvation.

Early in Mark's Gospel (1:35–39), Jesus excuses himself from a crowd of those in need and spends a night in prayer, perhaps to ensure clarity for his messianic task. When his disciples finally find him, Jesus tells them he must move on to the next village and preach there, since it was for this reason that he came out (Mark 1:38).[81] The parallel account in Luke (4:42–43) discussed above connects the purpose of Jesus's being sent to the necessity (*dei*) of his preaching. If the work of Jesus incarnate is necessary for salvation, then texts such as these show us that his work includes his preaching. Luke's Gospel grants further clarity to this perspective in Jesus's first sermon in Nazareth (4:16–30). Jesus identifies his mission as fulfilling Isaiah 61, which prominently includes the mission of proclamation: *preaching* good news to the poor, *preaching* freedom and the recovery of sight, and *preaching* the year of the Lord's favor (Luke 4:18–19; cf. 24:44–47).

Jesus's word ministry is therefore part of the divine necessity of salvation, and Jesus's preaching corresponds to his actions in Luke. Jesus preaches release (*aphesis*) for the captives (Luke 4:18), which Luke associates with the forgiveness of sins (e.g., Luke 1:77; 24:47; Acts 2:38; 5:31; 10:43; 13:38; 26:18; cf. Luke 3:3). Jesus preaches the recovery of sight to the blind, which is physically fulfilled (Luke 7:21–22; 18:42–43) as well as spiritually fulfilled in Jesus's revelation to his disciples (Luke 8:10; 10:21–24). The preaching of good news must therefore in some way be related to Jesus himself (Luke 2:10; Acts 8:35; 10:36), just as it is related to the kingdom (Luke 8:1; 16:16; Acts 8:12; cf. Mark 1:15).

We will consider in more detail how the good news relates to the kingdom and to Jesus in chapter 6. At this juncture it is important to consider Jesus's parables, which are also integrally tied to the coming of the kingdom. A comparison with the modes of prophetic speech in the Old Testament, especially the use of *məšālîm*, indicates that Jesus's parables are a prophetic mode of speech (cf. Ps. 78:2; Ezek. 17:1–2; 24:3).[82] Indeed, in all three Synoptics, Jesus associates his use of parables with the double-sided message of Isaiah

---

80. On the "I have come" statements and Jesus's entire mission, see Gathercole, *Preexistent Son*, 85, 107.

81. This most likely refers to the cosmic purpose of Jesus's mission and not simply a "local" one. Cf. ibid., 156.

82. See the discussion in Klyne R. Snodgrass, *Stories with Intent: A Comprehensive Guide to the Parables of Jesus* (Grand Rapids: Eerdmans, 2008), 572–74.

(6:9–10)—many would see and not see, and hear and not hear—which further reinforces the nature of parables as prophetic speech. Parables both reveal and conceal,[83] and these contrasting possibilities show why Jesus's parables are part of his necessary mission. The wider context of Isaiah 6 reveals additional connections between Jesus's teaching ministry and the coming of the kingdom of God. In the parable of the sower, which is the immediate context for Jesus's explanation of his parables, the sower sows the seed of the word of God (Matt. 13:19; Mark 4:14; Luke 8:11), and in the parable there is an interplay between the word and those that respond positively to the word (Matt. 13:19–23 // Mark 4:15–20 // Luke 8:12–15).[84] Significantly, in Isaiah 6 the seed is the stump, which refers to the remnant of Israel.[85] Thus, it is by the sowing of the word through Jesus's prophetic ministry that the end-time remnant of Israel is planted.[86]

Matthew's Gospel further confirms the need for Jesus to speak in parables. In Matthew 13:34–35 a fulfillment quotation indicates that Jesus's teaching in parables fulfills Psalm 78. Since the fulfillment quotations likely show how Jesus fits into, and indeed brings, God's scripturally shaped, eschatological salvation, Jesus's fulfillment of Psalm 78 through his use of parables further indicates that Jesus's teaching was part of God's scriptural paradigm for salvation. One further aspect of Jesus's citation of Psalm 78 is worth considering: I have argued elsewhere that the fulfillment quotations in Matthew employ texts that contrast the disobedience of Israel with the wide-ranging obedience of Jesus.[87] Interestingly, Psalm 78 also fits this paradigm, as it details at length the waywardness of Israel. If Matthew's fulfillment quotation is to be taken in light of the larger context of Psalm 78, then it is quite possible that what is being revealed in Matthew 13 is the way in which Jesus's wide-ranging obedience is contrasted to and overcomes the perennial recalcitrance of Israel. Admittedly, this reading is far from conclusive, but if Jesus were contrasting his own obedience with the disobedience of Israel, it would be consistent with the argument that Jesus's scriptural obedience is necessary for salvation.

In sum, the Synoptics manifest a shared perspective that Jesus's teaching ministry was part of the reason Jesus had to come and was necessary for

---

83. Ridderbos, *Coming of the Kingdom*, 129.

84. See also William L. Lane, *The Gospel according to Mark*, NICNT (Grand Rapids: Eerdmans, 1974), 161–63.

85. Wright, *Jesus*, 232 and 232n128; Brevard S. Childs, *Isaiah: A Commentary*, OTL (Louisville: Westminster John Knox, 2001), 58–59. This imagery likely also should be understood in light of the stump of Jesse, the true seed (cf. Isa. 11:1), and the new exodus language of the powerful Word of God (Isa. 55:10–11).

86. Snodgrass, *Stories with Intent*, 169.

87. Crowe, "Fulfillment in Matthew," 118–19.

salvation. We see this perhaps most clearly in the centrality of the preaching of the good news in Luke-Acts and in the role and purpose of Jesus's parables. But we also must not miss the centrality of Jesus himself in his preaching. Jesus often preaches about his own role in bringing the kingdom, which becomes clearer the closer he gets to the passion in Jerusalem.[88] In light of the close relationship between the preaching of Jesus and his actions, it is best to conclude that one reason the preaching of Jesus is necessary is that it is a message about the things Jesus himself is doing (e.g., Matt. 11:2–6; Luke 7:18–23).[89] Put differently, the role of Jesus's preaching in the Gospels indicates that "the announcement of redemption cannot be separated from the history of redemption itself."[90]

Jesus's Mission to Fulfill the Law and Prophets

The unity of Jesus's life and teachings leads to another significant text in which Jesus identifies a reason for his coming. In Matthew 5:17 Jesus declares that he has not come to abolish the Law and the Prophets but to fulfill them. As I argued earlier, Jesus's statement most likely entails his mission as a whole—his teaching as well as his actions—which is a distinctly *christological* accomplishment in association with his unique righteousness. Similar to the Lukan *dei* statements, Jesus's mission in Matthew is portrayed as a salvation-historical necessity.[91]

Seek, Save, and Ransom

As we have seen, in Luke 19:10 the Son of Man came to seek and save the lost, which is described in Luke 19:5 as necessary (*dei*). Luke 19 thus provides additional corroboration that the *dei* statements are corollary to the statements that speak of the purposes for Jesus's coming.

The interaction between Jesus and Zacchaeus in Luke 19 is unique to Luke, but Matthew (20:28) and Mark (10:45) contain the so-called ransom logion that is in many ways similar to Luke 19:10. In the ransom logion Jesus declares that the Son of Man (Jesus) did not come to be served but to serve and to give his life as a ransom (*lytron*) for many. By all accounts these statements are highly significant in the contexts of Matthew and Mark, as Jesus

---

88. See, e.g., Matt. 19:16–30 // Mark 10:17–31 // Luke 18:18–30; Thomas R. Schreiner, *New Testament Theology: Magnifying God in Christ* (Grand Rapids: Baker Academic, 2008), 185.

89. Ridderbos, *Coming of the Kingdom*, 76.

90. Herman N. Ridderbos, *Redemptive History and the New Testament Scriptures*, trans. H. de Jongste, rev. Richard B. Gaffin Jr. (Phillipsburg, NJ: P&R, 1988), 15.

91. Deines, "Not the Law," 75–77.

explicitly identifies something central to his mission.[92] Thus Craig Evans can claim without hyperbole that Mark 10:45 is "by far the most remarkable . . . saying in Mark."[93] The ransom statement is therefore worthy of more detailed attention, which will be given in chapter 7. At this point I simply observe that Jesus had to come to give his life as a ransom for many, which is necessary for salvation.

Summary: Purposes of Jesus's Coming

The pluriformity of statements that speak of the purposes for Jesus's coming indicates that Jesus had much to do in order to accomplish salvation. Additionally, the various reasons given for Jesus's coming indicate that the mission and obedience of Jesus must be viewed holistically; it is not prudent to view some aspects of Jesus's obedience as being more necessary than others.

The Holy and Righteous One

Thus far in this chapter we have considered some of the ways that Jesus's life accords with Scripture and the divine necessity in conjunction with the accomplishment of eschatological salvation. As we conclude this chapter, it is fitting to include some reflections on the attribution of *holy* and *righteous* to Jesus, and how these relate to early christological confessions of Jesus's character and work. These attributions are best taken in conjunction with the passages that identify Jesus's life in full conformity to Scripture and as the bringer of eschatological salvation.

The Holy One of God

The identification of Jesus as the Holy One of God (Mark 1:24; Luke 4:34; John 6:69; Acts 2:27; 3:14; 13:35) is relevant, since Jesus's holiness is corollary to Jesus's obedience, and this holiness benefits others. First, when considering the import of holiness in the Gospels, we must consider issues of cultic purity.[94] This emphasis is seen in the way that Jesus is contrasted with the unclean (*akathartos*) spirits throughout Mark (1:23–28; 3:11; 5:1–12; 6:7; 7:25; 9:25;

---

92. See, e.g., Elizabeth E. Shively, *Apocalyptic Imagination in the Gospel of Mark: The Literary and Theological Role of Mark 3:22–30*, BZNW 189 (Berlin: Walter de Gruyter, 2012), 1.

93. Craig A. Evans, *Mark 8:27–16:20*, WBC 34B (Nashville: Thomas Nelson, 2001), 120.

94. Marcus, *Mark 1–8*, 188; Arseny Ermakov, "The Holy One of God in Markan Narrative," *HBT* 36 (2014): 159–84.

cf. 3:30).[95] Jesus's first Markan encounter with an unclean, demonic spirit is instructive, since the unclean spirit explicitly identifies Jesus as the Holy One of God (1:24). In response, Jesus commands the unclean spirit to come out of the possessed man. Thus, as the Holy One of God, Jesus possesses a unique authority (1:27) and is able throughout Mark to transcend the boundaries of cultic expectations, such as when he touched the leper and not only healed him but made him clean (cf. 1:40–42).[96] Jesus also touches others—the dead daughter of Jairus, along with a woman with a blood-flow malady (Mark 5:21–43)—who would be deemed ritually unclean, but does not thereby compromise his own holiness as the Holy One of God.[97]

Surprisingly, whereas uncleanness was considered to be "contagious," Jesus's holiness transcends expected limitations of ritual purity,[98] and his touch renders clean the unclean. Jesus's contagious holiness may even be in view in two uniquely Markan healings in which Jesus utilizes his own spittle to heal a deaf man (7:33) and a blind man (8:23). In both healings, which seem to have an illustrative and prophetic sign act function in Mark's narrative (cf. 8:18), Jesus's palpable actions follow his explanation of what does and does not make one unclean (7:14–23). Could it be that Jesus's spittle not only plays a role in *healing* the men but is also viewed as making those with ritual blemishes "clean" (cf. Lev. 21:16–24)?[99] In other words, as the Holy One of God, could it be that Jesus's spittle is not only *not* unclean, but actually cleanses, even as it anticipates those who spit at Jesus in the passion (14:65; 15:19)?[100] If so, it could reveal the perspective that Jesus's incarnate work as the Holy

95. *Unclean* is another way for Mark to speak of *demonic* spirits. Marcus, *Mark 1–8*, 187; Larry W. Hurtado, *Mark*, NIBCNT 2 (Peabody, MA: Hendrickson, 1989), 32–33.

96. As a significant skin disease, leprosy would have likely been considered a "major impurity" in accord with the skin diseases included in Lev. 13. See Philip Peter Jenson, *Graded Holiness: A Key to the Priestly Conception of the World*, JSOTSup 106 (Sheffield: JSOT Press, 1992), 225–26; Jay Sklar, *Leviticus: An Introduction and Commentary*, TOTC 3 (Downers Grove, IL: IVP Academic, 2014), 183–84; cf. m. *Neg.*

97. Of course, the *woman* actually touches Jesus, but the principle remains. If the bleeding of the woman in Mark 5 was perpetual—or even only once every week (cf. Mark 5:25)—she would have been in a perpetual state of uncleanness (cf. Lev. 15:19–27; Josephus, *J.W.* 5.227; m. *Zabim* 1–5, noted in James R. Edwards, *The Gospel according to Mark*, PNTC [Grand Rapids: Eerdmans, 2002], 163). Touching a dead body (cf. Mark 5:41) would also typically have been considered to result in a "major impurity" (cf. Sklar, *Leviticus*, 199; Jenson, *Graded Holiness*, 226).

98. Cf. Sklar, *Leviticus*, 45–47.

99. See Lev. 15:8; m. *Zabim* 5.7; b. *Nid.* 55b. Spittle was also thought to have magical or healing power. Cf. J. R. Edwards, *Mark*, 225–26; Marcus, *Mark 1–8*, 473–74, 478; Karelynne Gerber Ayayo, "Magical Expectations and the Two-Stage Healing of Mark 8," *BBR* 24 (2014): 385–86. The role of Lev. 21:16–24 is noted by Ermakov, "Holy One of God," 17.

100. Marcus, *Mark 1–8*, 478.

One of God is a *priestly* work[101] and is the means by which his people are made acceptable to God.

The power Jesus displays in his conflicts with the unclean spirits in Mark is also related to Jesus's authority as Son of God. Similar to the account in Mark 1:24 (cf. Luke 4:34), in Mark 3:11 the unclean spirits identify Jesus as Son of God, and in Mark 5:7 the unclean spirit cries out that Jesus is the Son of the Most High God. From this we see that the Holy One of God in Mark's narrative is closely related to Jesus's status as Son of God, which is (at least) a messianic category. Though the term "Holy One of God" is not clearly a messianic title in the Old Testament (cf. 2 Kings 4:9; Ps. 106:16; Judg. 16:17 LXX [B]), it does seem to carry messianic connotations in Mark's Gospel in accord with Jesus's identity as Son of God (cf. Luke 1:35; Acts 2:27; 3:14; 13:35).

Significantly, as I argued in the previous chapter, Son of God denotes a relationship that is to be distinctly characterized by *obedience*. Thus, Jesus's identity as the Holy One of God deals not simply with ritual or cultic imagery but is at the same time language for *moral* holiness toward God. The Synoptics teach that the two greatest commands are to love God and to love one's neighbor (Matt. 22:37–38 // Mark 12:29–31 // Luke 10:27), the second of which comes from Leviticus 19, where God's people are called to a holy way of life. Thus, full-hearted obedience to God includes not only cultic practices but also love (= obedience) for God (Deut. 6:5) and love for one's neighbor (Lev. 19:18). The holiness of Leviticus, in other words, has in view not only the need for ritual purity but the need for heartfelt devotion to God and love for others, and these were to be manifested in one's actions.[102] Thus, Jesus's holiness as Son of God entails a moral dimension.[103] Similarly, Adolf Schlatter observes that Jesus's "authority was based on his purity; evil does not overcome what is good."[104] The ritual and moral aspects of holiness are therefore conjoined in Mark's narrative presentation of Jesus as holy, obedient, messianic Son of God.

In sum, Jesus's holiness evokes ritual and priestly imagery (cf. Mark 2:10, 25–28), but also the obedience as Son of God in contrast to the demonic, unclean spirits. The actions of Jesus, including his authoritative teaching and miracles, indicate that his entire mission can be described as one of holiness. Jesus's obedience transcends the dichotomy between cultic purity and a holy

---

101. See Ermakov, "Holy One of God," 169.

102. See also Sklar, *Leviticus*, 247; cf. James 2:8, 19, 24.

103. See also Ermakov, "Holy One of God," 168–69.

104. Adolf Schlatter, *The History of the Christ: The Foundation for New Testament Theology*, trans. Andreas J. Köstenberger (Grand Rapids: Baker, 1997), 78.

love for God and neighbor. We find Jesus, as the Holy One of God, in full accord with God's will in every way.[105]

The Righteous One

Closely related to Jesus's identity as the Holy One of God is his identity as the righteous one. Indeed, Luke tightly links these predications for Jesus in Acts 3:14 (*ton hagion kai dikaion*), where they are best taken not as hendiadys but as complementary perspectives on Jesus's full-hearted, incarnate obedience that conforms to Scripture.

We begin with righteousness in accord with Mark's Christology. In Mark, not only is Jesus the Holy One of God but he is also identified as the righteous sufferer, especially in the events leading up to and including the passion. Joel Marcus has outlined what he calls Psalms of the Righteous Sufferer (e.g., Pss. 10; 22; 41; 69), along with verbal parallels to Isaiah's Servant Songs, in Mark's Passion Narrative and Jesus's predictions of his impending passion (e.g., Isa. 50:6; 53:5, 7, 12).[106] Taken together, these underscore the obedience of Jesus as the righteous one in his death. Additionally, the allusions to Psalms and Isaiah are readily applied to a representative figure in light of the royal and corporate dimensions of the relevant texts.[107] Thus the righteous Servant, as a representative, gives his life vicariously for many in Mark (cf. 10:45; Isa. 53:10–12).

Indeed, a pattern we see throughout the Gospels is Jesus's identification as righteous in the climactic events pertaining to the cross. In Matthew 27:19 Pilate's wife identifies Jesus as a righteous man, and Pilate's ceremonial washing of hands after he refuses to release Jesus (27:24) is ironic since Pilate is guilty of shedding *innocent* blood (cf. Deut. 21:6–8). Similarly, in Luke 23:47 the centurion confesses that Jesus was righteous (*ontōs ho anthrōpos outos dikaios ēn*).[108] Though Jesus's righteousness is most assuredly implied in the centurion's confession in Matthew 27:54 // Mark 15:39 in light of the overarching narratives of Matthew and Mark, it is noteworthy that in Luke the centurion explicitly identifies Jesus as righteous. Certainly this righteousness entails Jesus's sinlessness on the cross, but in Luke-Acts "Righteous One" is probably a christological title

105. See also Ermakov, "Holy One of God," 181.
106. Joel Marcus, *The Way of the Lord: Christological Exegesis of the Old Testament in the Gospel of Mark*, SNTW (Edinburgh: T&T Clark, 1992), 172–98.
107. Marcus discusses both individual and corporate dimensions of the Psalms and Isaiah. *Way of the Lord*, 184–85, 190–91; note the diagram on 190n140.
108. For the translation "righteous" as opposed to "innocent," see Kyle Scott Barrett, "Justification in Lukan Theology" (PhD diss., Southern Baptist Theological Seminary, 2012), 149–53.

(Luke 23:47; Acts 3:14; 7:52).[109] Additionally, since Jesus's suffering in the passion is not an entirely new event in Luke but is the culmination of Jesus's lifelong suffering, and since Jesus's entire life accords with Scripture and God's eschatological necessity for salvation, then Jesus must have been the Righteous One throughout the totality of his life (cf. Matt. 5:10–11). Moreover, one should also see the principle of vicarious righteousness in Luke. Since Jesus as the baptized Messiah represents and identifies with people in their sin, he also identifies and represents them in his identity as Righteous One[110] who justifies the many (Isa. 53:11).[111]

In sum, the Synoptics, drawing upon language from Isaiah, portray Jesus as "righteous," especially in relation to his death (cf. Luke 23:47). However, though proportionately more emphasis does fall on the saving death of the Servant,[112] more needs to be said of the righteousness of the entire mission of the Servant (see further chap. 7). That Jesus's righteousness for others extends beyond only his death is further implied in Acts 3:14–15, which identifies Jesus as the Holy and Righteous One who was raised from the dead and to whom we must listen (3:22–23; cf. 2:27). Full of the Holy Spirit (cf. Luke 4:1–13; Acts 10:37–38), Jesus remained holy and fully righteous in both his life and death (cf. Luke 1:35, 75; 23:47). Significantly, Jesus's status as the Holy One in Acts is consistently tied to his resurrection: Jesus's full righteousness and holiness in accord with Scripture was met with the ultimate vindication of life from the dead.

Conclusion

In this chapter I have traced various ways that Jesus's life is described as obedient and in full accord with Scripture throughout the Synoptic Gospels. The language of fulfillment and necessity is key in this regard, as are the concepts of holiness and righteousness. Taken together, the Synoptics view Jesus as one who has come to accomplish a righteous mission, and this mission includes, but is not limited to, his sacrificial death. Instead, Jesus's entire ministry, and

---

109. Cf. ibid., 150; Larry W. Hurtado, *Lord Jesus Christ: Devotion to Jesus in Earliest Christianity* (Grand Rapids: Eerdmans, 2003), 189–90; Matthew C. Easter, "'Certainly This Man Was Righteous': Highlighting a Messianic Reading of the Centurion's Confession in Luke 23:47," *TynBul* 63 (2012): 35–51; Richard N. Longenecker, *The Christology of Early Jewish Christianity*, SBT 2/17 (London: SCM, 1970), 46–47.

110. Cf. Gaffin, "Justification in Luke-Acts," 110–11.

111. K. S. Barrett, "Justification in Lukan Theology," 151; David Seccombe, "Luke and Isaiah," *NTS* 27 (1981): 256–57.

112. See Marcus, *Way of the Lord*, 194–95.

indeed entire life, is viewed as being in full accord with Scripture and God's eschatological salvation. The righteousness that characterized the life and mission of Jesus as the messianic representative was not for himself but for others.

We also must not miss the relationship between Jesus's full obedience and the lack of perfect obedience from all who preceded Jesus. This is evident not only in the *dei* statements (cf. Matt. 23:23; Luke 11:42) but in Jesus's uniqueness throughout the Gospels. Jesus confronts the reader as one who is wholly without sin, one whom John the Baptist hesitated to baptize for the repentance of sins (Matt. 3:14). Jesus himself calls others to repentance, and he has the authority to forgive sins. Jesus is righteous (Luke 23:47), the Son of God (Matt. 26:54; Mark 15:39). He demonstrates a life of full conformity to his Father's will.[113] Since the sin of Adam, no one had ever fulfilled God's will in the way that Jesus does in the Gospels. Jesus's royal, filial obedience is set in contrast to the royal, filial disobedience of Adam and Israel. Indeed, Jesus's obedience entails a lifelong obedience to suffering on his way to the cross, which is set in contrast to and overcomes the sin of previous generations. The blessedness of life that was held out to Adam is realized by means of the perfect righteousness of the Christ, which ironically comes through his death.

However, to consider only the death of Christ as his righteous act for others would be to truncate the mission of Jesus. As we continue to consider how to connect the dots between the life and death of Christ, we find help from John's Gospel. In the next chapter we will see additional ways that Jesus's work before the cross was necessary, and how this glorious work—which culminates in Jesus's death and resurrection—is communicated through Adamic imagery.

113. Cf. Geerhardus Vos, *The Self-Disclosure of Jesus: The Modern Debate about the Messianic Consciousness*, ed. J. G. Vos, 2nd ed. (1953; repr., Phillipsburg, NJ: P&R, 2002), 191.

The Glory of the Last Adam
in the Gospel of John

In the previous chapter I argued that the Synoptic Gospels portray Jesus as the one who perfectly fulfills Scripture and the divine will, which is necessary for salvation. Despite obvious differences between the Synoptics and John, we find similar themes pertaining to the obedience of Jesus. For example, in John, Jesus is often said to have been sent by his Father to accomplish specific work(s), recalling the "I have come" statements in the Synoptics. Similarly, in John, Jesus's obedience is seen in the Son's full conformity to the will of the Father throughout his earthly ministry, and this is similar to the emphasis on Jesus's righteousness and fulfillment of Scripture in the Synoptics. In this chapter I will focus to a large extent on the works Jesus does prior to the cross in John, though one cannot sharply distinguish between phases of the obedience of Jesus since his work is ultimately one unified work. Stated simply, Jesus's obedience stands in the foreground of John's narrative,[1] and this obedience is necessary for salvation. Additionally, the obedience of Jesus is tethered to an underlying Adam Christology in John, which emerges more clearly toward the end of the Fourth Gospel where we encounter the climax of the Son's work. Thus, I will address Adam Christology more explicitly

1. See D. A. Carson, *The Gospel according to John*, PNTC (Grand Rapids: Eerdmans, 1991), 95.

toward the end of this chapter, though I will observe numerous other possible Adamic resonances in the footnotes.

The Work of the Son, Sent from the Father

One of the emphases of Johannine Christology is the identity of Jesus as the one sent from his Father (*apostellō*, *pempō*), which appears more than forty times.[2] By way of example, the need for Jesus's disciples to recognize that he has been sent from the Father reverberates throughout Jesus's climactic prayer in John 17 (17:3, 8, 21, 23, 25). Certainly, on the one hand, this "sent" language reveals the preexistence of the Son, which is explicit in John's prologue (1:1–18). The Word was in the beginning, and the Word was God (1:1). He was in the beginning with God (1:2) and became flesh and dwelt among us (1:14). Readers of John's Gospel are thus confronted with the divinity of the Son from the outset. Yet, on the other hand, the "sent" language points forward to the ultimate purpose of Jesus's coming, namely, to be lifted up unto death that he might draw all people to himself (3:14–15; 12:32–33). These two features—the divinity of the Son alongside his humanity—could seem to be in conflict. Indeed, the crowds ask: if Jesus is the Son of Man and Christ sent from the Father, and if the Christ is to remain forever, how could he die (12:34–36)? This quandary points to the mystery of the incarnation in John. The loftiness of Johannine Christology underscores the extraordinary humiliation of the Son, for in the incarnation the Son comes to deal with the problem of sin (1:29, 34; 8:34–36; 20:23; cf. 16:7–11)[3] through the laying down (and taking up) of his own life (3:14–15; 10:11, 17–18; 12:24, 32–33; 17:19; cf. 19:36). The Son who had always been with the Father is therefore sent into the world for a particular work,[4] which implies that the Son came to realize something that had not yet been accomplished. Jesus's mission in John can thus be described in various ways: it is to glorify the Father, establish a new community, overcome the world, bring life, and so on. But I suggest that we do well to think of the work of Jesus in John inclusively as the work of *salvation* (cf. 3:17; 4:22, 42; 5:34; 10:9; 12:47).

In accord with his necessary accomplishment of salvation, Jesus also serves in a *representative* capacity in John. On this point, we could emphasize Jesus

2. E.g., John 3:17, 34; 4:34; 5:23–24, 30, 36–38; 6:29, 38–39, 44, 57; 7:16, 18, 28–29, 33; 8:16, 18, 26, 29, 42; 9:4; 10:36; 11:42; 12:44–45, 49; 13:20; 14:24; 15:21; 16:5; 17:3, 8, 18, 21, 23, 25; 20:21; cf. 9:7, 11.

3. See Andreas J. Köstenberger and Scott R. Swain, *Father, Son, and Spirit: The Trinity and John's Gospel*, NSBT 24 (Downers Grove, IL: InterVarsity, 2008), 160.

4. I will discuss the relationship between "work" (*ergon*) and "works" (*erga*) below.

as the true representative of his Father as the sent one.[5] However, for the present purposes I am more interested in investigating how Jesus's *obedience* as Son can be seen in a representative light—Jesus's actions benefit his people.[6] As Christ and Son of Man, Jesus represents his people (e.g., 1:17, 41, 51; 3:14; 4:26; 9:22; 11:27; 12:32–34; 17:3; 20:31). Jesus is the Lamb of God who takes away the sin of the world (1:29). However one construes the lamb imagery in John 1, a vicarious taking away of sin is implied, especially if one sees the lamb imagery to be drawn in part from the Passover lamb imagery and possibly also Isaiah 53.[7] Jesus is not only the Lamb of God but also the Good Shepherd who lays down his life on behalf of his sheep (10:11). He is the source of life (1:4; 5:26),[8] and those who abide in Christ, feeding on him by faith, have life (6:29, 35, 51, 58; 15:1–11). In his prayer in John 17, Jesus emphasizes the work he has done for the benefit of others (17:2–4, 19). In sum, Jesus acts representatively, accomplishing salvation for his people. In order to demonstrate this claim in more detail, we turn now to consider some of the key texts in which the mission of Jesus is explained, particularly as it relates to the will of the Father and the work(s) of Jesus.

John 4: Jesus's Food and Completing the Work

The first text in which Jesus explicitly speaks of his work is John 4:34: "Jesus said to them, 'My food [*brōma*] is to do the will [*thelēma*] of him who sent me and to complete [*teleiōsō*] his work [*ergon*].'" Jesus's language here is reminiscent of Deuteronomy 8:3, which is cited in the temptation accounts of Matthew and Luke (Matt. 4:4; Luke 4:4),[9] and a similar point may be in view in John 4:34.[10] Whereas Israel failed in the wilderness to rely on the word of God, Jesus demonstrates wholehearted obedience to his Father by choosing faithfulness to the will of God over physical hunger. The coordination of

5. Craig S. Keener, *The Gospel of John: A Commentary*, 2 vols. (Peabody, MA: Hendrickson, 2003), 1:315–16.

6. Köstenberger and Swain, *Father, Son, and Spirit*, 169–70.

7. See Keener, *Gospel of John*, 1:453–54; Raymond E. Brown, *The Gospel according to John*, 2 vols., AB 29–29A (Garden City, NY: Doubleday, 1966–70), 1:63.

8. I take *en autō* in 1:4 as the beginning of a new sentence. Cf. Bruce M. Metzger, *A Textual Commentary on the Greek New Testament*, 2nd ed. (Stuttgart: Deutsche Bibelgesellschaft, 1994), 167–68; Geerhardus Vos, "The Range of the Logos Title in the Prologue to the Fourth Gospel," in *Redemptive History and Biblical Interpretation: The Shorter Writings of Geerhardus Vos*, ed. Richard B. Gaffin Jr. (Phillipsburg, NJ: P&R, 1980), 72.

9. See also C. K. Barrett, *The Gospel according to St. John: An Introduction with Commentary and Notes on the Greek Text*, 2nd ed. (Philadelphia: Westminster, 1978), 240; Carson, *Gospel according to John*, 228.

10. If so, then Adamic imagery may also be in view here.

will and *work* in 4:34 indicates that doing the *will* of the Father is doing the *work* of the Father.[11]

A similar collocation, this time of will (*thelēma*) and food (*brōsis*), is found in John 6, where Jesus says he has come down from heaven to do the will (*thelēma*) of the one who sent him (6:38). Interestingly, in John 6:27, after Jesus provides bread in the wilderness (6:11–13), he also speaks of food (*brōsis*), as he does in John 4:32.[12] Similarly, Jesus says in 6:55 that his flesh is true food (*brōsis*; cf. 4:32) and his blood is true drink. Later we read that the will (*thelēma*) of the one who sent Jesus is to provide eternal life, raising everyone up on the last day (6:39–40).[13] Taking into view the overall picture of the relationship between will, work, and food in John, we can conclude that Jesus's completion of the will and work of God, through his obedience, yields eternal life. We also find the principle of representation: since Jesus completes the will of God (= his food), those who want eternal life should believe in Jesus (6:29, 40), which means feeding on the body (= true food [6:55], and the bread of life [6:35]) and blood of Jesus. In other words, Jesus imparts salvation to others because of his accomplishment of the Father's will.

John 5: Completing the Works

A second text to consider (5:36) comes from Jesus's extended discourse on his relationship to the Father in John 5. In 5:30 we read that the Son came to seek (*zēteō*) not his own will (*thelēma*) but the will of the one who sent him, and in 5:36 Jesus states that he has been given works (*erga*) from the Father to complete (*teleiōsō*). Again Jesus speaks of the purpose of his task, which is not to do his own will but to do the works of his Father. Significantly, Jesus is responding to critiques leveled against him for healing the lame man on the Sabbath (5:1–16), which is one of the signs that Jesus had been doing (cf. 6:2; 7:31).[14] Though there seems to be a difference between Jesus's signs and Jesus's works—signs are singularly impressive feats[15]—we can subsume the

11. See also Johannes Riedl, *Das Heilswerk Jesu nach Johannes*, FTS 93 (Freiburg: Herder, 1973), 63.

12. It is also possible that the divine provision of bread in the wilderness is to be construed as the answer to Adam's first sin (of eating), which resulted in the curse that yielded the wilderness.

13. J. Ramsey Michaels, *The Gospel of John*, NICNT (Grand Rapids: Eerdmans, 2010), 261.

14. Cf. the survey in Andreas J. Köstenberger, *A Theology of John's Gospel and Letters: The Word, the Christ, the Son of God*, BTNT (Grand Rapids: Zondervan, 2009), 324–28.

15. Though not all affirm that signs are necessarily miraculous, I believe they are. Cf. Herman N. Ridderbos, *The Gospel of John: A Theological Commentary*, trans. John Vriend (Grand Rapids: Eerdmans, 1997), 113; Richard Bauckham, *Gospel of Glory: Major Themes in Johannine Theology* (Grand Rapids: Baker Academic, 2015), 55; Carson, *Gospel according to John*, 175; Keener, *Gospel of John*, 1:251–52, 272; Brown, *Gospel according to John*, 1:528; Hans

signs under the rubric of Jesus's works more broadly. Thus, all of Jesus's signs are works, but not all of Jesus's works are signs.[16] Therefore, the works of Jesus in 5:36 include everything Jesus had been doing, including (but not limited to) his signs.

Signs serve several purposes in John, and it is not my aim to study this topic in depth. One can observe, for example, the role of signs in authenticating God's prophet and eliciting faith.[17] I will discuss the miracles of Jesus in the Synoptics at greater length in chapter 6, but at this point I observe that if signs in John are miraculous, then they are likely to be taken as God's mighty interventions in the world, through Jesus, to bring deliverance.[18] This is consistent with the Old Testament, where "signs and wonders" referred to God's mighty deeds, especially in the exodus through Moses, to deliver his people.[19] In Deuteronomy 34:10–12 we read that no one was like Moses, not least because of the signs and wonders that the Lord did through him,[20] by which Israel was redeemed from Egypt and given the promised land as an inheritance (see Deut. 4:32–40, esp. 4:34).[21] Similarly, in John signs are means of salvation that call people to faith. This is consistent with the Mosaic resonances in many of the Johannine signs, however one delimits them.[22] By

Förster, "Die johanneischen Zeichen und Joh 2:11 als möglicher hermeneutischer Schlüssel," *NovT* 56 (2014): 2–4. Cf. Köstenberger, *Theology*, 328; Paul A. Rainbow, *Johannine Theology: The Gospel, the Epistles and the Apocalypse* (Downers Grove, IL: IVP Academic, 2014), 196; Daniel H. Fletcher, *Signs in the Wilderness: Intertextuality and the Testing of Nicodemus* (Eugene, OR: Wipf & Stock, 2014), 38–41, 80.

16. Keener, *Gospel of John*, 1:275; Francis J. Moloney, SDB, *Love in the Gospel of John: An Exegetical, Theological, and Literary Study* (Grand Rapids: Baker Academic, 2013), 48–49; cf. Köstenberger, *Theology*, 326–27n42.

17. See Richard Bauckham, "Messianism according to the Gospel of John," in *Challenging Perspectives on the Gospel of John*, ed. John Lierman, WUNT 2/219 (Tübingen: Mohr Siebeck, 2006), 43–46; Keener, *Gospel of John*, 1:272–79.

18. Bauckham ("Messianism," 43–46) discusses several texts relating signs to messianic expectations, including the testimony of Josephus, where we read in *J.W.* 6.285 of *ta sēmeia tēs sōtērias*; cf. the *sēmeia* of Moses in *Ant.* 2.275–76. Bauckham concludes that signs not only attest God's prophet but also show that God will deliver his people (ibid., 46).

19. Ridderbos, *Gospel of John*, 113; cf. Fletcher, *Signs in the Wilderness*, 38–41.

20. See John Lierman, "The Mosaic Pattern of John's Christology," in *Challenging Perspectives on the Gospel of John*, ed. John Lierman, WUNT 2/219 (Tübingen: Mohr Siebeck, 2006), 213–14; Wayne A. Meeks, *The Prophet-King: Moses Traditions and the Johannine Christology*, NovTSup 14 (Leiden: Brill, 1967), 162–64.

21. Cf. Duane L. Christensen, *Deuteronomy 21:10–34:12*, WBC 6B (Nashville: Thomas Nelson, 2002), 873; Peter C. Craigie, *The Book of Deuteronomy*, NICOT (Grand Rapids: Eerdmans, 1976), 406–7.

22. I believe we most likely find seven signs in John—six signs in John 1–12, with the seventh and ultimate sign coming in the glorification of Jesus in his death and resurrection (cf. 2:18–19; 12:27–43; 19:34–35; 20:30–31). See further Marc Girard, "La composition structurelle des 'signes' dans le quatrième évangile," *ScRel* 9 (1980): 317–20; Joseph A. Grassi, "Eating

way of example, following John's prologue that contrasts the law that came through Moses with the grace and truth that comes through Jesus Christ (1:17), Jesus turns water into wine (2:1–11). This first (*archē*) sign recalls the first miracle of Moses, in which he turned water into blood (Exod. 7:20).[23] The miraculous provision of bread in the wilderness (John 6:1–15) also recalls the signs and wonders done through Moses, since it excels the manna given through Moses in the wilderness (6:31–34, 49–51). Particularly noteworthy is the christological significance of the feeding—Jesus refers *to himself* as the true bread that comes down from heaven and gives life (6:32–40, 47–59). In John 6 the people connect the sign in the wilderness with deliverance and try to make Jesus king (6:14–15); Jesus had a different understanding of the way deliverance would come.

Some additional Mosaic possibilities are also worth considering. First, if the death and resurrection of Jesus is a sign, then this sign is correlated to Moses's lifting up of the serpent in the wilderness (John 3:14–15).[24] Second, and less likely, whereas the climactic plague against Egypt was the death of the firstborn, the climactic sign in the so-called Book of Signs (John 1:19–12:50) is the raising of Lazarus (11:1–41). Thus, whereas the sign through Moses was the *death* of the firstborn, the "better" sign through Jesus was *life* for the dead. Lazarus's resuscitation further anticipates the decisive granting of life over death, which comes by means of the one and only Son's resurrection. Third, some have seen the sign in John 5:1–16, in which a man lame for thirty-eight years was healed, to be redolent of the thirty-eight years the Israelites wandered in the wilderness (cf. Deut. 2:14).[25] This reading is possible, especially in light of the negative portrayal of the lame man in the narrative (contrast him with the man born blind in 9:1–27), but the length of the man's infirmity must not bear undue exegetical weight.

Regardless of how far we should press these possible resonances, it is clear we have a number of indications throughout John that the salvation Jesus brings—seen climactically in his signs—is greater than the signs and wonders God did through Moses. The primary point I wish to emphasize in relation to John 5 is that the Johannine signs, which are constitutive of the works Jesus has come to do (5:30, 36), are means by which a greater salvation is being

---

Jesus' Flesh and Drinking His Blood: The Centrality and Meaning of John 6:51–58," *BTB* 17 (1987): 25; Carson, *Gospel according to John*, 661; C. H. Dodd, *The Interpretation of the Fourth Gospel* (Cambridge: Cambridge University Press, 1953), 368–79; Köstenberger, *Theology*, 329n57.

23. Keener, *Gospel of John*, 1:278.

24. Fletcher (*Signs in the Wilderness*, 152–53) points out that Num. 21:8–9 (LXX) identifies Moses's bronze serpent as a sign (*sēmeion*). See further note 22 above.

25. See Förster, "Die johanneischen Zeichen," 13 and 13n59; C. K. Barrett, *John*, 253.

accomplished. Therefore, they call for faith in Jesus (5:39, 45–47; cf. 2:11).[26] Furthermore, in John 5 the deliverance that Jesus brings comes through his *obedience* (5:19–20). The works of Jesus discussed in John 5 are indications not that Jesus was rogue (5:16, 18) but that the Father works salvation through the obedient Son whom he loves (5:21–29, 36).

John 17: Completion of the Work

A third text that explains the purpose of Jesus's coming is John 17:4: "I glorified you on the earth, having completed the work that you gave me to do." The prayer of Jesus in John 17 is worthy of many monographs in itself, but I would like to make a few observations particularly about 17:4 in the context of Jesus's prayer, in relation to the Farewell Discourse (John 13:31–16:33), and in John's Gospel more broadly.[27] In particular, it is striking in 17:4 that Jesus can say, even *before* the cross, that he has completed the work that the Father had given him to do and that he has glorified the Father. Yet later Jesus will cry out "It is finished" from the cross (19:30; cf. 19:28). In what sense, then, could Jesus state that he had completed his work *before* the finality of the cross? One possible answer is that Jesus is speaking in 17:4 proleptically of the work that is "as good as finished."[28] Certainly we must read 17:4 in light of the finality of the completion in view at the cross in 19:30, but the emphasis on completion in 17:4 (*teleiōsas*), along with the glory that Jesus has already brought to the Father (*edoxasa*), seems rather to indicate the full accomplishment of Jesus's work thus far. Thus the aorist indicative in 17:4 (*edoxasa*) may stand in contrast to the aorist subjunctive in 17:1 (*doxasē*):[29] Jesus *has glorified* the Father by completing the task he had been given throughout his ministry (17:4), and Jesus *will glorify* his Father through his impending death (17:1).[30] This is similar to 12:27–28, where we read that the Father had glorified (*edoxasa*) his name in all that Jesus had done to that point (especially the signs [2:11]), and he will glorify (*doxasō*) his name again in the climactic work of Jesus in Jerusalem (cf. 12:41).[31]

---

26. Cf. Carson, *Gospel according to John*, 248; Ridderbos, *Gospel of John*, 113; Brown, *Gospel according to John*, 1:529–31.

27. "The importance of Jesus' words in his final prayer (17:4) cannot be overestimated" (Moloney, *Love*, 40).

28. Carson, *Gospel according to John*, 557.

29. C. K. Barrett, *John*, 504.

30. See Leon Morris, *The Gospel according to John*, rev. ed., NICNT (Grand Rapids: Eerdmans, 1995), 638.

31. On the glory of Isaiah and Jesus's glory as (suffering) servant, see Daniel J. Brendsel, *"Isaiah Saw His Glory": The Use of Isaiah 52–53 in John 12*, BZNW 208 (Berlin: Walter de

In other words, already in 17:4 Jesus had "attained the full goal of the mandate . . . that the Father had given him to fulfill."[32] We can see this by noting similarities between 17:4 and the other two texts we have considered where Jesus speaks of his mission (4:34; 5:36). The language of 17:4 recalls 4:34, which similarly speaks of doing (*poieō*) the will of the Father and completing (*teleioō*) his work (*ergon*). John 17:4 further recalls 5:36, where Jesus speaks of the need to complete (*teleioō*) the works (*erga*) the Father had given him (*didōmi*).

John 4:34b	John 5:36b	John 17:4
emon brōma estin hina <u>poieō</u> to thelēma tou pempsantos me kai <u>teleiōsō</u> autou <u>to ergon</u>	*ta gar erga **ha dedōken moi** ho patēr hina **teleiōsō** auta*	*egō se edoxasa epi tēs gēs <u>to ergon</u> **teleiōsas** ho dedōkas **moi** hina <u>poieō</u>*
My food is to <u>do</u> the will of him who sent me and to <u>complete</u> his <u>work</u>.	For the works **that** the Father **has given me**, to complete them.	I glorified you on the earth, having **completed** <u>the work</u> **that you gave me** to <u>do</u>.

<u>Underline</u>: Correlations between John 4:34 and 17:4.
Bold: Correlations between John 5:36 and 17:4.

John 4:34 and 17:4 may even serve as something like an *inclusio* for Jesus's ministry, emphasizing the need for Jesus to complete the work of the Father.[33] Further, 5:36 expands upon 4:34 by speaking of the works (*erga*) that the Father had given to Jesus. Thus, in 17:4 we can conclude that Jesus has completed the work that he had been given by his Father (including but not limited to the signs) and has therefore glorified the Father through his obedience. If 4:34 and 17:4 serve as an *inclusio* for Jesus's ministry, then this most likely indicates that Jesus has been fully obedient to discharge the entire task that he had been given to that point. In this sense Jesus can speak of his work as being completed, even though the cross stands before him.

In this light, Jesus approaches the cross as one who has already overcome the world for the benefit of his disciples (16:33). Though the climactic work remains to be finished after the prayer of Jesus, this does not lessen the necessity of all that Jesus had obediently accomplished in the preceding chapters. Understood this way, Jesus in John 17:4 is reflecting over the perfection of his task in his ministry, which was part of the requisite glorification of the Father that was necessary for salvation.[34] However, to affirm this one need not deny

---

Gruyter, 2014); Richard Bauckham, *God Crucified: Monotheism and Christology in the New Testament* (Grand Rapids: Eerdmans, 1999), 49–51, 63–68.

32. Ridderbos, *Gospel of John*, 549.

33. Though I have modified his discussion, I have gleaned much here from Moloney, *Love*, 39–54; see also Riedl, *Heilswerk*, 43.

34. This possibility is underscored even more if we find in 17:1–5 a reference to the *pactum salutis* or *covenant of redemption*, referring to the eternal, trinitarian plan of salvation. See

that the final completion of Jesus's work, the casting out of the ruler of this world, comes through the lifting up of the Son of Man (12:31–32). Jesus could go to the cross already as a conqueror (16:33),[35] even as his ultimate victory and glorification lay in the future.

Unity of Jesus's Work(s)

As the discussion above reveals, Jesus's work permeates the Gospel of John and is not limited to the cross. Instead, the diverse work of Jesus is viewed ultimately as a unity. In what follows I consider how Jesus in John is always working, the way the plural "works" (*erga*) relates to the one "work" (*ergon*) throughout the Gospel, the divine necessity (*dei*) of Jesus's work(s), and how the hour of Jesus arrives prior to the final hour.

Always Working

Jesus is always working in John, which fits well with the argument above— that the work of Jesus prior to the cross can be spoken of as a completed task. More than fifteen times in John we read that Jesus is working (or some variant of this), which underscores the ongoing task of Jesus throughout his ministry.[36] In John 5:17 Jesus observes that his Father is working until now (*heōs arti*), and Jesus himself is also working. Jesus's comment highlights the work that he does on the Sabbath, but it also implies his ongoing, perpetual work that does not cease on the Sabbath.[37] Of course, Jesus is also doing the divine works of God, yet he does so as the obedient Son (5:19). Similarly, in John 8 Jesus again says that he does only what he has learned from the Father (8:29), and he *always* does what pleases the Father (8:29; cf. Ign. *Magn.* 8.2). The point is that Jesus is without sin (8:46; cf. 9:24–25) and perpetually pleases his heavenly Father through his devotion and perfect execution of what he has been given to do, even to the point of death (8:28). Later in what becomes a rather intense exchange, Jesus affirms his intimate knowledge of God and states that he (in contrast to his interlocutors) truly keeps God's word (8:55).

---

further Köstenberger and Swain, *Father, Son, and Spirit*, 169–73; Turretin, *Inst.* 12.2.13–15; Herman Bavinck, *Reformed Dogmatics*, ed. John Bolt, trans. John Vriend, 4 vols. (Grand Rapids: Baker Academic, 2003–8), 3:212–16; Geerhardus Vos, *Reformed Dogmatics*, ed. and trans. Richard B. Gaffin Jr., 5 vols. (Bellingham, WA: Lexham Press, 2012–16), 2:84–92.

35. Morris, *Gospel according to John*, 633.

36. Cf. 4:34; 5:17, 20, 36; 7:3–4, 21; 9:4; 10:25, 32, 37–38; 14:10–12; 15:24; 17:4.

37. See Carson, *Gospel according to John*, 247–48; C. K. Barrett, *John*, 256; Edwyn Clement Hoskyns, *The Fourth Gospel*, ed. Francis Noel Davey, 2nd ed. (London: Faber and Faber, 1947), 267; Morris, *Gospel according to John*, 274.

It is revealing that Jesus speaks both of keeping God's word (8:55) and of doing the things that please the Father (8:29). We could paraphrase this to say that Jesus always delights to do the will of the Father.

Work and Works

The continual working of Jesus also points to the unity of Jesus's work. We have seen that John's Gospel speaks both of Jesus's singular "work" (*ergon* [4:34; 7:21; 10:32; 17:4]) and of Jesus's plural "works" (*erga* [5:20, 36; 9:3–4; 10:25, 32, 37–38; 14:10–12; 15:24]). The work and the works of Jesus are closely related, though the singular *work* tends to focus more (but not entirely) on Jesus's death and resurrection, which marks the completion of his work.[38] Yet this final work is intimately united to the many *works* that lead to the final work in Jerusalem. It would therefore be artificial to separate Jesus's *work* from his *works*. Throughout his ministry Jesus accomplishes the requisite works that constitute the one all-encompassing work. This is consistent with the divine voice in 12:28, which we considered above: the Father had already glorified his name in all that Jesus had done, and he would glorify it again. There is, in other words, the same divine response to the works done before the cross as there is to the one final work in the lifting up of the Son. The many works are just as necessary for the entire completion of Jesus's task as is the one work. Thus, as we have seen, there is a sense in which Jesus can speak of the completion of his work even before the cross (17:4; cf. 16:33). We can therefore agree with Bultmann's statement that in John "the 'works' which Jesus does at his Father's behest . . . are ultimately one single work."[39]

"It Is Necessary" in John

We also find the language of divine necessity (*dei*) in John. The divine necessity is particularly clear in relation to the climactic work of Jesus on the cross (3:14; 12:34) and the resurrection (20:9). In John 3:14 Jesus speaks of the necessity of the Son of Man being lifted up as Moses lifted up the serpent in the wilderness, in order that all who believe in him may have eternal life and

38. Cf. Moloney, *Love*, 48–49; Hoskyns, *Fourth Gospel*, 246; Morris, *Gospel according to John*, 246; Riedl, *Heilswerk*, 43.

39. Rudolf Bultmann, *Theology of the New Testament*, trans. Kendrick Grobel, 2 vols. (New York: Scribner, 1951–55), 2:52 (§47.2); see also Marinus de Jonge, "Signs and Works in the Fourth Gospel," in vol. 2 of *Miscellanea Neotestamentica*, ed. T. Baarda, A. F. J. Klijn, and W. C. van Unnik, NovTSup 48 (Leiden: Brill, 1978), 122–23; Bavinck, *Reformed Dogmatics*, 3:337–38.

be saved from condemnation (3:16–18). Likewise in 12:34 Jesus states that it is necessary for the Son of Man to be lifted up, which is the ultimate means by which the ruler of this world is cast out (12:31). As noted earlier, the lifting up of the Son of Man signifies not only the death he was to die (12:33) but also the glorification that is indissolubly linked with the crucifixion (12:32). Thus it was also necessary for the Christ to rise from the dead (20:9).

However, divine necessity can also be predicated of Jesus's works more extensively, beyond his death and resurrection. In John 9:4 we read that it was necessary for Jesus (along, it seems, with his disciples) to work the works of the one who sent him while it was day. Though the plural "we" is used in 9:4, this does not lessen the force of the uniqueness of the salvation Jesus accomplishes.[40] Instead, it underscores the lofty calling given to Jesus's disciples to continue and join in Jesus's works through the Spirit (14:12–14), though in a derivative fashion given the uniqueness of Jesus's work and Jesus's promise to work through his disciples (14:14). John also speaks of the necessity (*edei*) for Jesus to pass through Samaria (4:4). Though this could simply indicate the necessity to take the most appropriate route, in light of John's use of *dei* elsewhere and Jesus's later comment while in Samaria that his food is to do the will of the one who sent him (4:34), we are on firm exegetical ground to posit a more profound reason that Jesus had to go through Samaria.[41] Jesus's actions in Samaria are part of the necessary works of salvation that describe his ministry as a whole. Additionally, by passing through Samaria, Jesus is sent to seek worshipers of God who must (*dei*) worship God in spirit and truth (4:24).[42] Indeed, if we view the activity of Jesus in John as one unified whole, why would we need to separate theological from geographical necessity, since it is all part of one grand work of salvation? A more "theological" reading of *dei* in relation to Samaria in 4:4 also accords with the necessity of Jesus's calling other sheep from another fold in 10:16, which likely refers to sheep outside the fold of Israel (cf. Ezek. 37:15–28).[43] Even though in John 10 Jesus apparently speaks of sheep who

---

40. See Carson, *Gospel according to John*, 362. Some manuscripts read *eme*, but *hēmas* is the more difficult reading and is to be preferred. *Hēmas* also has impressive manuscript support and best accords with intrinsic probability; cf. Ridderbos, *Gospel of John*, 334. Also note the role of John the Baptist as part of the "we" in Matt. 3:15.

41. See Morris, *Gospel according to John*, 226; George R. Beasley-Murray, *John*, 2nd ed., WBC 36 (Nashville: Thomas Nelson, 1999), 59; Keener, *Gospel of John*, 1:590; and more cautiously Ridderbos, *Gospel of John*, 153. See alternatively Michaels, *Gospel of John*, 234–35.

42. See Keener, *Gospel of John*, 1:590.

43. Cf. Ridderbos, *Gospel of John*, 362–63; Morris, *Gospel according to John*, 455; C. K. Barrett, *John*, 376; Köstenberger, *Theology*, 183; Carson, *Gospel according to John*, 388; Keener, *Gospel of John*, 1:818–19; Michaels, *Gospel of John*, 590.

have not yet heard his voice,[44] it is not difficult to see how his statement in 10:16 also applies to Samaritan believers (cf. John 4:39–42).[45] The divine necessity of Jesus's life therefore extends beyond his death and resurrection to his ministry more broadly.

One other passage from John 3 may also be relevant. In John 3:30, John the Baptist says that it is necessary (*dei*) for Jesus to increase (*auxanein*), whereas John must decrease. Though John's emphasis is not on a specific work of Jesus per se, it is likely that he is speaking of the coming era of salvation through Christ that must take precedence, whereas John's ministry of anticipation must recede with the arrival of the Messiah. If so, this interpretation would comport well with the view that *dei* refers in John (as in the Synoptics) to the divine necessity of salvation wrought through the obedience of Jesus as the Christ.

The Hour of Jesus

Another way we can see the unity of Jesus's work unto salvation through-out John is that the hour of Jesus, which is ultimately his hour on the cross (7:30; 8:20; 12:23–27; 13:1; 17:1), nevertheless arrives before the final hour.[46] Before John 12 the hour is still future.[47] As Jesus states at the wedding in Cana, his hour has not yet come (2:4b). And yet Jesus does turn the water into wine, though his response to his mother indicates he is not in thrall to any person (2:4a).

To understand why Jesus turns the water into wine when his hour had apparently not yet come, it is helpful to consider the terminology of "now" (*nyn, arti*) in John. Jesus's sign at the wedding in Cana marks the beginning of the eschatological "nowness" of the great age of salvation. It is therefore significant that when Jesus tells the servants to draw wine from the stone water jars, he prefaces his command with "now" (2:8; cf. 2:10). The *now* of the wedding in Cana marks a significant turning point in the history of redemption, as *now* the greater glory of Jesus is beginning to be revealed (2:11) and will culminate in the cross. Jesus's ultimate hour would lead to his greatest glorification (12:23), but already in his signs before the cross, Jesus had begun to reveal the glory that would be more fully revealed toward the end of his

44. See Keener, *Gospel of John*, 1:818.

45. On the Samaritans, see Keener, *Gospel of John*, 1:584–601. Edward W. Klink III (*John*, ZECNT [Grand Rapids: Zondervan, forthcoming]) suggests that Jesus's knowledge of each of his disciples by name in 10:3 is an Adamic reference.

46. On the eschatology of the hour in John, see Stefanos Mihalios, *The Danielic Eschatological Hour in the Johannine Literature*, LNTS 436 (London: T&T Clark, 2011).

47. Carson, *Gospel according to John*, 437.

work (cf. 12:27–28).[48] It is therefore in the shadow of the cross that Jesus can speak of the nowness of the final hour (12:27).

Other Johannine texts confirm this perspective, namely, that the final hour is preceded by the eschatological hour that has already been inaugurated. In John 4 Jesus speaks of a coming hour in which the Father will be worshiped in spirit and truth (4:21, 24). Indeed, because Jesus himself has come, Jesus can say that the hour had already arrived when the Father would seek true worshipers (4:23). Similarly, in John 5:17 Jesus states that his Father is working "until now" (*heōs arti*), which underscores the eschatological current of Jesus's own divine actions on the Sabbath. A few verses later Jesus speaks of an hour coming that is already present (*erchetai hōra kai nyn estin*), in which Jesus would do a greater work than healing a lame man on the Sabbath—it would be a day when the dead would hear the voice of the Son of God and live (5:25). This statement is provisionally fulfilled in the raising of Lazarus (11:1–53), which anticipates the decisive resurrection of Jesus (2:19–21; 10:18; 19–21). The great day of eschatological life had already dawned during the ministry of Jesus. As Ramsey Michaels observes, Jesus's "extraordinary claim is not only that he is the Son who will awaken the dead, but that the future is *now*."[49]

Similarly, in John 9 the blind man is *now* able to see (9:19, 21, 25; cf. 9:41). Regardless of how far one reads the situation of John's original audience or a posited Johannine community in John 9,[50] from a narrative perspective the healing of the blind man points the reader to the nowness of the eschatological day of salvation during the ministry of Jesus (cf. Isa. 29:18; 35:5; 42:7, 16). One could consider many other uses of *arti* or *nyn* in John, but the survey provided here aims simply to underscore the present nowness that had already become a reality in the ministry of Jesus before the cross. This language, along with the Johannine conception of *hour*, encourages the reader to consider the unity and necessity of Jesus's entire work as an integrated whole in the Gospel of John. Though the final hour comes when the Son of Man is raised up, the glory of the Father is already revealed during the ministry of Jesus. In the next section we will consider in more detail how the works of Jesus, which always please the Father, benefit his people.

---

48. Girard ("La composition," 320) shows correlations between Jesus's first sign at the wedding in Cana and the final sign on the cross. In Girard's structure, which has much to commend it, these two signs form the outer frame of a chiasm.

49. Michaels, *Gospel of John*, 317 (emphasis added). See also the great faith of Martha in John 11:22, who knew already that God would give Jesus whatever he asked, and that he was already the resurrection and the life (11:27).

50. See the influential study of J. Louis Martyn, *History and Theology in the Fourth Gospel*, rev. ed., NTL (Louisville: Westminster John Knox, 2003).

Union with Christ and Salvation

Union with Christ is a central theological concept in John[51] and is particularly relevant for the present volume on the saving character of Jesus's life. The fourth Evangelist communicates union most prominently through the terminology of abiding or remaining (*menō*) in Jesus, and this union is tied to the character of Jesus as the one who abides in his Father's love and keeps the commandments. The Fourth Gospel's emphasis on salvation through union with Christ again entails the principle of representation, since Jesus's obedience yields salvation for those who believe in the Son.

Bread of Life Discourse (John 6:22–58)

In John 6 Jesus's miraculous feeding of the multitudes in the wilderness points to the deeper reality that Jesus himself, as Son of Man, is the bread of life who has come down from heaven (6:33, 35, 40, 48, 51, 53–58).[52] In this discourse Jesus speaks the scandalous words (6:60, 66) that all who wish to have life must eat the flesh of the Son of Man and drink his blood (6:51–54). Further, Jesus states that everyone who feeds on him abides (*menei*) in him, and he in them (6:56). Though it is difficult to separate the imagery of eating the flesh of the Son of Man and drinking his blood from a sacramental understanding in a post-Easter context, in John 6 the emphasis is not on the ritual per se, but on believing in the Son of Man (6:29, 35, 40, 47). To have eternal life, one must feed in faith on the Son of Man who has come down from heaven. Partaking of the bread of heaven unto life communicates participation, and indeed union, with the Son of Man. Feeding in faith on the Son of Man means deriving life from the Son in whom is all life, as Jesus explained earlier (1:4; 5:21, 25–26). The imagery of eating implies union, as does the language of remaining (*menō*) in the Son of Man (6:56).[53] The verb *menō*, most often translated as "abiding" or "remaining," is a favorite Johannine term and is employed to a greater extent in the Farewell Discourse to explain the nature of this union.

Before considering the Farewell Discourse, it is important to recognize the emphasis on Jesus's obedience in John 6. The union that the disciples have

51. See also Robert A. Peterson, "Union with Christ in the Gospel of John," *Presb* 39 (2013): 9–29.

52. If the feeding of the multitude is counted as the fourth of seven Johannine signs, then it would serve as the pivot of a chiastic arrangement of signs. See Girard, "La composition," 320; Grassi, "Eating Jesus' Flesh," 25.

53. See similarly Grant Macaskill, *Union with Christ in the New Testament* (Oxford: Oxford University Press, 2013), 215; Bauckham, *Gospel of Glory*, 94–103.

with Jesus is, in the context of John, union with the supremely obedient one. Jesus is obedient as the one sent from the Father to do his will. The narrative foundation for Jesus's obedience to his Father's will is most explicitly set forth in John 4:34 and 5:36,[54] and we find a similar statement in 6:38: "For I have come down from heaven not to do my will but the will of him who sent me." Partaking of the bread of life therefore means partaking of the Son who always obeys his Father. In John 6 the will of the Father includes the Son granting life and raising up on the last day all that the Father has given him (6:39–40), but by implication it also entails all that Jesus does in obedience to his Father. Because Jesus's food is to do the will of his Father, those who feed on Jesus by faith receive the life that flows from Jesus as the supremely obedient one.

Farewell Discourse (John 13:31–16:33)

Union with Christ is already in view in John 6, but receives further elaboration from Jesus on the final night of his life. The verb *menō* is found fourteen times in the Farewell Discourse, specifically in John 14–15,[55] though the imagery of union is not limited to the presence of that term. What I particularly wish to highlight in the Farewell Discourse is the interrelatedness of love, keeping the commandments, and abiding.

We begin in John 14:10–12, where Jesus instructs his disciples that the Father is in him and he is in the Father, and the Father who abides (*menei*) in Jesus does his works through Jesus (14:10). Jesus further states in 14:11 that he is in the Father and the Father is in him, and again draws attention to the works that he has done. In the next verse (14:12) Jesus speaks of the works that his disciples will do, which are the same works that Jesus himself does. At this point we encounter a crucial move: if Jesus does the works of the Father because the Father abides in the Son and vice versa, it is likely that Jesus speaks of the works that his disciples will do in light of the corresponding reality that the disciples will abide in Jesus. In other words, the disciples will do the works of Jesus after Jesus's departure inasmuch as they abide in Jesus. Key in this regard is the relationship between abiding and the works, which must be works of obedience to the Father.

In addition, abiding in Christ means loving him, which in turn means keeping his commandments (14:15). Similarly, in 14:20–21 the disciples are to be encouraged that in the coming day, when Jesus lives, they will know

---

54. To be sure, other texts in the early chapters of John also show Jesus's obedience to his Father's will, such as the Spirit's abiding on Jesus (John 1:32) and Jesus's lack of compulsion to his mother's request (2:4).

55. John 14:10, 17, 25; 15:4–7, 9–10, 16.

that Jesus is in the Father and they are in Jesus and he in them (14:20). Jesus further states again that the one who has the commandments and keeps them is the one who loves Jesus and will therefore be loved by Jesus's Father (14:21, 23). It is striking that the disciples' relationship to Jesus mirrors to some degree Jesus's relationship to his Father. Jesus is in the Father, and the Father is in the Son, and the Father loves the Son and is pleased by his obedience in doing the will of the Father (3:35; 4:34; 5:20, 36; 8:29, 42; 10:17; 17:23–26). Likewise, the disciples are to abide in Christ and keep his commandments, and by so doing will also be loved by Jesus's Father. The salient emphasis here is the way in which Jesus's words to his disciples are built on the christological foundation that Jesus is the obedient Son who keeps his Father's commandments. What the disciples are to do is to be done in light of what Jesus has done, though obviously without displacing his works (see, e.g., 14:12–14). The Son's abiding in the Father entails his full obedience to the Father, which is the presupposition for the disciples' abiding in Christ.

In John 15:1–17, where we find the most extensive Johannine discussion of union with Christ, we also see the interrelatedness of love, commandments, and abiding in Christ. Again the disciples are instructed to abide in the love of Jesus just as the Father loved the Son (15:9), which is further defined as keeping the commandments (15:10a). Jesus remained in his Father's love by keeping the commandments (15:10b). Love and obedience were perfectly united in Jesus. Indeed, we find elsewhere, in the Synoptics, that the two greatest commandments are love for God and love for neighbor (Matt. 22:37–40 // Mark 12:29–31 // Luke 10:27; cf. Rom. 13:8; Gal. 5:14; James 2:8, 19). In a covenantal context, love is tantamount to obedience. Therefore, to do what God commands is to love God and to love one's neighbor. In this light, the emphasis on Jesus's *love* in the Farewell Discourse also underscores the *obedience* of Jesus. Indeed, we read explicitly that Jesus loved God (14:31; 15:10; cf. 17:23–24) and loved his neighbor (13:34; 15:12–13).

We also find in John 15 the image of the vine and the branches. Jesus is the true vine, and those who remain in him will (and must) bear fruit (15:1–6; cf. Isa. 5:1–7; Ezek. 15:1–8).[56] This fruit is best taken, in light of broader New Testament usage, as the fruit of faithful obedience, which is necessary for salvation.[57] The source of this fruit is Jesus, the true vine who nourishes his

56. Harald Sahlin ("Adam-Christologie im Neuen Testament," *ST* 41 [1987]: 25) suggests that being "in Christ" in John 15 could be new-Adam imagery. This is an intriguing possibility but must remain tentative.

57. E.g., Matt. 3:8, 10; 7:16–18; 12:33; Luke 3:8–9; 6:43–44; Rom. 6:22; 7:4–5; Gal. 5:22–23; Eph. 5:9; Phil. 1:11; Col. 1:6, 10; Heb. 12:11; James 3:17; cf. John 15:6, 8.

people.[58] Jesus, in other words, is the source of true salvation for those who remain in him. This image likely also assumes Jesus is the chief fruit-bearer, especially in light of 12:24: "Truly, truly I say to you, unless a grain of wheat dies by falling to the earth, it remains alone; but if it dies, it bears much fruit." This statement could refer to a principle that is true for any follower of Jesus, but since it follows the key statement in 12:23 of the arrival of the hour of the Son of Man's glorification, the death in view in 12:24 most likely refers primarily to Jesus's own death (cf. 12:33).[59] Significantly, this death produces much fruit (12:24), and this is the presupposition of the disciples' fruit-bearing that comes by abiding in Christ.

In sum, Jesus's instructions to his disciples in the Farewell Discourse are based on strongly christological presuppositions. Jesus is the source of life, and he is the one who has loved God and neighbor fully, keeping God's commandments. The disciples must abide in Christ in order to bear fruit unto life (cf. 14:6). This is consistent with the Bread of Life Discourse in which the disciples must feed on the Son of Man to live forever (6:51). These texts therefore speak of salvation in terms of union with Christ, which points to Jesus's status as representative and life-giver. Because Jesus loved God and neighbor and laid down his life for his friends, his disciples are able to experience eternal life (3:14–15; 6:54; 12:23–24, 50). Few have summarized the importance of union with Christ better than John Calvin: "As long as Christ remains outside of us, and we are separated from him, all that he has suffered and done for the salvation of the human race remains useless and of no value to us."[60]

Jesus's Life and Eternal Life

In the previous section we considered the way John describes salvation as union with Christ. Life comes through Jesus, who has the authority to grant life as the unique Son of God. Additionally, the connections between keeping the commandments, love, and abiding, coupled with the emphasis throughout John on Jesus's obedience leading to life, indicate that the life Jesus imparts in John is also related to his unique obedience. As we conclude our study of John's Gospel, I would like to mention a few other ways in John that Jesus's life is viewed as important to salvation.

58. See, e.g., Keener, *Gospel of John*, 2:998.
59. So, e.g., Ridderbos, *Gospel of John*, 430; C. K. Barrett, *John*, 423; Carson, *Gospel according to John*, 438; Morris, *Gospel according to John*, 527; Keener, *Gospel of John*, 2:873; see alternatively Michaels, *Gospel of John*, 689.
60. Calvin, *Inst.* 3.1.1, in John Calvin, *Institutes of the Christian Religion*, ed. John T. McNeill, trans. Ford Lewis Battles, 2 vols., LCC 20 (Louisville: Westminster John Knox, 1960), 1:537.

First, Jesus is portrayed in John's Gospel as sinless. This is implied in John the Baptist's testimony that Jesus is the Lamb of God who takes away the sin of the world (1:29).[61] This "Lamb of God" proclamation, as suggested earlier, most likely entails sacrificial imagery at least in part.[62] What the Passover lamb represented by way of type, Jesus fulfills by way of reality: a perfect, sinless substitute sacrificed for sin. This makes good sense of John's portrayal of the Passion Narrative, in which some have suggested that Jesus was sacrificed at the same time that the lambs were being sacrificed in the temple (19:14),[63] but even more certain is the Passover imagery that the bones not be broken (19:31–37; cf. Exod. 12:46; Num. 9:12).[64] Jesus is thus portrayed as the perfect, sinless sacrifice in John's Passion Narrative. Similarly, in John 8:46 Jesus challenges his interlocutors to find sin in him, but they cannot. Neither were the Pharisees correct to accuse Jesus of sin (9:25–26; cf. 7:18–19). The baselessness of these accusations corresponds to Jesus's full obedience throughout John—no charge of wrongdoing can stick to him; he is wholly without sin.

Second, John often speaks of (eternal) life in conjunction with believing and abiding in Jesus.[65] The Johannine emphasis on life, as many have noted, is closely related to what the Synoptics communicate by way of kingdom.[66] Life in John means fullness of life, and ultimately eternal life, which fits well

61. Some church fathers saw an Adamic reference in the Spirit descending and remaining on the obedient Jesus in John 1:32–34. See, e.g., Cyril of Alexandria, *Commentary on John* 182–84, in *Commentary on John*, trans. David R. Maxwell, ed. Joel C. Elowsky, 2 vols., ACT (Downers Grove, IL: IVP Academic, 2013–15), 1:81–82; Bede, *Homily* 1.15 [John 1:29–34], in *Homilies on the Gospels*, trans. Lawrence T. Martin and David Hurst, CSS 110 (Kalamazoo, MI: Cistercian Press, 1991), 155. See also the authority of Jesus in John to give the Spirit (15:26; 16:7; 20:22), which Paul associates with the last Adam (1 Cor. 15:45); cf. Klink, *John* (forthcoming); Benjamin L. Gladd, "The Last Adam as the 'Life-Giving Spirit' Revisited: A Possible Old Testament Background of One of Paul's Most Perplexing Phrases," *WTJ* 71 (2009): 297–309; Geerhardus Vos, "The Eschatological Aspect of the Pauline Conception of the Spirit," in *Redemptive History and Biblical Interpretation: The Shorter Writings of Geerhardus Vos*, ed. Richard B. Gaffin Jr. (Phillipsburg, NJ: P&R, 1980), 91–125.

62. See Ridderbos, *Gospel of John*, 73–74; Carson, *Gospel according to John*, 150; Keener, *Gospel of John*, 1:454.

63. See, e.g., C. K. Barrett, *John*, 545; Bauckham, *Gospel of Glory*, 153–54; Craig R. Koester, *The Word of Life: A Theology of John's Gospel* (Grand Rapids: Eerdmans, 2008), 112–13. For those who demur, see Carson, *Gospel according to John*, 603–4; Andreas J. Köstenberger, "John," in *Commentary on the New Testament Use of the Old Testament*, ed. G. K. Beale and D. A. Carson (Grand Rapids: Baker Academic, 2007), 500.

64. See variously Keener, *Gospel of John*, 2:1130–31, 1156; Koester, *Word of Life*, 112–13; Brown, *Gospel according to John*, 2:883, 953; Carson, *Gospel according to John*, 627; Köstenberger, "John," 503–4. Alternatively, see Ridderbos, *Gospel of John*, 622.

65. E.g., John 1:4; 3:15–16, 36; 4:14; 5:26; 6:40; 8:12; 11:25; 14:6; 20:31.

66. So, e.g., Koester, *Word of Life*, 137; Thomas R. Schreiner, *New Testament Theology: Magnifying God in Christ* (Grand Rapids: Baker Academic, 2008), 27; Köstenberger, *Theology*, 285–86. I will discuss the kingdom of God in the Synoptics in chap. 6.

with Jewish anticipations of eternal life in the resurrection.[67] Though the consummation of the kingdom remains future (cf. 1 Cor. 15:24; 2 Pet. 1:11), John's realized-eschatological outlook indicates that already, because of the coming of the Son, believers experience eternal life through Jesus himself (see, e.g., John 17:3).

Indeed, it is not just who Jesus is but what he does that establishes kingdom life. We see this in the two Johannine passages that feature the language of kingdom (3:3, 5; 18:36). To have life, one must be a part of the kingdom that Christ brings, and this kingdom ultimately comes through the death of the Son of God. Thus, to Nicodemus Jesus emphasizes the need to be born again or from above (*anōthen* [3:3]) and then speaks of the necessity of the Son of Man being lifted up for eternal life (3:14–16). The second passage that speaks of the kingdom is Jesus's encounter with Pilate in John 18. When Jesus is presented before Pilate as a rival king (18:33–34, 37, 39; 19:14–15), Jesus responds that his kingdom is not of this world (18:36). Again we see that Jesus is, ironically (cf. 19:15), a rejected king before Pilate, though he will demonstrate his kingship not by being delivered from the cross but by being lifted up on the cross. Thus, Pilate's inscription is apropos: "Jesus of Nazareth, the King of the Jews" (19:19).

These two kingdom texts in John, coupled with John's broader emphasis on life, show the reader that eschatological life comes through the work of Jesus, who brings the kingdom through his death. At the same time, we have also seen that the work of Jesus in John is ultimately one integrated work, so we can conclude that all that Jesus does from the beginning of the Gospel contributes to the implementation of this kingdom of life. Jesus lays down his own life that he might overthrow the ruler of this world, since he will take up his life again (10:17–18; 12:24, 31; 14:30; 16:11; cf. 1 John 3:8). Jesus himself is free from sin, but the evil of sin leads to his death.[68] Yet he remains obedient even unto death, overcoming death through his resurrection.

At this point we might also ponder whether John's Passion Narrative presents an Adam Christology. The kingship of Jesus is clearly a driving emphasis of the Passion Narrative, with the charge leveled at Jesus revolving around the legitimacy of his purported kingship. From a canonical perspective, Adam should be considered the first king as one made in the image of God. Indeed, when Pilate presents Jesus to the crowd, his word choice is quite suggestive: "Behold the man!" (*idou ho anthrōpos* [Vulgate: *ecce homo*] [19:5]).[69] This

---

67. Keener, *Gospel of John*, 1:328–29; cf. Dodd, *Interpretation*, 144–50.
68. See Koester, *Word of Life*, 70.
69. Pilate's proclamation in 19:5 is omitted by 𝔓66 and some Latin witnesses, and *ho anthrōpos* is omitted by Vaticanus. However, these readings can credibly be identified as omissions; "behold

dramatic scene is rich with significance, showing the humanity of Jesus, along with Pilate's ridiculing the perceived kingship of Jesus.[70] Yet there could also be a Johannine double entendre here, linking Jesus with the first royal man. Whereas the first man was not obedient to cast out the serpent authoritatively, is Jesus being portrayed as the royal Son who by his obedience unto death is casting out the ancient serpent (cf. 12:31; 1 John 3:8)?[71] It has, in fact, been argued that John intends in 19:5 to contrast Jesus with Adam.[72] This possibility should be considered in light of the glory theme, which brings us to our third point.

Third, the glory of Jesus reflects his obedience. To be sure, the glory of Jesus is most climactically seen in his death and resurrection. However, Jesus can also say in 17:4 that he *has* glorified the Father, having completed the work that he had been given. Though the glory of Jesus is preeminently manifested in the cross, God's glory through Jesus permeates the entire Gospel of John in all that Jesus does.[73] This raises the possibility that we find in John's theology of glory an Adamic resonance, namely, that Jesus's glory, in conjunction with his filial obedience, is the eschatological realization of the glory that was not realized by Adam. As I noted in chapter 2, Jewish sources are rich with traditions relating Adam to protological glory, though the relevant biblical texts do not speak of Adam having attained this glory. It seems more likely, in view of the overarching canonical witness, that Adam's created state was a probationary administration that held out the possibility of glory and everlasting life, which was not yet realized in his prelapsarian state. Thus, even though Adam was created upright, he stood at the beginning of his course and had not yet reached the *telos* of his existence.[74] Nevertheless, many Jewish

---

the man" is strongly attested in the manuscript tradition (see, e.g., Sinaiticus). Additionally, James R. Royse (*Scribal Habits in Early Greek New Testament Papyri*, NTTSD 36 [Leiden: Brill, 2008], 511, 544) has observed a slight tendency for the scribe of 𝔓66 to omit more often than he adds.

70. See C. K. Barrett, *John*, 541; Keener, *Gospel of John*, 2:1123–24; Ridderbos, *Gospel of John*, 600–601.

71. See, e.g., Alan Richardson, *The Gospel according to St. John*, TBC (London: SCM, 1959), 197; Gerald L. Borchert, *John 12–21*, NAC 25B (Nashville: Broadman & Holman, 2002), 250; Richard D. Phillips, *John*, 2 vols., REC (Phillipsburg, NJ: P&R, 2014), 2:527; cf. Sahlin, "Adam-Christologie," 25. One might also ask if the serpent imagery from Num. 21, which is used for Jesus's lifting up on the cross (John 3:14), is itself an inner-biblical allusion to the diabolical serpent in the garden.

72. M. David Litwa, "Behold Adam: A Reading of John 19:5," *HBT* 32 (2010): 142; Klink, *John* (forthcoming). Litwa (followed by Klink) points particularly to Gen. 3:22 and *LAE* 13:3.

73. So, e.g., Köstenberger, *Theology*, 294–95; Bauckham, *Gospel of Glory*, 43–75.

74. See, e.g., Bavinck, *Reformed Dogmatics*, 2:564, 3:395; Geerhardus Vos, *Biblical Theology: Old and New Testaments* (1948; repr., Edinburgh: Banner of Truth, 1975), 31–40; Vos, *Reformed Dogmatics*, 2:16–20.

traditions reflect the rather widespread association of Adam with glory, which helps us understand the prominence of glory in association with Jesus as the last Adam. By associating the glory of Jesus with his climactic obedience, the Gospel of John shows its readers that Jesus was achieving the goal that had, to that point, not yet been fulfilled since the days of Adam.[75]

A contrast between Adam and Jesus in John 19 would also be appropriate in light of John's emphasis on the glory of the cross. Now, at the end of the course of Jesus's obedience, readers encounter the reality that Christ is a greater king than Adam. Whereas after Adam's sin we read "Behold Adam" (Gen. 3:22; LXX: *idou Adam*; MT: *hen hā'ādām*), which points to Adam's mortality and lack of glory, in John 19:5 we read "Behold the man" (*idou ho anthrōpos*), which though intended by Pilate to disparage Jesus, reveals John's underlying theology that the cross is the glorification of the Son (cf. John 12:23). What Pilate meant to be reviling, John means for the reader to understand as the true glory of the last Adam who overcomes the sin of Adam through his own death as true king.[76] Though Jesus's death may seem like a failure to the world, in John's Gospel the cross is the glorification of the Son. Thus, at this climactic moment in the Fourth Gospel, the Son's glorification that leads to life is portrayed as the obedience of the last Adam.[77] I will argue in chapter 7 that Jesus's resurrection in John may also evoke the Adamic context of the first garden. Humanity's original creation and fall takes place in a garden, and Christ as the last Adam overcomes the death of the first Adam in a garden.[78]

Conclusion

One can only scratch the surface of the deep wonders of John's Gospel in a chapter of this length, but I hope to have shown that Jesus's lifelong, filial

75. Some church fathers even associated Jesus's supposed age in John 2:20 (forty-six years; cf. Irenaeus, *Haer.* 2.22.5) with the value of Adam's name using gematria, thus leading to the view that "Jesus recapitulated by his age the numerical value of Adam's name" (Oskar Skarsaune, "Fragments of Jewish Christian Literature Quoted in Some Greek and Latin Fathers," in *Jewish Believers in Jesus: The Early Centuries*, ed. Oskar Skarsaune and Reidar Hvalvik [Peabody, MA: Hendrickson, 2007], 334). It is also of note that John 2 is the context for Jesus first revealing his glory (2:11), which was greater than Adam's.

76. Note that Jesus's crown consists of thorns (19:2, 5), which resulted from the curse of Adam (Gen. 3:18). This is also noted in Litwa, "Behold Adam," 142n26.

77. Here I draw from Litwa, "Behold Adam"; Klink, *John* (forthcoming). For additional possible parallels between John 18–19 and Gen. 3, see Litwa, "Behold Adam," 142n26.

78. See also Klink, *John* (forthcoming), who observes Adamic themes throughout John (e.g., 1:14; 10:3; 18:1–2; 19:5; 20:1, 22).

obedience was necessary for salvation. Jesus fully discharged the task given to him by his Father and is the source of eternal life for all who would believe in him. Jesus manifested the Father's glory in a way that no one else ever had since the days of Adam. This was not only because Jesus was by nature God (1:1) but also because the Son remained lovingly in the Father and was always in conformity with the Father's will. The eternal life that Jesus brings through his obedient life and death can also be described in terms of the kingdom. We turn our attention now to the way that Jesus brings this kingdom in the Synoptic Gospels.

The Last Adam and the Kingdom
of Righteousness

We have seen that Jesus's incarnate work is described as necessary for salvation and for the fulfillment of Scripture. Moreover, these actions are the actions of Jesus as the baptized Messiah who is anointed with the Holy Spirit. In this chapter we will consider Jesus's messiahship more explicitly through the lens of royal imagery. Jesus's obedient sonship should be viewed in relation to Adam and Israel, but it is also presented in Davidic terms. As king, Jesus inaugurates and establishes the kingdom of God, not only at his death, but already during his ministry. Moreover, the inauguration of the kingdom of God must be viewed in tandem with the ongoing, messianic obedience of Jesus even before the cross. To be sure, the death of Jesus is crucial for understanding the full establishment of the kingdom, but the focus of the present chapter is on the ways in which the kingdom is inaugurated prior to the cross, in conjunction with the incarnate actions of Jesus as the last Adam and the Messiah. In this chapter I will discuss Jesus's role in implementing the kingdom of God, his authority in binding the strong man, and the relation of his miracles to his messianic obedience. Consistent with what we have seen in previous chapters, the authority of Jesus to implement the kingdom of righteousness is often portrayed in Adamic terms.

Kingdom of Righteousness

King and Kingdom

As Son of God and son of David, Jesus is identified in royal terms through-out the Gospels (e.g., Matt. 1:1; 22:45; Mark 12:37; Luke 1:32; 20:44; John 18:36), and this royal identity is tied to Jesus's role as Messiah and servant. Jesus's royal sonship is declared at his baptism (Matt. 3:17 // Mark 1:11 // Luke 3:22; cf. Ps. 2:7), and his obedience as messianic Son is explained in terms of servanthood (cf. Isa. 42:1). As the king and representative of his people, Jesus is anointed with the Holy Spirit, who empowers him for his messianic ministry that is often described in Isaianic terms (e.g., Matt. 12:17–21). The narrative structure of the Gospels also reveals the close connection between the messianic sonship of Jesus and the kingdom, since immediately after his baptism and temptation Jesus announces the inaugu-ration of the kingdom (Matt. 4:17; Mark 1:14–15; Luke 4:16–21; cf. 4:43). Thus, even if one were to demur at the concept of a unified servant figure in Jesus's day, it is beyond doubt that the Evangelists utilize language quite prominently from Isaiah 40–66 to describe the work of Jesus, not least in relation to the establishment of the kingdom of God. Put simply, royal and servant imagery are intermingled in the Gospels' presentation of the coming of the kingdom. Certainly much can be said about the relationship of Jesus's death to suffering servant texts, but we also must not miss the emphasis on the servant language throughout the entire ministry of Jesus. The task of the servant is realized not only in the death of Jesus but also in his life and ministry more extensively.

Before considering in more detail the relationship of the kingdom to Isa-iah and other prophetic texts, it is important to observe that the kingdom is already present during the ministry of Jesus.[1] In Matthew and Mark, Jesus's first announcement of the kingdom indicates that the kingdom has drawn near, or is at hand (*ēngiken* [Matt. 4:17 // Mark 1:15]), which indicates the initial inbreaking of the messianic kingdom of God into the world.[2] This

1. On the "already/not yet" nature of the kingdom of God in the Gospels, see Herman N. Ridderbos, *The Coming of the Kingdom*, trans. H. de Jongste, ed. Raymond O. Zorn (Philadel-phia: P&R, 1962); Thomas R. Schreiner, *New Testament Theology: Magnifying God in Christ* (Grand Rapids: Baker Academic, 2008), 45–68.

2. In Matt. 3:2, John the Baptist also indicates that the kingdom is at hand, which points to two features of John's ministry. First, John's ministry is very closely tied to Jesus's ministry. Second, though John belongs to the old order of prophets (Matt. 11:11), as an eschatological prophet like Elijah (11:14) he leans forward toward the new age that comes with Christ. Thus, though Jesus himself brings the kingdom, John's preaching closely resembles and anticipates Jesus's preaching and actions.

announcement comes at the beginning of Jesus's ministry—immediately after Jesus's baptism, anointing with the Holy Spirit, and obedience in the face of the devil's three temptations. These events, along with John's preparatory ministry, provide foundational prerequisites for the inbreaking of God's kingdom. Before announcing the kingdom's arrival, Jesus is anointed as king and vicariously overcomes temptation.

Jesus's announcement of the kingdom implies a conflict of kingdoms—where the kingdom of God comes, the kingdom of Satan is under attack. Interestingly, after the beginning of his ministry, Jesus does not generally speak of the kingdom as having *come near*, but he does tell his disciples to proclaim in their traveling ministry that the kingdom has come near (*ēngiken*) to the cities they visit (Matt. 10:7; Luke 10:9, 11). Though Jesus himself apparently was not initially bringing the kingdom to these areas (cf. Luke 10:1), he had authorized his disciples to act and speak with his authority (Matt. 10:5–8; Luke 10:1–11; cf. Mark 6:7–13). Therefore, in their itinerant ministry the disciples could, as Jesus himself did, proclaim the nearness of the kingdom, through their actions and message, as they represented Jesus.

Thus, I propose that as the kingdom initially comes to an area, the Gospels describe it as being near. However, once the kingdom draws near, it appears from that point to be more fully established as the message and the activity of the kingdom take root. We see this dynamic in Jesus's rebuke to the Pharisees in Matthew 12. When accused of casting out demons by the power of the devil (Matt. 12:24), Jesus responds that he casts out demons by the Spirit of God, which is proof that the kingdom of God had come upon them (12:28). Instead of the term *engizō*, the term *phthanō* is found in Matthew 12:28, which indicates at least two things. First, the kingdom actions of Jesus should have been clear to the Pharisees, and Jesus was therefore rebuking them for their lack of belief given the clarity with which the kingdom had come upon them. Second, the slightly stronger verb (*phthanō*) for the presence of the kingdom may indicate the fuller establishment of the kingdom than when Jesus initially announced the kingdom earlier in the narrative (cf. 4:17).[3] As the kingdom had been advancing powerfully (Matt. 11:12; cf. Luke 7:16), evil, sin, and sickness were overcome, which led Jesus to speak more forcefully later in his ministry of the kingdom's "already" presence.

---

3. BDAG, "φθάνω," 1053, #2: "arrive, reach"; cf. BDAG, "ἐγγίζω," 270, #2: "draw near, come near, approach." Cf. Dan G. McCartney, "*Ecce Homo*: The Coming of the Kingdom as the Restoration of Human Viceregency," *WTJ* 56 (1994): 9–10; George R. Beasley-Murray (*Jesus and the Kingdom of God* [Grand Rapids: Eerdmans, 1986], 75–80), who critiques those who would use the term to deny the reality of the kingdom's presence in Jesus's ministry; cf. R. T. France, *The Gospel of Matthew*, NICNT (Grand Rapids: Eerdmans, 2007), 480n23.

A similar dynamic is evident in the parallel account in Luke 11:20 and also in the explanation of the kingdom in Luke 17:20–21. In response to the Pharisees' inquiry as to the timing of the kingdom of God, Jesus answers that the kingdom does not come in the ways they were anticipating,[4] but it had in fact already come. Though some have argued that *entos hymōn* indicates that the kingdom of God is "within you," this option is extremely unlikely. Instead, Jesus rebukes the Pharisees for not understanding that the kingdom was already *among* them.[5] Despite their lack of faith, the works of Jesus were clear (e.g., the healing of the ten lepers in the previous pericope) and corresponded to the expectations of the messianic age expounded in Isaiah (Luke 7:20–23). The kingdom was not elsewhere or strictly yet to come; the key to understanding the kingdom was Jesus's presence among the Pharisees at that moment.[6]

It is important to recognize that this emphasis on the present reality of the kingdom, which comes through the person and work of Jesus, prominently includes Jesus's obedience. In contrast to the Pharisees who were looking ahead for something they thought was yet to come, Jesus proclaims, in light of his Spirit-wrought works and his own presence, that the kingdom of God had already arrived. Thus the kingdom does not *only* come by means of the cross; the kingdom was already a present reality through the obedience and work of the Son of God even before the crucial events in Jerusalem.

Righteous King and Righteous Kingdom

We further see that the obedience of Jesus is necessary for the establishment of the kingdom in the way that the Evangelists build on prophetic imagery, especially from Isaiah, to explain the nature of Jesus's kingdom work. The kingdom is often described in Isaianic terms, especially in relation to righteousness and justice. And these aspects of the kingdom are closely related to both king and servant in Isaiah. In light of this background, it seems that *righteousness* and *kingdom* are virtually synonymous in the message of Jesus.[7] One of the clearest Isaianic servant texts applied to Jesus is Isaiah 42:1–4 in Matthew 12:17–21. The questions one might ask of these texts are legion,[8] but

4. See Darrell L. Bock, *Luke*, 2 vols., BECNT (Grand Rapids: Baker Academic, 1994–96), 2:1412–14; Joel B. Green, *The Gospel of Luke*, NICNT (Grand Rapids: Eerdmans, 1997), 629.
5. Thus taking *entos hymōn* as "in your midst." Cf. BDAG, "ἐντός," 340, #1.
6. Bock (*Luke*, 2:1414–18) notes that *estin* is in an emphatic position; contra John Nolland, *Luke*, 3 vols., WBC 35A–C (Dallas: Word, 1989–93), 2:852.
7. Ridderbos, *Coming of the Kingdom*, 286.
8. Cf., e.g., Richard C. Beaton, *Isaiah's Christ in Matthew's Gospel*, SNTSMS 123 (Cambridge: Cambridge University Press, 2002).

it is clear that the servant in Isaiah 42 is crucial for understanding the work of Jesus in Matthew. This is not to say that "servant" is necessarily a title for Jesus in Matthew but it is to say that the task of the servant describes the work of Jesus as obedient Son of God.[9] Moreover, the citation of Isaiah 42 in Matthew 12 emphasizes the work of Jesus in proclaiming and establishing justice (12:18, 20). It is helpful to note that the term "justice" (*krisis*) used by Matthew correlates to *mišpāṭ* in the MT, and these respective terms (or their cognates) are often paired in both the MT and the LXX with "righteousness" (*ṣedeq, dikaiosynē*; Isa. 1:21, 26; 5:7, 16; 9:6[9:7 EVV]; 16:5; 32:1, 16; 33:5; 54:17; 56:1; 58:2; 59:9, 14; cf. 63:1 LXX). Thus, it is likely that the *justice* in view in Matthew 12:18–21 should be understood in tandem with *righteousness*, and therefore in light of Matthew's emphasis on righteousness throughout the Gospel. If we take this approach, then it is not difficult to see that the justice that Jesus brings must be understood in relation to his definitive embodiment of justice, just as we have seen with Jesus's embodiment of righteousness in Matthew.

Moreover, it is striking that justice and righteousness are often paired in Isaiah when speaking of the need for a Davidic king to rule justly and righteously (Isa. 9:6[9:7 EVV]; 16:5; 32:1, 16; cf. Jer. 33:15–16). These terms encapsulate what God desires for the people (e.g., Isa. 1:26; 33:15; 56:1) and reflect God's own character (Isa. 5:16; 33:5). Thus it is fitting for Matthew to relate the *justice* of the servant to the coming of the *kingdom* of God in Matthew 12. Jesus's kingdom work as Son of God is explained in terms of the righteousness and justice that are indicative not only of the servant but also the Davidic king.[10] Although Jesus often withdrew and behaved in a way that must have been surprising for those anticipating a powerful political ruler (cf. Matt. 12:15–16), already during his ministry he was instituting and carrying forth the justice of the kingdom of God that corresponds to the hopes of Isaiah, in which the king would rule justly and rightly. Additionally, Jesus's rule as Davidic king is for all nations (Isa. 42:1; Matt. 12:18, 21; cf. Isa. 11:9–10), which also corresponds to the work of the servant (Isa. 42:4, 6; 49:6).[11]

Another key in relating the work of the servant to the work of the kingdom is the role of the Holy Spirit, who anoints the servant (Matt. 12:18; cf. Isa. 42:1) and whose power reveals that the kingdom of God has come (Matt.

---

9. Ibid., 176.

10. Matthew does not explicitly identify Jesus as Son in 12:17–21, but *agapētos* in 12:18 most likely entails filial imagery (cf. 3:17; 17:5).

11. I will say more below about the gentile mission in Matthew, but certainly by the end of the Gospel (Matt. 28:18–20) the mission to the gentiles is clear.

12:28). It is as the one supremely anointed with the Spirit that the servant proclaims and leads forth justice.[12] This imagery evokes earlier portions of Isaiah in which the king would be anointed with the Holy Spirit and reign in righteousness and justice, bringing peace (Isa. 9:3–6 [9:4–7 EVV]; 11:1–10). Indeed, the way Matthew relates the kingdom, justice, and Holy Spirit should caution us from a reading of Isaiah that dichotomizes the first thirty-nine chapters from the last twenty-seven (or further between Isaiah 40–55 and 56–66).[13] Reading Isaiah as if it were two or three separate books is a modern phenomenon, and this approach would not have been shared by the Gospel writers. Therefore, it is important to consider ways in which earlier chapters of Isaiah provide a context for understanding later chapters.

When we read Isaiah as a unity, we can identify similarities between the work of the servant and the work of the king, both of whom are anointed with the Spirit. Indeed, the role of the servant overlaps significantly with the role of the king, which is consistent with the way that Matthew correlates these themes in relation to Jesus. Matthew's fulfillment quotations include texts not only from the so-called Servant Songs (Isa. 42:1–4; 53:4) but also from royal-messianic contexts in Isaiah 7–9 (Isa. 7:14 in Matt. 1:23 [cf. Isa. 8:10]; Isa. 9:1–2 in Matt. 4:12–16). Given the prominence of these royal expectations in the early church, Matthew would certainly have been aware of the wider context of these passages[14] and therefore was most likely consciously linking the Spirit's role in Jesus's kingdom ministry to the justice of the king in Isaiah. In addition, Jesus's identification as *Nazōraios* in Matthew 2:23 alludes on some level to the branch (*netser*) of Isaiah 11:1–5 on whom the Spirit rests and who judges the poor with righteousness.[15]

At this point it may be helpful to summarize how Matthew 12 sheds light on the importance of the life of Jesus for Matthew. First, through Jesus's ministry the kingdom has already come. Second, as the one supremely anointed with the Holy Spirit, Jesus's task of executing justice fits the prophetic hopes for the actions of the Davidic king. Third, the justice that Jesus effects in Matthew is an aspect of his obedient sonship. Matthew 12 portrays Jesus as the servant-like royal Son who executes justice and righteousness for the

---

12. Cf. David Seccombe, "Luke and Isaiah," *NTS* 27 (1981): 253. For justice as the theme of the first Servant Song, see J. Alec Motyer, *The Prophecy of Isaiah: An Introduction and Commentary* (Downers Grove, IL: IVP Academic, 1993), 318.

13. See, e.g., Brevard S. Childs, *Isaiah: A Commentary*, OTL (Louisville: Westminster John Knox, 2001), xi, 3.

14. C. H. Dodd, *According to the Scriptures: The Substructure of New Testament Theology* (London: Nisbet, 1952), 79–80.

15. See Brandon D. Crowe, "Fulfillment in Matthew as Eschatological Reversal," *WTJ* 75 (2013): 115–16.

benefit of his people and all the nations. In so doing, he brings eschatological salvation.[16]

The citation of Isaiah 53:4 in Matthew 8:17 also indicates the influence of the Isaianic servant in Matthew's presentation of Jesus's ministry. Significantly, Jesus fulfills the task of the suffering servant—namely, taking weaknesses and bearing diseases—in his ministry of healing. Thus, while we should certainly recognize the role of the suffering servant in relation to the cross of Jesus in Matthew (see, e.g., Matt. 26:28), we also must recognize that Jesus executes his task as suffering servant, and therefore bears the burden of sin, in the midst of his ministry.[17] This is similar to what I argued in chapter 4 for Luke, that Jesus's sufferings extended beyond the cross to his suffering throughout his life and ministry. We are therefore cautioned against dichotomizing the life of Jesus in a way that limits the suffering, and indeed sin-bearing capacity, of Jesus only to his death.[18]

Luke's Gospel also relates the anointing of Jesus with the Holy Spirit to Isaianic expectations. A key text in this regard is Isaiah 61:1–2, cited in Luke 4:18–21. This passage is part of Jesus's opening sermon in Nazareth, but this is by no means the first text that relates the Spirit to Jesus. Luke has already laid the royal framework for the relationship of the Holy Spirit to Jesus in his Gospel. For example, Jesus is proclaimed to be the son of David through the conception by the Holy Spirit (Luke 1:32–35), and the Spirit empowers Jesus for his filial, messianic obedience in the face of temptation (3:21–22; 4:1–12). It is therefore fitting that the Spirit is central to Jesus's explanation of his own ministry in the Nazareth sermon (4:14–30), which is programmatic for the rest of the Gospel. Indeed, one would not be wide of the mark to view Isaiah 61:1–4, which speaks of the Spirit-inspired announcement of good news manifested in various ways, as a summary of Jesus's message throughout Luke.[19]

---

16. See Herman Bavinck, *Reformed Dogmatics*, ed. John Bolt, trans. John Vriend, 4 vols. (Grand Rapids: Baker Academic, 2003–8), 2:223–24.

17. See John P. Meier, *The Vision of Matthew: Christ, Church, and Morality in the First Gospel* (1991; repr., Eugene, OR: Wipf & Stock, 2004), 69; G. K. Beale, *A New Testament Biblical Theology: The Unfolding of the Old Testament in the New* (Grand Rapids: Baker Academic, 2011), 906.

18. See, e.g., the concern of Mark Randall Jackson, "Atonement in Matthew's Gospel" (PhD diss., Southern Baptist Theological Seminary, 2011), 67–70. Additionally, Matthew most likely does not dichotomize sharply between sin and sickness. See W. D. Davies and Dale C. Allison Jr., *A Critical and Exegetical Commentary on the Gospel according to St. Matthew*, 3 vols., ICC (Edinburgh: T&T Clark, 1988–97), 2:38.

19. See further Seccombe, "Luke and Isaiah." Note also *aphesis* in the context of Luke's Jubilee imagery (cf. Lev. 25); cf. Green, *Luke*, 207; C. Kavin Rowe, *Early Narrative Christology: The Lord in the Gospel of Luke*, BZNW 139 (2006; repr., Grand Rapids: Baker Academic, 2009), 80–82.

Key for the present purposes is the role of the Spirit's anointing on Jesus. This is significant because the Spirit anoints Jesus not only for the preaching of the message as summarized by Isaiah 61 but also for the embodiment of that message. As Kavin Rowe states, "The fulfillment is thus tied to the person of Jesus even as it is tied to the coming events of his ministry."[20] The freedom or release (*aphesis*) in view in Isaiah 61 is wide-ranging in the sense that it entails not only economic relief but also the forgiveness of sins (cf. 11Q13 II, 6) and release from demonic oppression,[21] and the actualization of this release occurs throughout the life and ministry of Jesus.[22] Thus, for example, in the midst of his ministry Jesus already pronounces the forgiveness of sins (Luke 5:20, 24), which we should associate with the anointing of the Holy Spirit in light of 4:18–21.[23] Moreover, all these Isaianic themes speak of the way that the kingdom comes through the power of the Holy Spirit in Luke (4:43; 8:1; 9:2, 11; 10:9; 11:20; 17:20–21).

In Acts, Luke further emphasizes the role of the Holy Spirit in relation to Isaiah and Jesus's incarnate work. An important text in this regard is Acts 10:34–43, especially 10:36–38. The identification of Jesus of Nazareth as the one anointed with the Holy Spirit and power, who went around doing good, recalls Jesus's own explanation of his mission in Luke 4:14–30, and therefore recalls Isaiah 61.[24] It is in this light that we must consider what specifically Peter has in mind when he recounts the deeds of Jesus in Acts 10. In other words, the "good" that Jesus did in Galilee, Judea, and Jerusalem (10:38) refers to the wide-ranging description of Jesus's ministry in Isaiah 61:1–2, which summarizes all that Jesus does in Luke to accomplish salvation.

Further supporting the interpretation that Jesus was accomplishing salvation through his wide-ranging obedience is the recognition that the rare word for doing good (*euergeteō*)—strictly speaking, a *hapax legomenon* in the New Testament[25]—evokes the language of benefaction.[26] More specifically, and significant for the present argument, this terminology is elsewhere used

20. Rowe, *Early Narrative Christology*, 81. Note also the royal dimensions of 11Q13 II, 15–25.

21. See Christopher R. Bruno, "'Jesus Is Our Jubilee' . . . But How? The OT Background and Lukan Fulfillment of the Ethics of Jubilee," *JETS* 53 (2010): 97–99.

22. Rowe, *Early Narrative Christology*, 82.

23. Rowe (ibid., 104) argues that Jesus's authority to forgive sins in Luke is tied to Jesus's divine identity (cf. 5:21).

24. So, e.g., Eckhard Schnabel, *Acts*, ZECNT (Grand Rapids: Zondervan, 2012), 501; I. H. Marshall, "Acts," in *Commentary on the New Testament Use of the Old Testament*, ed. G. K. Beale and D. A. Carson (Grand Rapids: Baker Academic, 2007), 580.

25. Related noun forms are found in Luke 22:25; Acts 4:9; 1 Tim. 6:2.

26. BDAG, "εὐεργετέω," 405; Darrell L. Bock, *Acts*, BECNT (Grand Rapids: Baker Academic, 2007), 397–98.

to describe the salvific benefits of God. *Euergeteō* occurs three times in the Psalms (LXX), and in every case it appears in the context of God's saving actions (Pss. 12:6; 56:3; 114:7; cf. Wis. 3:5; *Diogn.* 10:6). Indeed, one of these psalms (Ps. 114 LXX [116 EVV])—which speaks of God doing good and saving the psalmist, delivering his soul from death—may provide part of the scriptural rationale for Jesus's resurrection in Acts 2:24.[27] For all these reasons, it seems eminently likely that Acts 10:36–38 provides additional substantiation that Jesus's actions during his ministry were means by which salvation was being accomplished.

All told, the message of Peter in Acts 10 emphasizes various aspects of the work of Jesus beyond the cross. To be sure, Peter's summary of the life of Jesus climaxes with his death and resurrection (10:39–41), but it includes more than only the final events of his life. Peter's emphasis on the entire work of Jesus as the anointed one fits with Scot McKnight's contention that we considered earlier, that Jesus's identification as the anointed one of Israel is an abbreviated way to evoke all that Jesus did in his ministry as Messiah.[28] Peter emphasizes that he and his apostolic colleagues were witnesses to *all* that Jesus did in Judea and Jerusalem, which includes more than just the death of Jesus.[29] Thus, when the apostles replaced Judas Iscariot, they looked not only for one who was an eyewitness to the death and resurrection of Jesus, but for one who was with Jesus beginning with the baptism of John (Acts 1:22–23). The replacement for Judas, who would spread the apostolic message, had to be an eyewitness of Jesus's ministry. We should therefore conclude, in light of the overarching narrative of Luke-Acts, that Jesus's actions before Jerusalem were vital for the accomplishment of salvation.

In addition, to relate these themes back to the kingdom, in Acts 10 Luke indicates that Jesus is Lord of all (10:36). This is clearly a confession of the supreme authority of Jesus, and in the context of a discussion with the Roman centurion Cornelius, it is hard not to imagine that Peter's claim should be viewed, at least to some degree, as a corrective to the exalted claims of Caesar.[30] In other words, in Acts 10:36–38 Luke again links the role of the

---

27. See the cross reference in *Novum Testamentum Graece*, 28th ed., edited by Barbara Aland et al. (Stuttgart: Deutsche Bibelgesellschaft, 2012).

28. Scot McKnight, *The King Jesus Gospel: The Original Good News Revisited* (Grand Rapids: Zondervan, 2011), 122.

29. The references to Judea (Acts 10:37) and the regions of Judea (10:39) most likely include all the regions where Jesus went around preaching and doing good. In other words, Galilee is likely in view as well. Cf. Bock, *Acts*, 398; Schnabel, *Acts*, 501; Craig S. Keener, *Acts: An Exegetical Commentary*, 4 vols. (Grand Rapids: Baker Academic, 2012–15), 2:1801.

30. Cf. C. Kavin Rowe, *World Upside Down: Reading Acts in the Graeco-Roman Age* (Oxford: Oxford University Press, 2009), 112.

servant who is powerfully anointed with the Holy Spirit with the kingdom authority of Jesus. This is not surprising since Isaianic texts are often invoked by the Evangelists to describe the kingdom. Moreover, it is consistent with the vision of Isaiah as a whole, which anticipates the kingdom coming by means of a Spirit-anointed king who would lead the people in righteousness for their benefit.[31]

Similarly, Luke connects servant and royal imagery by identifying Jesus as *pais* in several texts. The term *pais* is often translated simply as "child" or "servant," but it is also used in a robustly christological way. Israel is identified as the Lord's covenantal *pais* in Luke 1:54, as is David in Zechariah's Benedictus (Luke 1:69). As a child Jesus is also identified as *pais* (Luke 2:43), but Luke uses this term of Jesus more often in Acts. Again David is identified as God's anointed *pais* in Acts 4:25, in connection with Psalm 2, and Jesus himself is twice identified as the anointed *pais* just a few verses later (4:27, 30). The identification of Jesus as *pais* is consistent with Peter's speech in Acts 3 that also identifies Jesus twice as *pais*, which has royal and national connotations (3:13, 26).[32] In light of the Davidic and corporate connotations of *pais*, we should also note that the servant figure(s) in Isaiah is often identified in the LXX as *pais* (Isa. 42:1; 49:6; 52:13). As the anointed servant like David (Acts 3:13), Jesus is also the Holy and Righteous One who corresponds to the Isaianic servant (Acts 3:14) and will establish righteousness on the earth. These themes are held together in Luke's theology just as they are in Matthew. It would be anachronistic to posit that Matthew or Luke viewed the Psalms and Isaiah as having separate and discrete messages. Instead, these New Testament authors reveal a shared perspective that the Davidic king will rule in righteousness and establish the righteousness on earth that brings comfort, hope, and salvation to the people of God.

To emphasize further the present point, throughout the Gospels we find that the Isaianic age of justice, righteousness, and blessing is already becoming a reality during the ministry of Jesus. This is Jesus's point in response to the messengers sent from John the Baptist while John is in prison (Matt. 11:2–6 // Luke 7:18–23). In response to John's inquiry regarding whether Jesus is really the Messiah (*ho erchomenos*), Jesus replies with a litany of deeds he had already performed that indicate the age of blessing has already dawned. The blind see (Matt. 9:27–31; Luke 7:21; cf. Isa. 35:5; 42:18), the lame walk (Matt. 9:1–8 // Luke 5:17–26; cf. Isa. 35:6; Acts 3:6–8), the deaf hear (Matt.

---

31. See the texts noted above (e.g., Isa. 9:6 [9:7]; 11:1–4; 16:5; 32:1).

32. Larry W. Hurtado (*Lord Jesus Christ: Devotion to Jesus in Earliest Christianity* [Grand Rapids: Eerdmans, 2003], 191) observes that *pais* is "a specifically Israel-oriented and royal-messianic" identifier for Jesus.

9:32–33; cf. Isa. 29:18; 35:5; 42:18; Luke 11:14), the dead are raised (Matt. 9:18–26;[33] Luke 7:11–17; cf. Isa. 26:19), the gospel is preached to the poor (Matt. 5:3 // Luke 6:20; cf. Isa. 61:1–2), and even lepers are cleansed (Matt. 8:1–4 // Luke 5:12–16; cf. Isa. 33:24; 2 Kings 5). Therefore, Jesus concludes with the admonition "blessed is the one who does not take offense at me" (*makarios estin hos ean mē skandalisthē en emoi* [Matt. 11:6 // Luke 7:23]). Implicit in John's question is, if Jesus is bringing the age of salvation, where is the freedom for the captives and judgment on God's enemies (Isa. 61:1–2)? Jesus responds that John must not doubt that Jesus is indeed the Messiah who is already effecting the fullness of eschatological blessings set forth in Isaiah. The age of salvation had already dawned, though it had not yet been brought to consummation.

Thus, Isaiah anticipates a day of salvation in which curses will be overcome through the righteous servant-king.[34] Part and parcel of the new salvation is the coming of a better righteousness that reflects God's own character and prominently includes the forgiveness of sins (cf. Isa. 40:2; 43:25; 44:22).[35] The actions of God to save his needy people are thus manifestations of his righteousness (e.g., Isa. 1:27; 46:13; 51:5–8; 56:1; 59:16–17; 61:10; 62:1; 63:1). This righteousness comes either by means of the king (Isa. 9:6 [9:7 EVV]; 11:4; 16:5; 32:1, 16–17) or the servant (53:11), and benefits the people (51:6–8). Additionally, Isaiah speaks of the benefits of keeping God's commandments, which would lead to a righteousness for all time (48:18; 60:21).

Similarly, Jeremiah indicates a righteous Branch will be raised up as king, executing righteousness and justice in the land, which will lead to lasting security and blessing (Jer. 23:5–6). Indeed, the Branch will be called "the LORD is our righteousness," which recalls God's faithfulness to save his people. To be noted here as well is the relationship between the execution of righteousness and the security of blessings. The prophecy of Jeremiah 23 is reiterated in Jeremiah 33:15–16, which recounts the same promise. In addition, we should note the textual links between the refrain "Behold, the days are coming" in Jeremiah 33:14 (also found in 23:5) with the proximate occurrence of this phrase in Jeremiah, which prophesies a new covenant (31:31). The righteous Branch will thus execute righteousness and justice in the land, and thereby bring salvation for the people. Zechariah reveals a similar perspective in which the righteous king comes bringing salvation (Zech. 9:9; cf. 8:8). Zechariah 9:9 is

33. Luke 8:40–56 also recounts the raising of Jairus's daughter, but in Luke's narrative this comes after the messengers are sent from John the Baptist (7:18–23).

34. See also H. G. M. Williamson, *Variations on a Theme: King, Messiah and Servant in the Book of Isaiah* (Carlisle: Paternoster, 1998).

35. See, e.g., Bavinck, *Reformed Dogmatics*, 2:223–24.

cited explicitly in Matthew's Gospel (Matt. 21:5; cf. John 12:15), revealing the perspective that Jesus's actions bring salvation.[36] Key again is the relationship between righteousness and salvation, and the corresponding identification of Jesus as the righteous king.

In sum, in several Old Testament passages we find prophetic hopes in which God's righteousness and salvation would be revealed and executed through the righteous king. This was necessary to bring about security and peace, given the covenant people's perennial lack of covenant fidelity (e.g., Isa. 1:21; 5:7; 46:12; 58:2; 59:14; Jer. 9:24; Hosea 10:2; Amos 5; cf. Micah 6:8).

We find similar expectations in noncanonical texts. In *Psalms of Solomon* 17, which was likely written close to the time of the New Testament, we read of a righteous, godly king in opposition to the conquering gentile (Pompey?).[37] The *Psalms of Solomon* anticipate a king (17:21) who will lead in righteousness (17:26) and who will not tolerate unrighteousness (17:27). There will be no unrighteousness among the people all his days (17:32), and the king himself is, remarkably, described as sinless (17:36). The king (= "Lord Messiah") will be powerful in the Holy Spirit, characterized by wisdom, strength, and righteousness (17:37). No one will be able to stand against the beautiful king of Israel (17:39–42). The similarities between the messianic king in *Psalms of Solomon* and the prophetic texts discussed above are not difficult to see. What is perhaps most striking in *Psalms of Solomon* is the way in which the king is described as *completely* righteous, entirely free from sin (17:36). In addition to the *Psalms of Solomon*, other texts speak of a righteous, eschatological figure (*1 En.* 38:2; 53:6; cf. 92:3–4),[38] and in numerous texts we encounter the eschatological hope that the people will be righteous (e.g., *1 En.* 10:16–21; *Jub.* 1:23–24; *Pss. Sol.* 17:26, 32, 40–41; 18:4–9).[39]

The Kingdom of the Last Adam

The point of this survey is to illustrate the biblical and Jewish hopes of God's coming, righteous salvation that would lead to righteousness among God's people. As righteous king and servant, Jesus embodies God's saving righteousness and leads his people in righteousness. The Evangelists' emphasis on the obedience of Jesus underscores that Jesus, through his actions,

36. To be sure, in Matt. 21 the actions are specifically those of the passion. Yet the actions of Jesus's final week are ultimately of a piece with his obedience as a whole.

37. See R. B. Wright, introduction to "*Psalms of Solomon*," in *OTP*, 2:640–41.

38. Cf. Hurtado, *Lord Jesus Christ*, 189–90.

39. For the logic of *Pss. Sol.* 18, see Brandon D. Crowe, *The Obedient Son: Deuteronomy and Christology in the Gospel of Matthew*, BZNW 188 (Berlin: Walter de Gruyter, 2012), 142–43.

accomplishes the mighty righteousness of the Lord to save. The reign of the Messiah is linked in Isaiah and the prophets to a kingdom that will never end, and significantly, this kingdom is related to the full establishment of righteousness. At this point we need to broaden our horizons to understand the protological underpinnings for this eschatological hope of everlasting righteousness. Again it is relevant to consider the role of Adam. Earlier (chap. 3) I argued that the promise held out to Adam was fullness of life in the original administration God gave to him. Adam did not persist in righteousness (cf. Eccles. 7:29) and therefore experienced the curse of death instead of the blessing of life. This begins the recurring principle throughout Scripture that obedience to God's commands is wed to blessing and life, whereas cursing and death derive from disobedience.[40]

Thus, the everlasting rule of the Messiah, which is realized in Jesus, builds on a foundational Adamic protology. The kingship of Jesus in the Gospels, which corresponds to the early Jewish anticipations of an everlasting kingship (cf. Isa. 9:6 [9:7 EVV]), portrays Jesus as a new and better Adam. Thus, for example, in *Jubilees* 4:30 Adam is said to have lived for only 930 years—or seventy years less than the ideal of one thousand—because of his sin.[41] Additionally, Adam was not only viewed as a priestly figure due to his working (*'ābad*) and protecting (*šāmar*) the garden (Gen. 2:15), but also as a royal figure as one made in the image of God, the great King (Gen. 1:26–28; 5:1). Jewish texts consistently identify Adam as kinglike,[42] yet Adam did not bring the lasting kingdom, and sin cut his time short (*Jub.* 4:30; *4 Ezra* 7:118–19). Likewise, in Revelation 20:4–6 Adamic imagery may be in view in the thousand-year reign of Christ.[43] In contrast to Adam, Jesus established the eschatological kingdom, and was free from the sin that hindered Adam's reign. The messianic kingdom of righteousness has no end.[44]

In light of these expectations, a key move in the Gospels is the way the obedience of Jesus as messianic Son and servant is the means by which the righteous kingdom is established (e.g., Matt. 12:17–32). The allusions throughout the Gospels to Isaiah 53:11 indicate that the actions of the servant—which as

40. The texts here are too numerous to list, but some include Lev. 18:5; Deut. 6:1–3; 26–28; Ps. 19:7–11; Prov. 6:23; 19:16; 28:13.

41. See here esp. Charles E. Hill, *Regnum Caelorum: Patterns of Millennial Thought in Early Christianity*, 2nd ed. (Grand Rapids: Eerdmans, 2001), 91–92; G. K. Beale, *The Book of Revelation*, NIGTC (Grand Rapids: Eerdmans, 1999), 1018–19.

42. See Beale, *New Testament Biblical Theology*, 30–46.

43. Adamic imagery may also be in view in the binding of the ancient serpent in Rev. 20:2. See also Beale, *Book of Revelation*, 985, 1018.

44. For texts that speak of the righteousness of the coming age, see Richard J. Bauckham, *Jude, 2 Peter*, WBC 50 (Waco: Word, 1983), 326.

we have seen include more than Jesus's death—constitute the people as righteous. The righteousness of Jesus is, in other words, a *vicarious* righteousness. Jesus fulfills the role of the righteous king and servant (and thereby embodies national Israel), and as the representative of his people also overcomes their perennial lack of obedience.[45] Thus, unlike the covenant people of Israel who were consistently (and tragically) identified as disobedient children—Isaiah describes them as dumber than an ox or a donkey who did not know the manger (Isa. 1:3)—Jesus as the last Adam and Son of God is fully obedient, even from his earliest days in the manger (Luke 1:35; 2:1–14).

One further possibility should be suggested at this point. If Jesus as king is the righteous one in a representative way, can we say more about *how* this can be a reality? To be sure, Jesus as the anointed one is chosen by God to represent the people, and this at one level explains his representative capacity. But in line with this, there is also an Adamic reason. Just as the reality of the first man's sin had negative consequences for his offspring, so does the reality of the last Adam's righteousness have positive consequences for his people. This construal, of course, recalls Paul's explanation of the significance of the two-Adam schema (Rom. 5:12–21; 1 Cor. 15:42–49). However, in light of the royal-Adamic connections we have observed in the Gospels, and in light of the biblical-theological approach of the present volume, such parallels are not out of bounds. The Evangelists nowhere explain the significance of the two-Adam schema in quite the same way that Paul does, but the Gospel narratives rarely expound matters in the manner of the epistles. Therefore, we must not assume the Evangelists' ignorance of Paul's teaching on the matter (especially for Luke), since (at least most of) Paul's writings preceded the writing of the Gospels.

To put the matter more starkly: Jesus's righteousness benefits his people because of his unique status as the last Adam, preserved from birth by the holiness of the Spirit.[46] As one who was uniquely born, Jesus can uniquely

---

45. On the king as a representative for the people, see Gerald A. Cooke, "The Israelite King as Son of God," *ZAW* 73 (1961): 202–25; Joachim Bieneck, *Sohn Gottes als Christusbezeichnung der Synoptiker*, ATANT 21 (Zürich: Zwingli, 1951), 58–68; cf. N. T. Wright, *Jesus and the Victory of God*, COQG 2 (Minneapolis: Fortress, 1996), 477, 595.

46. Recently, Andrew T. Lincoln (*Born of a Virgin? Reconceiving Jesus in the Bible, Tradition, and Theology* [Grand Rapids: Eerdmans, 2013]) has argued that we need to reassess the virginal conception of Jesus and suggests that the creeds on this point intend to emphasize the full humanity of Jesus rather than a virginal conception per se. However, Lincoln's view is not persuasive. See my review in *New Horizons* 35, no. 6 (2014): 22. Others, such as Mark Strauss (*Four Portraits, One Jesus: A Survey of Jesus and the Gospels* [Grand Rapids: Zondervan, 2007], 415), suggest that the virginal conception has little to do with the *sinlessness* of Jesus. However, the emphasis on holiness in Luke 1:35 suggests that Jesus's sinlessness and his virginal conception are related concepts. Traditionally the virginal conception has often been closely related to the

serve as a righteous representative, inaugurating and establishing an everlasting kingdom of righteousness, thereby overcoming the problem of sin and death introduced by Adam.

Kingdom, Righteousness, and the Gospel

The above survey leads us to speak of some ways in which the kingdom relates to the gospel. We truncate the good news if we do not consider the positive aspects of righteousness that are central to the message of the kingdom. This is the case for several reasons.

First, the gospel is the message of the kingdom (e.g., Mark 1:14–15).[47] Second, the message of the kingdom is intricately related to the righteousness that defines the kingdom.[48] That is, the kingdom of God is a kingdom of righteousness, which demands repentance (Matt. 4:17; Mark 1:15). Third, the righteousness of the kingdom is realized by Jesus, the messianic king and last Adam, through his lifelong obedience. Significantly, it is because of the righteousness of the king that the benefits of the kingdom accrue to the people of God. Therefore, to speak most fully of the good news of the kingdom is to emphasize the obedience of the king who embodies the will of God and makes the blessings of the kingdom possible. To be sure, the death of Jesus is of vital importance in this regard, but the message of the kingdom was already being preached during the ministry of Jesus. This was possible because Jesus was inaugurating the kingdom even before his death and resurrection.

Binding the Strong Man

One of the ways we see Jesus accomplishing salvation in his life is through the powerful work of the Holy Spirit that evinces a clash of kingdoms. When Jesus engages in spiritual conflict, he does so through the power of the Holy Spirit. Such a clash is evident in the binding of the strong man (Matt. 12:22–37 // Mark 3:22–30; cf. Luke 11:14–23), which further reveals how Jesus accomplishes salvation even before the cross. In what follows I will argue that Jesus, as the stronger one, casts out Satan, binds demons, and therefore brings salvation. Additionally, this binding must be viewed in tandem with Jesus's incarnate obedience.

---

sinlessness of Jesus. See, e.g., Turretin, *Inst.* 13.11.3; Bavinck, *Reformed Dogmatics*, 3:286–95; J. Gresham Machen, *The Virgin Birth of Christ* (1930; repr., Grand Rapids: Baker, 1985), 395.

47. See also Jonathan T. Pennington, *Reading the Gospels Wisely: A Narrative and Theological Introduction* (Grand Rapids: Baker Academic, 2012), 11; McKnight, *King Jesus Gospel*.

48. Ridderbos, *Coming of the Kingdom*, 286.

Binding the Strong Man in Mark

We begin in Mark's Gospel (3:22–30), where the binding of the strong man plays a crucial role in the unfolding of the narrative. This has recently been argued by Elizabeth Shively, who observes that Mark 3:22–30 is one of two places in Mark where Jesus identifies the purpose of his mission (cf. 10:45).[49] Though we have seen some other texts that may also fit this description (e.g., 1:38), Shively's observation is instructive. To understand Jesus's mission in Mark, therefore, we must wrestle with the significance of the binding of the strong man. This passage should be viewed in light of the building conflict in Mark that is moving quickly toward the passion (cf. 3:6). The binding of the strong man (3:27) forms part of the center of a Markan intercalation (3:22–30), bracketed on either side by the misunderstanding of Jesus's family (3:20–21, 31–35).[50] The conflict that Jesus encounters comes from both the earthly and the cosmic realms,[51] and Jesus's parable of the strong man explains the opposition. As Joel Marcus states, Jesus explains "the ineradicable division and fierce enmity between him and the demonic forces that hold the human race in thrall and blind it to its true good."[52] Jesus's explanation of the conflict should be viewed in light of Jesus's works thus far in Mark 1–3. Additionally, the Beelzebul controversy in Mark 3:22–30 forms a frame with the temptation of Jesus (1:12–13); in both accounts the key characters are Jesus, Satan, and the Holy Spirit.[53] Thus, we do well to understand the binding of the strong man in light of Jesus's obedience in the face of temptation. As Ernest Best rightly observes, "It was in the Temptation that the strong man met the stronger."[54] More specifically, Jesus's victory in the temptation through the power of the Holy Spirit corresponds to the initial binding of the strong man that Jesus speaks of in 3:27.

Before arguing for this position further, it will be helpful to survey the details in Mark's account. When accused of casting out demons by the prince of demons (Beelzebul = Satan),[55] Jesus says that if he were empowered by

---

49. Elizabeth E. Shively, *Apocalyptic Imagination in the Gospel of Mark: The Literary and Theological Role of Mark 3:22–30*, BZNW 189 (Berlin: Walter de Gruyter, 2012), 1–2.

50. See James R. Edwards, *The Gospel according to Mark*, PNTC (Grand Rapids: Eerdmans, 2002), 11, 117–26. Joel Marcus (*Mark 1–8: A New Translation with Introduction and Commentary*, AB 27 [New York: Doubleday, 2000], 278–79) argues more specifically that the parable of the strong man in 3:27 is the middle of a chiastic structure of 3:20–35.

51. Shively, *Apocalyptic Imagination*, 26, 48–49.

52. Marcus, *Mark 1–8*, 279.

53. Shively, *Apocalyptic Imagination*, 43.

54. Ernest Best, *The Temptation and the Passion: The Markan Soteriology*, 2nd ed., SNTSMS 2 (Cambridge: Cambridge University Press, 1990), 12.

55. See the discussions in Shively, *Apocalyptic Imagination*, 57–62; Marcus, *Mark 1–8*, 272.

Satan, his actions would be self-defeating and Satan's kingdom could not stand. Jesus therefore denies the accusation that he cast out demons through the power of Satan. Instead, Jesus indicates that it is necessary first to bind the strong man, and then his house (= kingdom [3:24–25]) can be plundered. In all likelihood we can take the strong man to be Satan, whom Jesus, as the stronger one, binds (cf. John's prophecy in 1:7). The might of Jesus over Satan likely corresponds to the obedience of Jesus in the temptation, which serves as the complementary section of the literary frame. Jesus's unfettered presence with the wild animals in Mark 1:13 implies a fettering of the foremost foe. The narrative structure of Mark therefore suggests that the *initial* binding of the strong man has already occurred before 3:22–30—namely, in Jesus's obedience in the face of temptation—and now the strong man's house is being plundered. This plundering likely correlates to the exorcisms of Jesus and indeed *all* that Jesus has already done from the temptation to this point in the narrative (exorcisms; healings of the leper, the sick, the fever-stricken, the lame; Sabbath healing; etc.).

Further linking this account to the temptation is the keyword *ekballō*. Commentators regularly note the force of Mark's use of this term for the Holy Spirit driving Jesus into the wilderness to be tempted, and we noted earlier that this term also recalls Adam's expulsion from the garden (Gen. 3:24; cf. *anagō* in Matt. 4:1; *agō* in Luke 4:1). *Ekballō* also occupies a key role in the lead-up to the parable of the binding of the strong man. In Mark 3:22–23 *ekballō* is employed to narrate the powerful exorcisms of Jesus, and this term is again linked with the Holy Spirit, as Jesus concludes this controversy with a warning against blaspheming the Holy Spirit. Though much ink has been spilled over the "eternal sin" (Mark 3:29), the linkage between the power of the Holy Spirit and the powerful actions of Jesus is fairly clear: to claim that Jesus's works were wrought by the power of Satan is to deny that they were works of the Holy Spirit. Therefore, the plundering of Satan's kingdom comes through Jesus's Spirit-empowered deeds, including his Spirit-empowered obedience in the wilderness. To be clear, this does not mean that Satan's kingdom had been completely eclipsed at the beginning of Mark's Gospel.[56] Indeed, Jesus's statements in 3:24–26 assume that Satan's kingdom has not yet met its final end. However, in contrast to the present

---

56. Best (*Temptation and the Passion*, 15) considers the temptation the decisive first act of Jesus's ministry, and the subsequent exorcisms are a "mopping up" project of isolated units of Satan's host. One can agree with the spirit of Best's comment—that Satan is decisively defeated from the beginning of Jesus's ministry—but Jesus's initial victory is not yet the final victory, which comes through Jesus's death and resurrection (cf. Mark 8:33). See also Shively, *Apocalyptic Imagination*, 75–76.

reign of Satan's kingdom, Jesus indicated that the despoiling of the strong man's house was already taking place because of the initial binding of the strong man. The obedient work of Jesus incarnate, even before the cross, overcomes the kingdom of Satan.[57]

In sum, the obedience of Jesus in the temptation is an epochally significant event that marks the initial binding of the strong man, which leads to the plundering of his kingdom.[58] To commandeer Oscar Cullmann's famous D-day analogy, we could say that the initial "invasion" that leads to Jesus's victory is his obedience in the temptation, and throughout his ministry—climaxing in his death and resurrection—Jesus continues to advance the kingdom.[59] Thus throughout Mark, though additional exorcisms and healings are necessary, Jesus's authority is never in question; the demons regularly acknowledge that they are subject to Jesus as the stronger one (1:24, 34; 3:11; 5:7–13; cf. 3:15; 6:7). And as the correlations with the temptation suggest, the victory of Jesus over the demonic realm is characterized not by usurping authority but by humble obedience.[60]

Further underscoring the obedience of Jesus in relation to the binding of the strong man is the likely Adamic imagery bound up with this pericope. We see this, first of all, in the verbal parallels between the binding of the strong man and the temptation account noted above. In chapter 2, I argued, following many others, that Jesus's temptation in Mark is portrayed in Adamic terms. If the temptation and binding of the strong man in Mark are indeed to be viewed as two aspects of a frame, then there is a prima facie likelihood that Adamic imagery is also in view in Mark 3:22–30. Second, and even more significant, the victory of Jesus in 3:22–30 is Jesus's victory over Satan (as it also is in 1:12–13), which stands in contrast to Adam's failure to defeat the

---

57. See also Ridderbos, *Coming of the Kingdom*, 61–63, 106–13; Sinclair B. Ferguson, *The Holy Spirit*, CCT (Downers Grove, IL: InterVarsity, 1996), 50–51. Yet we also need to leave room for the suffering of Jesus in his obedience throughout his life and ministry (as noted in chap. 3), and there may be a sense in which "the demands became more extensive and exacting as [Jesus] went on to the climactic demand [of death]." See John Murray, "The Obedience of Christ," in *Collected Writings of John Murray*, 4 vols. (Edinburgh: Banner of Truth, 1976–82), 2:153, noting Heb. 5:8.

58. See also Geerhardus Vos, *Biblical Theology: Old and New Testaments* (1948; repr., Edinburgh: Banner of Truth, 1975), 330–31; Best, *Temptation and the Passion*, 13, 15, 106.

59. See Oscar Cullmann, *Christ and Time: The Primitive Christian Conception of Time and History*, trans. Floyd V. Filson, rev. ed. (Philadelphia: Westminster, 1964), 84–87, 141–46. Cullmann emphasizes the cross and resurrection as the "*already concluded decisive battle*" (ibid., 84, emphasis original). To be sure, Jesus's death and resurrection are decisive, and yet Jesus's victory in the temptation is also a decisive moment for the opposition encountered throughout Mark.

60. Ridderbos, *Coming of the Kingdom*, 61.

deceiver in the garden.[61] When Adam disobeyed God's command, he forfeited the original state of righteousness. As last Adam, Jesus obeys in the face of temptation (1:12–13), exercising obedient dominion over the entrenched kingdom of Satan.[62] This is similar to *Testament of Levi*, where the eschatological priest would overcome the sin of Adam, reopen paradise, and bind Beliar (*T. Levi* 18:12).[63] Third, and closely related to the preceding point, in the binding of Satan we may have royal connotations associated with Adam. Instead of Adam as God's vice-regent ruling over the world, the parable of the strong man indicates that Satan's kingdom held sway. Thus it was fitting for Jesus, as Son of Man, to exercise the authority and dominion that Adam did not by binding the devil.[64] Fourth, the role of the Holy Spirit may also bespeak Adamic imagery, since in both the temptation and the binding Jesus is empowered by the Holy Spirit, and the creation of Adam is closely associated with the Spirit (Gen. 2:7).[65]

Fifth, viewing the binding of the strong man as last-Adam imagery fits well with the history of interpretation. Irenaeus closely linked the power of Jesus in the binding of the strong man with Jesus's obedience in the face of temptation, which he related to Jesus's role as recapitulation of Adam (*Haer.* 3.18.6–7; 3.23.1; 5.21.1, 3; 5.22.1; cf. 3.8.2; 3.23.7; 4.33.4).[66] Calvin, commenting on this parable, also relates the binding to the sin of Adam, stating that Satan held sway "because Adam, having withdrawn from the dominion of God, has subjected all his posterity to this foreign sway."[67] The victory of Christ as last Adam releases his people from the tyranny of Satan.

Jesus's Obedient Authority in Matthew and Luke

Additional textual links between the binding of the strong man and Jesus's obedience, along with other Adamic resonances, are found in Matthew. Matthew's account of the binding of the strong man (Matt. 12:22–37) is quite

---

61. As noted in chap. 2, in the first century it was widely accepted that the serpent was an embodiment of Satan.

62. See also Eric Grässer, "ΚΑΙ ΗΝ ΜΕΤΑ ΤΩΝ ΘΗΡΙΩΝ (Mk 1,13b): Ansätze einer theologischen Tierschutzethik," in *Studien zum Text und zur Ethik des Neuen Testaments: Festschrift zum 80. Geburtstag von Heinrich Greeven*, ed. Wolfgang Schrage, BZNW 47 (Berlin: Walter de Gruyter, 1986), 154.

63. See also *T. Mos.* 10:1; *T. Sol.* 15:10–12; 22:20.

64. See Joel Marcus, "Son of Man as Son of Adam," *RB* 110 (2003): 59–60; McCartney, "*Ecce Homo*," 9–10; Beale, *New Testament Biblical Theology*, 420.

65. See the discussion of Luke 1:35 in chap. 2.

66. See Agnès Bastit, "L'apologue synoptique du 'Fort ligoté' (Mt 12,29 et par.) dans la théologie d'Irenée et la première littérature chrétienne," *LTP* 70 (2014): 299–314.

67. John Calvin, *Commentary on a Harmony of the Evangelists, Matthew, Mark, and Luke*, trans. and ed. William Pringle, 3 vols. (repr., Grand Rapids: Baker, 2003), 2:72.

similar to Mark's and is linked narratively to the Spirit-anointed servant (12:17–21) and the kingdom of God (12:28). Additionally, Matthew explicitly relates the binding of the strong man to Jesus's identity as the Son of Man (12:32), which, though implicit in Mark, underscores the Adamic connections with the coming of the kingdom in Matthew. Matthew makes more explicit something else that is implicit in Mark's narrative, namely, the casting out of the demonic spirits by the Spirit of God (12:28). The Spirit who enables Jesus to cast out demons in Matthew is the same Spirit who empowers Jesus's obedience.

Another distinctive of Matthew in relation to Mark is the expanded space devoted to the temptation account. Whereas the temptation is presented with an economy of words in Mark 1:12–13, Matthew (along with Luke) gives a threefold structure of the temptation, which recalls both Israel and Adam. In all three Synoptics, the temptation is the first action of Jesus after being baptized and anointed as Messiah; before Jesus heals any diseases or casts out any demons, he first overcomes Satan's opposition. After this initial victory, Jesus begins to demonstrate his victory over Satan's realm in various ways. As with Mark, these victories are likely the plundering of the strong man's house, which follows the binding of the strong man (Matt. 12:29). Additionally, the emphasis in Matthew on the kingdom of God that comes by the casting out of demons (12:28) indicates a kingdom conflict between Satan and Jesus, and the kingdom is also in view in the third temptation (4:8–10). Only after this initial victory does Jesus proclaim the imminence of the coming of the kingdom (4:17).[68] From this we should conclude that the kingdom comes after the initial victory over Satan, which Jesus later identifies as the binding of the strong man (12:28–29).[69] In this light, when the obedient Jesus commanded Satan to be gone (*hypage* [4:10]), the devil did indeed flee (*aphiēsin*) from him (4:11).

Before considering Luke's contribution, one further aspect of Matthew's distinctive contribution to the binding of the strong man is noteworthy. In Matthew 12 royal and servant imagery are combined, particularly from Isaiah, with regard to the mission of Jesus. It is therefore striking that the servant's humility and lack of querulousness is indicative of the authority of the one who

---

68. See similarly Adolf Schlatter, *Der Evangelist Matthäus: Seine Sprache, sein Ziel, seine Selbständigkeit* (Stuttgart: Calwer, 1929), 407.

69. Others who suggest that Matthew's temptation narrative may be the initial binding of the strong man include Craig S. Keener, *The Gospel of Matthew: A Socio-Rhetorical Commentary* (Grand Rapids: Eerdmans, 2009), 365; John Nolland, *The Gospel of Matthew*, NIGTC (Grand Rapids: Eerdmans, 2005), 502; Davies and Allison, *Matthew*, 2:343; Joachim Jeremias, *The Parables of Jesus*, trans. S. H. Hooke, 2nd ed. (New York: Scribner, 1972), 122; Beale, *New Testament Biblical Theology*, 421.

binds the strong man. In other words, Jesus is at once the obedient Messiah who cares for the weakest among God's people (12:19–21), and the stronger one who binds the devil in conjunction with the coming of God's powerful kingdom (12:28–29). The close proximity of these themes underscores that it is through the humiliation and obedience of the messianic king that the kingdom comes; thus we again see that the binding of the strong man and the coming of salvation are linked to the holiness and character of Jesus. The presence of the kingdom already in Matthew 12 (cf. 12:28) is a result of the already-existing state of Jesus in his humiliation and selfless dedication to the messianic task of suffering.

Luke's Gospel includes additional connections between Jesus's obedience and the overcoming of Satan. Although Luke does not explicitly mention the binding of the strong man, he does include an account that is at least conceptually parallel. In fact, Luke's Gospel may include even stronger language for Jesus's victory over Satan. In place of the binding of the strong man, Luke 11:21–23 mentions a strong man who is fully armed (*kathōplismenos*), and the stronger man who gains victory (*nikēsē*) over this armed man takes away his armor (*tēn panoplian autou airei*) and divides his spoil (*ta skyla autou diadidōsin*). As in Matthew and Mark, this parable is best taken as a metaphor for the work of Christ: Satan is portrayed in warrior-like fashion, but he is overcome by Jesus, the stronger man.

Another uniquely Lukan contribution to this discussion is found in Luke 10:18–19, where Jesus states that he saw (*etheōroun*) Satan fall (*pesonta*) like lightning from heaven.[70] Historically, many have viewed this text, in association with Isaiah 14:12, as referring to a prehistoric fall of Satan from heaven.[71] Though one cannot completely dismiss this possibility, the vision of Jesus in the context of the present authority of Jesus over Satan (10:17–20; cf. 11:21–23) suggests a more proximate reason for Satan's downfall.[72] If so, this

70. Though the imperfect verbal form is used here (*etheōroun*), which could emphasize an iterative or imperfective aspect (so apparently Norval Geldenhuys, *Commentary on the Gospel of Luke*, NICNT [Grand Rapids: Eerdmans, 1951], 305n22), one should be cautious since *theōreō* does not generally appear in the aorist. See, e.g., BDF §101; I. H. Marshall, *The Gospel of Luke*, NIGTC (Grand Rapids: Eerdmans, 1978), 428; Nolland, *Luke*, 2:564. Additionally, the *falling* refers to Satan, not lightning.

71. See Simon J. Gathercole, "Jesus' Eschatological Vision of the Fall of Satan: Luke 10.18 Reconsidered," *ZNW* 94 (2003): 144–48.

72. See also Samuel Vollenweider, "'Ich sah den Satan wie einen Blitz vom Himmel fallen' (Lk 10,18)," *ZNW* 79 (1988): 196–98; George Eldon Ladd, *The Presence of the Future: The Eschatology of Biblical Realism* (Grand Rapids: Eerdmans, 1974), 157; Anthony A. Hoekema, *The Bible and the Future* (Grand Rapids: Eerdmans, 1994), 46. Others suggest a vision of a future event yet to occur. See Gathercole, "Jesus' Eschatological Vision," 153–63; Susan R. Garrett, *The Demise of the Devil: Magic and the Demonic in Luke's Writings* (Minneapolis:

would provide additional corroboration for interpreting the victory of Jesus as already inaugurated during his ministry, commencing particularly with Jesus's obedience in the temptation (4:1–13).[73] Again it is significant that, as important as the death and resurrection of Christ are for the final defeat of Satan, Jesus already speaks of the downfall of Satan before these climactic events. In other words, the obedient work of Jesus during his life is a vital part of what brings the ultimate downfall of Satan.

The victory of Jesus over Satan during his ministry also explains the authority Jesus gives to his disciples over snakes and scorpions already during his ministry (Luke 10:17–20). Of course, when Jesus gives his disciples this authority, he is not simply granting zoological authority over reptiles and arachnids, but he is granting them spiritual authority—serpents and scorpions, often found in the wilderness, represent the curse of sin and the authority of Satan, the ancient serpent (Rev. 9:1–11; 12:1–17; 20:2). Such authority correlates well to the *Testaments of the Twelve Patriarchs*, where we read that in the messianic age the sin of Adam will be overcome, Beliar will be bound, and authority will be given to trample on evil spirits (*T. Sim.* 6:6; *T. Levi* 18:12).[74]

The spiritual authority given to the disciples also evokes Psalm 91, which is a key text in Luke's temptation account, since it is from Psalm 91 that Satan presents Jesus with his climactic, final test.[75] Indeed, Psalm 91 is the only biblical text quoted by Satan in the exchange. In Psalm 91 the foot of the one who dwells in the shadow of the Almighty is protected (91:12), and authority is given for him to tread on the lion and serpent (91:13; cf. Deut. 8:15). This is the authority that Jesus, as obedient Son and last Adam, manifests throughout Luke. Jesus refuses to put God to the test (Luke 4:9–13) and thereby overcomes the devil and establishes his authority as the stronger man (11:21–23), likewise granting similar authority to his disciples.

The authority of Jesus and his disciples over the serpent(s) may also evoke the promise in Genesis 3:15 that the seed of the woman would crush the head of the serpent.[76] It is thus possible that Psalm 91:13 (trampling the serpent underfoot) is also an allusion to crushing the head of the serpent in Genesis

Fortress, 1989), 49–54. However, even if Jesus speaks here of a future fall of Satan, the disciples' authority over snakes and scorpions during Jesus's ministry seems to indicate that the effects of Satan's future fall were already beginning to be realized before his end.

73. See also Geldenhuys, *Gospel of Luke*, 302; Garrett, *Demise of the Devil*, 42–43 and 131n25, citing Justin, *Dial.* 125; Beale, *New Testament Biblical Theology*, 421.

74. See also Beale, *New Testament Biblical Theology*, 422.

75. See the earlier discussion in chap. 3.

76. Bock, *Luke*, 2:1008; cf. David B. Sloan, "Interpreting Scripture with Satan? The Devil's Use of Scripture in Luke's Temptation Narrative," *TynBul* 66 (2015): 247–48.

3:15.[77] Regardless of one's view on this matter, we are on firm ground to see Adamic imagery in Luke. Luke's temptation is tightly connected to an Adamic genealogy (3:23–4:13), and we have seen other Adamic resonances in Luke (e.g., role of Holy Spirit, Son of Man, bent-over woman, paradise). The authority of Jesus as the last Adam over Satan, along with the authority he grants to his disciples to tread on serpents and scorpions, is likely the inauguration of the crushing of the head of the serpent (cf. Rom. 16:20). Thus, "the disciples are reasserting humanity's vice-regent role in creation."[78] Jesus's obedience during the course of his life already begins to bring the downfall of Satan, which underscores the necessity of Jesus's life for the accomplishment of salvation.

Messianic Victory and Salvation

In the preceding discussion I observed that the binding of the strong man is tantamount to the accomplishment of salvation. I would like to suggest several ways this may be the case, though these should not be viewed as the final word on the subject. Instead, I am attempting to tease out more explicitly what may often be left implicit in discussions of the binding of the strong man in conjunction with what Jesus accomplishes during his ministry.

First, the binding of the strong man is closely associated with the authority of Jesus to forgive sins.[79] We see this especially in Mark 3:22–30 where the authority of Jesus over the strong man (3:27) appears to stand in a causal relationship to the promise that all sins and blasphemies will be forgiven (3:28). In other words, *because* Jesus binds the strong man, *therefore* every sin and blasphemy will be forgiven (excepting the qualification in 3:29). Or, as Joel Marcus puts it, "the promise of forgiveness of sins . . . can be taken as one of the fruits of the Stronger One's victory over Satan."[80] Since Jesus initially defeated Satan in the temptation (1:12–13 with 3:22–30), Jesus already exercised authority to forgive sins during his ministry (2:1–12). We find a similar relationship in Matthew between the initial victory over Satan and Jesus's authority during his ministry (Matt. 4:1–11; 9:1–8; cf. 1:21). Though the logical relationship between the binding of the strong man and the forgiveness of sins in Matthew 12 is arguably not as clear as it is in Mark 3, we nevertheless find

77. Beale, *New Testament Biblical Theology*, 420.

78. Bock, *Luke*, 2:1008.

79. On which see Daniel Johansson, "Jesus and God in the Gospel of Mark: Unity and Distinction" (PhD diss., University of Edinburgh, 2011), 41–58; Johansson, "'Who Can Forgive Sins but God Alone?' Human and Angelic Agents, and Divine Forgiveness in Early Judaism," *JSNT* 33 (2011): 351–74.

80. Marcus, *Mark 1–8*, 283. Cf. Irenaeus, *Haer.* 5.21.3.

strong support for understanding forgiveness of sins to come in conjunction with Jesus's victory over Satan (cf. Matt. 12:28–31).

If Matthew and Mark view the forgiveness of sins to come in conjunction with the binding of the strong man, this would accord with some Jewish traditions in which Satan held *people* in captivity (*T. Naph.* 8:6; cf. *Jub.* 48:15).[81] Likewise, the spoil (*ta skeuē*) of the devil in Jesus's parable most likely refers to *people* who are freed from diabolic captivity.[82] Freedom for people also seems to be in view in Luke 11:22 (*ta skyla*).[83] Though Darrell Bock identifies the spoils as the entirety of the benefits of salvation,[84] these are benefits experienced personally by those who have been freed. Indeed, the salvation that Jesus brings in the Synoptics is largely deliverance of *people* from demons, sicknesses, and sins.[85] Moreover, in Luke we find perhaps an even stronger emphasis on the release from captivity that Jesus brings, in light of the programmatic citation of Isaiah 61:1–2, with its emphasis on release for the captives (*aichmalōtois aphesin*) and sending forth in freedom those who are oppressed (*aposteilai tethrausmenous en aphesei*), at the beginning of his ministry (Luke 4:18; cf. 13:16).[86] Additionally, we find in all these accounts—though it is strongest in Luke—an allusion to Isaiah 53:12, which speaks of dividing the spoil of the strong (*tōn ischyrōn meriei skyla*).[87] This comes in the context of the work of the suffering servant, who bears the iniquities of the many and pours out his life unto death (Isa. 53:5–6, 11–12). Allusions to Isaiah 53:12 in the binding of the strong man accounts provide additional support for understanding forgiveness of sins to be a benefit of Jesus's victory over the strong man. Finally, we find something similar in 11Q13, where deliverance from Belial and evil spirits is associated with the forgiveness of sins (11Q13 II, 6, 11–12, 25).

Second, the binding of the strong man is necessary for the establishment of God's kingdom. We see this most clearly in Matthew and Luke, where the casting out of demons is associated with the increasing realization of the

81. Cf. Davies and Allison, *Matthew*, 2:342; Rikk E. Watts, "Mark," in *Commentary on the New Testament Use of the Old Testament*, ed. G. K. Beale and D. A. Carson (Grand Rapids: Baker Academic, 2007), 145. For other Jewish texts that speak of the binding of evil spirits, see Best, *Temptation and the Passion*, 12.

82. Irenaeus, *Haer.* 3.8.2; R. Watts, "Mark," 145; C. E. B. Cranfield, *The Gospel according to St. Mark: An Introduction and Commentary*, CGTC (Cambridge: Cambridge University Press, 1959), 138; Keener, *Gospel of Matthew*, 364; Davies and Allison, *Matthew*, 2:342; France, *Matthew*, 481; cf. *Ques. Ezra* 31.

83. Geldenhuys, *Gospel of Luke*, 330.

84. Bock, *Luke*, 2:1083.

85. I will discuss the interplay of these below, in association with miracles.

86. Cranfield, *Gospel according to St. Mark*, 138.

87. Seccombe, "Luke and Isaiah," 256–67; R. Watts, "Mark," 146.

kingdom of God (esp. in Matt. 12:28; Luke 11:20), though kingdom language features significantly in Mark as well (Mark 3:24–25). A likely allusion to Isaiah 49:24–25 further underscores the kingdom emphasis of the binding of the strong man. In this passage God promises to intervene and save those who are captive, which is part of Isaiah's vision of eschatological salvation.[88] The Lord is the Savior, the Redeemer, the Mighty One of Jacob (Isa. 49:26), and his salvation is couched in royal imagery. Thus, the kings of this world who have held God's people in captivity will lick the feet of those they formerly ruled (49:23; cf. 49:9), and God's people will be restored to their kingdom's land (49:16–18; cf. 49:7). In Isaiah the power of God to save his people is greater than that of any earthly monarch,[89] and this correlates well with the kingdom emphasis of the binding of the strong man in the Synoptics.[90] It also accords with the need for the forgiveness of sins, since in Isaiah 50:1 the people are in bondage because of transgressions.[91] Additionally, the likely allusion to Isaiah 53:12 in dividing the spoil employs the language of a warrior overcoming the kingdom of a lesser power.[92] We similarly see the eschatological triumph of God's kingdom over the dominion of Belial in the Dead Sea Scrolls. For example, the War Scroll speaks of the final defeat of Belial and his evil angels (1QM I, 14–15), and in 4Q285, frag. 7 the Branch of David will judge the forces of Belial.[93] These canonical and noncanonical texts provide a context for understanding that in the Gospels the binding of the strong man means the kingdom of God has come near.[94]

Third, closely related to the supremacy of God's kingdom, the binding of Satan is linked with the spread of the gospel to all nations. In Isaiah 49 the calling home of Zion's children means overcoming the strength of the nations,[95] but Isaiah also envisions the inclusion of the nations as well, depending on

88. On the allusion in Mark, see R. Watts, "Mark," 145–48. See also Isa. 22:17–25, where the Lord of Hosts casts out (LXX: *ekballō*) the strong man (Shebna) and entrusts the key of David to his successor, Eliakim.

89. "Just as YHWH is stronger than the strong man Babylon (Isa. 49:24–25), so is Jesus stronger than Satan" (Johansson, "Jesus and God," 36).

90. See also *Pss. Sol.* 5:5 (no one can plunder the strong man) with *Pss. Sol.* 17 (no one can stand against Israel's king, who will distribute his people to their land).

91. See Childs, *Isaiah*, 393.

92. R. Watts, "Mark," 146.

93. Cf. Michael Wise, Martin Abegg Jr., and Edward Cook, *The Dead Sea Scrolls: A New Translation*, rev. ed. (New York: HarperOne, 2005), 368–70. What is now labeled as frag. 7 has in the past been identified as frag. 5. See the reconstruction of Philip Alexander and Geza Vermes in Stephen J. Pfann et al., eds., *Qumran Cave 4.XXVI: Cryptic Texts and Miscellanea, Part 1*, DJD 36 (Oxford: Clarendon, 2000).

94. Cf. Ridderbos, *Coming of the Kingdom*, 61–64, 108–10.

95. Motyer, *Prophecy of Isaiah*, 395.

the purpose of the oracle (cf. Isa. 45:22–25).[96] The mission to the nations is, of course, a subject of much discussion in Matthew's Gospel particularly. By the end of the Gospel we find a clear mission to all nations (Matt. 28:19; cf. 24:14), though during his ministry Jesus states that he was sent only to the lost sheep of the house of Israel (15:24; cf. 10:5–6). In spite of Matthew's emphasis on the redemptive-historical priority of Israel, however, the gentile mission is anticipated already from the opening verses (e.g., "son of Abraham" [1:1]; four gentiles in the genealogy [1:2–17]; positive role of the magi [2:1–12]). Nevertheless, in Matthew, Jesus rarely interacts with gentiles, and therefore it is noteworthy when he does. Prominent examples of gentiles with whom Jesus interacted include the centurion of faith (8:5–13), the Canaanite woman (15:21–28), and the Gadarene demoniacs (8:28–34).[97] An interesting question in this last account is how to take Matthew's redactional phrase "before the time" (pro kairou) in 8:29, which refers to the demons' apparent surprise at being overcome by the stronger one before their ultimate end (cf. Luke 8:31).[98] The demons' final destruction had not yet come, but they were nevertheless not free to inhabit the possessed men when Jesus commanded otherwise. Thus, while the demons were apparently not tormented pro kairou, they were sent out from their present realm (Matt. 8:32). Additionally, the authority of Jesus over the demons is mentioned in a gentile region (Gadara/Gerasa). Thus, Matthias Konradt has argued that pro kairou refers primarily to the surprise of the demons at meeting Jesus among the gentiles before the gentile mission, which comes after Jesus's death and resurrection.[99]

The question thus arises: does the term kairos in the phrase pro kairou refer to the time of final victory or to the era of the gentile mission? I propose that we find both aspects intertwined—that is, an anticipation of Jesus's final victory over the demonic realm and the mission to the gentiles—in Matthew's use of pro kairou. Jesus had already begun to exercise eschatological authority over the demons, but he had not yet completely destroyed them.[100] At the same

96. Childs, Isaiah, 392–93.
97. See the significant study by Matthias Konradt, Israel, Kirche, und die Völker im Matthäus-evangelium, WUNT 215 (Tübingen: Mohr Siebeck, 2007), ET: Israel, Church, and the Gentiles in the Gospel of Matthew, trans. Kathleen Ess, BMSEC (Waco: Baylor University Press, 2014).
98. Keener, Gospel of Matthew, 365; Ridderbos, Coming of the Kingdom, 111–13.
99. Konradt, Israel, Church, and the Gentiles, 56–59.
100. Konradt (ibid., 57) argues that Jesus offers no concession to the demons, and they perish as a result of falling into the sea. This means that Jesus does mete out final destruction to the demons. However, it is not clear that apethanon applies to the demons rather than the pigs (see Mark 5:13 // Luke 8:33; Davies and Allison, Matthew, 2:84). It is better to see in this account the clear display of Jesus's greater authority, with a delay of the demons' final destruction because the time of their end had not yet come.

time, Jesus occasionally interacts with gentiles, though he does not engage in a full-fledged gentile mission himself. The fuller binding of Satan comes later, in conjunction with Jesus's death and resurrection, and this leads to a fuller mission to the gentiles. And yet already during Jesus's ministry he begins to rein in the reign of Satan, and already this begins to be manifested among the gentiles.[101] In other words, in the midst of Jesus's ministry the realities of the end (Satan's defeat and the mission to the gentiles) are already beginning to be realized. It is further instructive that Jesus's statements regarding the binding of the strong man and the coming of the kingdom in Matthew 12:25–32 follow on the heels of the Isaiah 42 quotation that emphasizes the servant's relevance *for the gentiles* (12:18, 21).

The relationship between the binding of Satan and the gospel going to the gentiles also seems to be in view in Revelation 20:1–3. In 20:1 the angel holds the key, which is representative of the resurrection authority of Jesus (1:18; 3:7; 9:1), and Satan (= the dragon = the ancient serpent) is bound for a thousand years (20:2).[102] Significantly, this binding is specifically identified as restraint from deceiving the nations (20:3), which entails the preaching of the gospel to the nations and their coming to faith (cf. Acts 14:16; 17:30). In Revelation 20 this initial binding of Satan comes through Jesus's death and resurrection, though it is also quite possible that this binding had already begun during Jesus's ministry.[103] If so, then Revelation 20 may betray a similar perspective to the binding of the strong man in Matthew, since the binding of the devil leads to the spread of the gospel among the nations, though his final demise has not yet come.[104]

Fourth, the binding of the strong man is one aspect of the positive accomplishment of righteousness intended from the beginning of creation. In other words, binding the strong man is Adamic imagery. The correlation between the temptation of Jesus and the initial binding of Satan would point in this direction, since the temptation of Jesus presents the reader with an Adamic trope. Another way we see Adamic imagery comes via the relationship between Satan and serpent imagery that was commonplace by the first century (e.g., Luke 10:19; Rev. 12:9; 20:2). Adam was created to serve and guard in the garden

---

101. If we view the release of people from demonic bondage as a form of real deliverance, we do not need to deny that Jesus was in some sense advancing the kingdom of God already in gentile territory. Contrast Konradt, *Israel, Church, and the Gentiles*, 59.

102. For a defense of this exegesis of Rev. 20, see Beale, *Book of Revelation*, 984–89.

103. See ibid., 985; William Hendriksen, *More than Conquerors: An Interpretation of the Book of Revelation* (Grand Rapids: Baker, 1998), 187; Hoekema, *Bible and the Future*, 46.

104. Even if one were to view the binding in Rev. 20:2 as an event yet to happen, it is still plausible that this text is intended to evoke Jesus's earlier binding of the strong man.

(Gen. 2:15)—which could be described as judicial-military language[105]—but he failed to overcome the serpent. When Jesus binds the strong man through his obedience in the face of Satan's temptation, he exercises the dominion over the devil that Adam should have exercised. This comports with the interpretation of Irenaeus, who understood the obedience of Jesus to be the binding of the strong man, which overcame the sin of Adam.[106]

In sum, the binding of the strong man points to the necessity of the obedience of Jesus incarnate in order to defeat Satan's kingdom and overcome the sin of Adam.[107] Jesus's authority as the stronger one flows from his obedience and empowering by the Holy Spirit. As the last Adam, Jesus cast out Satan through his obedience in the face of temptation and began to institute the kingdom of God, along with its salvific blessings, during his ministry, though we will see in the next chapter that Jesus's death and resurrection were necessary for the full establishment of the kingdom.[108]

Mighty, Saving Acts of Jesus

Jesus's kingdom authority is seen also in his miracles. Much could be said about the miracles of Jesus, but I am interested specifically in Jesus's mighty acts and the accomplishment of salvation. First, Jesus's powerful works incarnate were evidence that the messianic age had dawned (Matt. 11:2–6 // Luke 7:18–23; cf. 4Q521), which meant that God's promised salvation had arrived. The promise of salvation in Isaiah is concomitantly the promise for the deaf to hear, the blind to see, the lame to leap, the mute to sing, and the dead to be raised (Isa. 26:19; 29:18; 35:5–6; 61:1–2), which are all apparent in the ministry of Jesus.[109] Even Jesus's miraculous feeding of the five thousand in the wilderness (Matt. 14:13–21 // Mark 6:30–44 // Luke 9:10–17 // John 6:1–15)

105. Meredith G. Kline, *Kingdom Prologue: Genesis Foundations for a Covenantal Worldview* (Overland Park, KS: Two Age Press, 2000), 85–87; cf. Bruce K. Waltke with Cathi J. Fredricks, *Genesis: A Commentary* (Grand Rapids: Zondervan, 2001), 87.

106. Irenaeus, *Haer.* 3.18.6–7; 3.21.10; 3.22.4; 5.21.1–5.22.2. Cf. Ronald E. Heine, *Classical Christian Doctrine: Introducing the Essentials of the Ancient Faith* (Grand Rapids: Baker Academic, 2013), 121; Gustaf Aulén, *Christus Victor: An Historical Study of the Three Main Types of the Idea of the Atonement*, trans. A. G. Hebert (London: SPCK, 1931), 45–46, though see the critique of Aulén's interpretation of Irenaeus in Douglas F. Kelly, *Systematic Theology: Grounded in Holy Scripture and Understood in the Light of the Church*, vol. 2, *The Beauty of Christ: A Trinitarian Vision* (Fearn, UK: Mentor, 2014), 437–39.

107. See also *T. Levi* 18:10–12; Arseny Ermakov, "The Holy One of God in Markan Narrative," *HBT* 36 (2014): 169, 176–77.

108. See Ridderbos, *Coming of the Kingdom*, 171.

109. Konradt, *Israel, Church, and the Gentiles*, 41; France, *Matthew*, 423–24.

is a fulfillment of Isaiah's vision of salvation (cf. Isa. 25:6–9).[110] From Mark's account, William Lane suggests that Jesus's arrangement of the people into groups on the green grass, in association with the provision of bread, recalls the first exodus under Moses and indicates that Jesus is the eschatological shepherd leading his people on a new exodus.[111] Through Jesus's mighty acts, the kingdom of God was being realized.[112]

Second, Jesus's miracles are indications of his kingdom authority and are part of the holistic way in which the power of Satan's kingdom is overcome.[113] Sickness, disease, and infirmity in the Gospels are portrayed as much a part of the realm of Satan as are demon possession and sin. We see this, for example, in the way that demonic possession can be associated with bodily ailments (Matt. 9:32–33; 12:22–32;[114] Mark 9:25). More specifically, Satan can apparently be the cause for bodily ailments (Luke 13:10–17). In addition, sin and sickness are related more broadly in the Gospels, so that Jesus identifies the need for forgiveness of sins with the need for healing (Matt. 9:1–8 // Mark 2:1–12 // Luke 5:17–26). Sometimes sin and sickness are rather clearly related, and sometimes they are not (cf. John 5:1–15 with 9:1–3), but in every case sickness results from the entrance of sin into the world. This is preeminently seen in the curse of death that Jesus overcomes by raising the dead several times before his own resurrection (Matt. 9:18–25; Mark 5:35–43; Luke 7:11–17; 8:49–56; John 11:1–44). Therefore, for Jesus to overcome sicknesses and ailments is for Jesus to overcome the consequences of sin. Moreover, miracles are often performed in conjunction with the preaching of the kingdom (Matt. 4:23; 9:35; 10:7–8; Luke 9:11; 10:9, 17; 11:20),[115] which further underscores miracles as acts of kingdom conflict.

Therefore, Jesus's plundering of the strong man's house (or the dividing of his spoil) should be associated not only with Jesus's exorcisms but with all the powerful ways that Jesus overcomes the kingdom of Satan. Not only do serpents and scorpions belong to the enemy's power, but so also do disease

110. William L. Lane, *The Gospel according to Mark*, NICNT (Grand Rapids: Eerdmans, 1974), 232. See further Marcus, *Mark 1–8*, 420; Davies and Allison, *Matthew*, 2:481–82.

111. Lane, *Gospel according to Mark*, 229–30.

112. See Schreiner, *New Testament Theology*, 64.

113. In this paragraph I am indebted particularly to Ridderbos, *Coming of the Kingdom*, 65–70. See also Scot McKnight, "Matthew as 'Gospel,'" in *Jesus, Matthew's Gospel and Early Christianity: Studies in Memory of Graham N. Stanton*, ed. Daniel M. Gurtner, Joel Willitts, and Richard A. Burridge, LNTS 435 (London: T&T Clark, 2011), 74.

114. Note that the charge in Matt. 9:34 is echoed in Matt. 12:24. In this second context Jesus identifies the power to bind the strong man as that of the Holy Spirit (12:28; cf. 12:32). Thus, viewed in light of Matt. 12, Jesus's ability to heal every sickness in Matt. 9:35 is, like his exorcistic authority, empowered by the Holy Spirit.

115. Schreiner, *New Testament Theology*, 65; Ridderbos, *Coming of the Kingdom*, 65.

and death. Jesus's struggle against Satan is fought not only in a spiritual or ethical realm but also "in the whole of the physical domain."[116] Where Jesus performs miracles, there we find proof that the kingdom has come.

Third, Jesus's kingdom miracles are ways in which eschatological salvation is beginning to be realized. Put differently, miracles are often redemptive acts.[117] These acts can be either positive (salvation) or negative (judgment), depending on one's posture toward God, but both ultimately serve the redemption of God's people.[118] Jesus's healing miracles and granting new life to the dead are positive, indicating the inauguration of new creation.[119] Even exorcisms are signs of new creation, since they point to the overcoming of evil and sin and the restoration to fullness of life.[120] Jesus also performs miracles with a more negative function of judgment, but even these seem to serve a redemptive purpose. An example here is Jesus's cursing of the fig tree,[121] which represented the spiritual state of many in Israel toward Jesus or the present temple structure (or both). This is likely because fig trees could represent Israel (see esp. Jer. 8:13), and Mark's intercalation of Jesus's cursing of the temple between the pronouncement of the curse on the fig tree and its realization (Mark 11:12–21; cf. Matt. 21:18–22) indicates that the two accounts are to be read together.[122] Jesus's cursing of the fig tree indicates the coming destruction of the present, idolatrous temple system (cf. Jer. 7:8–15), which confirms a new way of forgiveness, through Jesus himself, that does not come through the cultic means of Jesus's day (cf. Matt. 24:2; 26:61; Mark 13:1; 14:58; Luke 21:6; John 2:19).[123]

Similarly, Jesus's miracles point toward new creation, as they demonstrate Jesus's mastery over the created realm. In this light, it is striking that several of Jesus's miracles occur on the Sabbath, which evokes God's original creational

116. Ridderbos, *Coming of the Kingdom*, 67. Cf. Geerhardus Vos, *The Self-Disclosure of Jesus: The Modern Debate about the Messianic Consciousness*, ed. Johannes G. Vos, 2nd ed. (1953; repr., Phillipsburg, NJ: P&R, 2002), 26–27, 71, 258–60.

117. See Bavinck, *Reformed Dogmatics*, 1:337, 345. Miracles are not *only* redemptive acts; some, for example, point to the work of Christ but may not be in themselves redemptive (cf. John 2:1–11). See also John M. Frame, *The Doctrine of God*, TL 2 (Phillipsburg, NJ: P&R, 2002), 259–60.

118. For example, the plagues in Egypt were negative events for the Egyptians, but they served the deliverance of God's people.

119. Ridderbos, *Coming of the Kingdom*, 65; Beale, *New Testament Biblical Theology*, 423.

120. See similarly Schreiner, *New Testament Theology*, 66.

121. Ridderbos, *Coming of the Kingdom*, 68–69.

122. See further J. R. Edwards, *Mark*, 338–46; Klyne R. Snodgrass, *Stories with Intent: A Comprehensive Guide to the Parables of Jesus* (Grand Rapids: Eerdmans, 2008), 259.

123. See variously James D. G. Dunn, *Jesus Remembered*, CM 1 (Grand Rapids: Eerdmans, 2003), 787–88; Wright, *Jesus*, 273–74, 333–36, 434–35.

design (cf., e.g., Luke 13:10–17). Jesus's nature miracles, such as his calming of the storms (Matt. 8:23–27; 14:22–33; Mark 4:35–41; 6:45–52; Luke 8:22–25), are perhaps most impressive in their portrayal of Jesus as Lord of creation. When Jesus calms the sea, he brings peace and order out of chaos, recalling God's original supremacy over formlessness and voidness (Gen. 1:2). Jesus's calming of the waters also recalls the deliverance of the Israelites through the waters of the sea in the exodus (Exod. 14:26–31), the paradigm for salvation in the Old Testament (cf. Ps. 66; Jer. 16:14–16). Similarly, when Jesus calms the storms, he concomitantly saves his disciples from destruction (Matt. 8:25; 14:30; Mark 4:38; Luke 8:24). Jesus's miracles, in other words, serve a salvific purpose for his disciples, recalling the mighty deeds of Yahweh in the Old Testament.

Fourth, we also see the way that salvation comes through Jesus's miracles by returning to Acts 10:36–38. Earlier we saw that in this text Peter describes Jesus as the one who went around doing good by the power of the Holy Spirit, healing all who were oppressed by the devil. I argued that this "doing good" may be conceived as salvifically benefiting his people. In conjunction with this interpretation, the good that Peter has in view was most likely primarily Jesus's miraculous works. If so, then the miracles of Jesus would need to be understood as part of the salvific benefits bestowed by Jesus in his doing good.

Fifth, Jesus's miracles are part of the accomplishment of salvation because they are integral to his messianic obedience. Again it is significant that Jesus's obedience in the face of temptation—which I have argued is his initial binding of the strong man—precedes Jesus's exorcisms and miracles, which are associated with plundering the spoil of the strong man. This is further confirmed by the role of the Holy Spirit in the miracles of Jesus (Matt. 12:15–18; Luke 4:18; cf. Acts 10:38), which is the same Holy Spirit that empowered Jesus's obedience. Jesus's task as obedient Son of God is described in terms of the servant, and this involves even his healing ministry (cf. Isa. 53:4; Matt. 8:14–17). Thus, in Matthew 8 and 12 Jesus's obedience as the servant entails his bearing of illnesses and diseases. And as I have argued Jesus's obedience, which includes his bearing of the sins of many, is not limited to his death.[124]

Finally, closely related to miracles as a sign of new creation and Jesus's obedience are the Adamic features of Jesus's miracles. Miracles are ways in which Jesus overcomes the curse of sin, and this highlights Jesus's overarching

---

124. See also Irenaeus, *Haer.* 4.8.2: "For He did not make void, but fulfilled the law, by performing the offices of the high priest, propitiating God for men, and cleansing the lepers, healing the sick, and Himself suffering death, that exiled man might go forth from condemnation, and might return without fear to his own inheritance" (*ANF* 1:471).

obedience as that which overcomes the sin of Adam.[125] In addition to the new life that Jesus bestows in raising people from the dead (noted above), we can again observe the imagery of the provision of bread in the wilderness. When Jesus feeds the four thousand and five thousand, he does so in desolate places that recall the curse of the ground on account of Adam's sin (Matt. 14:13; 15:33; Mark 6:31–32; 8:4; Luke 9:12; John 6:31, 49; cf. Gen. 3:17–19). And yet Jesus overcomes their hunger and the desolation in his abundant provision of food that does not come from their toiling over the ground but from divine provision.[126] Jesus's miracles are part of the way that he, as the last Adam, overcomes the curse of the first Adam.

Conclusion

In this chapter I have argued that Jesus is the messianic servant-king who is anointed and empowered by the Holy Spirit to establish righteousness, bind the strong man, cast out demons, perform miracles, and defeat the kingdom of Satan in various ways. Jesus establishes the kingdom of righteousness through his mission as a whole, manifesting an obedience that overcomes the disobedience of Adam and the effects of Adam's sin.

However, the kingdom is not yet fully established in the Gospels before the death and resurrection of Jesus. So long as the final suffering and death of Christ had not yet occurred, the kingdom could only be partially realized.[127] The victory that Christ gains in his earthly ministry is decisive but not yet final. A foundational presupposition for the present study is that one cannot dichotomize Jesus's obedience in his life and his obedience in death. Instead, these must be seen as two aspects of his integrated obedience. Therefore, in the following chapter we will turn to the ways in which Jesus's life and death are interrelated as we consider in more detail the role of the death of Jesus in establishing the kingdom.

125. See Beale, *New Testament Biblical Theology*, 423, 906; McCartney, "*Ecce Homo*," 10; Joel William Parkman, "Adam Christological Motifs in the Synoptic Traditions" (PhD diss., Baylor University, 1994), 96.

126. See also the suggestions of Harald Sahlin, "Adam-Christologie im Neuen Testament," *ST* 41 (1987): 17–18. See possibly *4 Ezra* 6:52–54.

127. Ridderbos, *Coming of the Kingdom*, 109, 171.

The Death and Resurrection
of the Last Adam

Thus far we have looked at various ways that the life, ministry, and deeds of Jesus incarnate are necessary for the full realization of salvation. In the Gospels, Jesus demonstrates wholehearted obedience to his Father, in contrast to Adam and Israel. He fulfills the will of God in Scripture, doing what was necessary for salvation. He overcomes the devil, inaugurating the righteous kingdom of God. Throughout this study I have argued that Jesus accomplishes salvation through his life and ministry. However, in no way do I desire to undersell the significance of Jesus's death and resurrection. I have not been arguing that less importance should be attributed to the death of Jesus; rather, I have been arguing that the life of Jesus in the Gospels is more important than is often recognized.

In this chapter I aim to show how the life and death of Jesus are organically interwoven, so we must think of his work as a unified whole. Just as we cannot fully appreciate the significance of Jesus's death apart from the character of his life, neither can we fully appreciate the life of Jesus apart from his death. Jesus's lifelong obedience climaxes in his obedience unto death. The salvation accomplished by Jesus must be viewed in light of the finality of his death and resurrection, even as we await the consummation of his work when he returns. What might have appeared to be the ultimate defeat for Jesus (his death on the cross) becomes through the resurrection the greatest victory, with death itself being defeated. In what follows we will consider especially four angles related to Jesus's obedience unto death and salvation: the relation of mercy and sacrifice, Jesus's life as ransom, the blood of the new covenant, and Jesus's vindication in his resurrection. In this chapter we will see again various ways that Adam's legacy has cast a long shadow over humanity, yet the curse of Adam's sin is definitively overcome in the glorious resurrection of the perfectly obedient last Adam.

Mercy and Sacrifice

Mercy and Love in Matthew

The Gospel of Matthew emphasizes that true sacrifice is not simply a matter of externals but is a matter of one's inner disposition, and these are perfectly united in Christ. Twice in Matthew Jesus challenges the Pharisees with the words of Hosea 6:6: "I desire mercy, not a sacrifice" (Matt. 9:13; 12:7).[1] These encounters point to the embodiment of mercy in the actions of Jesus, who calls sinners (9:11) and considers his disciples guiltless for eating grain plucked on the Sabbath (12:7). In these contexts Jesus uses Hosea 6:6 to rebuke the Pharisees for outward observance of the law only, to the neglect of the weightier matters of mercy (cf. 23:23).[2] In the MT of Hosea, God desires *hesed*, which is rendered *eleos* in the LXX. Both terms can be translated "mercy," though *hesed* communicates more explicitly covenant love and faithfulness.[3] In the Old Testament *hesed* consistently characterizes the Lord's faithfulness to his covenant.[4] Likewise, in the Prophets in particular, *hesed* can also refer to the need for God's covenant people to demonstrate covenant love toward the Lord (Jer. 2:2; Hosea 4:1; 10:12; Jon. 2:8), which is

1. Indeed, Hosea 6:6 is the only Old Testament text that Matthew explicitly quotes more than once. See Dale C. Allison Jr., "The Configuration of the Sermon on the Mount and Its Meaning," in *Studies in Matthew: Interpretation Past and Present* (Grand Rapids: Baker Academic, 2005), 213–14.

2. Cf. R. T. France, *The Gospel of Matthew*, NICNT (Grand Rapids: Eerdmans, 2007), 354; W. D. Davies and Dale C. Allison Jr., *A Critical and Exegetical Commentary on the Gospel according to St. Matthew*, 3 vols., ICC (Edinburgh: T&T Clark, 1988–97), 2:105, 315; cf. Irenaeus, *Haer.* 4.17.4.

3. See variously R. Laird Harris, "חסד," *TWOT* §698 (1:305–7); K&D 10:66; David Hill, "On the Use and Meaning of Hosea 6:6 in Matthew's Gospel," *NTS* 24 (1977): 107–19; cf. France, *Matthew*, 354.

4. Cf., e.g., Exod. 15:13; 20:6; 34:6–7; Num. 14:18–19; Deut. 5:10; 7:9, 12; 2 Sam. 7:15; 22:51; 1 Kings 8:23; 2 Chron. 6:14; Pss. 6:4; 18:50; 23:6; 40:11; 89:33; Isa. 54:8, 10; Jer. 9:24; 31:3; 32:18; 33:11; Hosea 2:19; Joel 2:13; Jon. 4:2; Mic. 7:18, 20.

closely related to the need to deal in love with their neighbors (Prov. 19:22; 20:28; Hosea 4:1–2; 6:4–11; 12:1–15 [11:12–12:14 EVV]; Zech. 7:9). Indeed, it is striking how closely interrelated are one's commitment to the Lord and one's commitment to practicing righteousness: lack of *ḥesed* toward God manifests itself in lack of *ḥesed* toward others. Micah 6:8 illustrates the prophetic vision well: God's people must practice justice, love covenant faithfulness [*ḥesed*], and walk humbly with their God. In other words, love for God and love for neighbor are concomitants.

It is the infelicitous dichotomy between love/mercy and sacrifice that is addressed in Hosea 6:4–11, with 6:6–7 forming something like a Janus in the passage. In Hosea 6:4–6 the emphasis falls primarily on the people's lack of *ḥesed* toward the Lord. In contrast to the *ḥesed* of Ephraim and Judah, which is like the disappearing dew of the morning (6:4), verse 6 serves as a climax for 6:4–6 and speaks positively of the true *ḥesed* that the Lord desires. Closely related to Hosea 6:4–6, verses 7–11 provide further insight into the lack of *ḥesed* that characterized God's people in interpersonal relationships.[5] Instead of demonstrating covenant loyalty, God's covenant people were characterized by thievery, murder, and sexual infidelity (6:8–11). Hosea 6:6 is thus positioned at a key juncture in a passage that lays bare the lack of *ḥesed* among God's covenant people who did not show the requisite love for God or neighbor.

Matthew's use of Hosea 6:6 to underscore the necessity of mercy reveals something close to the heart of my argument: Jesus embodies the mercy that God requires. In Matthew 9:9–13 Jesus demonstrates mercy by calling Matthew and subsequently eating with tax collectors and sinners. Later in Matthew 9, Jesus heals a bleeding woman (9:22), a girl who had died (9:24–25), and two blind men (9:29–30). Since Jesus's healing of these blind men is narrated in response to their plea for mercy (9:27), we can by extension understand all of Jesus's dealings in this context as acts of mercy. Indeed, the repetition of *mercy* in 9:13 and 9:27 frames this section of the narrative. By extending mercy toward sinners and mercifully healing those in dire need (cf. 9:36), Jesus embodies the sort of mercy God requires in Hosea 6:6.[6] This is also consistent with the reading of the Sermon on the Mount offered in chapter 4, where I argued that Jesus realizes throughout Matthew what is commanded in the Sermon on the Mount. Indeed, in the Beatitudes those who show mercy are blessed (5:7), and it is this sort of mercy that consistently characterizes Jesus throughout Matthew (9:27–30; 15:22–28; 17:15–18; 20:30–34; cf. 9:13;

---

5. See also Mary Hinkle Edin, "Learning What Righteousness Means: Hosea 6:6 and the Ethic of Mercy in Matthew's Gospel," *WW* 18 (1998): 357–59.

6. One might also note the anticipation of God's healing in Hosea 6:1–2. Cf. Richard B. Hays, "The Gospel of Matthew: Reconfigured Torah," *HvTSt* 61 (2005): 180.

12:7; 18:33; 23:23). As the ultimate covenant sacrifice (cf. Matt. 26:28), Jesus overcomes bare sacrifice in his full-fledged delight to do his Father's will (cf. 1 Sam. 15:22; Ps. 40:6–8; Prov. 21:3; Amos 5:21–24).

The Matthean emphasis on mercy in Jesus's teaching and actions also fits well with Jesus's summary of the Law and Prophets in response to the Pharisees' challenge. When asked what the greatest commandment is, Jesus gives a twofold response: love God wholeheartedly (Matt. 22:37–38; cf. Deut. 6:5) and love one's neighbor as oneself (Matt. 22:39; Lev. 19:18). Significantly, Jesus gives this response not only as a summary of the Torah but as the pillars on which hang all the Law *and* the Prophets (Matt. 22:40).[7] In other words, Leviticus, Deuteronomy, and Hosea all agree that what is required is to love God and love one's neighbor. The location of Jesus's response in Matthew's narrative is also instructive, as it comes in the passion week when the conflict between Jesus and the Pharisees is most intense. Not only does Jesus confound them with his answer, along with the question about David's son (22:41–46), but he also pronounces woes upon the scribes and Pharisees. Of particular relevance is the fourth woe for neglecting justice (*krisis*), mercy (*eleos*), and faithfulness (*pistis*) (23:23; cf. Luke 11:42). Though the tithing of mint, dill, and cumin was not wrong, merely conforming to outward rites to the neglect of the weightier matters of the law (*ta barytera tou nomou*) indicated hypocrisy and demonstrated the validity of the critique from Hosea 6:6 found in Jesus's first two conflicts with the Pharisees (Matt. 9:13; 12:7). Moreover, the mercy required in Hosea 6:6 can just as easily be described as covenantal love, especially in light of the semantic range of *ḥesed*.[8] Just as the mercy of Hosea 6:6 requires love of God and love of neighbor, so Jesus identifies love of God and neighbor as the requirement of all the Law and Prophets.

By identifying love for God and neighbor as the key to the Law and Prophets, Jesus emphasizes that God desires not only obedience to external rites but also obedience that arises from true devotion. Deuteronomy (quoted in Matt. 22:37) is instructive in this regard. On the one hand, love is tantamount to obedience in Deuteronomy: to love God is to do what he commands (Deut. 7:9; 11:1, 13). On the other hand, by focusing on love, Deuteronomy emphasizes the affective aspects of loyalty to God, which go beyond merely external obedience (Deut. 6:5; 10:12; 13:3; 30:6; cf. 8:2).[9] Likewise, Hosea manifests

---

7. See also France, *Matthew*, 847; Hays, "Gospel of Matthew," 179.

8. Cf. *HALOT*, 1:336–37; *DCH*, "חֶסֶד," 3:277–81.

9. See further Brandon D. Crowe, *The Obedient Son: Deuteronomy and Christology in the Gospel of Matthew*, BZNW 188 (Berlin: Walter de Gruyter, 2012), esp. 114–15; Geerhardus Vos, "The Scriptural Doctrine of the Love of God," *PRR* 13 (1902): 1–37.

a similar interest in covenantal love (cf. Hosea 11:1–4).[10] The Law and the Prophets agree that one cannot be truly devoted to God if one's heart is not pure and if one does not love one's neighbor. To love God in a covenantal context is to do all that he commands. In this light, Jesus identifies his true family as those who do the will of his Father (Matt. 12:46–50), which is based on the presupposition that Jesus does the will of his Father, even unto death (26:42; cf. 7:21). In sum, Jesus not only teaches us what the Law and the Prophets are really all about, but he embodies them by positively loving God and loving his neighbor.

Matthew's use of Hosea 6:6 underscores what we have seen in various ways throughout this study: what God requires (in this case, mercy) is realized through the obedience of Jesus. Jesus embodies not merely the formal acts of obedience but also "the disposition, will, determination, and volition which lie back of" the formal acts.[11] Matthew's Gospel indicates that doing what God requires must come through a total commitment to God, which leads to an obedience that comes from the heart.[12] Thus we read in the Beatitudes of the blessing of those with the proper heart attitudes: poor in spirit (Matt. 5:3), meek (5:5), merciful (5:7), pure in heart (5:8), and so on. In the so-called antitheses (5:21–48) Jesus emphasizes that obedience to God's requirements is not only about the letter of the law but also the spirit of the law. It is not enough simply not to commit adultery (5:27); instead, a man must not even look lustfully at a woman (5:28). Other antitheses speak of the positive requirements that are entailed in scriptural prohibitions. One not only must not murder (5:21), but one must not even be angry with a brother or sister (5:22). What is more, one should positively seek reconciliation (5:23–25). Likewise, not only must one not invoke the *lex talionis* for personal vengeance, but one must positively turn the other cheek and go the extra mile, offering more than what is being sought, not refusing the one who asks (5:38–42). Disciples must not only not hate their enemies, but they must love them and pray for them, in order to reflect the perfection of their Father's loving character (5:43–48).

These antitheses follow on the staggering statement of Jesus in 5:20 that one's righteousness must exceed that of the scribes and Pharisees in order to enter the kingdom of heaven. We have seen already that this greater righteousness must not be read in isolation from Jesus, who fulfills all righteousness, but at the same time righteousness in Matthew calls for rigorous obedience. The greater righteousness is to be characterized by mercy and

---

10. Crowe, *Obedient Son*, 120–24.
11. John Murray, *Redemption Accomplished and Applied* (Grand Rapids: Eerdmans, 1955), 22.
12. See Hays, "Gospel of Matthew," 177.

love.[13] These are the standards for the disciples of Jesus, even as they describe the actions of Jesus himself. Jesus's rebuke of the Pharisees in Matthew 23 underscores that what had been rent asunder in Pharisaic practice was joined together in Jesus: scrupulous righteousness derived from a true love for God, which issued forth in mercy toward others.[14]

Put differently, in Matthew we find that Jesus performs mercy *and* sacrifice, and his full obedience to the Father uniquely qualifies him to save his people from their sins (Matt. 1:21), serving as the (new) covenant sacrifice (26:28). As I have argued at various points, Jesus's ability to save his people from their sins is built on the presupposition of his sinlessness. For the purposes of the present argument, it is important to draw attention to something significant about sinfulness that is often left unstated: sin encompasses not only unlawful acts but also the failure to do positively what God requires (which, as the Sermon on the Mount shows us, is deeper than we might expect). Indeed, in rabbinic tradition the 613 commandments of the Torah included 248 positive commandments.[15] Or, to use a more contemporary turn of phrase, Matthew's Gospel shows us the problem not only of sins of commission but also of sins of omission (Matt. 7:12; 22:34–40; 23:23; cf. James 4:17). Indeed, the act of abstaining from something proscribed is itself a positive act of obedience. Not grumbling against the Lord, for example, entails the correspondent reality of trusting in the Lord's provision (cf. Deut. 1:26–27; 8:1–6). The greater righteousness means that it is not sufficient to meet the lowest common denominator of the law's interpretation; rather, one must positively seek the proper goal (cf. Matt. 6:33). The greater righteousness means that even those who adhere to the minutiae of the law externally are breaking God's law if they have not truly loved God, shown mercy, and positively practiced the weightier matters of the law. In this sense, Matthew 23:23 provides a foil that clarifies the work of Jesus unto death: Jesus did not neglect any aspect of the law of righteousness (cf. 3:15), including (but not limited to) the weightier matters of the law.

We have seen that the mercy (*eleos*) God desires in Matthew 9:13 and 12:7 is a translation of the covenantal love conveyed by *ḥesed* in Hosea 6:6. Matthew's contrast between the Pharisees and Jesus, highlighted by his use of Hosea 6:6, raises an interesting possibility that is worth considering further: might Matthew's use of Hosea 6 reveal an implicit Adam Christology

---

13. Cf. ibid., 182; D. Hill, "Hosea 6:6," 110, 117.

14. See similarly Matthias Konradt, *Israel, Kirche, und die Völker im Matthäusevangelium*, WUNT 215 (Tübingen: Mohr Siebeck, 2007), ET: *Israel, Church, and the Gentiles in the Gospel of Matthew*, trans. Kathleen Ess, BMSEC (Waco: Baylor University Press, 2014), 132–33.

15. The 248 positive commandments corresponded to the 248 parts of one's body, whereas the 365 prohibitions corresponded to the days of the year (*b. Mak.* 23b–24a).

for Jesus, who faultlessly shows true covenant love? This possibility arises in light of the wider context of Hosea 6. As I discussed in chapter 3, Hosea 6:7 may speak of God's people transgressing the covenant like Adam. Lending plausibility to this suggestion is Matthew's contextual use of Scripture elsewhere, which renders it quite likely that he was aware of the wider context of Hosea, especially since he quotes from or alludes to Hosea elsewhere in his Gospel.[16] As Richard Hays has memorably stated, "If the Pharisees go to learn what Hosea 6:6 means, they will have to read more than one verse."[17]

As noted above, the *ḥesed* of Hosea 6:6 focuses on both the lack of *ḥesed* shown toward the Lord (Hosea 6:4–6) and the need to deal in *ḥesed* in interpersonal relationships (6:6–11).[18] To fail to show *ḥesed* (6:6) is to transgress the covenant (6:7). Thus, many commentators discuss the close relationship between Hosea 6:6 and 6:7.[19] In light of the lack of mercy shown by the Pharisees and the woes that Jesus pronounces upon them, the Pharisees are likely portrayed as *covenant* breakers (cf. Matt. 3:7–10), which is consistent with Hosea's equation of lack of *ḥesed* and the transgression of the *covenant*. Further supporting the view that the Pharisees are portrayed as covenant breakers is the wording of Matthew 15:3, where Jesus rebukes the Pharisees because they transgress (*parabainō*) the commandments of God. The Matthean redactional term *parabainō*, used only three times in the New Testament, is also found in Hosea 6:7 (LXX) to describe covenantal transgression, like that of Adam (cf. Josh. 7:11, 15; 23:16; 2 Kings 18:12; Hosea 8:1; also Heb. 9:15). The transgression of the commandments of God in Matthew 15 in favor of the traditions of men reveals a hypocrisy that is captured by the words of Isaiah 29:13 ("This people honors me with their lips, but their heart is far away from me"), which, much like Hosea 6:6, diagnoses the dichotomy between the Pharisees' outward piety and their lack of heart devotion.

Perhaps we can take this one step further: if the Pharisees are portrayed as covenant breakers in light of Hosea 6, and if Jesus is portrayed as one who demonstrates true *ḥesed* according to Hosea 6 (and does not break the

16. In addition to Hosea 6:6 in Matt. 9:13 and 12:7, see Hosea 11:1 in Matt. 2:15; Hosea 2:1 [1:10 EVV] in light of Matt. 16:16. On Matthew's awareness of the wider context, see Crowe, *Obedient Son*, 29–30; for the prevalence of the entire book of Hosea in early Christian thought, see C. H. Dodd, *According to the Scriptures: The Substructure of New Testament Theology* (London: Nisbet, 1952), 74–78.

17. Hays, "Gospel of Matthew," 181.

18. Davies and Allison (*Matthew*, 2:104) and D. Hill ("Hosea 6:6," 109) suggest that Matthew may have made his own translation from the Hebrew, though John Nolland (*The Gospel of Matthew*, NIGTC [Grand Rapids: Eerdmans, 2005], 387) is probably correct that we cannot say for sure. Nevertheless, we know Matthew elsewhere refers to both the OG and Hebrew texts, so it's likely he was aware of the covenantal connotations of *eleos* in Hosea 6:6.

19. See, e.g., Douglas J. Stuart, *Hosea–Jonah*, WBC 31 (Waco: Word, 1987), 110–11; K&D 10:66.

covenant), then perhaps Jesus is being portrayed in Matthew as the one who did not transgress the covenant *like Adam* did. By exhibiting true *ḥesed* Jesus fulfills God's requirement of humanity, overcoming the dichotomy between sacrifice and full devotion to God (Isa. 29:13; Hosea 6:6). Thus, Matthew's use of Hosea 6:6 may be the tip of the iceberg of a more thoroughgoing Adam-Christ parallel, and may provide additional reason for viewing Jesus's obedience in representative and vicarious terms.[20] Likewise, an Adamic understanding of Jesus's covenantal faithfulness in Matthew is also consistent with Jesus's fulfillment of the two great covenantal commands: love of God and love of neighbor. To love God and neighbor fully is to keep God's law, since obeying the Law (and Prophets) is a matter of the heart.[21]

Thus, loving God means keeping his commands, and this leads to life. Therefore, to gain fullness of life one must keep the commandments. This is what Adam failed to do, and therefore he failed to attain the promise of life that was set before him. This failure is apparent in the history of Israel, especially in light of Deuteronomy. Although the choice of blessing and curse, life and death, was held out to Israel, the unfortunate reality is that God's people too often chose the path of cursing and not the path of life (Deut. 11:26–28; 26–28; cf. Prov. 19:16). In the same way, the path of the Pharisees was not the path of life, but according to Jesus they were like whitewashed tombs from which emanated the miasma of spiritual decay (Matt. 23:27). Jesus's positive embodiment of covenant mercy, in contrast to the Pharisees who transgressed the covenant, underscores the polarity between true, devoted obedience to God on the one hand and mere externality on the other. The path of blessing, as we see in the Beatitudes, is the path of scriptural conformity. The blessed life Adam failed to achieve was attained by the obedient life of the last Adam, who was uniquely qualified to serve as the perfect covenant sacrifice.

Love and Mercy in Mark, Luke, and John

I have been focusing on the fulfillment of God's covenantal requirements in Matthew, but we find similar emphases in the other three Gospels. One of the clearest ways we see Jesus's supreme covenantal obedience is in the discussion of the two great commands across the Synoptics. Both Mark (12:28–31) and

---

20. It may also be relevant that eating is in view in Matt. 9:9–13 (table fellowship), 12:1–8 (eating grain plucked on the Sabbath), and 15:1–9 (ritual washings before eating). If so, *eating* could provide additional warrant for reading these texts in light of Adam, whose notorious sin was eating the forbidden fruit.

21. See Herman N. Ridderbos, *The Coming of the Kingdom*, trans. H. de Jongste, ed. Raymond O. Zorn (Philadelphia: P&R, 1962), 317–19.

Luke (10:25–28) include a discussion on the two great commands, which call for love of God and love of neighbor, and in both Mark and Luke we find similarities to the Matthean perspective outlined above. For example, when Jesus explains the two great commands to the scribe in Mark 12, the scribe responds positively with the recognition that loving God and loving one's neighbor is better than burnt offerings and sacrifices (12:33).

The discussion of the two great commandments in Luke 10:25–28 is perhaps even more significant given its wider context in relation to the parable of the good Samaritan (10:25–37) and the emphasis on "do this and live" (10:28; cf. Lev. 18:5). The lawyer initially asks what he must do to inherit eternal life. After Jesus's prompting, the lawyer responds with the two great commands. Jesus affirms his answer, concluding "do this and you will live" (10:28). But what did Jesus mean by this biblical turn of phrase? Did he really mean that eternal life could be inherited by loving God and loving one's neighbor? Or was he perhaps speaking in hypothetical terms to further the conversation? I argue that Jesus is at once challenging the lawyer (and all readers by extension) and assuming that Leviticus 18:5 reveals the underlying principle that life and keeping God's commandments are logically and necessarily intertwined. The use of Leviticus 18:5 in the New Testament is swirling in eddies of interpretive complexity, but I would suggest several points moving forward.

First, the interaction between the lawyer and Jesus in Luke 10:25–29 sets the stage for the parable of the good Samaritan (10:30–37), and 10:25–37 is therefore best taken as a unit. This is less controversial today than it would have been a hundred or even fifty years ago, when many suggested that the best way to interpret the parables was to disentangle them from their contexts in the Gospels.[22] However, from a literary perspective, the contexts in which the parables are found are of the utmost importance for careful interpretation. Thus, the interaction between Jesus and the lawyer provides the context for understanding who is one's neighbor. Additionally, the entire episode is framed by terminology of "doing" (*poiēsas*) (10:25, 37),[23] and Jesus's directive in 10:28 is "do [*poiei*] this and you will live." We see, then, a clear emphasis on "doing" in the context of this parable, which graphically illustrates the need positively to show mercy (10:37), much as we saw with Matthew's use of Hosea 6:6.[24]

22. Cf. Joachim Jeremias, *The Parables of Jesus*, trans. S. H. Hooke, 2nd ed. (New York: Scribner, 1972), 96–114.
23. Klyne R. Snodgrass, *Stories with Intent: A Comprehensive Guide to the Parables of Jesus* (Grand Rapids: Eerdmans, 2008), 349.
24. Likewise, Luke 11:42 mirrors Matt. 23:23 in the need to demonstrate true love and justice, which Jesus did without fault.

Second, the parable in light of the broader context strongly suggests that the lawyer's understanding of his ability to keep the two great commands was insufficient. Though his answer was correct (10:27–28), in practice the lawyer had an inadequate perspective on who was worthy to receive mercy. Moreover, it is not irrelevant that the lawyer desired to justify himself (*ho de thelōn dikaiōsai heauton* [10:29]). One need not import a Pauline doctrine of justification to see that the lawyer was trying to vindicate himself (cf. Luke 18:9–14), whereas Jesus challenged the man's rectitude in light of the radical demands of the law. For Jesus, then, the two great love commands are of a piece with the principle of "do this and live" (Lev. 18:5). Thus, though the principle of "do this and live" is true, Jesus's challenge indicates that neither the lawyer nor anyone else in the hearing of Jesus had fully met the demands of Leviticus 18:5 because of the presence of sin.[25] That Jesus concludes the parable with "go and do [*poiei*] likewise" (Luke 10:37) does not undermine this interpretation,[26] since the validity of the requirement to show mercy is consistent with the ongoing relevance of the two great commands.

Third, in light of Luke's overall narrative we can affirm that Jesus did love God and neighbor perfectly and so fulfilled the principle of "do this and live." Luke's fulfillment of the two great commands is consonant with all that we have seen thus far in Jesus's thoroughgoing conformity to Scripture, his fulfillment of the divine necessity of salvation, the mercy that he shows throughout his ministry, and his role in saving the lost. Indeed, it is of particular interest that the lawyer's question about inheriting eternal life appears to be tantamount to "What must I do to participate in the resurrection of the righteous?"[27] If this is the intent of the lawyer's question, then it is most interesting in light of Jesus's own resurrection in Luke. The lawyer's powerlessness to secure life by his actions provides a foil for the perfect obedience of Christ. Is Jesus then providing a glimpse into the rationale for his own experience of resurrection

---

25. See John Murray, *The Epistle to the Romans*, NICNT, 2 vols. (Grand Rapids: Eerdmans, 1959–65), 2:249–51. Though Murray's discussion focuses on Lev. 18:5 in Romans, it remains instructive for a consideration of Luke 10. Additionally, readers will observe that although the term *sin* is not used in the parable of the good Samaritan, Luke's Gospel—and indeed all the Gospels—is built on the presupposition of the problem of sin, which is why Jesus came as Savior (cf., e.g., Luke 1:77; 2:11; 19:9–10; Acts 5:31). Cf. Adolf Schlatter, *The History of the Christ: The Foundation for New Testament Theology*, trans. Andreas J. Köstenberger (Grand Rapids: Baker, 1997), 74–78, 120.

26. See also Geldenhuys, *Gospel of Luke*, 312.

27. Darrell L. Bock, *Luke*, 2 vols., BECNT (Grand Rapids: Baker Academic, 1994–96), 2:1023, who notes Dan. 12:2 and the discussions in Str-B 1:808–9, 829; cf. Kenneth E. Bailey, *"Poet and Peasant" and "Through Peasant Eyes": A Literary-Cultural Approach to the Parables in Luke*, combined ed. (Grand Rapids: Eerdmans, 1983), 35–36; C. F. Evans, *Saint Luke* (London: SCM; Philadelphia: Trinity Press International, 1990), 465.

life? Did his resurrection follow logically upon his fully loving God and neighbor? Did he *live* in the resurrection because he "did this"—namely, *all* that God required? A strong case can be made that Jesus's own resurrection life follows necessarily from his perfect adherence to God's commands.[28]

Fourth, and quite significant, an emphasis on Jesus's fulfillment of the two great commands and Leviticus 18:5 also comports with the Adam Christology of Luke (cf. Luke 3:38), since the principle of "do this and live" appears to have been distinctly possible for Adam. It is as the last Adam—as one not in need of redemption—that Jesus is able to "do this and live." Though Leviticus 18:5 was originally addressed to Israel, Israel could only "do this and live" in an analogous way to Adam. Whereas perfect obedience was possible for Adam in his created state—and eternal life would have been, by implication, offered to him were he to meet this covenantal condition[29]—Israel was a people decidedly in need of redemption and forgiveness of sins.[30] Simply put, it was never possible for Israel to attain eternal life through perfect obedience. Nor were they called to do so. After the entrance of sin into the world, it is only the last Adam, uniquely conceived by the Holy Spirit as the head of new creation, who can deliver resurrection life through perfect conformity to all that God requires. I propose that we find in Luke's account of the parable of the good Samaritan implicit indications that Jesus, as the last Adam, fulfills the principle of "do this and live," thereby securing resurrection life.

I readily acknowledge that not all will be convinced of my suggestions. I also concede that I have said more about the theology presupposed in the context of the parable than the parable itself. However, I do think the parable has more to say about the way one comes to participate in eternal life than is sometimes allowed,[31] though I do not think eternal life is the main point of the parable per se. I am also not suggesting that we should only read the parable in such a way that Jesus is the good Samaritan. Instead, while leaving room for (at least) implicit Christology in the parables,[32] the imperatival force of the parable ("go and do [*poiei*] likewise" [10:37]) is not to be discounted.

28. Cf. Herman Bavinck, *Reformed Dogmatics*, ed. John Bolt, trans. John Vriend, 4 vols. (Grand Rapids: Baker Academic, 2003–8), 3:174, 225–26; 4:601–2. For ways in which this parable relates to the life of Jesus, see Craig A. Evans, *Luke*, NIBCNT (Peabody, MA: Hendrickson, 1990), 178; William Hendriksen, *Exposition of the Gospel according to Luke* (Grand Rapids: Baker, 1978), 596. Cf. also François Bovon, *Luke*, trans. Christine M. Thomas, Donald S. Deer, and James Crouch, 3 vols., Hermeneia (Minneapolis: Fortress, 2002–13), 2:53, 60, 64.

29. See the discussion in chap. 3 of the proposed Adamic covenant.

30. One need only consider the various sacrifices set forth in Leviticus.

31. Cf., e.g., Snodgrass, *Stories*, 358–59; Simon J. Gathercole, *Where Is Boasting? Early Jewish Soteriology and Paul's Response in Romans 1–5* (Grand Rapids: Eerdmans, 2002), 121–23.

32. Cf. Davies and Allison, *Matthew*, 2:382.

Nevertheless, Luke 10:25–28 is an important passage to consider when reflecting upon the significance of Jesus's life for salvation. If the suggested reading of Luke 10:25–28 is correct, then we find an implicit reference to Jesus's perfect obedience to the law (which entails true love for God), leading inexorably to eternal life.

A consideration of the parable of the good Samaritan leads one to consider Jesus's encounter with the rich young ruler (Matt. 19:16–22 // Mark 10:17–22 // Luke 18:18–23).[33] Similar to the lawyer in Luke 10, the young ruler asks Jesus what he must do to inherit eternal life (Matt. 19:17 // Mark 10:17 // Luke 18:18). Again Jesus challenges the young man's understanding of what is required. Whereas the young man wants to know which commandments have to be kept, and then affirms he has kept them, Jesus highlights the young man's lack of meeting the radical demands of the commandments by pointing out his need to give to the poor. It is not difficult to see how the man's unwillingness to meet this demand can be viewed as a failure to conform to the commandment not to steal (Matt. 19:18 // Mark 10:19 // Luke 18:22). The depth of commitment required by the law called not for nominal conformity but for sincere love for neighbor even if it meant personal loss (cf. Eph. 4:28). Additionally, the young man's refusal to part with his many possessions revealed a heart that was not fully committed to the Lord, which means he also broke the first commandment to have no other gods before the Lord. It is further instructive that in Matthew's account Jesus urges the man to be perfect (*teleios* [19:21]), which recalls the perfection of God's loving character in Matthew 5:48. Matthew's account, therefore, rather clearly links the commands Jesus gives to the rich young man to the need to love as God loves. Whereas the rich young ruler was unable to meet these demands, Jesus himself can offer eternal life (cf. Matt. 19:29 // Mark 10:30 // Luke 18:30), which presupposes Jesus's unique ability to do that which is required for life.[34]

Summary: Mercy and Sacrifice

God desires mercy, not bare sacrifice. In Jesus the dichotomy between these is overcome, so that perfect devotion to God and perfect sacrifice are united. Sacrifice is not bad, of course, but the danger is to engage in outward conformity to rites in a way that is divorced from sincere devotion to God. Matthew's use of Hosea 6:6 emphasizes the need for true, entire covenant faithfulness, as

33. As is commonly noted, no one account includes all three attributions (rich, young, ruler), but it is a composite description.

34. Cf. Thomas R. Schreiner, *New Testament Theology: Magnifying God in Christ* (Grand Rapids: Baker Academic, 2008), 185.

does Jesus's emphasis on the two great commands, which find their realization in Jesus's life. Both the lawyer, whose questions prompt the parable of the good Samaritan, and the rich young ruler illustrate how difficult it is to meet God's demands, and they simultaneously serve as a foil for the perfect character of Jesus. Jesus was uniquely qualified to serve as the ultimate sacrifice, because as the last Adam he was free from sin—whether sins of omission or sins of commission. Perfection of life and perfection of sacrifice are united in Jesus, something we will consider further under the following headings.

Jesus's Life as Ransom

We turn now to some key texts that speak of the nature of Jesus's sacrifice, which we do well to consider in light of the unity of his life's work. Earlier, in chapter 2, I discussed the intersection of Adam Christology and the so-called ransom logion in Matthew 20:28 and Mark 10:45:

Matthew 20:28	Mark 10:45
hōsper ho huios tou anthrōpou ouk ēlthen diakonēthēnai alla diakonēsai kai dounai tēn psychēn autou lytron anti pollōn	*kai gar ho huios tou anthrōpou ouk ēlthen diakonēthēnai alla diakonēsai kai dounai tēn psychēn autou lytron anti pollōn*
Just as the Son of Man did not come to be served but to serve, and to give his life as a ransom for many	For even the Son of Man did not come to be served but to serve, and to give his life as a ransom for many

More remains to be said concerning the import of these crucial passages as they relate to the life and death of Jesus. By way of foundation, the ransom logion quite clearly communicates the idea of substitution: the Son of Man gives his life over to death in place of the many.[35] Supporting this reading is the preposition *anti*, which most often indicates "in place of." Indeed, Murray Harris argues that the primary meaning of *anti* in the LXX and nonbiblical Greek is that of a substitutionary exchange.[36] Beyond the preposition, which can only bear so much exegetical weight, is the concept itself. Leon Morris argues persuasively in a classic work that even if one were to doubt the significance of the preposition *anti*, on a conceptual level ransom (*lytron*)

35. Cf. Murray, *Redemption*, 32–40. Also recall that Mark 10:45 is one of the clearest places Jesus identifies his mission in Mark; cf. Elizabeth E. Shively, *Apocalyptic Imagination in the Gospel of Mark: The Literary and Theological Role of Mark 3:22–30*, BZNW 189 (Berlin: Walter de Gruyter, 2012), 1.

36. Murray J. Harris, *Prepositions and Theology in the Greek New Testament: An Essential Reference Resource for Exegesis* (Grand Rapids: Zondervan, 2012), 49–56.

necessitates the idea of an exchange, since it derives from the framework of a ransom price rendered.[37]

Further supporting the concept of substitution is Jesus's role as a representative.[38] Jesus speaks in the ransom logion of his role as the royal Son of Man (cf. Dan. 7:13–14), the one man who gives his life as a ransom for many. This is consistent with the argument made earlier, that Jesus's baptism should be viewed in light of his identification and representation of his people in their need for repentance and forgiveness of sins (Matt. 3:2; Mark 1:4; Luke 3:3).

In addition, other aspects of the Old Testament background(s) for the ransom logion strongly suggest a substitutionary understanding of *lytron* and may also provide additional support for the present focus on the *life* of Jesus. Along with the Danielic resonances noted in chapter 2, the ransom logion most likely evokes the servant's role from Isaiah 53. Though the verbal parallels between Isaiah 53 and Matthew 20:28 // Mark 10:45 are not overwhelming, they are sufficient, in conjunction with the conceptual parallels, to provide exegetical warrant for reading the ransom logion in light of Isaiah 53.[39] Specifically, in Isaiah 53:11–12 the servant makes many (LXX: *polloi*) righteous, bearing their iniquities and giving his own life (LXX: *psychē*) in their place. In Matthew 20:28 // Mark 10:45 Jesus's life is given for many (*pollōn*). This is narratively related to Jesus's death on the cross poured out for many (*pollōn* [Matt. 26:28; Mark 14:24]), which Matthew states explicitly is for the forgiveness of sins (*eis aphesin hamartiōn*). Moreover, Isaiah 53 features prominently elsewhere in both Matthew and Mark. By way of example, Matthew 8:17 quotes Isaiah 53:4 in relation to the healing ministry of Jesus, and (as noted earlier) Joel Marcus has identified many verbal parallels between Isaiah 40–55 and Mark's Gospel.[40] As Son of Man, Jesus (surprisingly) serves, giving his own life as the ransom for many through his death on the cross.

We can say even more about how the ransom logion may reveal an indissoluble connection between the life and death of Jesus since it is specifically

---

37. Leon Morris, *The Apostolic Preaching of the Cross* (Grand Rapids: Eerdmans, 1955), 26–35. Cf. M. Harris, *Prepositions and Theology*, 54: "What λύτρον already implies, ἀντί simply reinforces—the idea of vicariousness."

38. See also G. K. Beale, *A New Testament Biblical Theology: The Unfolding of the Old Testament in the New* (Grand Rapids: Baker Academic, 2011), 196–97, 398.

39. See the chart in Joel Marcus, *Mark 8–16: A New Translation with Introduction and Commentary*, AYB 27A (New Haven: Yale University Press, 2009), 753; cf. Davies and Allison, *Matthew*, 3:96; France, *Matthew*, 762.

40. Joel Marcus, *The Way of the Lord: Christological Exegesis of the Old Testament in the Gospel of Mark*, SNTW (Edinburgh: T&T Clark, 1992), 188–90. Cf. N. T. Wright, *Jesus and the Victory of God*, COQG 2 (Minneapolis: Fortress, 1996), 588–91. See also the discussion in chap. 6 on Luke 11:21–22.

the *life* (*psychē*) that is given in place of others.[41] This may be surprising, since Numbers 35:31–32 warns against offering a ransom for a murderer, and Psalm 49:8–9 [48:8–10 LXX; 49:7–8 EVV] indicates that no one is able to give anything that would be sufficient to ransom the life (LXX: *psychē*) of another. Likewise, earlier in Matthew and Mark Jesus asks what a man can give in exchange for his soul (*psychē*; Matt. 16:26 // Mark 8:37). The implied answer to Jesus's question, much like Psalm 49, is that nothing can be found that is more important than one's soul (cf. *Sipre* Deut. §329).[42] Humanity is made in the image of God, which means that the taking of a person's life by the hands of another is a tragedy of the highest degree (Gen. 9:6). In several Old Testament texts we read about laws pertaining to the ransom price for one's life (Exod. 30:12; cf. Num. 35:31–33), which seems to illustrate the need for atonement.[43] And yet in the ransom logion Jesus states that he, as Son of Man, has come to give his own life as a ransom for many. It appears, then, that what was thought to be impossible as a matter of proverbial wisdom (cf. Ps. 49:4)—that no person possesses anything of sufficient worth to redeem another person from death—was nevertheless possible with the Son of Man. By serving even to the point of laying down his priceless life in exchange for others, Jesus is able to redeem the many.[44]

I suggest, then, that the ransom logion reveals the unity of the life and death of Jesus in that his life is in fact able to serve as a ransom, which points to its qualitatively perfect character. This comes by viewing the ransom logion in light of the Gospels more broadly, since Jesus comes to save his people from their sins (Matt. 1:21) and identifies with John's baptism of repentance for the forgiveness of sins (Matt. 3:11–17 // Mark 1:4–11). Moreover, we have also seen connections between Isaiah 53:10–12, which states that the servant is put to death for the transgressions of many, and the ransom logion. The servant is an offering for guilt, bears the transgressions of others, makes others righteous, and makes intercession for transgressors. Old Testament sacrificial imagery involved with this description, which necessitates a spotless sacrifice (e.g., Lev. 5:15, 18; 6:6), further supports the view that Jesus is viewed as holy, distinct from transgressors. Jesus is able to provide the sufficiently valuable ransom because he is uniquely qualified to serve as the spotless, sacrificial

41. See also Cilliers Breytenbach, "Narrating the Death of Jesus in Mark: Utterances of the Main Character, Jesus," *ZNW* 105 (2014): 166–67.
42. Adolf Schlatter, *Der Evangelist Matthäus: Seine Sprache, sein Ziel, seine Selbständigkeit* (Stuttgart: Calwer, 1929), 523.
43. Cf. M. Harris, *Prepositions and Theology*, 54.
44. Nolland (*Gospel of Matthew*, 693) is probably correct to draw attention to the hope of God's deliverance in Ps. 49:15. I will discuss the resurrection below.

ransom. And as we have seen, sinlessness entails not only avoiding lawless deeds but also positively doing what the law requires.

As a Son of Man passage, the ransom logion may also entail Adamic imagery (see chap. 2)—the Son of Man is a representative person who is able to give his life vicariously on behalf of many. The salvific work of the Son of Man, as an Adamic figure, in conjunction with probable allusions to Isaiah 53:10–12, may also complement Paul's similar statements in Romans 5:18–19.[45] In both the ransom logion and Romans 5 the obedience of Christ is described in language reminiscent of the servant of Isaiah 53:10–12, who qualifies transgressors to be counted righteous, and in both contexts Christ is the one man who gives his life for the transgressions of the many. Though my argument does not necessitate that one recognize these possible parallels between Romans and the ransom logion, it is intriguing that in Romans Christ's obedience is clearly set in contrast to Adam's disobedience, and in the Gospels it is quite likely that the work of Christ is also portrayed in Adamic terms.

To be sure, a strong emphasis is placed on the obedient *death* of Christ in the ransom logion. And yet we risk truncating the significance of the life that is given as a ransom if we try to limit the ransom logion to speaking *only* of Jesus's death. We can see the significance of Jesus's life in the ransom logion in light of the overarching Adam-Christ imagery in the Gospels: by portraying Jesus in Adamic terms, the Evangelists underscore the obedience of Jesus in contrast to Adam's disobedience. The obedience of the (Adamic) Son of Man in the ransom logion surely emphasizes the death of Jesus as the last Adam, but this is only the most climactic aspect of his wide-ranging obedience that is to be viewed as an integrated whole. Indeed, the ransom logion assumes full conformity to the law, which is necessary to serve as a ransom for transgressors.

Moreover, how would one delimit the obedience of Jesus's death? Do those actions of Jesus that involved suffering before the cross, and seem to have ensured Jesus's continued faithfulness to the mission of dying on the cross, constitute in some way the obedience of Jesus unto death? In other words, limiting Jesus's sacrifice of his life only to his obedience unto death would lead to numerous exegetical quandaries, since we would be forced to delimit what counts and what does not count as constitutive of Jesus's sacrificial death in a way that Scripture does not. Is Jesus's suffering *on the cross*, before his death, to be considered constitutive of his sacrificial death, or does only the act of dying itself count? If we perhaps conclude that Jesus's entire suffering on the

45. Yongbom Lee (*The Son of Man as the Last Adam: The Early Church Tradition as a Source of Paul's Adam Christology* [Eugene, OR: Pickwick, 2012], 97–112) argues that the ransom logion tradition in the early church underlies Paul's statements in Rom. 5.

cross in some way is constitutive of his death, what about his suffering on the Via Dolorosa? What about the blood Jesus shed during his scourging? What about Jesus's obedience to the path of suffering at Caesarea Philippi, when Peter would have hindered his path that led toward the cross? The question could be pushed back even further: was Jesus's baptism of repentance of a piece with his obedience unto death, since Jesus himself connects his baptism to his death?[46] I do not wish to belabor the point, but simply propose that the life in view in the ransom logion summarily speaks of Jesus's unified obedience, which *must* have included both positive fulfillment of the law and suffering unto death, since these are two sides of one reality (I will return to this issue below, and in the theological synthesis of chap. 8). The life of Jesus, given as a ransom for many, was a life devoid of sin and therefore a life of positive obedience to God. And this life of obedience that is given representatively and vicariously is the life of the last Adam, whose actions overcome the deathly effects of the sin of the first Adam.[47]

An early work in the history of Christian interpretation may provide further support for the relationship between the ransom logion, the entire obedience of Jesus, and Adam Christology. In the (probably) second-century *Epistle to Diognetus*, the notion of ransom (*lytron*) features prominently, apparently echoing both the ransom logion (Matt. 20:28 // Mark 10:45) and Romans 5:18–19.[48] I have argued elsewhere that the *lytron* in view in *Diognetus* 9:2

---

46. Recall the discussion from chap. 4; cf. Luke 12:49–50.

47. Recently Nathan Eubank (*Wages of Cross-Bearing and Debt of Sin: The Economy of the Kingdom of Heaven in Matthew's Gospel*, BZNW 196 [Berlin: Walter de Gruyter, 2013]) has argued that the economic dimensions of the ransom logion in Matthew should be taken into greater consideration in light of Matthew's emphasis on economic language to describe salvation. For Eubank, Jesus is able to ransom the many (Matt. 20:28) because he has amassed a heavenly treasury of righteousness (cf. Matt. 6:19–21) (ibid., 107–8, 121–32). Though Eubank has done readers a service to highlight Matthew's economic language, I am not convinced by all of his conclusions. For example, it is not as uncommon as Eubank suggests to find economic language lacking in relation to Jesus's *lytron* sayings (see, e.g., the classic works of Morris, *Apostolic Preaching*, 9–59; Murray, *Redemption*, 42–50). It is also not clear that one must envision Matthew's language as a rather literal(?) treasury of merit that is amassed (see Geerhardus Vos, *Reformed Dogmatics*, ed. and trans. Richard B. Gaffin Jr., 5 vols. [Bellingham, WA: Lexham Press, 2012–16], 3:116–24; cf. Eubank, *Wages of Cross-Bearing*, 124–25). The price in view is not financial payment but rather the price (= value) of the lifeblood of Jesus (Morris, *Apostolic Preaching*, 44; Lev. 17:11, 14). Additionally, the covenantal blood of Jesus poured out for the forgiveness of sins (Matt. 26:28) underscores the interrelatedness of the sacrifice of Jesus's life and the penalty of death due to sin. This penalty is tantamount to the wrath of God, which Eubank does not see in Matthew's view of atonement (*Wages of Cross-Bearing*, 129). Economic language in Matthew must therefore be more fully integrated with what Matthew says about the death of Jesus and forgiveness of sins, which I will address in the next section.

48. For what follows, see Brandon D. Crowe, "Oh Sweet Exchange! The Soteriological Significance of the Incarnation in the *Epistle to Diognetus*," ZNW 102 (2011): 96–109; cf. J. Christopher

refers to the entire obedience of the Son that is given in exchange for the many unrighteous (*Diogn.* 9:5), which includes both the positive accomplishment of righteousness and his serving as a sacrificial *lytron* in his death.[49] In *Diognetus*, therefore, we find an interpretation of the ransom logion that understands the ransom to include the positive character of Jesus's life in association with his death. Moreover, these themes may also be collocated with Adamic imagery, since in *Diognetus* language from the ransom logion is combined with language from Romans 5:18–19.[50] If this interpretation is correct, then *Diognetus* provides additional support for the present argument that the ransom logion in Matthew and Mark envisions the positive character of Jesus's life—all that which was accomplished in the incarnation—as that which is given as a ransom for many.

Regardless of how one reads *Diognetus*, the emphasis in Matthew (especially) of the need for a greater righteousness that entails love, justice, and mercy—which Jesus himself exhibits fully—in conjunction with the role of Jesus as a *lytron* for many, strongly suggests that Jesus was uniquely qualified to serve in this capacity because of his positive obedience of all that was required throughout his life. Were Jesus to have failed in any way, he would not have been qualified to serve as a (perfect) ransom for many. In other words, one must view the obedience of Jesus in his life and death as an integrated whole.

Blood of the Covenant

In the preceding section I alluded to the fact that Jesus's blood was valuable because of the sinlessness of his life. This statement warrants additional explanation. To begin, we should acknowledge that some of the most important sources we have for the nature and purpose of Jesus's death come from Jesus's words of institution during the Last Supper (Matt. 26:26–29 // Mark 14:22–25 // Luke 22:15–20). Moreover, these words in Matthew and Mark exhibit verbal parallels to the ransom logion, as evidenced by the giving of Jesus's life for "many" (*pollōn*) in both contexts. Therefore the ransom logion must be read in light of the words of Jesus the night before his death. Indeed, Jesus's discussion of the blood of the covenant most likely expands upon the life given in the ransom (Matt. 26:28 // Mark 14:24; cf. Luke 22:20).[51]

Edwards, *The Ransom Logion in Mark and Matthew: Its Reception and Its Significance for the Study of the Gospels*, WUNT 2/327 (Tübingen: Mohr Siebeck, 2012), 61–66.

49. Crowe, "Oh Sweet Exchange!," 100–107.

50. Ibid., 108–9.

51. See, e.g., Breytenbach, "Death of Jesus," 165–67.

In other words, the blood of Jesus is tantamount to the life in view in the ransom logion, and the words of institution specifically identify this blood as the blood of the covenant (cf. Exod. 24:8; Jer. 31:31 [38:31 LXX]; Zech. 9:11). Therefore, the blood of the covenant that is poured out for many (for the forgiveness of sins) is immensely valuable and invokes the character of Jesus's entire life.[52] To be clear, I am not saying that the blood is *only* about Jesus's life and not his death. Rather, it is the lifeblood of Jesus poured out in his covenantal death.[53] At the Last Supper Jesus institutes a (new) covenant, which is built upon the foundation of his own blood and therefore the obedience of his entire life.[54] It is striking that in the new covenant, the blood of the covenant is the blood of the covenant mediator himself. This is expounded in Hebrews, but the principles are also present in the Gospels. In the covenant ceremony of Exodus 24, for example, Moses is the mediator of the Sinaitic covenant but does not pour out his own blood in its ratification. Instead, Moses employs the blood of sacrificial oxen (Exod. 24:5–8). In contrast, Jesus pours out his own blood for the forgiveness of sins, which indicates that, as the covenant mediator, Jesus himself had met the requirements of the covenant.[55]

This interpretation requires further explanation. In Jeremiah 31 we read that a new covenant was necessary because of the people's persistent covenantal rebellion. This new covenant recalls Sinai but is better than the Mosaic covenant because God's law will be written on the hearts of his people (Jer. 31:33 [38:33 LXX]). Part of the problem with the Mosaic covenant was the dichotomy between heart and ritual, obedience and sacrifice.[56] True forgiveness of sins (Jer. 31:34), and not simply rituals (Jer. 7:1–34), would come with the new covenant, which was necessary since the old covenant had been

52. Cf. Davies and Allison, *Matthew*, 3:473; J. P. Meier, *The Vision of Matthew: Christ, Church, and Morality in the First Gospel* (1991; repr., Eugene, OR: Wipf & Stock, 2004), 183; James R. Edwards, *The Gospel according to Mark*, PNTC (Grand Rapids: Eerdmans, 2002), 426.

53. Cf., e.g., Morris (*Apostolic Preaching*, 108–22), who takes great care to emphasize that death is in view in most relevant biblical references where the blood is mentioned. He also acknowledges the close connection between the *life* and the *blood* (Lev. 17:11, 14), though he wishes to emphasize that death is virtually always in view. One can agree with Morris's desire to emphasize the death of Jesus by mention of his blood, without having to deny that Jesus's blood is valuable because of the character of his life. Curiously, Morris does not mention Matt. 26:28 // Mark 14:24 // Luke 22:20 in his discussion of the blood. See also Donald Macleod, *Christ Crucified: Understanding the Atonement* (Downers Grove, IL: IVP Academic, 2014), 68–71.

54. Only Luke 22:20 specifies a "new" covenant, but we can scarcely imagine that Matthew and Mark intend something different, particularly since all three Synoptics invoke the new covenant language of Jer. 31. Cf. Ridderbos, *Coming of the Kingdom*, 200.

55. See Meredith G. Kline, "The Old Testament Origins of the Gospel Genre," *WTJ* 38 (1975): 1–27.

56. See C. John Collins, "The Eucharist as Christian Sacrifice: How Patristic Authors Can Help Us Read the Bible," *WTJ* 66 (2004): 12; cf. Jer. 11:10.

broken by God's faithless children who had experienced the covenantal curse of exile.[57] True circumcision of heart was necessary (Jer. 4:4, 14; 9:25–26; cf. 3:10; 5:23; 7:24; 9:8, 14; 11:20; 17:5–10; 18:12; 29:13), which would come through the work of God in the new covenant (Jer. 31:31–34; cf. Deut. 30:6; Jer. 24:7; 32:39–41). A similar view is found in Isaiah 1:11, where the Lord says: "What is the abundance of your sacrifices to me? . . . I do not delight in the blood of rams or of lambs or of goats." In other words, the prophets bemoan hollow ritual and anticipate the day when there will be no discrepancy between heart commitment and external actions. While this hope is still *not yet* a perfect reality in the present age in which sin and death remain, the new covenant has *already* been established on the basis of Jesus's perfect accomplishment in history of all of God's covenantal requirements. By fully loving God and neighbor, Jesus has overcome the dichotomy between sacrifice and obedience, thereby grounding the benefits of the new covenant in his own life's work.[58] And as covenant mediator, Jesus has sealed with his blood the new, better covenant.[59]

Jesus's words of institution in many ways summarize his entire work and give us warrant for viewing his actions throughout the Gospels as covenantal actions.[60] To be sure, the term "covenant" (*diathēkē*) is used sparingly in the Gospels. However, as noted in chapter 3, the concept is present even where the terminology may be lacking. A few examples will suffice to illustrate this principle. Jesus is the son of Abraham (Matt. 1:1) and the son of David (Matt. 1:1; Luke 1:32–33), which denotes his covenantal heritage and his status as royal Son of God (as does his circumcision [Luke 2:21]). As Son of God, Jesus recalls the nation, the king, and even Adam. Jesus's choice of twelve disciples serves a covenantal purpose, as the covenant people are re-formed around Jesus himself.[61] Matthew features an Immanuel *inclusio* focused on Jesus as "God with us" (Matt. 1:23; 28:20; cf. 18:20), recalling the highest covenant blessing of God's dwelling with his people (cf. Lev. 26:12). In Luke the birth of Jesus proves that God has remembered his covenantal mercy and is providing salvation for his people (Luke 1:50, 54–55, 68–79; 2:11, 26–32). So it is quite fitting for Jesus to invoke the language of covenant in the words of institution, since his entire life and ministry were shaped by God's covenant dealings with his people. More specifically, Jesus's life was characterized by

57. See Deut. 28; Jer. 3:14, 19, 22; 4:4, 22; 11:1–17; 25:1–24; 27:1–22; 29:1–32; 31:15–22.

58. See also William L. Lane, *Hebrews 9–13*, WBC 47B (Dallas: Word, 1991), 266.

59. For the unity of heart motive of the offerer and ritual sacrifice in Leviticus, see Nobuyoshi Kiuchi, "Spirituality in Offering a Peace Offering," *TynBul* 50 (1999): 23–31.

60. See Ridderbos, *Coming of the Kingdom*, 200–201.

61. E.g., Wright, *Jesus*, 169, 300.

complete, wholehearted covenantal faithfulness in all that he did. This was no small thing in light of Israel's history, where covenantal faithfulness was often found lacking, and where the covenant mediator himself was in need of atonement. Not so with Jesus.

In sum, though one cannot sufficiently mine the significance of Christ's death in a chapter of this length, we can at least say that Jesus's covenantal blood places him in the context of Israel's history and underscores the uniqueness of his life as covenant mediator.[62] In light of the role of covenantal blood in the Old Testament (e.g., Exod. 24:8–9), we can say with confidence that Jesus's blood sanctifies the members of the new covenant community, making them acceptable to approach God.[63] The words of institution recall God's previous covenantal relations with his people and indicate that a new day was dawning in which the sins of previous generations were being overcome through the sinless covenant mediator.[64]

The unity of sacrifice and perfect delight in the Father's will gives us opportunity to reflect on the unity of Christ's work, especially in light of the traditional categories of the active and passive obedience of Christ. These distinctions have been taken in various ways, and some have understood the passive obedience of Christ as referring to Jesus's death, and the active obedience of Christ as referring to his righteous life.[65] In light of this supposed two-stage approach, some have suggested we should retain Christ's *passive* obedience as sufficient for salvation, while perhaps jettisoning the need to speak of Christ's *active* obedience for salvation.[66] However, a better way to understand the active and passive obedience of Christ is to view them as *aspects* of the integrated, single work of Christ. From this perspective, Jesus's entire life is his active obedience, and his entire life is his passive obedience (though one does not therefore need to deny the intensification of suffering at the end of Jesus's earthly life). Thus, Christ's active obedience refers to his perfect accomplishment of all that God requires of humanity, whereas his

62. See also the discussion of the suffering servant and the (new) covenant in Oscar Cullmann, *The Christology of the New Testament*, trans. Shirley C. Guthrie and Charles A. M. Hall, rev. ed. (Philadelphia: Westminster, 1963), 64.

63. Cf. Amy L. B. Peeler, "Desiring God: The Blood of the Covenant in Exodus 24," *BBR* 23 (2013): 187–205.

64. See similarly, but with a different emphasis, Wright, *Jesus*, 560–61.

65. See, e.g., N. T. Wright, *Justification: God's Plan and Paul's Vision* (London: SPCK, 2009), 204.

66. Cf. Bavinck, *Reformed Dogmatics*, 3:378, discussing Christ's whole obedience: "It is totally contrary to Scripture . . . to restrict the 'satisfactory' (atoning) work of Christ to his suffering or even, as Jacob Alting did, to his suffering only during the three hours of darkness on the cross." See further the discussion in chap. 8.

passive obedience refers to his suffering the penalty of God's law.[67] Both are necessary for salvation, and both are found in the Gospels: Jesus obeys his Father perfectly at all times, and his obedience entails suffering.

In other words, the passive obedience of Christ does not refer only to his death, nor does his active obedience refer only to some events in his life. Instead, Jesus's *entire* obedience has both active and passive dimensions. Thus, Jesus was quite active in the passion and the events leading up to it, struggling in prayer that God's will would be done (Matt. 26:39 // Mark 14:36 // Luke 22:42). Jesus's passive obedience was thus willful obedience and does not imply that Jesus was merely passive.[68] Instead, it refers to his lifelong suffering.[69] Jesus's full love for God and neighbor (which denotes his perfect fulfilling of the law) constitutes his active obedience.[70] The positive obedience of Jesus in the temptation accounts of Matthew and Luke, in which Jesus also suffered the effects of sin, not only anticipates his obedient death on the cross,[71] but also illustrates well the unity of the active and passive dimensions of Jesus's obedience throughout his life.

In sum, the unity of Jesus's delight in doing all of the Father's will, including his willing embracing of sufferings (especially those in the final week of his life), should warn us against dividing the unified work of Christ. I will have more to say about this in the final chapter.

Resurrection and Kingdom Victory

With the death of Jesus as covenant mediator, we encounter a major turning point. Now the kingdom is firmly established, having been sealed with Jesus's blood.[72] Though Jesus inaugurated the kingdom already during his ministry, the kingdom could only be partially realized before his death and

---

67. See, e.g., Murray, *Redemption*, 21–22; Turretin, *Inst.* 14.13; Vos, *Reformed Dogmatics*, 3:127–31, 4:154–55; Bavinck, *Reformed Dogmatics*, 3:394–95; Louis Berkhof, *Systematic Theology*, 4th ed. (Grand Rapids: Eerdmans, 1941), 379–81; Macleod, *Christ Crucified*, 180–81.

68. *Passive* means "to suffer" (from Latin: *patior* [Greek: *paschō*]), not "passivity." See Robert Letham, *The Work of Christ*, CCT (Downers Grove, IL: IVP Academic, 1993), 130.

69. See Vos, *Reformed Dogmatics*, 3:128; Calvin, *Inst.* 2.16.5; Letham, *Work of Christ*, 130.

70. Jesus also demonstrated love for God and neighbor by his suffering, which underscores the unity of his active and passive obedience; because Jesus's obedience is a unity, the active and passive obedience always coincide in Jesus's life and death (so Bavinck, *Reformed Dogmatics*, 3:395).

71. See, e.g., Konradt, *Israel, Church, and the Gentiles*, 301; Terence L. Donaldson, "The Mockers and the Son of God (Matthew 27:37–44): Two Characters in Matthew's Story of Jesus," *JSNT* 41 (1991): 3–18; cf. Mikeal C. Parsons, *Luke*, Paideia (Grand Rapids: Baker Academic, 2015), 318–20.

72. Cf. Macleod, *Christ Crucified*, 25–26.

resurrection.[73] With the death and resurrection of Jesus comes, in the words of John's Gospel, the casting out of the ruler of this world (John 12:31–32).[74] Thus there is a close connection between the blood of the covenant and the fuller flowering and spread of the kingdom, particularly since Jesus's obedience unto death results in resurrection. Indeed, in the events relating to the Last Supper, we find after the words of institution that Jesus will not drink from the fruit of the vine again until he does so in the consummated kingdom (Matt. 26:29 // Mark 14:25 // Luke 22:18), which among other things anticipates Jesus's continued rule over the kingdom after his death. Moreover, in Luke, Jesus follows the words of institution with the promise to the Twelve that they had been given a kingdom and will judge the twelve tribes of Israel (Luke 22:29–30), thus indicating a close connection between the blood of the new covenant with the coming of the kingdom.

The Gospels, in other words, not only mention the death of Jesus but also are built on the presupposition of Jesus's resurrection. Three of the four Gospels clearly end with resurrection appearances of Jesus (Matt. 28:1–20; Luke 24:1–53; John 20–22). Moreover, the so-called longer ending of Mark (16:9–20), which exhibits a secondary character, also includes a resurrection account.[75] But even without this longer ending, Mark implies the resurrection already by 16:8 in light of Jesus's threefold prediction of his resurrection (Mark 8:31; 9:31; 10:33–34; cf. 8:29–9:8) and the angelic reminder that Jesus told his disciples he would meet them in Galilee (16:7).[76] Indeed, not only in Mark but in all four Gospels, Jesus predicts both his death and his resurrection (Matt. 16:21; 17:22–23; 20:18–20; Luke 9:22; 18:33; John 2:19–21; 10:17–18; cf. Matt. 17:1–8; Luke 9:28–36). In Luke Jesus explains that the resurrection was part of what was spoken of in the Old Testament that was

73. Ridderbos, *Coming of the Kingdom*, 171.

74. Cf. Macleod, *Christ Crucified*, 238; Craig R. Koester, *The Word of Life: A Theology of John's Gospel* (Grand Rapids: Eerdmans, 2008), 119.

75. For the argument that Mark 16:9–20 was composed in light of (at least) Matthew, Luke, and John, see James A. Kelhoffer, *Miracle and Mission: The Authentication of Missionaries and Their Message in the Longer Ending of Mark*, WUNT 2/112 (Tübingen: Mohr Siebeck, 2000), esp. chaps. 2–3.

76. Of course, Mark may have intended to include a resurrection account, but for whatever reason it is no longer extant (N. T. Wright, *The Resurrection of the Son of God*, COQG 3 [Minneapolis: Fortress, 2003], 617–24). However, it is more likely that 16:8 is the original ending of Mark. See variously William L. Lane, *The Gospel according to Mark*, NICNT (Grand Rapids: Eerdmans, 1974), 590–92; Larry W. Hurtado, "The Women, the Tomb, and the Climax of Mark," in *A Wandering Galilean: Essays in Honour of Seán Freyne*, ed. Zuleika Rodgers, Margaret Daly-Denton, and Anne Fitzpatrick McKinley, JSJSup 132 (Leiden: Brill, 2009), 427–50; Ned B. Stonehouse, *The Witness of Matthew and Mark to Christ* (Grand Rapids: Eerdmans, 1958), 86–118. Marcus (*Mark 8–16*, 1088–96) leans this way as well.

necessary to be fulfilled (Luke 24:26–27, 46). Without the resurrection the Gospel narratives would be unresolved, with the opponents of Jesus having the last word.[77] The resurrection therefore is the vindication of Jesus, that he was in the right and that his lifelong obedience, even in the face of suffering, was not in vain.

All this is to emphasize that the resurrection does indeed factor significantly in the Gospels, which is significant for the present focus on the obedience of Christ because Jesus's resurrection vindicates his obedience throughout his life; his suffering was not in vain.[78] Indeed, the uniqueness of Jesus's resurrection is consonant with the uniqueness of his obedience. Whereas David as God's anointed died and was buried, Peter's words in Acts 2:27 (cf. Ps. 16:10 [15:10 LXX]) indicate that Jesus's resurrection is the resurrection of God's supremely Holy One.[79] The lack of Jesus's decay in the tomb is due to his perfect sinlessness, since decay was often viewed as a penalty for sin.[80] A similar connection between Jesus's righteousness and his vindication in the resurrection appears to be in view in Acts 3:14–15 ("But you denied the Holy and Righteous One . . . and you killed the *archēgos* of life, whom God raised from the dead").[81] Additionally, Acts 17:31 seems to assume that Jesus as resurrected Lord will judge in righteousness *because* he is proved to be righteous through the resurrection.[82] The resurrection is the final indication that Jesus's obedience was obedience unto life.[83] The perfect obedience of Jesus leads to perfect experience of resurrection life. The words of Geerhardus Vos are apropos in this regard: "Had something been lacking in the suffering of Christ, then it would have been impossible that the violence of death had

77. See Davies and Allison, *Matthew*, 3:673.

78. François Vouga, *Une théologie du Nouveau Testament*, MdB 43 (Geneva: Labor et Fides, 2001), 228; James D. G. Dunn, *Jesus Remembered*, CM 1 (Grand Rapids: Eerdmans, 2003), 867; Wright, *Resurrection*, 726–28; cf. Marcus, *Way of the Lord*, 180. See also Luke 23:46 in light of Ps. 31:5 (Kyle Scott Barrett, "Justification in Lukan Theology" [PhD diss., Southern Baptist Theological Seminary, 2012], 150). This connection is spelled out in more detail in the Pauline corpus, on which see Rom. 1:4; 4:25; 1 Cor. 15:20–28, 42–49; 1 Tim. 3:16; Beale, *New Testament Biblical Theology*, 493–97, who also cites Geerhardus Vos, *The Pauline Eschatology* (1930; repr., Grand Rapids: Baker, 1979), 151.

79. See also Geerhardus Vos, *The Self-Disclosure of Jesus: The Modern Debate about the Messianic Consciousness*, ed. Johannes G. Vos, 2nd ed. (1953; repr., Phillipsburg, NJ: P&R, 2002), 109–12.

80. Martin Pickup, "'On the Third Day': The Time Frame of Jesus' Death and Resurrection," *JETS* 56 (2013): 533–34.

81. *Archēgos* is notoriously difficult to translate, so I have transliterated it here. Some options for translation include leader, prince, ruler, founder, champion, author. Cf. BDAG, "ἀρχηγός," 138–39; William L. Lane, *Hebrews 1–8*, WBC 47A (Dallas: Word, 1991), 56–57.

82. Beale, *New Testament Biblical Theology*, 494.

83. See ibid., 906.

ceased even for a moment. Had there been something imperfect in the active obedience of the Mediator, then in no way could an enlivening have taken place in his soul and body. The resurrection must be viewed as God's *de facto* declaration of the perfection of Christ's work in both respects."[84]

The resurrection, then, is a vindication of Jesus's obedience and is therefore tantamount to a legal proclamation of Jesus's being in the right. Put even more starkly, the resurrection was the just verdict of God for Jesus perfectly meeting the demands of "do this and live." In Jesus's resurrection we see that perfect obedience does indeed lead to everlasting life.

If the resurrection shows that Jesus's obedience leads to life, this also accords with the Adamic imagery of the resurrection in the Gospels. As I argued in chapter 3, it is likely that life was promised to Adam in the garden for perfect obedience, though this was not realized in Adam's day. Similarly, it is also likely that the resurrection accounts are replete with Adamic resonances. First, we see this in the overarching new-creational imagery associated with the resurrection.[85] Jesus is raised to life as the last Adam, overcoming the curse of sin and death that entered the world through the first Adam. Jesus's miracles are often indications of the inbreaking of new creation, and the most definitive new-creational miracle is the resurrection life experienced by Jesus himself.[86]

Second, as mentioned briefly in chapter 5, the garden imagery in John's resurrection account (John 20:15; cf. 19:41) may be last-Adam imagery. The tomb is specifically identified as a new tomb in a garden, and when Jesus appeared to Mary, she mistook him for the gardener. The Adamic resonances in John, along with the history of interpretation, encourage us to consider the possibility that the Johannine garden recalls Adam's original paradisal estate. Just as the first Adam received life in the garden, so Jesus emerges as the last Adam in resurrection life out of the garden tomb. Francis Moloney notes this reading in the history of interpretation—that "what was lost in a garden is restored in a garden"—and suggests there may be more to this proposed biblical parallel than much current scholarly interpretation would allow.[87] As the one who came to do his Father's will, Jesus does better than Adam and experiences resurrection life.

---

84. Vos, *Reformed Dogmatics*, 3:221; cf. Vos, "The Eschatological Aspect of the Pauline Conception of the Spirit," in *Redemptive History and Biblical Interpretation: The Shorter Writings of Geerhardus Vos*, ed. Richard B. Gaffin Jr. (Phillipsburg, NJ: P&R, 1980), 109.

85. Beale, *New Testament Biblical Theology*, 423, 906; Ridderbos, *Coming of the Kingdom*, 65, 115.

86. Indeed, in John, Jesus taking up his own life (in addition to laying it down) is even presented as part of his requisite obedience (John 10:17–18). See Macleod, *Christ Crucified*, 179.

87. Francis J. Moloney, SDB, *Love in the Gospel of John: An Exegetical, Theological, and Literary Study* (Grand Rapids: Baker Academic, 2013), 141n19; cf. Alistair Begg and Sinclair B.

Third, the authority of the resurrected Jesus in Matthew's narrative (28:18–20) recalls the authority of the Son of Man in Daniel 7 and is therefore also Adamic imagery. Just as Adam was created with authority over the created world but failed through his willful disobedience, now Jesus, through his wide-ranging obedience and vindication/exaltation in the resurrection, has *all* authority in heaven and earth (cf. Acts 1:4; 2:32–33). It seems, then, that the authority of Jesus is to be viewed in Adamic terms as a direct result of Jesus's full-fledged obedience. The eternal life that Adam was unable to realize through obedience has been attained through the resurrection of the obedient second man, Jesus Christ. This is also consonant with the kingdom language in Paul, where Jesus as the last Adam receives the kingdom from the Father, having defeated every enemy (1 Cor. 15:24; cf. Luke 22:29). Additionally, John includes the authority of the resurrected Christ to grant the Spirit (John 20:22), which Paul associates with Christ as life-giving last Adam (1 Cor. 15:45). Similarly, Acts recounts how Jesus of Nazareth, whom God has made both Lord and Christ (Acts 2:36), has the resurrection authority to grant the Spirit (Acts 1:4–11; 2:1–36; cf. Luke 3:16), which we have seen in Luke is the Spirit of holiness who empowered the last Adam (Luke 3:38–4:14; cf. 1:35). In sum, the resurrection glory of Jesus, which results from his perfect obedience, excels the glory of Adam.

Thus, with the death and resurrection of Jesus we encounter a significant moment in redemptive history. Now the victory of Christ is ensured, as he has persevered in obedience throughout his life, even unto death. With the resurrection comes the expansion of the gospel to all nations. For example, in Matthew the mission of Jesus is primarily to Israel during his earthly ministry (Matt. 9:36–10:5; 15:24). That is not, of course, to say that Jesus had no room for gentiles throughout his ministry or that the inclusion of the gentiles was a completely new development, but Jesus's focus was the lost sheep of the house of Israel.[88] Matthew concludes, however, with the clear command after the resurrection to go to all nations (Matt. 28:18–20). The good news that will be for all the people in Luke 2:10 is likely for Israel, though it is in the promises of Israel that the gentiles will hope (Luke 2:29–32), and this is more fully expounded in Acts (cf. Acts 1:8). In John, Jesus says if he is lifted up from the earth—a double entendre that includes his physical lifting up on the cross and his resurrection/exaltation—he will draw *all* people to himself (John 12:32). In Mark it is at the death of Jesus that the Roman centurion

---

Ferguson, *Name Above All Names* (Wheaton: Crossway, 2013), 34–35; Mary L. Coloe, PBVM, "The Garden as a New Creation in John," *TBT* 53 (2015): 158–64.

    88. See further Konradt, *Israel, Church, and the Gentiles*.

(rightly) confesses that Jesus is the Son of God, which indicates (along with other elements in Mark) that the gospel is for the gentiles. Though Mark does not apparently include a resurrection appearance of Jesus, Jesus's resurrection is clearly announced by the angel at the empty tomb (Mark 16:7), and the resurrection is the *sine qua non* that best explains the presence and proliferation of the church by the middle of the first century. Moreover, it is also helpful to remember, in light of the widespread belief in the resurrection in early Christianity, that Jesus's death often serves as a synecdoche that includes Jesus's resurrection.[89] The cosmic events associated with the crucifixion and resurrection of Jesus in the Gospels (darkness at noon, tearing of the veil, earthquake[s], opening of tombs, angelic participation, etc.) further corroborate the singular significance of Jesus's death in the history of redemption.[90]

In conjunction with Jesus's death and resurrection, we return to the possible Adamic allusion noted in chapter 6. Adam was originally tasked with guarding and serving in the garden and should have cast out the serpent when he challenged the command of God. When Adam failed, death resulted. However, Jesus bound the strong man throughout his ministry, and consummately in his death and resurrection. Revelation speaks of the binding of the ancient serpent (= Satan) from deceiving the nations (Rev. 20:2–3),[91] which dovetails with the redemptive-historical significance of the death and resurrection of Christ in the Gospels: through his death and resurrection Jesus has overcome the sin of Adam, definitively bound the strong man (= Satan), and inaugurated the age of resurrection life for all nations.

Conclusion

As we conclude the exegetical investigation, it is important again to emphasize the unity of Jesus's obedience, encompassing both his life and his death. In the Gospels we not only find that God desires love and mercy but also that Jesus himself realizes these divine requirements. Too often sacrifice and love

---

89. Cf. Calvin, *Inst.* 2.16.13; Douglas F. Kelly, *Systematic Theology: Grounded in Holy Scripture and Understood in the Light of the Church*, vol. 2, *The Beauty of Christ: A Trinitarian Vision* (Fearn, UK: Mentor, 2014), 477; Darrell L. Bock, *Recovering the Real Lost Gospel: Reclaiming the Gospel as Good News* (Nashville: B&H, 2010), 3.

90. See also, e.g., Davies and Allison, *Matthew*, 3:622, 628, 639; Marcus, *Mark 8–16*, 1061–68; James R. Edwards, *The Gospel according to Luke*, PNTC (Grand Rapids: Eerdmans, 2015), 694; G. K. Beale and Dane Ortlund, "Darkness over the Whole Land: A Biblical-Theological Reflection on Mark 15:33," *WTJ* 75 (2013): 221–38.

91. See G. K. Beale, *The Book of Revelation*, NIGTC (Grand Rapids: Eerdmans, 1999), 985; D. Kelly, *Systematic Theology*, 2:400–401.

have been dichotomized, but Jesus points us to the spirit of love required by the Law and Prophets, even as he lays down his own life sacrificially. By offering himself up unto death, Jesus definitively unites true circumcision of heart with perfect sacrifice. Jesus's resurrection is his vindication as God's Messiah and is predicated on the perfection of his life. Indeed, the resurrection not only is the vindication of Jesus as Messiah but also ensures the full salvation of all those who place their faith in him. In the final chapter I will explore some of these theological themes in more detail.

The Last Adam and Salvation

Theological Synthesis and Conclusions

Summary of Argument

In this volume I have argued that Jesus is the last Adam who lived a life of vicarious obedience necessary for salvation. To recap, in chapter 1, I argued that the two-Adam structure that is prominent in the history of interpretation provides a helpful compass for those today who are interested in the theology of the Gospels. Jesus is consistently identified in the history of interpretation as the second and last Adam whose obedience overcomes the disobedience of the first Adam. In chapter 2 we considered the multifaceted Adam Christology in the Gospels. The Gospels present Jesus as the last Adam in various ways, including in the temptation narratives, by means of the role of the Holy Spirit, and through the Son of Man imagery. These observations provided momentum for chapter 3, where the focus was specifically on Jesus's sonship—a central theme in the Gospels, with numerous implications. First, Jesus's filial identity relates Jesus to Israel, the typological son of God. Second, Jesus's sonship also relates Jesus to Adam, the first covenantal son of God. Third, in light of these canonical links, Jesus's sonship strongly emphasizes his obedience. We also considered in chapter 3 the key roles of the baptism and temptation narratives, noting how these accounts draw attention to Jesus's sonship and obedience and set the stage for Jesus's obedience throughout the Gospels.

In chapter 4 we considered in more detail some of the ways in which Jesus fulfills Scripture, along with statements that speak of the divine necessity of Jesus's obedient life for salvation. Jesus is portrayed as the Holy and Righteous One whose obedience excels that of Adam. In chapter 5 we looked in greater detail at the contours of John's Gospel, which portrays Jesus's glory as greater than Adam. In John, Jesus is also portrayed as the obedient Son who was always working and always doing the will of his Father, accomplishing salvation for those who believe in the Son of Man. Jesus's work in John must be viewed as a unity, which means his life and death are both necessary for the perfect completion of his work. In chapter 6 we considered the work of Jesus that was necessary to inaugurate the kingdom of God, which is a kingdom of righteousness instituted by the righteous king. Jesus's power is corollary to his holiness and includes his binding of the strong man, by which he overcomes the sin of Adam. In chapter 7 we looked more explicitly at the death of Jesus and considered how the perfection of Jesus's life enabled him to serve as the perfect sacrifice for sin, since in Jesus we find the unity of heart devotion and outward obedience. Jesus's blood is therefore uniquely able to serve as a ransom for many. We also considered the judicial nature of the resurrection. The last Adam embodied perfect obedience through his life and was therefore crowned with new-creational, resurrection life.

In this study I have not provided a thorough definition of *salvation*. Instead, I have preferred to consider inductively some of the ways that Jesus's multifaceted work is necessary for salvation. As we approach the end of this study, I repeat the simple, working gloss on salvation from chapter 1: deliverance from sin unto everlasting life in fellowship with the Triune God.[1] In light of the preceding discussion, it should be emphasized that Jesus's lifelong obedience as the (divine) Son of God leads to *resurrection* life, and all those who trust in Christ likewise will participate in resurrection life. Thus, to say that Jesus's perfect obedience is necessary for salvation is to say that Jesus's perfect obedience is necessary for participation in eternal/resurrection life.

In sum, I have argued that Jesus's life is necessary for salvation. However, the complexity of Jesus's mission renders it impossible to say all that needs to be said in one volume. By no means should this study be considered exhaustive; I do not claim to have covered every possible angle of the richness of what

---

1. As I noted in chap. 1, for fuller discussions see John Murray, *Redemption Accomplished and Applied* (Grand Rapids: Eerdmans, 1955); Herman Bavinck, *Reformed Dogmatics*, ed. John Bolt, trans. John Vriend, 4 vols. (Grand Rapids: Baker Academic, 2003–8), esp. vols. 3–4.

Christ has done to accomplish salvation. Additionally, I have focused almost exclusively in this volume on the *accomplishment* of salvation and have said little about the *application* of salvation, though the latter is equally as necessary as the former.[2] My hope is that this study will interject new life (and some new arguments) into some old conversations as exegetes, theologians, pastors, professors, students, and others wrestle with the soteriological significance of the life of Jesus in the Gospels. Woe betide me if I were to suggest that the revelation that comes through Christ or his death is somehow less important. However, another danger is failing to appreciate the theological significance of the life of Jesus, which makes the Gospels such fertile ground for theological reflection. Jesus does many things in the Gospels, including (quite prominently, as I have argued) vicariously accomplishing salvation as a representative man. In what follows I offer a synthesis of some salient points and suggest some implications moving forward.

Incarnation and Salvation

I opened this volume by echoing the question many others have asked: what is the theological significance of the incarnate work of Jesus, particularly in the Gospels? Various answers to this question have been articulated through the centuries. For example, the so-called mystical theory of the atonement looks to Jesus's assumption of flesh at the incarnation, and the resulting union of God and man, as an atonement by which humanity is saved—it focuses more on *who Jesus is*, one could say, than on *what he does*.[3] The Gospels certainly emphasize the importance of the real incarnation of the Son of God in relation to salvation. However, the Gospels' emphasis on the *work* of Jesus should caution us from stating that the incarnation *is* the accomplishment of salvation *tout simple*. Instead, the incarnation is a *necessary*, but not a *sufficient*, condition for salvation.[4] At the beginning of his earthly life, Jesus stands at the beginning of his course of lifelong obedience, but much remains to be done for the full accomplishment of salvation. The

---

2. Bavinck: "The application of salvation is no less an essential constituent of redemption than the acquisition of it" (*Reformed Dogmatics*, 3:523; cf. 3:466–68). See also Murray, *Redemption*, 79–181.

3. See Bavinck, *Reformed Dogmatics*, 3:392; Geerhardus Vos, *Reformed Dogmatics*, ed. and trans. Richard B. Gaffin Jr., 5 vols. (Bellingham, WA: Lexham Press, 2012–16), 3:162–65. Of course, there are many permutations of this theory; I simply intend to provide a general summary.

4. See Turretin, *Inst.* 13.3; cf. Robert A. Peterson, *Salvation Accomplished by the Son: The Work of Christ* (Wheaton: Crossway, 2012), 28; Donald Macleod, *Christ Crucified: Understanding the Atonement* (Downers Grove, IL: IVP Academic, 2014), 80; Vos, *Reformed Dogmatics*, 3:130. This pithy phrasing was first suggested to me by Scott Swain.

incarnation marks the beginning of Jesus's subjection to the law.[5] For the shepherds, the magi, and Simeon, to rejoice in seeing the child Jesus was the proper response; to see the child was to see salvation (Luke 2:38). However, salvation was not fully accomplished on the day of Jesus's birth; the Gospels go on to show all the ways in which Jesus had to be fully obedient in order to accomplish salvation. Yet we can also say that Jesus was vicariously obedient even from his infancy.[6] To accomplish salvation in a representative way, Jesus had to be fully human. He had a human nature just like the rest of humanity, yet he was wholly without sin. Jesus was therefore fully qualified to serve as an obedient substitute.[7] Yet it is not the mere *fact* of the incarnation that accomplishes salvation but the *actions* of the Son of God in his incarnate state.

The Necessary Obedience of the Last Adam

The incarnation through the agency of the Holy Spirit points to the uniqueness of Jesus as the head of new creation. I have argued throughout that Jesus is portrayed as the last Adam in the Gospels, not only in Luke's genealogy, but in all sorts of ways, including Jesus's role as Son of Man, the covenantal obedience he shows to his Father, the realization of eternal life through his death and resurrection, his binding of Satan, and so forth. Understanding Jesus as the last Adam pays dividends as we reflect upon the soteriological perspective of the Gospels vis-à-vis the life of Jesus. Jesus's obedience must be understood in light of Israel, but ultimately in light of Adam. Adam stood at the beginning of creation with a goal of eschatological life set before him, though he was not yet in possession of this life. Yet Adam failed his probation and suffered the penalty of death in place of life. As the last Adam, Jesus is the obedient Son who serves a representative capacity, vicariously attaining the life through obedience that Adam did not (see below). And Jesus also had a tougher course than Adam, since Jesus had to persevere in obedience in the postlapsarian world.

If it is indeed the case that eternal life for Adam was contingent upon his obedience, it would be mistaken to think this condition was simply set aside after the sin of Adam. Instead, a promise is given that the serpent

---

5. Vos, *Reformed Dogmatics*, 3:191–92; Louis Berkhof, *Systematic Theology*, 4th ed. (Grand Rapids: Eerdmans, 1941), 379; Bavinck, *Reformed Dogmatics*, 3:406–10.

6. Calvin, *Inst.* 4.16.18; Lombard, *Sentences* 3.18.2; Bavinck, *Reformed Dogmatics*, 3:378.

7. Murray (*Redemption*, 19) argues that Jesus's *obedience* is wide-ranging enough to be the integrating principle of his atoning work.

would eventually be overcome (Gen. 3:15), and God intervenes to redeem his people in various ways throughout his covenantal dealings in the Old Testament. The full obedience required of Adam was no longer possible for naturally born men and women in the postlapsarian order, since Adam's sin (and therefore death) had spread to all people. However, Jesus was uniquely conceived by the power of the Holy Spirit, and he uniquely realized the conditions for eschatological life that were originally given to Adam: life upon the execution of "personal, entire, exact, and perpetual obedience."[8] Upon the completion of his task, Jesus is resurrected unto new life (cf. 1 Cor. 15:21–22) and is able to grant life to those who believe in him. Life and the keeping of the commandments go hand in hand in Scripture, and this is most beautifully seen in the perfect obedience of Jesus and the benefits acquired by it.[9]

In addition, understanding Christ as the last Adam is prominent in the history of interpretation and provides ample precedent for identifying a pervasive Adam Christology in the Gospels. Likewise, Jesus's incarnate obedience for salvation features prominently in early articulations of the rule of faith (*regula fidei*). Again Irenaeus (ca. 130–ca. 202) is instructive, whose *Demonstration of the Apostolic Preaching* may be viewed as an exposition of the rule of faith (cf. *Epid.* 3).[10] In accord with the rule of faith, Irenaeus (*Epid.* 6) speaks of the recapitulation of all things in the flesh of Jesus for our salvation and to abolish death.[11] Similarly, the author of *Against Noetus* 17–18 (possibly Hippolytus of Rome, ca. 170–ca. 236), summarizing the "word of truth" in accord with the tradition of the apostles, uses new Adam terminology for the salvific work of Christ incarnate. Additionally, Novatian (fl. 249–251), in *A Treatise Concerning the Trinity* 9, also expounding on the rule of faith, speaks of the role of Christ incarnate fulfilling shadows and figures of the Old Testament in his life and ministry, in addition to his passion and resurrection. The point is simply that many early articulations of the rule of faith, which claim to preserve the teaching of the apostles, emphasize the importance of Jesus's life for salvation, often in association with (at least implicit) Adamic imagery. It is also significant that these discussions are placed in a trinitarian framework (since the rule of faith bears

8. Westminster Confession of Faith 19.1.

9. One must also, however, recognize the divinity of the Son in acquiring the benefits of eternal life, which helps us understand the infinite value of his perfect obedience. Cf. Vos, *Reformed Dogmatics*, 3:6–9.

10. On this point, and for the following articulations of the rule of faith, I glean from Everett Ferguson, *The Rule of Faith: A Guide*, CC (Eugene, OR: Cascade, 2015).

11. See also the well-known summary of the rule of faith in Irenaeus, *Haer.* 1.10.1.

a trinitarian character), thereby underscoring not only the humanity of the Son but also his divinity.

Vicarious Obedience

Additionally, Jesus's obedience serves as *vicarious* obedience. As the last Adam and Messiah, Jesus is a public person with corporate significance.[12] As the head of a new humanity, he acts not only for himself but for those he represents. Jesus's obedience benefits his people. What is explicit in Paul's epistolary exposition (Rom. 5:12–21)—that the actions of Adam and Christ have implications for those "in" each representative man—is also present in narrative form in the Gospels. The obedience of Jesus must be appreciated as a positive accomplishment of God's will in a way that extends beyond his death, but most certainly includes it. Jesus's entire obedience, which is vindicated in his resurrection, is the ground for believers' justification today.

If Jesus's obedience is vicarious unto salvation, it may also speak to the issue of the imputation of Christ's righteousness. This is most often discussed in relation to Pauline theology, but the Gospels also have something to add to this discussion. If the preceding argument has merit—that Jesus fulfills the Scriptures and righteousness vicariously on behalf of his people, granting salvation on the basis of his obedience—is this not tantamount to imputation? Of course the terminology is not used, but that is hardly an argument against it;[13] "one may doubt the word, provided the matter is safe (*de vocabulo dubitetur, re salva*)."[14] Jesus is vicariously obedient and fulfills God's requirements in a way that benefits his people. This fits hand in glove with the Reformed doctrine of imputation.[15] Stated simply, imputation means that believers are justified in God's sight not on the basis of any inherent worthiness or work wrought by themselves but on the basis of the righteousness of Christ's obedience.[16] Thus, one can speak of the imputation of Christ's *righteousness*,[17] though some have argued that it is better to speak of the imputation of Jesus's entire *obedience*, both active and passive.[18] This leads us to consider again the unity of Jesus's obedience.

12. Bavinck, *Reformed Dogmatics*, 3:379.
13. Ben C. Dunson, "Do Bible Words Have Bible Meaning? Distinguishing between Imputation as Word and Doctrine," *WTJ* 75 (2013): 239–60.
14. Bavinck, *Reformed Dogmatics*, 2:569.
15. See also Grant Macaskill, *Union with Christ in the New Testament* (Oxford: Oxford University Press, 2013), 298; Bavinck, *Reformed Dogmatics*, 3:591.
16. Murray, *Redemption*, 123–24.
17. Ibid., 124; Berkhof, *Systematic Theology*, 524.
18. Bavinck, *Reformed Dogmatics*, 4:223–24; cf. 3:102; Heidelberg Catechism 60; Westminster Confession of Faith 11.1.

The Unity of Jesus's Obedience

Continuing from the previous point, one of the recurring themes throughout this volume is that it would be artificial to separate the obedience of Jesus in his life and his obedience in his death. The two are woven together in an indissoluble unity. As we have seen, the active obedience and passive obedience of Jesus are not *two stages* of Jesus's obedience but are *two aspects* of the lifelong, integrated obedience of Jesus. Active obedience refers to Jesus's full realization of all that God requires of humanity, whereas passive obedience refers to his suffering the penalty due to humanity as a result of sin. Jesus's obedience was always active and always passive; the distinction is *logical*, not *temporal*.[19] We can no more divide the obedience of Christ into parts than we can separate ice cream from milk in a milkshake.[20] By his integrated obedience—active and passive—Jesus secured eternal life for his people.

Most of the focus in this study has been on the obedience of Jesus in his *ministry*, which receives the lion's share of attention in the Gospels. However, it is also appropriate to speak of Jesus's representative obedience throughout his incarnate life. Jesus is not a different person prior to his baptism, though he does embark more explicitly on his messianic task after his messianic anointing. Thus the glimpses we have into Jesus's obedience as a child are significant and must be considered part of his unified obedience as last Adam. As Calvin memorably observed, "From the time when [Christ] took on the form of a servant, he began to pay the price of liberation in order to redeem us."[21] Similarly, in the words of Geerhardus Vos: "[The] suffering of the Mediator does not date from the end of His stay on earth. . . . It appears from His circumcision that Christ, as concerns the requirement of the law, subjected Himself not only subsequently but *from the beginning*. And it is rightly observed that the blood of the Savior's circumcision is as much atoning blood for us as is the blood shed on Golgotha. His *entire life* was a continual suffering."[22]

---

19. Vos, *Reformed Dogmatics*, 3:127–31; J. Gresham Machen, *God Transcendent*, ed. Ned B. Stonehouse (1949; repr., Edinburgh: Banner of Truth, 1982), 190–91; Murray, *Redemption*, 21–22, cf. 17; Berkhof, *Systematic Theology*, 379–81.

20. Cf. Bavinck, *Reformed Dogmatics*, 3:394–95, 4:223–24; Turretin, *Inst.* 14.13; 16.4. Note also Turretin's careful discussion of various types of merit (*Inst.* 17.5.2–5); cf. Bavinck, *Reformed Dogmatics*, 2:587.

21. Calvin, *Inst.* 2.16.5, in John Calvin, *Institutes of the Christian Religion*, ed. John T. McNeill, trans. Ford Lewis Battles, 2 vols., LCC 20 (Louisville: Westminster John Knox, 1960), 1:507; see also Douglas F. Kelly, *Systematic Theology: Grounded in Holy Scripture and Understood in the Light of the Church*, vol. 2, *The Beauty of Christ: A Trinitarian Vision* (Fearn, UK: Mentor, 2014), 368.

22. Vos, *Reformed Dogmatics*, 3:192 (emphasis added).

The unity of Jesus's obedience also has implications for discussions of imputation, in accord with what I argued above. Some today argue that Jesus's righteous *death* (and resurrection) is reckoned or applied to believers, but not his righteous *life*.[23] This is by no means a new concept, having already been anticipated by theologians such as Johannes Piscator (1546–1625),[24] delegates to the Westminster Assembly, and others.[25] However, Piscator's position, for example, artificially bifurcates the unified obedience of Christ. More specifically (and perhaps more controversially), it would be out of step with the Gospels to say that the death of Jesus can ultimately be separated from his life, with only his death being reckoned or imputed to believers. We must not seek to divide the obedience of Jesus—as if one aspect of his obedience could be siphoned off from another. Instead, we must recognize his work as a unity. It is Jesus's entire obedience that saves. Certainly the death of Christ is emphasized in the New Testament, but as the climactic act of his integrated obedience, the death of Christ often serves synecdochically, and the cross metonymically, for Jesus's *entire* obedience.[26]

Jesus of Nazareth as a First-Century Jewish Man

I have argued throughout this study that Jesus is a unique individual—the representative, last Adam. But if so, how does this relate to the need to understand Jesus in his first-century Jewish context? If we focus on Jesus as the last Adam, do we thereby neglect the historical, cultural, and religious context of first-century Palestine in favor of more "ethereal" theological categories? I

23. A variety of perspectives could be mentioned here; this is often discussed particularly in relation to Pauline theology. See variously J. R. Daniel Kirk, "The Sufficiency of the Cross (II): The Law, the Cross, and Justification," *SBET* 24 (2006): 133–54; Mark A. Seifrid, *Christ, Our Righteousness: Paul's Theology of Justification*, NSBT 9 (Downers Grove, IL: InterVarsity, 2000), 175; N. T. Wright, *Justification: God's Plan and Paul's Vision* (London: SPCK, 2009), 204–5; Richard B. Hays, *The Faith of Jesus Christ: The Narrative Substructure of Galatians 3:1–4:11*, 2nd ed., BRS (Grand Rapids: Eerdmans, 2002), xxx–xxxiii; Michael F. Bird, *Evangelical Theology: A Biblical and Systematic Introduction* (Grand Rapids: Zondervan, 2013), 562–64. For discussions on justification and the right to eternal life, see Turretin, *Inst.* 16.4; Vos, *Reformed Dogmatics*, 4:151–54; cf. 3:128–31; Bavinck, *Reformed Dogmatics*, 3:395.

24. See F. L. Bos, *Johann Piscator: Ein Beitrag zur Geschichte der reformierten Theologie* (Kampen: J. H. Kok, 1932), 71–84; Turretin, *Inst.* 11.22.12–18; 14.13.1; Bavinck, *Reformed Dogmatics*, 3:347, 377–78; Vos, *Reformed Dogmatics*, 3:131–32, 4:153–54.

25. See Jeffrey K. Jue, "The Active Obedience of Christ and the Theology of the Westminster Standards: A Historical Investigation," in *Justified in Christ: God's Plan for Us in Justification*, ed. K. Scott Oliphint (Fearn, UK: Mentor, 2007), 99–130.

26. See Bavinck, *Reformed Dogmatics*, 3:378: "In his suffering and death, the whole of Christ's preceding life was incorporated, summed up, and completed." Cf. Turretin, *Inst.* 14.13.8.

would answer this question with an emphatic no! Jesus's historical context is vitally important for understanding the theological significance of his incarnate life and work.[27] What does it profit us to consider Jesus in the context of first-century Palestinian Judaism? Much in every way. I mention here a few reasons.

First, the reality of the incarnation demands that we take Jesus's flesh-and-blood experience seriously. If Jesus's entire life was one of perpetual obedience, then his life was one of constant obedience to the laws revealed to Israel. Jesus had to be truly obedient not just at some moments of his life but always, even as a child in Galilee (and Egypt!) under the authority of Mary and Joseph (cf. Luke 2:51). Additionally, if Jesus's entire life was one of suffering, then we can presume that his experiences of suffering would have been quite acute in the first century. Not only did Jesus bear the curse of sin in a representative capacity every day of his life, but we can also think of his suffering more "mundanely" by considering common human experience. Jesus lived without such modern amenities as electricity, relative ease and safety of travel, modern medicine, and the convenience of running water (at least as we know it today).[28] Jesus also lived at a politically volatile time, particularly in Palestine, which perpetually seemed to be in the crosshairs of clashing kingdoms. The territory of Judea was under the thumb of Rome, as Pilate's presence in the Gospels (along with Herod Antipas and others) starkly illustrates, and faithful Jews (especially the Messiah!) would have faced constant difficulties and temptations in a world of competing loyalties (cf. Matt. 22:21 and parr.). Indeed, the events of Jesus's day, in retrospect, seemed to be leading—as if inexorably—toward the clash between Rome and Jerusalem (and such chaotic events as the year of the four emperors in AD 68–69). The difficulties of life for faithful Jews in the first century were legion (cf. Matt. 24:21 and parr.). This also accords with Paul's statement that Jesus came in the "fullness of time" (Gal. 4:4), which denotes (among other things) a time of great spiritual evil. We see this, for example, in the constant opposition of the demonic and satanic to Jesus in his messianic work—even in the promised land. It is well documented that the first century was a time of effervescent messianic fervor, in opposition to the extending reach of the Roman Empire, and the opportunities for missteps and error were abundant. And yet Jesus never erred in any way, remaining faithful throughout his life, demonstrating his faithfulness all the way to Jerusalem and his ironic enthronement upon a Roman cross.

27. See also Christoph Stenschke, "The Apostles' Creed, the God of Israel and the Jew Jesus of Nazareth," *EuroJTh* 22 (2013): 110–23.
28. Cf. *Res gest. divi Aug.* 20; Frontinus, *De aquaeductu*.

Second, Jesus's first-century Jewish identity is indispensable for understanding his role in the context of God's covenantal dealings with his people. Jesus is the promised king from David's line who was prophesied to rule over an everlasting kingdom. David's line is, of course, Abraham's line, and Jesus is also the promised seed of Abraham, the one through whom blessings come to all the peoples of the earth. Thus stated, it makes sense why Matthew would begin by identifying Jesus as the son of David and son of Abraham (Matt. 1:1). The promise to Abraham is channeled through Moses and receives glorious prefiguration in the kingdom of David. The nascent nation in Exodus 19 becomes the grand nation under David (and Solomon), with the promise that Zion would be established as the highest of the mountains (Isa. 2:2–4; Mic. 4:1–3). This is not the place for a full-fledged biblical-covenantal theology, but it will suffice to note that Jesus's identity as a Jewish man goes hand in hand with his identity as son of David according to the flesh, who was declared Son of God in power by his resurrection from the dead (Rom. 1:3–4). Jesus is the chosen heir of God's promises to Abraham and the prophets; it is through Jesus that we receive the blessings anticipated in the latter days.

Third, there is a close connection between these covenantal administrations (from Abraham to Moses to David to Jesus) and Adam. Indeed, as we have seen, whereas Matthew traces his genealogy from Abraham to Jesus, Luke's genealogy traces Jesus back to Adam (and ultimately to God). Thus, Jesus as son of David, son of Abraham, and son of Adam are complementary perspectives on understanding the role of Jesus in the context of covenant history. We are speaking in preeminently *biblical* terms to identify Jesus as the last Adam and to understand Jesus's work in light of Adam. In Scripture, Adam leads organically to Abraham and Israel, though Adam is unique in being first of all a man created upright, having no need for redemption in his prelapsarian state. Adam, in his created state, was completely free from the taint of sin. All covenant administrations subsequent to Adam (and prior to Christ) are covenants made with people in need of redemption, and therefore their relation to Adam in his prelapsarian state can only be analogous. We can certainly identify strains of consistency between God's covenantal commands to Adam and subsequent commands throughout the Old Testament, but as I argued in chapter 3, we must also maintain the uniqueness of Adam and Christ. Jesus is a Jewish man, from the line of Judah, who stands squarely in the context of Israel's covenantal context. He was really born of Mary, having a true body and a reasonable soul. And yet Jesus is different from all the sons and daughters of Israel in being wholly without sin. In this regard, Adam is his closest parallel. Only Adam and Christ are the heads of creation and re-creation, respectively. Yet understanding the indissoluble link between Adam and subsequent covenant history—perhaps most strikingly in the universality of death after the entrance of sin into the world through Adam—ensures that we do not abstract Adam from the scriptural narrative but view him as the beginning of the narrative that finds its resolution in the last Adam. The historical reality of sin and death that came through Adam is overcome by the historical reality of the incarnate obedience and life-giving authority of Jesus.

Fourth, the traditional offices of Christ as prophet, priest, and king reinforce the idea that we must understand Jesus in his historical, Jewish context. For what are these offices if not most fundamentally the offices of God's *covenant* people? Whatever parallels we may find in other ancient Near Eastern cultures, these offices have very well-defined roles for God's people, and Jesus fulfills all three offices. In fact, they all anticipate the substance of Christ (cf. Col. 2:17; Heb. 10:1). Therefore, to speak of Jesus as prophet, priest, and king (see below) is to make claims about Jesus that must be understood in tandem with his identity as son of David, son of Abraham, and son of Adam.

Prophet, Priest, and King

The traditional offices of prophet, priest, and king also help us understand the wide-ranging obedience of Jesus in the Gospels.[29] Though the obedience of Christ cannot be reduced to or neatly partitioned into any one office in isolation from the others, as a summary these remain valuable categories to articulate the obedience of Jesus. For example, a necessary part of Jesus's mission was preaching the gospel, which corresponds to the prophetic office. Jesus also states he came to give his life as a ransom for many, which echoes priestly language from the Old Testament. Likewise, Jesus came to establish the kingdom of God as the righteous king, and he is the stronger man who bound the armor-laden strong man through the finger of God (Luke 11:20) and his entire obedience.[30] Stated simply, the consideration of the obedience of Christ unto salvation in this volume supports these traditional categories, and

29. See, e.g., Calvin, *Inst.* 2.15; Vos, *Reformed Dogmatics*, 3:85–182; D. Kelly, *Systematic Theology*, 2:61–64; Bavinck, *Reformed Dogmatics*, 3:364–68; Berkhof, *Systematic Theology*, 356–411; Karl Barth, *Dogmatics in Outline*, trans. G. T. Thomson (London: SCM, 1949), 77–90; Robert Letham, *The Work of Christ*, CCT (Downers Grove, IL: IVP Academic, 1993), 91–247; T. F. Torrance, *Incarnation: The Person and Life of Christ*, ed. Robert T. Walker (Downers Grove, IL: IVP Academic, 2008), 45–46; Richard P. Belcher Jr., *Prophet, Priest, and King: A Biblical Theology of the Offices of Christ* (Phillipsburg, NJ: P&R, 2016). These offices for Christ are utilized at least as early as Eusebius, *Hist. eccl.* 1.3; cf. Heb. 1:1–4.

30. All three offices may be in view in brief scope in Matt. 12: Jesus is greater than Jonah (= prophet [12:41]), temple (= priest [12:6]), and Solomon (= king [12:42]).

we can draw upon them with great profit for understanding the saving work of Christ. This construal also fits well with the identification of Jesus as the last Adam, since Adam can also be described as a prophet, priest, and king.[31]

These offices also help us consider the various theories of the atonement, which we cannot discuss at length. A number of atonement theories have been propounded through the centuries and have been identified with such nomenclature as the mystical, moral, governmental, ransom, *Christus Victor*, and penal substitutionary (or vicarious satisfaction) theories.[32] Though I am most persuaded by penal substitution or vicarious satisfaction as an overarching category,[33] understanding Christ's work in terms of prophet, priest, and king enables us to see that one can describe the richness of Christ's work from various angles, including, for example, *Christus Victor*. Yet *Christus Victor* must be understood in tandem with forensic categories since, for the victory of Christ to bring true deliverance, it must provide freedom from sin, guilt, and death, which necessarily entails a penal dimension.[34]

The Gospels in Biblical and Systematic Theology

By this point readers will no doubt have gathered that I believe in the legitimacy and importance of both biblical and systematic theology. Though they differ slightly in purpose, in practice both can and should interface rather seamlessly with one another. In my understanding, whereas biblical theology traces the development of ideas from the beginning to the end of Scripture, systematic theology takes more of a bird's-eye view and considers revelation as a whole. To use one analogy, biblical theology is like a line, whereas systematic theology is like a circle.[35] This approach that combines biblical and systematic theology has a long and reputable history in Christian interpretation. Many

31. See Bavinck, *Reformed Dogmatics*, 3:331; cf. G. K. Beale, *A New Testament Biblical Theology: The Unfolding of the Old Testament in the New* (Grand Rapids: Baker Academic, 2011), 31–38.

32. For concise discussions, see Vos, *Reformed Dogmatics*, 3:153–67; Bavinck, *Reformed Dogmatics*, 3:392–94; Berkhof, *Systematic Theology*, 384–91; D. Kelly, *Systematic Theology*, 2:421–42; cf. Anthony C. Thiselton, *The Thiselton Companion to Christian Theology* (Grand Rapids: Eerdmans, 2015), 60–89.

33. Bavinck, *Reformed Dogmatics*, 3:393–98; Berkhof, *Systematic Theology*, 372–82; Vos, *Reformed Dogmatics*, 3:135. Bavinck rightly relates this to Jesus's "full and complete obedience" (*Reformed Dogmatics*, 3:393).

34. See Richard B. Gaffin Jr., *No Adam, No Gospel: Adam and the History of Redemption* (Phillipsburg, NJ: P&R; Philadelphia: Westminster Seminary Press, 2015), 20.

35. This analogy comes from Geerhardus Vos, "The Idea of Biblical Theology as a Science and as a Theological Discipline," in *Redemptive History and Biblical Interpretation: The Shorter Writings of Geerhardus Vos*, ed. Richard B. Gaffin Jr. (Phillipsburg, NJ: P&R, 1980), 23.

of the best theologians have been some of the best exegetes. One thinks, for example, of the interplay between Calvin's commentaries and his *Institutes*; the two were to be read in tandem. Indeed, the early church's adherence to the rule of faith illustrates that those in the church have always had an impulse to articulate the teaching of Scripture in a topical way. In light of this pattern in the history of interpretation, students of the Gospels today have much to learn from biblically faithful exegetes who have wrestled with the overall structure of God's revelation.

I noted in chapter 1, echoing the perspective of Adolf Schlatter, that it is best to view the New Testament authors as bearing a unified witness. Here I repeat that sentiment and add to it the helpfulness of systematic theology alongside biblical theology. Again Schlatter is instructive, arguing that we find in the New Testament unified dogmas, and these are not impositions from the outside. Instead, the New Testament shows us a community that arose around particular doctrines.[36] The Gospels do not sound a discordant note to the rest of the New Testament; rather, the essence of what we find more fully expressed elsewhere is already present (at least in seed form) even in the Synoptic Gospels.[37] To be sure, one must not neglect to listen carefully to the individual witnesses, whether to the Fourfold Gospel as a whole or to each of the Gospels individually. However, it seems to me that the current scholarly landscape exhibits an abundance of studies that listen to discrete voices within the canon. As Grant Macaskill has recently argued, studies on the New Testament documents in light of background literature abound, but fewer studies today consider, for example, Paul in light of Peter.[38] Therefore, we need more studies that consider synthetically the witness of the Fourfold Gospel in light of the entire New Testament and indeed all of Scripture.[39] This volume therefore seeks to bring new life to the discussion of the theology of the Gospels by thinking systematically and synthetically about the Christology of the Fourfold Gospel.

To be clear, I am not saying that the Gospels tell us all there is to know about the work of Christ; many details remain to be articulated in the more didactic portions of the New Testament. The nature of the atonement is explained in more detail in Romans than it is in John.[40] I am arguing, however, that the

---

36. Adolf Schlatter, "The Theology of the New Testament and Dogmatics," in *The Nature of New Testament Theology: The Contribution of William Wrede and Adolf Schlatter*, ed. and trans. Robert Morgan, SBT 2/25 (Naperville, IL: Allenson, 1973), 140.

37. See Bavinck, *Reformed Dogmatics*, 3:233, 235, 252, 269, 272.

38. Macaskill, *Union with Christ*, 2.

39. See similarly Schlatter, "Theology of the New Testament," 140.

40. See recently D. A. Carson, "Adumbrations of Atonement Theology in the Fourth Gospel," *JETS* 57 (2014): 520–21.

four narratives of the life of Jesus in Matthew, Mark, Luke, and John offer a rich repository for theological reflection and communicate in narrative form the conviction that Jesus saves his people from their sins through his vicarious obedience.[41] We must take seriously the Gospels as an important theological part of the unified New Testament witness to Christ.

At this point it may also be helpful to note that many of the creeds and confessions, especially from the Reformed tradition (which I know the best), have more to say about the work of Christ than is sometimes recognized. Creeds and confessions are often thoughtful, pithy formulations that represent in short shrift years of wrestling with the biblical texts. In chapter 1, I gave several examples of the Adam-Christ parallel from the history of Christian interpretation that contrast the disobedience of Adam and the thoroughgoing obedience of Jesus. The church's creeds and confessions are not infallible, but inasmuch as they note Christ's relation to Adam and his role as prophet, priest, and king, they also contain at least implicit (and often explicit) references to God's covenantal dealings with Israel. Additionally, one must not neglect to recognize that Adam stands at the head of Old Testament covenantal administrations, and one could argue that all of Old Testament history can, from one perspective, be subsumed under the headship of Adam.

Thus, in many creeds and confessions we find that Jesus's obedience is set in contrast to the disobedience of Adam,[42] and Jesus's work is couched in terms of Israel's prophetic, priestly, and kingly institutions.[43] The active obedience and passive obedience of Christ are often mentioned as well,[44] which underscores his lifelong, incarnate obedience. By way of illustration, the Second Helvetic Confession (1566) 11 states:

> Furthermore, by His passion or death, *and by all those things which He did and suffered for our sakes from the time of His coming in the flesh,* our Lord

41. Compare the observations on the life of Jesus from Richard Bauckham (*Jesus and the Eyewitnesses: The Gospels as Eyewitness Testimony* [Grand Rapids: Eerdmans, 2006], 277): "The early Christian movement was interested in the genuinely past history of Jesus because they regarded it as *religiously relevant.* . . . Jesus was more than the founder of their movement; he was the source of salvation. . . . Thus, at the deepest level, it was for profoundly theological reasons—their understanding of God and salvation—that early Christians were concerned with faithful memory of the really past story of Jesus." See also Michael F. Bird, *The Gospel of the Lord: How the Early Church Wrote the Story of Jesus* (Grand Rapids: Eerdmans, 2014), 25.

42. Westminster Confession of Faith 7, 8.5; Westminster Larger Catechism 31; Heidelberg Catechism 16, 20; Second London Confession 7.

43. Westminster Confession of Faith 8.1; D. Kelly, *Systematic Theology,* 2:516–21.

44. Savoy Declaration 11.1 ("active obedience to the whole Law"); cf. Westminster Confession of Faith 8.4–5.

reconciled His heavenly Father unto all the faithful (Rom. 5:10), purged their sin (Heb. 1:3), spoiled death, broke asunder condemnation and hell, and by His resurrection from the dead, brought again and restored life and immortality (2 Tim. 1:10). For He is our righteousness, life, and resurrection (John 6:44); and, to be short, He is the fullness and perfection, the salvation and most abundant sufficiency of all the faithful.[45]

And the Scottish Confession of 1616 reads:

This blessed Lord has fulfilled the whole law for us to our benefit; both doing all that the law requires of us, and suffering the punishment due to our disobedience, even to the curse of the law and death of the cross; where, by the fulfilling of the law, our redemption was sealed and consummated.[46]

Reformational creeds also provide insight into the richness of the Apostles' Creed. Calvin's catechism of 1545, for example, unpacks the richness of the doctrine of Christ in the Apostles' Creed that is not expanded upon in the creed itself but is included in the creed's pregnant language. For example, Calvin notes that the second head of the creed ("I believe in Jesus Christ his only Son, our Lord") entails all the work of Christ by which he has come to redeem us (Q. 31). One way we know this is because the title "Christ," as an honorific title of anointing, implicitly includes the threefold office of prophet, priest, and king and all the incarnate works of Jesus that are represented by those institutions (Q. 34–45). Indeed, even the name *Jesus*, in light of Scripture's teaching, carries with it the theological significance of Matthew 1:21: Jesus is the *Savior* (Q. 32). Calvin proceeds to explain how the creed's discussion of the supernatural birth of Jesus by the Holy Spirit communicates that Jesus assumed human flesh and accomplished all that was necessary for salvation (Q. 49), which was necessary because the sin that was committed by a man against God had to be redressed in human nature (Q. 51–52). Jesus's conception by the Holy Spirit thus includes more than simply the means by which Jesus was conceived; it also includes his perfect holiness, being free from all stain of sin, that he might truly redeem humanity cursed by the sin of Adam (Q. 53–54). Readers may particularly be interested in Calvin's answer to question 55: "Why do you go immediately from his birth to his death, passing over the whole history of his human life?" Calvin's catechism responds, "Because nothing is said here about what belongs properly to the substance of our

45. James T. Dennison Jr., ed., *Reformed Confessions of the 16th and 17th Centuries in English Translation*, 4 vols. (Grand Rapids: Reformation Heritage, 2008–14), 2:830 (emphasis added).

46. Dennison, *Reformed Confessions*, 4:111, cf. 4:112–13.

redemption."[47] By this Calvin does not mean that the obedient life of Jesus is not necessary for our redemption—after all, he has just discussed the need for a perfect human to redeem humanity (Q. 49–54), and elsewhere he expounds the necessity of Jesus's full obedience for salvation.[48] Instead, Calvin simply means that the creed at this point does not expound upon what belongs to the substance of our salvation. He may also intend that the definitive moment of redemption comes through the death (and resurrection) of Christ, which follows in the creed. Yet Calvin's catechism does address how the history of Jesus's life is necessary for salvation, and he also illustrates how the Apostles' Creed is not completely silent on such matters.[49]

Christian creeds, confessions, and catechisms also mention the obedience of Christ in various other ways, including the resurrection life that Jesus attained because of his perfect fulfillment of the law[50] and the requirement for man to accomplish all righteousness in order to be glorified.[51] The point is simply that we have many rich formulations to draw from in creedal traditions that point us to the necessity of Christ's obedience for our salvation. Creeds and confessions are purposefully pithy, but they communicate a great deal in an economy of words, not least where they address the person and work of Christ. Our appropriation of the Gospels for theology can thus be greatly helped by careful consideration of the richness of the church's creedal traditions.

Finally: The Grace of the Last Adam

At points in this study I have referred, in passing, to the definition and contours of the gospel message. As we conclude, I submit that we do indeed find much good news in the Gospels by focusing on the life of Jesus unto salvation. As the last Adam, Jesus vicariously realizes the obedience necessary for eternal life, overcoming the problem of sin and death. One would need many, many

47. Translations from Dennison, *Reformed Confessions*, 1:476.
48. Cf. Calvin, *Inst.* 2.16.5; 4.16.18.
49. See esp. Q. 49–54, see also Q. 103, 118–19, and Calvin's catechism of 1538, §20.4. But see also Henri Blocher, "The Atonement in John Calvin's Theology," in *The Glory of the Atonement: Biblical, Historical and Practical Perspectives. Essays in Honor of Roger Nicole*, ed. Charles E. Hill and Frank A. James III (Downers Grove, IL: IVP, 2004), 293.
50. Emden Catechism (1554) 38, which explains the resurrection in the Apostles' Creed.
51. Echoing the language in the Confession of Theodore Beza (1560) 19. For some other relevant texts, see Belgic Confession (1561) 22; the Hungarian *Confessio Catholica* (1562): "In What Way Do the Justified Fulfill the Law?"; the Confession of Tarcal and Torda (1562–1563) 3.19, 24; Heidelberg Catechism (1563) 36–37; Second Helvetic Confession (1566) 19; Bohemian Confession (1575, 1609) 8; London Baptist Confession (1644) 16–21; Westminster Confession of Faith (1646) 7–8; London Baptist Confession (1677) 8.4–5.

volumes to discuss the grace that is manifested to us through Jesus Christ; indeed, I suppose that the whole world would not be able to contain the books that could be written.

I finish, then, with a few brief reflections on the wonders of the grace of Jesus Christ that is revealed in the Gospels. In the Gospels we see that Jesus accomplishes the righteousness that characterizes the kingdom of God, and this righteousness is a gift.[52] The kingdom demands a better righteousness than that of the scribes and Pharisees for those who would enter it (Matt. 5:20), yet it is also the Father's good pleasure to grant the kingdom (Luke 12:32). The stringency in entering the kingdom is ultimately answered by the full obedience of Jesus himself, who establishes and opens the gates of the kingdom through his perfect obedience—both active and passive. Jesus shows us the unity of obedience and love that the covenantal law of God always required. Jesus's people, then, must be united to him by faith, and so receive the blessings of salvation through the work of the last Adam. By following in the righteous steps of the Messiah, we learn how to truly love God and love our neighbor. Jesus is definitively and representatively obedient as the last Adam and Son of God, and his people are obedient in a derivative sense, through faith in him. Jesus is the mediator of the new covenant, which is sealed in his blood. The full measure of the law has been met, and the penalty of sin has been overcome through Jesus's death and resurrection. Our faith and hope must therefore be in Jesus Christ, who has proven obedient on our behalf.

I conclude with the confidence expressed by New Testament scholar J. Gresham Machen. As he lay dying in a North Dakota hospital, Machen's last recorded words came via telegram: "I'm so thankful for [the] active obedience of Christ. No hope without it."[53] Machen's hope is gloriously narrated for us in the Fourfold Gospel, where we read of salvation accomplished by the fully obedient last Adam. As Jesus delighted to do his Father's will, may we delight to trust in and follow a gracious Savior.

---

52. Cf. Bavinck, *Reformed Dogmatics*, 4:183.
53. John Murray, *Collected Writings of John Murray*, 4 vols. (Edinburgh: Banner of Truth, 1976–82), 3:64.

Bibliography

Abernethy, Andrew T. *The Book of Isaiah and God's Kingdom: A Thematic-Theological Approach.* NSBT 40. Downers Grove, IL: IVP Academic, 2016.

Achtemeier, Elizabeth. *Deuteronomy, Jeremiah.* PC. Philadelphia: Fortress, 1978.

Agan, C. D. "Jimmy," III. *The Imitation of Christ in the Gospel of Luke: Growing in Christlike Love for God and Neighbor.* Phillipsburg, NJ: P&R, 2014.

Allison, Dale C., Jr. *A Critical and Exegetical Commentary on the Epistle of James.* ICC. London: Bloomsbury T&T Clark, 2013.

———. *Studies in Matthew: Interpretation Past and Present.* Grand Rapids: Baker Academic, 2005.

Andersen, Francis I., and David Noel Freedman. *Hosea: A New Translation with Introduction and Commentary.* AB 24. Garden City, NY: Doubleday, 1980.

Armstrong, Jonathan J. "Victorinus of Pettau as the Author of the Canon Muratori." *VC* 62 (2008): 1–34.

Aulén, Gustaf. *Christus Victor: An Historical Study of the Three Main Types of the Idea of the Atonement.* Translated by A. G. Hebert. London: SPCK, 1931.

Ayayo, Karelynne Gerber. "Magical Expectations and the Two-Stage Healing of Mark 8." *BBR* 24 (2014): 379–91.

Bailey, Kenneth E. *Jesus through Middle Eastern Eyes: Cultural Studies in the Gospels.* Downers Grove, IL: IVP Academic, 2008.

———. *"Poet and Peasant" and "Through Peasant Eyes": A Literary-Cultural Approach to the Parables in Luke.* Combined ed. Grand Rapids: Eerdmans, 1983.

Baldwin, Joyce G. *Daniel: An Introduction and Commentary.* TOTC. Downers Grove, IL: InterVarsity, 1978.

Barrett, C. K. *The Gospel according to St. John: An Introduction with Commentary and Notes on the Greek Text.* 2nd ed. Philadelphia: Westminster, 1978.

Barrett, Kyle Scott. "Justification in Lukan Theology." PhD diss., Southern Baptist Theological Seminary, 2012.

Barth, Karl. *Church Dogmatics* IV/1. Edited by T. F. Torrance. Translated by Geoffrey W. Bromiley. Edinburgh: T&T Clark, 1956.

———. *Dogmatics in Outline*. Translated by G. T. Thomson. London: SCM, 1949.

Bastit, Agnès. "L'apologue synoptique du 'Fort ligoté' (Mt 12,29 et par.) dans la théologie d'Irenée et la première littérature chrétienne." *LTP* 70 (2014): 291–314.

Bauckham, Richard. *God Crucified: Monotheism and Christology in the New Testament*. Grand Rapids: Eerdmans, 1999.

———. *Gospel of Glory: Major Themes in Johannine Theology*. Grand Rapids: Baker Academic, 2015.

———. *Jesus and the Eyewitnesses: The Gospels as Eyewitness Testimony*. Grand Rapids: Eerdmans, 2006.

———. "Jesus and the Wild Animals." In *Jesus of Nazareth: Lord and Christ; Essays on the Historical Jesus and New Testament Christology*, edited by Joel B. Green and Max Turner, 3–21. Grand Rapids: Eerdmans, 1994.

———. *Jesus: A Very Short Introduction*. VSI 275. Oxford: Oxford University Press, 2011.

———. *Jude, 2 Peter*. WBC 50. Waco: Word, 1983.

———. "Messianism according to the Gospel of John." In *Challenging Perspectives on the Gospel of John*, edited by John Lierman, 34–68. WUNT 2/219. Tübingen: Mohr Siebeck, 2006.

Bauckham, Richard, James R. Davila, and Alexander Panayotov, eds. *Old Testament Pseudepigrapha: More Noncanonical Scriptures*. Vol. 1. Grand Rapids: Eerdmans, 2013.

Bauer, Walter. *A Greek-English Lexicon of the New Testament and Other Early Christian Literature*. Revised and edited by Frederick William Danker. 3rd ed. Chicago: University of Chicago Press, 2000.

Bavinck, Herman. *Reformed Dogmatics*. Edited by John Bolt. Translated by John Vriend. 4 vols. Grand Rapids: Baker Academic, 2003–8.

Beale, G. K. *The Book of Revelation*. NIGTC. Grand Rapids: Eerdmans, 1998.

———. *A New Testament Biblical Theology: The Unfolding of the Old Testament in the New*. Grand Rapids: Baker Academic, 2011.

———. *The Temple and the Church's Mission: A Biblical Theology of the Dwelling Place of God*. NSBT 17. Downers Grove, IL: InterVarsity, 2004.

———. "The Use of Hosea 11:1 in Matthew 2:15: One More Time." *JETS* 55 (2012): 697–715.

Beale, G. K., and D. A. Carson, eds. *Commentary on the New Testament Use of the Old Testament*. Grand Rapids: Baker Academic, 2007.

Beale, G. K., and Dane Ortlund. "Darkness over the Whole Land: A Biblical-Theological Reflection on Mark 15:33." *WTJ* 75 (2013): 221–38.

Beasley-Murray, George R. *Jesus and the Kingdom of God*. Grand Rapids: Eerdmans, 1986.

———. *John*. 2nd ed. WBC 36. Nashville: Thomas Nelson, 1999.

Beaton, Richard C. *Isaiah's Christ in Matthew's Gospel*. SNTSMS 123. Cambridge: Cambridge University Press, 2002.

Bede. *Homilies on the Gospels*. Translated by Lawrence T. Martin and David Hurst. CSS 110. Kalamazoo, MI: Cistercian Press, 1991.

Begg, Alistair, and Sinclair B. Ferguson. *Name Above All Names*. Wheaton: Crossway, 2013.

Belcher, Richard P., Jr. *Prophet, Priest, and King: A Biblical Theology of the Offices of Christ*. Phillipsburg, NJ: P&R, 2016.

Berkhof, Louis. *Systematic Theology*. 4th ed. Grand Rapids: Eerdmans, 1941.

Best, Ernest. *The Temptation and the Passion: The Markan Soteriology*. 2nd ed. SNTSMS 2. Cambridge: Cambridge University Press, 1990.

Bieneck, Joachim. *Sohn Gottes als Christusbezeichnung der Synoptiker*. ATANT 21. Zürich: Zwingli, 1951.

Bingham, D. Jeffrey. *Irenaeus' Use of Matthew's Gospel in "Adversus Haereses."* TEG 7. Leuven: Peeters, 1998.

Bird, Michael F. *Evangelical Theology: A Biblical and Systematic Introduction*. Grand Rapids: Zondervan, 2013.

———. *The Gospel of the Lord: How the Early Church Wrote the Story of Jesus*. Grand Rapids: Eerdmans, 2014.

Blackwell, Ben C. *Christosis: Pauline Soteriology in Light of Deification in Irenaeus and Cyril of Alexandria*. WUNT 2/314. Tübingen: Mohr Siebeck, 2011.

Blass, Friedrich, and Albert Debrunner. *A Greek Grammar of the New Testament and Other Early Christian Literature*. Edited and translated by Robert W. Funk. Chicago: University of Chicago Press, 1961.

Blocher, Henri. "The Atonement in John Calvin's Theology." In *The Glory of the Atonement: Biblical, Historical and Practical Perspectives. Essays in Honor of Roger Nicole*, edited by Charles E. Hill and Frank A. James III, 263–303. Downers Grove, IL: IVP, 2004.

Block, Daniel I. *Deuteronomy*. NIVAC. Grand Rapids: Zondervan, 2012.

Bock, Darrell L. *Acts*. BECNT. Grand Rapids: Baker Academic, 2007.

———. *Luke*. 2 vols. BECNT. Grand Rapids: Baker Academic, 1994–96.

———. *Recovering the Real Lost Gospel: Reclaiming the Gospel as Good News*. Nashville: B&H, 2010.

———. "The Use of Daniel 7 in Jesus's Trial, with Implications for His Self-Understanding." In *"Who Is This Son of Man?" The Latest Scholarship on a Puzzling Expression of the Historical Jesus*, edited by Larry W. Hurtado and Paul L. Owen, 78–100. LNTS 390. London: T&T Clark, 2011.

Bockmuehl, Markus. "The Baptism of Jesus as 'Super-Sacrament' of Redemption." *Theology* 115 (2012): 83–91.

Bonnard, Pierre. *L'Évangile selon Saint Matthieu.* 2nd ed. CNT 1. Neuchatel: Delachaux & Niestlé, 1963.

Borchert, Gerald L. *John 12–21.* NAC 25B. Nashville: Broadman & Holman, 2002.

Bos, F. L. *Johann Piscator: Ein Beitrag zur Geschichte der reformierten Theologie.* Kampen: J. H. Kok, 1932.

Bovon, François. *Luke.* Translated by Christine M. Thomas, Donald S. Deer, and James Crouch. 3 vols. Hermeneia. Minneapolis: Fortress, 2002–13.

Bräutigam, Michael. *Union with Christ: Adolf Schlatter's Relational Christology.* Eugene, OR: Pickwick, 2015.

Brendsel, Daniel J. *"Isaiah Saw His Glory": The Use of Isaiah 52–53 in John 12.* BZNW 208. Berlin: Walter de Gruyter, 2014.

Breytenbach, Cilliers. "Narrating the Death of Jesus in Mark: Utterances of the Main Character, Jesus." *ZNW* 105 (2014): 153–68.

Brown, Raymond E. *The Birth of the Messiah: A Commentary on the Infancy Narratives in Matthew and Luke.* Rev. ed. ABRL. New York: Doubleday, 1993.

———. *The Gospel according to John.* 2 vols. AB 29–29A. Garden City, NY: Doubleday, 1966–70.

Bruce, F. F. *Romans.* 2nd ed. TNTC. Grand Rapids: Eerdmans, 1985.

Bruno, Christopher R. "'Jesus Is Our Jubilee' . . . But How? The OT Background and Lukan Fulfillment of the Ethics of Jubilee." *JETS* 53 (2010): 81–101.

Bultmann, Rudolf. *The History of the Synoptic Tradition.* Translated by John Marsh. Rev. ed. New York: Harper & Row, 1968.

———. *Jesus and the Word.* Translated by Louise Pettibone Smith and Erminie Huntress Lantero. New York: Scribner, 1958.

———. *Theology of the New Testament.* Translated by Kendrick Grobel. 2 vols. New York: Scribner, 1951–55.

Burridge, Richard A. *What Are the Gospels? A Comparison with Graeco-Roman Biography.* 2nd ed. BRS. Grand Rapids: Eerdmans, 2004.

Calvin, John. *Commentary on a Harmony of the Evangelists, Matthew, Mark, and Luke.* Translated and edited by William Pringle. 3 vols. Reprint, Grand Rapids: Baker, 2003.

———. *Institutes of the Christian Religion.* Edited by John T. McNeill. Translated by Ford Lewis Battles. 2 vols. LCC 20. Louisville: Westminster John Knox, 1960.

Caneday, Ardel B. "Mark's Provocative Use of Scripture in Narration: 'He Was with the Wild Animals and Angels Ministered to Him.'" *BBR* 9 (1999): 19–36.

Carson, D. A. "Adumbrations of Atonement Theology in the Fourth Gospel." *JETS* 57 (2014): 513–22.

———. *The Gospel according to John.* PNTC. Grand Rapids: Eerdmans, 1991.

Charlesworth, James H. *Old Testament Pseudepigrapha*. 2 vols. ABRL. Garden City, NY: Doubleday, 1983–85.

Chiarot, Kevin. *The Unassumed Is the Unhealed: The Humanity of Christ in the Theology of T. F. Torrance*. Eugene, OR: Pickwick, 2013.

Childs, Brevard S. *The Book of Exodus: A Critical, Theological Commentary*. OTL. Philadelphia: Westminster, 1974.

———. *Isaiah: A Commentary*. OTL. Louisville: Westminster John Knox, 2001.

Christensen, Duane L. *Deuteronomy 1:1–21:9*. WBC 6A. Nashville: Thomas Nelson, 2001.

———. *Deuteronomy 21:10–34:12*. WBC 6B. Nashville: Thomas Nelson, 2002.

Clements, R. E. *God's Chosen People: A Theological Interpretation of the Book of Deuteronomy*. London: SCM, 1968.

Clines, D. J. A., ed. *Dictionary of Classical Hebrew*. 9 vols. Sheffield: Sheffield Phoenix, 1993–2014.

———. "The Image of God in Man." *TynBul* 19 (1968): 53–103.

———. *Job 21–37*. WBC 18A. Nashville: Thomas Nelson, 2006.

Collins, Adela Yarbro. *Mark*. Hermeneia. Minneapolis: Fortress, 2007.

Collins, C. John. "The Eucharist as Christian Sacrifice: How Patristic Authors Can Help Us Read the Bible." *WTJ* 66 (2004): 1–23.

Collins, John J. "The Son of Man in First-Century Judaism." *NTS* 38 (1992): 448–66.

Coloe, Mary L., PBVM. "The Garden as a New Creation in John." *TBT* 53 (2015): 158–64.

Cooke, Gerald A. "The Israelite King as Son of God." *ZAW* 73 (1961): 202–25.

Craigie, Peter C. *The Book of Deuteronomy*. NICOT. Grand Rapids: Eerdmans, 1976.

Cranfield, C. E. B. *The Gospel according to St. Mark: An Introduction and Commentary*. CGTC. Cambridge: Cambridge University Press, 1959.

Crowe, Brandon D. "Fulfillment in Matthew as Eschatological Reversal." *WTJ* 75 (2013): 111–27.

———. *The Message of the General Epistles in the History of Redemption: Wisdom from James, Peter, John, and Jude*. Phillipsburg, NJ: P&R, 2015.

———. *The Obedient Son: Deuteronomy and Christology in the Gospel of Matthew*. BZNW 188. Berlin: Walter de Gruyter, 2012.

———. "Oh Sweet Exchange! The Soteriological Significance of the Incarnation in the *Epistle to Diognetus*." *ZNW* 102 (2011): 96–109.

———. "The Song of Moses and Divine Begetting in Matt 1,20." *Bib* 90 (2009): 47–58.

———. "The Sources for Luke-Acts: Where Did Luke Get His Material (And Why Does It Matter)?" In *Issues in Luke-Acts: Selected Essays*, edited by Sean A. Adams and Michael W. Pahl, 73–95. GH. Piscataway, NJ: Gorgias, 2012.

———. *Was Jesus Really Born of a Virgin?* CAHQ. Phillipsburg, NJ: P&R, 2013.

Cullmann, Oscar. *Christ and Time: The Primitive Christian Conception of Time and History*. Translated by Floyd V. Filson. Rev. ed. Philadelphia: Westminster, 1964.

———. *The Christology of the New Testament*. Translated by Shirley C. Guthrie and Charles A. M. Hall. Rev. ed. Philadelphia: Westminster, 1963.

Cureton, Kenyn M. "Jesus as Son and Servant: An Investigation of the Baptism and Testing Narratives and Their Significance for Cohesion, Plot, and Christology in Matthew." PhD diss., Southern Baptist Theological Seminary, 1993.

Curtis, Byron G. "Hosea 6:7 and the Covenant-Breaking like/at Adam." In *The Law Is Not of Faith: Essays on Work and Grace in the Mosaic Covenant*, edited by Bryan D. Estelle, J. V. Fesko, and David VanDrunen, 170–209. Phillipsburg, NJ: P&R, 2009.

Cyril of Alexandria. *Commentary on John*. Translated by David R. Maxwell. Edited by Joel C. Elowsky. 2 vols. ACT. Downers Grove, IL: IVP Academic, 2013–15.

Daniélou, Jean, SJ. *From Shadows to Reality: Studies in the Biblical Typology of the Fathers*. Translated by Dom Wulstan Hibberd. London: Burns and Oates, 1960.

Davies, W. D. *Paul and Rabbinic Judaism: Some Rabbinic Elements in Pauline Theology*. London: SPCK, 1948.

Davies, W. D., and Dale C. Allison Jr. *A Critical and Exegetical Commentary on the Gospel according to St. Matthew*. 3 vols. ICC. Edinburgh: T&T Clark, 1988–97.

Davila, James R. *The Provenance of the Pseudepigrapha: Jewish, Christian, or Other?* JSJSup 105. Leiden: Brill, 2005.

Deines, Roland. *Die Gerechtigkeit der Tora im Reich des Messias. Mt 5,13–20 als Schlüsseltext der matthäischen Theologie*. WUNT 177. Tübingen: Mohr Siebeck, 2004.

———. "Not the Law but the Messiah: Law and Righteousness in the Gospel of Matthew—an Ongoing Debate." In *Built Upon the Rock: Studies in the Gospel of Matthew*, edited by Daniel M. Gurtner and John Nolland, 53–84. Grand Rapids: Eerdmans, 2008.

Deissler, Alfons. "Der 'Menschensohn' und 'das Volk der Heiligen des Höchsten' in Dan 7." In *Jesus und der Menschensohn: Für Anton Vögtle*, edited by Rudolf Pesch and Rudolf Schnackenburg, 81–91. Freiburg: Herder, 1975.

Dempster, Stephen G. *Dominion and Dynasty: A Theology of the Hebrew Bible*. NSBT 15. Downers Grove, IL: IVP Academic, 2003.

———. "From Slight Peg to Cornerstone to Capstone: The Resurrection of Christ 'On the Third Day' according to the Scriptures." *WTJ* 76 (2014): 371–409.

Dennison, James T., Jr., ed. *Reformed Confessions of the 16th and 17th Centuries in English Translation*. 4 vols. Grand Rapids: Reformation Heritage, 2008–14.

Derrett, J. Duncan M. "The Manger: Ritual Law and Soteriology." *Theology* 74 (1971): 566–71.

deSilva, David A. "The *Testaments of the Twelve Patriarchs* as Witnesses to Pre-Christian Judaism: A Re-Assessment." *JSP* 23 (2013): 21–68.

Dodd, C. H. *According to the Scriptures: The Substructure of New Testament Theology*. London: Nisbet, 1952.

———. *The Apostolic Preaching and Its Developments*. New York: Harper & Row, 1936.

———. *The Founder of Christianity*. London: Collins, 1971.

———. "The Framework of the Gospel Narrative." *ExpTim* 43 (1931–32): 396–400.

———. *The Interpretation of the Fourth Gospel*. Cambridge: Cambridge University Press, 1953.

Donaldson, Terence L. "The Mockers and the Son of God (Matthew 27:37–44): Two Characters in Matthew's Story of Jesus." *JSNT* 41 (1991): 3–18.

DuBose, William Porcher. *The Gospel in the Gospels*. New York: Longmans, Green, 1908.

Duguid, Iain M. *Ezekiel*. NIVAC. Grand Rapids: Zondervan, 1999.

Dunn, James D. G. *Christology in the Making: A New Testament Inquiry into the Origins of the Doctrine of the Incarnation*. 2nd ed. Grand Rapids: Eerdmans, 1989.

———. *Jesus Remembered*. CM 1. Grand Rapids: Eerdmans, 2003.

Dunson, Ben C. "Do Bible Words Have Bible Meaning? Distinguishing between Imputation as Word and Doctrine." *WTJ* 75 (2013): 239–60.

Easter, Matthew C. "'Certainly This Man Was Righteous': Highlighting a Messianic Reading of the Centurion's Confession in Luke 23:47." *TynBul* 63 (2012): 35–51.

Edin, Mary Hinkle. "Learning What Righteousness Means: Hosea 6:6 and the Ethic of Mercy in Matthew's Gospel." *WW* 18 (1998): 355–63.

Edwards, J. Christopher. *The Ransom Logion in Mark and Matthew: Its Reception and Its Significance for the Study of the Gospels*. WUNT 2/327. Tübingen: Mohr Siebeck, 2012.

Edwards, James R. *The Gospel according to Luke*. PNTC. Grand Rapids: Eerdmans, 2015.

———. *The Gospel according to Mark*. PNTC. Grand Rapids: Eerdmans, 2002.

Ehrman, Bart D., and Zlatko Pleše. *The Apocryphal Gospels: Texts and Translations*. Oxford: Oxford University Press, 2013.

Eissfeldt, Otto. "Πληρῶσαι πᾶσαν δικαιοσύνην in Matthäus 3,15." *ZNW* 61 (1970): 209–15.

Elliger, K., and W. Rudolph, eds. *Biblia Hebraica Stuttgartensia*. 5th ed. Stuttgart: Deutsche Bibelgesellschaft, 1977.

Ermakov, Arseny. "The Holy One of God in Markan Narrative." *HBT* 36 (2014): 159–84.

Eubank, Nathan. *Wages of Cross-Bearing and Debt of Sin: The Economy of the Kingdom of Heaven in Matthew's Gospel*. BZNW 196. Berlin: Walter de Gruyter, 2013.

Evans, C. F. *Saint Luke*. London: SCM; Philadelphia: Trinity Press International, 1990.

Evans, Craig A. *Luke*. NIBCNT. Peabody, MA: Hendrickson, 1990.

———. *Mark 8:27–16:20*. WBC 34B. Nashville: Thomas Nelson, 2001.

Evans, Craig A., and James A. Sanders. *Luke and Scripture: The Function of Sacred Tradition in Luke-Acts*. Minneapolis: Fortress, 1994.

Fairweather, Eugene R., ed. and trans. *A Scholastic Miscellany: Anselm to Ockham*. LCC: Ichthus Edition. Philadelphia: Westminster, 1966.

Fee, Gordon D. *Pauline Christology: An Exegetical-Theological Study*. Peabody, MA: Hendrickson, 2007.

Ferguson, Everett. *The Rule of Faith: A Guide*. CC. Eugene, OR: Cascade, 2015.

Ferguson, Sinclair B. *The Holy Spirit*. CCT. Downers Grove, IL: InterVarsity, 1996.

———. *John Owen on the Christian Life*. Edinburgh: Banner of Truth, 1987.

Fitzmyer, Joseph A. *The Gospel according to Luke*. 2 vols. AB 28–28A. Garden City, NY: Doubleday, 1981–85.

Fletcher, Daniel H. *Signs in the Wilderness: Intertextuality and the Testing of Nicodemus*. Eugene, OR: Wipf & Stock, 2014.

Förster, Hans. "Die johanneischen Zeichen und Joh 2:11 als möglicher hermeneutischer Schlüssel." *NovT* 56 (2014): 1–23.

Frame, John M. *The Doctrine of God*. TL 2. Phillipsburg, NJ: P&R, 2002.

———. *Systematic Theology: An Introduction to Christian Belief*. Phillipsburg, NJ: P&R, 2013.

France, R. T. "The Formula Citations of Matthew 2 and the Problem of Communication." *NTS* 27 (1981/1982): 233–51.

———. *The Gospel of Mark*. NIGTC. Grand Rapids: Eerdmans, 2002.

———. *The Gospel of Matthew*. NICNT. Grand Rapids: Eerdmans, 2007.

———. *Matthew: Evangelist and Teacher*. Exeter: Paternoster, 1989.

Fuller, R. H. *The Mission and Achievement of Jesus: An Examination of the Presuppositions of New Testament Theology*. SBT 12. London: SCM, 1954.

Gaffin, Richard B., Jr. "Justification in Luke-Acts." In *Right with God: Justification in the Bible and the World*, edited by D. A. Carson, 106–25. Grand Rapids: Baker, 1992.

———. *No Adam, No Gospel: Adam and the History of Redemption*. Phillipsburg, NJ: P&R; Philadelphia: Westminster Seminary Press, 2015.

———. *Resurrection and Redemption: A Study in Paul's Soteriology*. 2nd ed. Phillipsburg, NJ: P&R, 1987.

Garland, David E. *Luke*. ZECNT. Grand Rapids: Zondervan, 2011.

Garrett, Susan R. *The Demise of the Devil: Magic and the Demonic in Luke's Writings*. Minneapolis: Fortress, 1989.

Gathercole, Simon J. *Defending Substitution: An Essay on Atonement in Paul*. ASBT. Grand Rapids: Baker Academic, 2015.

———. "Jesus' Eschatological Vision of the Fall of Satan: Luke 10.18 Reconsidered." *ZNW* 94 (2003): 143–63.

———. *The Preexistent Son: Recovering the Christologies of Matthew, Mark, and Luke.* Grand Rapids: Eerdmans, 2006.

———. *Where Is Boasting? Early Jewish Soteriology and Paul's Response in Romans 1–5.* Grand Rapids: Eerdmans, 2002.

Geldenhuys, Norval. *Commentary on the Gospel of Luke.* NICNT. Grand Rapids: Eerdmans, 1951.

Gelston, Anthony, ed. *The Twelve Minor Prophets. BHQ* 13. Stuttgart: Deutsche Bibelgesellschaft, 2010.

Gibbs, Jeffrey A. "Israel Standing with Israel: The Baptism of Jesus in Matthew's Gospel (Matt. 3:13–17)." *CBQ* 64 (2002): 511–26.

Gibson, Jeffrey B. "Jesus' Wilderness Temptation according to Mark." *JSNT* 53 (1994): 3–34.

Gieschen, Charles A. "Why Was Jesus with the Wild Beasts (Mark 1:13)?" *CTQ* 73 (2009): 77–80.

Giesen, Heinz. *Christliches Handeln: Eine redaktionskritische Untersuchung zum* δικαιοσύνη-*Begriff im Matthäus-Evangelium.* EHS.T 181. Frankfurt: Peter Lang, 1981.

Gilbert, Allan H. "Σήμερον καὶ αὔριον, καὶ τῇ τρίτῃ (Luke 13:32)." *JBL* 35 (1916): 315–18.

Girard, Marc. "La composition structurelle des 'signes' dans le quatrième évangile." *ScRel* 9 (1980): 315–24.

Gladd, Benjamin L. "The Last Adam as the 'Life-Giving Spirit' Revisited: A Possible Old Testament Background of One of Paul's Most Perplexing Phrases." *WTJ* 71 (2009): 297–309.

Gnilka, Joachim. *Das Evangelium nach Markus.* 2 vols. EKKNT 2. Zürich: Benziger; Neukirchen-Vluyn: Neukirchener, 1978–79.

Goodwin, Thomas. *Christ Set Forth.* Vol. 4 of *The Works of Thomas Goodwin.* Edinburgh: James Nichol, 1862.

Grässer, Eric. "ΚΑΙ ΗΝ ΜΕΤΑ ΤΩΝ ΘΗΡΙΩΝ (Mk 1,13b): Ansätze einer theologischen Tierschutzethik." In *Studien zum Text und zur Ethik des Neuen Testaments: Festschrift zum 80. Geburtstag von Heinrich Greeven,* edited by Wolfgang Schrage, 144–57. BZNW 47. Berlin: Walter de Gruyter, 1986.

Grassi, Joseph A. "Eating Jesus' Flesh and Drinking His Blood: The Centrality and Meaning of John 6:51–58." *BTB* 17 (1987): 24–30.

Green, Joel B. *The Gospel of Luke.* NICNT. Grand Rapids: Eerdmans, 1997.

Guelich, Robert A. *Mark 1–8:26.* WBC 34A. Waco: Word, 1989.

Hagner, Donald A. *Matthew.* 2 vols. WBC 33A–B. Dallas: Word, 1993–95.

Hahneman, Geoffrey Mark. *The Muratorian Fragment and the Development of the Canon.* Oxford: Clarendon, 1992.

Hamm, M. Dennis, SJ. "The Freeing of the Bent Woman and the Restoration of Israel: Luke 13.10–17 as Narrative Theology." *JSNT* 31 (1987): 23–44.

Harder, Lydia. "Power and Authority in Mennonite Theological Development." In *Power, Authority, and the Anabaptist Tradition,* edited by Benjamin W. Redekop and Calvin W. Redekop, 73–94. Baltimore: Johns Hopkins University Press, 2001.

Harris, Murray J. *Prepositions and Theology in the Greek New Testament: An Essential Reference Resource for Exegesis.* Grand Rapids: Zondervan, 2012.

Harris, R. Laird, Gleason L. Archer Jr., and Bruce K. Waltke, eds. *Theological Wordbook of the Old Testament.* 2 vols. Chicago: Moody Press, 1980.

Hays, Richard B. *The Faith of Jesus Christ: The Narrative Substructure of Galatians 3:1–4:11.* 2nd ed. BRS. Grand Rapids: Eerdmans, 2002.

———. "The Gospel of Matthew: Reconfigured Torah." *HvTSt* 61 (2005): 165–90.

———. *Reading Backwards: Figural Christology and the Fourfold Gospel Witness.* Waco: Baylor University Press, 2014.

Heil, John Paul. "Jesus with the Wild Animals in Mark 1:13." *CBQ* 68 (2006): 63–78.

Heine, Ronald E. *Classical Christian Doctrine: Introducing the Essentials of the Ancient Faith.* Grand Rapids: Baker Academic, 2013.

Hendriksen, William. *Exposition of the Gospel according to Luke.* Grand Rapids: Baker, 1978.

———. *More than Conquerors: An Interpretation of the Book of Revelation.* Grand Rapids: Baker, 1998.

Hengel, Martin. *The Four Gospels and the One Gospel of Jesus Christ: An Investigation of the Collection and Origin of the Canonical Gospels.* Translated by John Bowden. Harrisburg, PA: Trinity Press International, 2000.

Hengel, Martin, and Daniel P. Bailey. "The Effective-History of Isaiah 53 in the Pre-Christian Period." In *The Suffering Servant: Isaiah 53 in Jewish and Christian Sources,* edited by Bernd Janowski and Peter Stuhlmacher, translated by Daniel P. Bailey, 75–146. Grand Rapids: Eerdmans, 2004.

Hill, Charles E. *Regnum Caelorum: Patterns of Millennial Thought in Early Christianity.* 2nd ed. Grand Rapids: Eerdmans, 2001.

———. *Who Chose the Gospels? Probing the Great Gospel Conspiracy.* Oxford: Oxford University Press, 2010.

Hill, David. "On the Use of Hosea 6:6 in Matthew's Gospel." *NTS* 24 (1977): 107–19.

Hodge, Charles. *Systematic Theology.* 3 vols. Reprint, Peabody, MA: Hendrickson, 2008.

Hoekema, Anthony A. *The Bible and the Future.* Grand Rapids: Eerdmans, 1994.

Holmes, Michael W., ed. and trans. *The Apostolic Fathers: Greek Texts and English Translations.* 3rd ed. Grand Rapids: Baker Academic, 2007.

Holsinger-Friesen, Thomas. *Irenaeus and Genesis: A Study of Competition in Early Christian Hermeneutics*. JTISup 1. Winona Lake, IN: Eisenbrauns, 2009.

Hood, Jason B. *Imitating God in Christ: Recapturing a Biblical Pattern*. Downers Grove, IL: IVP Academic, 2013.

———. *The Messiah, His Brothers, and the Nations (Matthew 1.1–17)*. LNTS 441. London: T&T Clark, 2011.

Hooker, Morna D. *Jesus and the Servant: The Influence of the Servant Concept of Deutero-Isaiah in the New Testament*. London: SPCK, 1959.

———. *The Son of Man in Mark: A Study of the Background of the Term "Son of Man" and Its Use in St. Mark's Gospel*. London: SPCK, 1967.

Horbury, William. "The Messianic Associations of 'the Son of Man.'" *JTS* 36 (1985): 34–55.

Hoskyns, Edwyn Clement. *The Fourth Gospel*. Edited by Francis Noel Davey. 2nd ed. London: Faber and Faber, 1947.

Howard, David M., Jr. *Joshua*. NAC 5. Nashville: Broadman & Holman, 1998.

Hugenberger, Gordon Paul. *Marriage as Covenant: A Study of Biblical Law and Ethics Governing Marriage Developed from the Perspective of Malachi*. VTSup 52. Leiden: Brill, 1994.

Huizenga, Leroy Andrew. "The Incarnation of the Servant: The 'Suffering Servant' and Matthean Christology." *HBT* 27 (2005): 25–58.

Hurtado, Larry W. *Lord Jesus Christ: Devotion to Jesus in Earliest Christianity*. Grand Rapids: Eerdmans, 2003.

———. *Mark*. NIBCNT 2. Peabody, MA: Hendrickson, 1989.

———. "The Women, the Tomb, and the Climax of Mark." In *A Wandering Galilean: Essays in Honour of Seán Freyne*, edited by Zuleika Rodgers, Margaret Daly-Denton, and Anne Fitzpatrick McKinley, 427–50. JSJSup 132. Leiden: Brill, 2009.

Hurtado, Larry W., and Paul L. Owen, eds. *"Who Is This Son of Man?" The Latest Scholarship on a Puzzling Expression of the Historical Jesus*. LNTS 390. London: T&T Clark, 2011.

Irons, Charles Lee. *The Righteousness of God: A Lexical Examination of the Covenant-Faithfulness Interpretation*. WUNT 2/386. Tübingen: Mohr Siebeck, 2015.

Jackson, Mark Randall. "Atonement in Matthew's Gospel." PhD diss., Southern Baptist Theological Seminary, 2011.

Janowski, Bernd. "He Bore Our Sins: Isaiah 53 and the Drama of Taking Another's Place." In *The Suffering Servant: Isaiah 53 in Jewish and Christian Sources*, edited by Bernd Janowski and Peter Stuhlmacher, translated by Daniel P. Bailey, 48–74. Grand Rapids: Eerdmans, 2004.

Jenson, Philip Peter. *Graded Holiness: A Key to the Priestly Conception of the World*. JSOTSup 106. Sheffield: JSOT Press, 1992.

Jeremias, Joachim. *Golgotha*. ANZK 1. Leipzig: Eduard Pfeiffer, 1926.

————. *The Parables of Jesus.* Translated by S. H. Hooke. 2nd ed. New York: Scribner, 1972.

Johansson, Daniel. "Jesus and God in the Gospel of Mark: Unity and Distinction." PhD diss., University of Edinburgh, 2011.

————. "'Who Can Forgive Sins but God Alone?' Human and Angelic Agents, and Divine Forgiveness in Early Judaism." *JSNT* 33 (2011): 351–74.

Johnson, Marshall D. *The Purpose of the Biblical Genealogies: With Special Reference to the Setting of the Genealogies of Jesus.* SNTSMS 8. Cambridge: Cambridge University Press, 1969.

Jones, Mark. *Why Heaven Kissed Earth: The Christology of the Puritan Reformed Orthodox Theologian, Thomas Goodwin (1600–1680).* RHT 13. Göttingen: Vandenhoeck & Ruprecht, 2010.

Jonge, Marinus de. "Signs and Works in the Fourth Gospel." In vol. 2 of *Miscellanea Neotestamentica,* edited by T. Baarda, A. F. J. Klijn, and W. C. van Unnik, 107–25. NovTSup 48. Leiden: Brill, 1978.

Jue, Jeffrey K. "The Active Obedience of Christ and the Theology of the Westminster Standards: A Historical Investigation." In *Justified in Christ: God's Plan for Us in Justification,* edited by K. Scott Oliphint, 99–130. Fearn, UK: Mentor, 2007.

Kähler, Martin. *The So-Called Historical Jesus and the Historic, Biblical Christ.* Translated by Carl E. Braaten. Philadelphia: Fortress, 1964.

Kaminsky, Joel S. *Corporate Responsibility in the Hebrew Bible.* JSOTSup 196. Sheffield: Sheffield Academic, 1995.

Keating, Daniel. "The Baptism of Jesus in Cyril of Alexandria: The Re-Creation of the Human Race." *ProEccl* 8 (1999): 201–22.

Kee, H. C. "*Testaments of the Twelve Patriarchs.*" In vol. 1 of *Old Testament Pseudepigrapha,* edited by James H. Charlesworth, 775–828. ABRL. New York: Doubleday, 1983.

Keener, Craig S. *Acts: An Exegetical Commentary.* 4 vols. Grand Rapids: Baker Academic, 2012–15.

————. *The Gospel of John: A Commentary.* 2 vols. Peabody, MA: Hendrickson, 2003.

————. *The Gospel of Matthew: A Socio-Rhetorical Commentary.* Grand Rapids: Eerdmans, 2009.

Keil, Carl Friedrich, and Franz Delitzsch. *Biblical Commentary on the Old Testament.* Translated by James Martin et al. 25 vols. Edinburgh, 1857–1978. Reprint, 10 vols., Peabody, MA: Hendrickson, 1996.

Kelhoffer, James A. *Miracle and Mission: The Authentication of Missionaries and Their Message in the Longer Ending of Mark.* WUNT 2/112. Tübingen: Mohr Siebeck, 2000.

Kelly, Douglas F. *Systematic Theology: Grounded in Holy Scripture and Understood in the Light of the Church.* Vol. 2, *The Beauty of Christ: A Trinitarian Vision.* Fearn, UK: Mentor, 2014.

Kelly, J. N. D. *Early Christian Doctrines*. 5th rev. ed. Peabody, MA: Prince Press, 2007.

Kennedy, Joel. *The Recapitulation of Israel: Use of Israel's History in Matthew 1:1–4:11*. WUNT 2/257. Tübingen: Mohr Siebeck, 2008.

Kidner, Derek. *Love to the Loveless: The Message of Hosea*. BST. Downers Grove, IL: InterVarsity, 1981.

Kingsbury, Jack Dean. "The Figure of Jesus in Matthew's Story: A Literary-Critical Probe." *JSNT* 21 (1984): 3–36.

———. *Matthew: Structure, Christology, Kingdom*. Philadelphia: Fortress, 1975.

Kirk, J. R. Daniel. "The Sufficiency of the Cross (II): The Law, the Cross, and Justification." *SBET* 24 (2006): 133–54.

Kittel, Gerhard, and Gerhard Friedrich, eds. *Theological Dictionary of the New Testament*. Translated by Geoffrey W. Bromiley. 10 vols. Grand Rapids: Eerdmans, 1964–76.

Kiuchi, Nobuyoshi. "Spirituality in Offering a Peace Offering." *TynBul* 50 (1999): 23–31.

Kline, Meredith G. *Kingdom Prologue: Genesis Foundations for a Covenantal Worldview*. Overland Park, KS: Two Age Press, 2000.

———. "The Old Testament Origins of the Gospel Genre." *WTJ* 38 (1975): 1–27.

Klink, Edward W., III. *John*. ZECNT. Grand Rapids: Zondervan, forthcoming.

Koehler, Ludwig, Walter Baumgartner, and Johann J. Stamm, eds. *The Hebrew and Aramaic Lexicon of the Old Testament*. Translated and edited under the supervision of Mervyn E. J. Richardson. 4 vols. Leiden: Brill, 1994–99.

Koester, Craig R. *The Word of Life: A Theology of John's Gospel*. Grand Rapids: Eerdmans, 2008.

Konradt, Matthias. *Israel, Kirche, und die Völker im Matthäusevangelium*. WUNT 215. Tübingen: Mohr Siebeck, 2007. ET: *Israel, Church, and the Gentiles in the Gospel of Matthew*. Translated by Kathleen Ess. BMSEC. Waco: Baylor University Press, 2014.

Köppen, Klaus-Peter. *Die Auslegung der Versuchungsgeschichte unter besonderer Berücksichtigung der Alten Kirche*. BGBE 4. Tübingen: Mohr Siebeck, 1961.

Köstenberger, Andreas J. "John." In *Commentary on the New Testament Use of the Old Testament*, edited by G. K. Beale and D. A. Carson, 415–512. Grand Rapids: Baker Academic, 2007.

———. *A Theology of John's Gospel and Letters: The Word, the Christ, the Son of God*. BTNT. Grand Rapids: Zondervan, 2009.

Köstenberger, Andreas J., and Scott R. Swain. *Father, Son, and Spirit: The Trinity and John's Gospel*. NSBT 24. Downers Grove, IL: InterVarsity, 2008.

Kruger, Michael J. *Canon Revisited: Establishing the Origins and Authority of the New Testament Books*. Wheaton: Crossway, 2012.

———. *The Question of Canon: Challenging the Status Quo in the New Testament Debate*. Downers Grove, IL: IVP Academic, 2013.

Kynes, William L. *A Christology of Solidarity: Jesus as the Representative of His People in Matthew*. New York: University Press of America, 1991.

Ladd, George Eldon. *The Presence of the Future: The Eschatology of Biblical Realism*. Grand Rapids: Eerdmans, 1974.

Lane, William L. *The Gospel according to Mark*. NICNT. Grand Rapids: Eerdmans, 1974.

———. *Hebrews 1–8*. WBC 47A. Dallas: Word, 1991.

———. *Hebrews 9–13*. WBC 47B. Dallas: Word, 1991.

Leder, Hans-Günter. "Sündenfallerzählung und Versuchungsgeschichte: Zur Interpretation von Mc 1,12f." *ZNW* 54 (1963): 188–216.

Lee, Yongbom. *The Son of Man as the Last Adam: The Early Church Tradition as a Source of Paul's Adam Christology*. Eugene, OR: Pickwick, 2012.

Legaretta-Castillo, Felipe de Jésus. *The Figure of Adam in Romans 5 and 1 Corinthians 15: The New Creation and Its Ethical and Social Reconfiguration*. Minneapolis: Fortress, 2014.

Leim, Joshua E. *Matthew's Theological Grammar: The Father and the Son*. WUNT 2/402. Tübingen: Mohr Siebeck, 2015.

Lengsfeld, Peter. *Die Adam-Christus-Typologie im Neuen Testament und ihre dogmatische Verwendung bei M. J. Scheeben und K. Barth*. KBOST 9. Essen: Ludgerus, 1965.

Letham, Robert. *Union with Christ: In Scripture, History, and Theology*. Phillipsburg, NJ: P&R, 2011.

———. *The Work of Christ*. CCT. Downers Grove, IL: IVP Academic, 1993.

Levison, John R. *Portraits of Adam in Early Judaism: From Sirach to 2 Baruch*. JSPSup 1. Sheffield: JSOT Press, 1988.

Lewis, Jack P. "The Woman's Seed (Gen. 3:15)." *JETS* 34 (1991): 299–319.

Lierman, John. "The Mosaic Pattern of John's Christology." In *Challenging Perspectives on the Gospel of John*, edited by John Lierman, 210–34. WUNT 2/219. Tübingen: Mohr Siebeck, 2006.

Lincoln, Andrew T. *Born of a Virgin? Reconceiving Jesus in the Bible, Tradition, and Theology*. Grand Rapids: Eerdmans, 2013.

Litwa, M. David. "Behold Adam: A Reading of John 19:5." *HBT* 32 (2010): 129–43.

Lloyd-Jones, D. Martyn. *Studies in the Sermon on the Mount*. 2nd ed. 2 vols. Grand Rapids: Eerdmans, 1971.

Lombard, Peter. *The Sentences*. Book 3, *On the Incarnation of the Word*. Translated by Giulio Silano. MST 45. Toronto: Pontifical Institute of Mediaeval Studies, 2009.

Longenecker, Richard N. *The Christology of Early Jewish Christianity*. SBT 2/17. London: SCM, 1970.

———. "The Obedience of Christ in the Theology of the Early Church." In *Reconciliation and Hope: New Testament Essays on Atonement and Eschatology*, edited by Robert Banks, 142–52. Exeter: Paternoster, 1974.

Luther, Martin. *Sermons on the Gospel of St. John Chapters 1–4*. Vol. 22 of *Luther's Works*. Edited by Jaroslav Pelikan. St. Louis: Concordia, 1957.

———. *Sermons on the Gospel of St. John Chapters 14–16*. Vol. 24 of *Luther's Works*. Edited by Jaroslav Pelikan. St. Louis: Concordia, 1957.

Luz, Ulrich. *Matthew*. Translated by James E. Crouch. 3 vols. Hermeneia. Minneapolis: Fortress, 2001–7.

———. *The Theology of the Gospel of Matthew*. Translated by J. Bradford Robinson. Cambridge: Cambridge University Press, 1995.

Macaskill, Grant. *Union with Christ in the New Testament*. Oxford: Oxford University Press, 2013.

Machen, J. Gresham. *God Transcendent*. Edited by Ned B. Stonehouse. 1949. Reprint, Edinburgh: Banner of Truth, 1982.

———. *The Virgin Birth of Christ*. 1930. Reprint, Grand Rapids: Baker, 1985.

Macintosh, A. A. *A Critical and Exegetical Commentary on Hosea*. ICC. Edinburgh: T&T Clark, 1997.

Macleod, Donald. *Christ Crucified: Understanding the Atonement*. Downers Grove, IL: IVP Academic, 2014.

Maher, Michael. *Targum Pseudo-Jonathan: Genesis*. ArBib 1B. Collegeville, MN: Liturgical Press, 1992.

Mahnke, Hermann. *Die Versuchungsgeschichte im Rahmen der synoptischen Evangelien: Ein Beitrag zur frühen Christologie*. BBET 9. Frankfurt: Peter Lang, 1978.

Marcus, Joel. *Mark 1–8: A New Translation with Introduction and Commentary*. AB 27. New York: Doubleday, 2000.

———. *Mark 8–16: A New Translation with Introduction and Commentary*. AYB 27A. New Haven: Yale University Press, 2009.

———. "Son of Man as Son of Adam." *RB* 110 (2003): 38–61.

———. "Son of Man as Son of Adam. Part II: Exegesis." *RB* 110 (2003): 370–86.

———. *The Way of the Lord: Christological Exegesis of the Old Testament in the Gospel of Mark*. SNTW. Edinburgh: T&T Clark, 1992.

Marshall, I. H. "Acts." In *Commentary on the New Testament Use of the Old Testament*, edited by G. K. Beale and D. A. Carson, 513–606. Grand Rapids: Baker Academic, 2007.

———. *The Gospel of Luke*. NIGTC. Grand Rapids: Eerdmans, 1978.

———. "Son of Man." In *Dictionary of Jesus and the Gospels*, edited by Joel B. Green and Scot McKnight, 775–81. Downers Grove, IL: InterVarsity, 1992.

Martyn, J. Louis. *History and Theology in the Fourth Gospel*. Rev. ed. NTL. Louisville: Westminster John Knox, 2003.

Mauser, Ulrich. *Christ in the Wilderness: The Wilderness Theme in the Second Gospel and Its Basis in the Biblical Tradition*. SBT 39. London: SCM, 1963.

Maximus the Confessor. *On the Cosmic Mystery of Jesus Christ.* Translated by Paul Blowers and Robert Louis Wilken. PPS 25. Crestwood, NY: St. Vladimir's Seminary Press, 2003.

May, David M. "The Straightened Woman (Luke 13:10–17): Paradise Lost and Regained." *PRSt* 24 (1997): 245–58.

McCartney, Dan G. "*Ecce Homo*: The Coming of the Kingdom as the Restoration of Human Viceregency." *WTJ* 56 (1994): 1–21.

McDonnell, Kilian. "Jesus' Baptism in the Jordan." *TS* 56 (1995): 209–36.

McKnight, Scot. *The King Jesus Gospel: The Original Good News Revisited.* Grand Rapids: Zondervan, 2011.

———. "Matthew as 'Gospel.'" In *Jesus, Matthew's Gospel and Early Christianity: Studies in Memory of Graham N. Stanton*, edited by Daniel M. Gurtner, Joel Willitts, and Richard A. Burridge, 59–79. LNTS 435. London: T&T Clark, 2011.

McNamara, Martin. *Targum Neofiti 1: Genesis.* ArBib 1A. Collegeville, MN: Liturgical Press, 1992.

Meeks, Wayne A. *The Prophet-King: Moses Traditions and the Johannine Christology.* NovTSup 14. Leiden: Brill, 1967.

Meier, John P. *A Marginal Jew: Rethinking the Historical Jesus.* 5 vols. ABRL. New York: Doubleday, 1991–2016.

———. *The Vision of Matthew: Christ, Church, and Morality in the First Gospel.* 1991. Reprint, Eugene, OR: Wipf & Stock, 2004.

Mell, Ulrich. "Jesu Taufe durch Johannes (Markus 1,9–15)—zur narrativen Christologie vom neuen Adam." *BZ* 40 (1996): 161–78.

Metzger, Bruce M. *The Canon of the New Testament: Its Origin, Development, and Significance.* Oxford: Clarendon, 1987.

———. *A Textual Commentary on the Greek New Testament.* 2nd ed. Stuttgart: Deutsche Bibelgesellschaft, 1994.

Michaels, J. Ramsey. *The Gospel of John.* NICNT. Grand Rapids: Eerdmans, 2010.

Mihalios, Stefanos. *The Danielic Eschatological Hour in the Johannine Literature.* LNTS 436. London: T&T Clark, 2011.

Moloney, Francis J., SDB. *Love in the Gospel of John: An Exegetical, Theological, and Literary Study.* Grand Rapids: Baker Academic, 2013.

Moltmann, Jürgen. *The Way of Jesus Christ: Christology in Messianic Dimensions.* Translated by Margaret Kohl. Minneapolis: Fortress, 1993.

Morris, Leon. *The Apostolic Preaching of the Cross.* Grand Rapids: Eerdmans, 1955.

———. *The Gospel according to John.* Rev. ed. NICNT. Grand Rapids: Eerdmans, 1995.

Motyer, J. Alec. *The Prophecy of Isaiah: An Introduction and Commentary.* Downers Grove, IL: IVP Academic, 1993.

Moule, C. F. D. "Fulfillment Words in the New Testament: Use and Abuse." In *Essays in New Testament Interpretation*, edited by C. F. D. Moule, 3–36. Cambridge: Cambridge University Press, 1982.

———. *An Idiom Book of New Testament Greek*. 2nd ed. Cambridge: Cambridge University Press, 1959.

Müller, Mogens. "Bundesideologie im Matthäusevangelium. Die Vorstellung vom neuen Bund als Grundlage der matthäischen Gesetzesverkündigung." *NTS* 58 (2011): 23–42.

Murray, John. *Collected Writings of John Murray*. 4 vols. Edinburgh: Banner of Truth, 1976–82.

———. *The Epistle to the Romans*. NICNT. 2 vols. Grand Rapids: Eerdmans, 1959–65.

———. *Redemption Accomplished and Applied*. Grand Rapids: Eerdmans, 1955.

Neyrey, Jerome. *The Passion according to Luke: A Redaction Study of Luke's Soteriology*. New York: Paulist, 1985.

Nielsen, J. T. *Adam and Christ in the Theology of Irenaeus of Lyons: An Examination of the Function of the Adam-Christ Typology in the "Adversus Haereses" of Irenaeus, against the Background of the Gnosticism of His Time*. Assen, Netherlands: Van Gorcum, 1968.

Nolland, John. *The Gospel of Matthew*. NIGTC. Grand Rapids: Eerdmans, 2005.

———. *Luke*. 3 vols. WBC 35A–C. Dallas: Word, 1989–93.

Novenson, Matthew V. *Christ among the Messiahs: Christ Language in Paul and Messiah Language in Ancient Judaism*. Oxford: Oxford University Press, 2012.

Novum Testamentum Graece. 28th ed. Edited by Barbara Aland et al. Stuttgart: Deutsche Bibelgesellschaft, 2012.

O'Brien, Peter T. *Colossians and Philemon*. WBC 44. Waco: Word, 1982.

Osborn, Eric. *Irenaeus of Lyons*. Cambridge: Cambridge University Press, 2001.

Owen, John. *The Glory of Christ*. Vol. 1 of *The Works of John Owen*. Edited by William H. Goold. Edinburgh: Banner of Truth, 1965.

Pao, David W., and Eckhard J. Schnabel. "Luke." In *Commentary on the New Testament Use of the Old Testament*, edited by G. K. Beale and D. A. Carson, 251–414. Grand Rapids: Baker Academic, 2007.

Parkman, Joel William. "Adam Christological Motifs in the Synoptic Traditions." PhD diss., Baylor University, 1994.

Parsons, Mikeal C. *Luke*. Paideia. Grand Rapids: Baker Academic, 2015.

Peeler, Amy L. B. "Desiring God: The Blood of the Covenant in Exodus 24." *BBR* 23 (2013): 187–205.

Pennington, Jonathan T. "Heaven, Earth, and a New Genesis." In *Cosmology and New Testament Theology*, edited by Jonathan T. Pennington and Sean M. McDonough, 28–44. LNTS 355. London: T&T Clark, 2008.

———. *Reading the Gospels Wisely: A Narrative and Theological Introduction.* Grand Rapids: Baker Academic, 2012.

Perkins, William. "The Combat between Christ and the Devil Displayed; or, A Commentary upon the Temptations of Christ." In vol. 1 of *The Works of William Perkins*, edited by J. Stephen Yuille, 71–165. Grand Rapids: Reformation Heritage, 2014.

Pesch, Rudolf. *Das Markusevangelium.* 2 vols. HThKNT 2. Freiburg: Herder, 1976–77.

Peterson, Robert A. *Salvation Accomplished by the Son: The Work of Christ.* Wheaton: Crossway, 2012.

———. "Union with Christ in the Gospel of John." *Presb* 39 (2013): 9–29.

Pfann, Stephen J., et al., eds. *Qumran Cave 4.XXVI: Cryptic Texts and Miscellanea, Part 1.* DJD 36. Oxford: Clarendon, 2000.

Phillips, Richard D. *John.* 2 vols. REC. Phillipsburg, NJ: P&R, 2014.

Pickup, Martin. "'On the Third Day': The Time Frame of Jesus' Death and Resurrection." *JETS* 56 (2013): 511–42.

Postell, Seth D. *Adam as Israel: Genesis 1–3 as the Introduction of the Torah and Tanakh.* Eugene, OR: Wipf & Stock, 2011.

Powell, Mark Allan. "The Plots and Subplots of Matthew's Gospel." *NTS* 38 (1992): 187–204.

———. *What Is Narrative Criticism?* GBSNT. Minneapolis: Fortress, 1990.

Pratt, Richard L., Jr. *He Gave Us Stories: The Bible Student's Guide to Interpreting Old Testament Narrative.* Phillipsburg, NJ: P&R, 1990.

Presley, Stephen O. *The Intertextual Reception of Genesis 1–3 in Irenaeus of Lyons.* BibAnChr 8. Leiden: Brill, 2015.

———. "The Lost Sheep Who Is Found: Irenaeus' Intertextual Reading of Genesis 3 in *Adversus Haereses* III 23.1–8." *StPatr* 52 (2010): 47–59.

Przybylski, Benno. *Righteousness in Matthew and in His World of Thought.* SNTSMS 41. Cambridge: Cambridge University Press, 1981.

Quarles, Charles L. *Sermon on the Mount: Restoring Christ's Message to the Modern Church.* NACSBT 11. Nashville: Broadman & Holman, 2011.

Rad, Gerhard von. *Genesis: A Commentary.* Translated by John H. Marks. Rev. ed. OTL. Philadelphia: Westminster, 1972.

Rainbow, Paul A. *Johannine Theology: The Gospel, the Epistles and the Apocalypse.* Downers Grove, IL: IVP Academic, 2014.

Ratzinger, Joseph [Pope Benedict XVI]. *Jesus of Nazareth: From the Baptism in the Jordan to the Transfiguration.* Translated by Adrian J. Walker. London: Bloomsbury, 2007.

Richardson, Alan. *The Gospel according to St. John.* TBC. London: SCM, 1959.

Ridderbos, Herman N. *The Coming of the Kingdom.* Translated by H. de Jongste. Edited by Raymond O. Zorn. Philadelphia: P&R, 1962.

———. *The Gospel of John: A Theological Commentary*. Translated by John Vriend. Grand Rapids: Eerdmans, 1997.

———. *Redemptive History and the New Testament Scriptures*. Translated by H. de Jongste. Revised by Richard B. Gaffin Jr. Phillipsburg, NJ: P&R, 1988.

Riedl, Johannes. *Das Heilswerk Jesu nach Johannes*. FTS 93. Freiburg: Herder, 1973.

Robertson, O. Palmer. *The Flow of the Psalms: Discovering Their Structure and Theology*. Phillipsburg, NJ: P&R, 2015.

Rowe, C. Kavin. *Early Narrative Christology: The Lord in the Gospel of Luke*. BZNW 139. 2006. Reprint, Grand Rapids: Baker Academic, 2009.

———. *World Upside Down: Reading Acts in the Graeco-Roman Age*. Oxford: Oxford University Press, 2009.

Royse, James R. *Scribal Habits in Early Greek New Testament Papyri*. NTTSD 36. Leiden: Brill, 2008.

Rubin, Nissan, and Admiel Kossman. "The Clothing of the Primordial Adam as a Symbol of Apocalyptic Time in Midrashic Sources." *HTR* 90 (1997): 155–70.

Sahlin, Harald. "Adam-Christologie im Neuen Testament." *ST* 41 (1987): 11–32.

Scaer, Peter J. "Lukan Christology: Jesus as Beautiful Savior." *CTQ* 69 (2005): 63–74.

Schlatter, Adolf. *Das Evangelium des Lukas: Aus seinen Quellen erklärt*. 2nd ed. Stuttgart: Calwer, 1960.

———. *Der Evangelist Matthäus: Seine Sprache, sein Ziel, seine Selbständigkeit*. Stuttgart: Calwer, 1929.

———. *The History of the Christ: The Foundation for New Testament Theology*. Translated by Andreas J. Köstenberger. Grand Rapids: Baker, 1997.

———. "The Theology of the New Testament and Dogmatics." In *The Nature of New Testament Theology: The Contribution of William Wrede and Adolf Schlatter*, edited and translated with introduction by Robert Morgan, 117–66. SBT 2/25. Naperville, IL: Allenson, 1973.

Schnabel, Eckhard. *Acts*. ZECNT. Grand Rapids: Zondervan, 2012.

———. "The Muratorian Fragment: The State of Research." *JETS* 57 (2014): 231–64.

Schramm, Christian. "Paradiesische Reminiszenz(en) in Mk 1,13?! Der Streit um die Adam-Christus-Typologie auf dem hermeneutischen Prüfstand." In *Theologies of Creation in Early Judaism and Ancient Christianity: In Honour of Hans Klein*, edited by Tobias Nicklas and Korinna Zamfir, 267–98. DCLS 6. Berlin: Walter de Gruyter, 2010.

Schreiner, Thomas R. *New Testament Theology: Magnifying God in Christ*. Grand Rapids: Baker Academic, 2008.

Schröter, Jens. *From Jesus to the New Testament*. Translated by Wayne Coppins. BMSEC. Waco: Baylor University Press, 2013.

Schweitzer, Albert. *The Quest of the Historical Jesus: A Critical Study of Its Progress from Reimarus to Wrede*. Translated by W. Montgomery. New York: MacMillan, 1968.

Scroggs, Robin. *The Last Adam: A Study in Pauline Anthropology*. Philadelphia: Fortress, 1966.

Seccombe, David. "Luke and Isaiah." *NTS* 27 (1981): 252–59.

Seifrid, Mark A. *Christ, Our Righteousness: Paul's Theology of Justification*. NSBT 9. Downers Grove, IL: InterVarsity, 2000.

Sharpe, John L., III. "The Second Adam in the Apocalypse of Moses." *CBQ* 35 (1973): 35–46.

Shively, Elizabeth E. *Apocalyptic Imagination in the Gospel of Mark: The Literary and Theological Role of Mark 3:22–30*. BZNW 189. Berlin: Walter de Gruyter, 2012.

Simonetti, Manlio, ed. *Matthew 1–13*. ACCS 1a. Downers Grove, IL: IVP Academic, 2001.

———, ed. *Matthew 14–28*. ACCS 1b. Downers Grove, IL: IVP Academic, 2002.

Skarsaune, Oskar. "The Ebionites." In *Jewish Believers in Jesus: The Early Centuries*, edited by Oskar Skarsaune and Reidar Hvalvik, 419–62. Peabody, MA: Hendrickson, 2007.

———. "Fragments of Jewish Christian Literature Quoted in Some Greek and Latin Fathers." In *Jewish Believers in Jesus: The Early Centuries*, edited by Oskar Skarsaune and Reidar Hvalvik, 325–78. Peabody, MA: Hendrickson, 2007.

———. *The Proof from Prophecy: A Study in Justin Martyr's Proof-Text Tradition: Text-Type, Provenance, Theological Profile*. NovTSup 56. Leiden: Brill, 1987.

Sklar, Jay. *Leviticus: An Introduction and Commentary*. TOTC 3. Downers Grove, IL: IVP Academic, 2014.

———. "Sin and Impurity: Atoned or Purified? Yes!" In *Perspectives on Purity and Purification in the Bible*, edited by Baruch J. Schwartz et al., 18–31. LHBOTS 474. New York: T&T Clark, 2008.

Sloan, David B. "Interpreting Scripture with Satan? The Devil's Use of Scripture in Luke's Temptation Narrative." *TynBul* 66 (2015): 231–50.

Snodgrass, Klyne R. *Stories with Intent: A Comprehensive Guide to the Parables of Jesus*. Grand Rapids: Eerdmans, 2008.

Söding, Thomas. "Der Gehorsam des Gottessohne: Zur Christologie der matthäischen Versuchungserzählung (4,1–11)." In *Jesus Christus als die Mitte der Schrift*, edited by Christof Landmesser, Hans-Joachim Eckstein, and Hermann Lichtenberger, 711–50. BZNW 86. Berlin: Walter de Gruyter, 1997.

Stanton, Graham N. Foreword to *What Are the Gospels? A Comparison with Graeco-Roman Biography*, by Richard A. Burridge. 2nd ed. BRS. Grand Rapids: Eerdmans, 2004.

———. "The Fourfold Gospel." *NTS* 43 (1997): 317–46.

———. *A Gospel for a New People: Studies in Matthew*. Edinburgh: T&T Clark, 1992.

———. *Jesus of Nazareth in New Testament Preaching*. SNTSMS 27. Cambridge: Cambridge University Press, 1974.

Stein, Robert H. *Mark*. BECNT. Grand Rapids: Baker Academic, 2008.

Steiner, Martin. *La tentation de Jésus dans l'interprétation patristique de Saint Justin a Origène*. Paris: Librairie Lecoffre, 1962.

Stenschke, Christoph. "The Apostles' Creed, the God of Israel and the Jew Jesus of Nazareth." *EuroJTh* 22 (2013): 110–23.

Stonehouse, Ned B. *Origins of the Synoptic Gospels: Some Basic Questions*. London: Tyndale Press, 1964.

———. *The Witness of Matthew and Mark to Christ*. Grand Rapids: Eerdmans, 1958.

Stott, John R. W. *The Message of the Sermon on the Mount*. BST. Downers Grove, IL: InterVarsity, 1978.

Strack, Hermann L., and Paul Billerbeck. *Kommentar zum Neuen Testament aus Talmud und Midrasch*. 6 vols. Munich: C. H. Beck, 1922–61.

Strauss, Mark L. *The Davidic Messiah in Luke-Acts: The Promise and Its Fulfillment in Lukan Christology*. JSNTSup 110. Sheffield: Sheffield Academic, 1995.

———. *Four Portraits, One Jesus: A Survey of Jesus and the Gospels*. Grand Rapids: Zondervan, 2007.

Strecker, Georg. *Der Weg der Gerechtigkeit: Untersuchung zur Theologie des Matthäus*. FRLANT 82. Göttingen: Vandenhoeck & Ruprecht, 1962.

Strimple, Robert B. *The Modern Search for the Real Jesus: An Introductory Survey of the Historical Roots of Gospels Criticism*. Phillipsburg, NJ: P&R, 1995.

Stuart, Douglas J. *Hosea–Jonah*. WBC 31. Waco: Word, 1987.

Stuhlmacher, Peter. "Isaiah 53 in the Gospels and Acts." In *The Suffering Servant: Isaiah 53 in Jewish and Christian Sources*, edited by Bernd Janowski and Peter Stuhlmacher, translated by Daniel P. Bailey, 147–62. Grand Rapids: Eerdmans, 2004.

Taylor, Vincent. *The Life and Ministry of Jesus*. Nashville: Abingdon, 1955.

Thiselton, Anthony C. *The Thiselton Companion to Christian Theology*. Grand Rapids: Eerdmans, 2015.

Thompson, Alan J. *The Acts of the Risen Lord Jesus: Luke's Account of God's Unfolding Plan*. NSBT 27. Downers Grove, IL: IVP Academic, 2011.

———. "The Trinity in Luke-Acts." In *The Essential Trinity: New Testament Foundations and Practical Relevance*, edited by Brandon D. Crowe and Carl R. Trueman, 62–82. London: Apollos, 2016.

Toepel, Alexander. "The Cave of Treasures: A New Translation and Introduction." In *Old Testament Pseudepigrapha: More Noncanonical Scriptures*, vol. 1, edited by Richard Bauckham, James R. Davila, and Alexander Panayotov, 531–84. Grand Rapids: Eerdmans, 2013.

Torgerson, Heidi. "The Healing of the Bent Woman: A Narrative Interpretation of Luke 13:10–17." *CurTM* 32 (2005): 176–86.

Torrance, T. F. *Incarnation: The Person and Life of Christ*. Edited by Robert T. Walker. Downers Grove, IL: IVP Academic, 2008.

Turretin, Francis. *Institutes of Elenctic Theology*. Translated by George Musgrave Giger. Edited by James T. Dennison Jr. 3 vols. Phillipsburg, NJ: P&R, 1992–97.

Van Maaren, John. "The Adam-Christ Typology in Paul and Its Development in the Early Church Fathers." *TynBul* 64 (2013): 275–97.

Verheyden, Joseph. "The Canon Muratori: A Matter of Dispute." In *The Biblical Canons*, edited by Jean-Marie Auwers and H. J. de Jonge, 487–556. Leuven: Leuven University Press, 2003.

Vollenweider, Samuel. "'Ich sah den Satan wie einen Blitz vom Himmel fallen' (Lk 10,18)." *ZNW* 79 (1988): 187–203.

Vos, Geerhardus. *Biblical Theology: Old and New Testaments*. 1948. Reprint, Edinburgh: Banner of Truth, 1975.

———. "The Eschatological Aspect of the Pauline Conception of the Spirit." In *Redemptive History and Biblical Interpretation: The Shorter Writings of Geerhardus Vos*, edited by Richard B. Gaffin Jr., 91–125. Phillipsburg, NJ: P&R, 1980.

———. *Grace and Glory: Sermons Preached in the Chapel of Princeton Theological Seminary*. Edinburgh: Banner of Truth, 1994.

———. "The Idea of Biblical Theology as a Science and as a Theological Discipline." In *Redemptive History and Biblical Interpretation: The Shorter Writings of Geerhardus Vos*, edited by Richard B. Gaffin Jr., 3–24. Phillipsburg, NJ: P&R, 1980.

———. *The Pauline Eschatology*. 1930. Reprint, Grand Rapids: Baker, 1979.

———. "The Range of the Logos Title in the Prologue to the Fourth Gospel." In *Redemptive History and Biblical Interpretation: The Shorter Writings of Geerhardus Vos*, edited by Richard B. Gaffin Jr., 59–90. Phillipsburg, NJ: P&R, 1980.

———. *Reformed Dogmatics*. Edited and translated by Richard B. Gaffin Jr. 5 vols. Bellingham, WA: Lexham Press, 2012–16.

———. "The Scriptural Doctrine of the Love of God." *PRR* 13 (1902): 1–37.

———. *The Self-Disclosure of Jesus: The Modern Debate about the Messianic Consciousness*. Edited by Johannes G. Vos. 2nd ed. 1953. Reprint, Phillipsburg, NJ: P&R, 2002.

Vouga, François. *Une théologie du Nouveau Testament*. MdB 43. Geneva: Labor et Fides, 2001.

Waltke, Bruce K., with Cathi J. Fredricks. *Genesis: A Commentary*. Grand Rapids: Zondervan, 2001.

Waltke, Bruce K., and Michael O'Connor. *An Introduction to Biblical Hebrew Syntax*. Winona Lake, IN: Eisenbrauns, 1990.

Waltke, Bruce K., with Charles Yu. *An Old Testament Theology: An Exegetical, Canonical, and Thematic Approach*. Grand Rapids: Zondervan, 2007.

Watts, John D. W. *Isaiah 34–66*. Rev. ed. WBC 25. Nashville: Thomas Nelson, 2005.

Watts, Rikk E. "Mark." In *Commentary on the New Testament Use of the Old Testament*, edited by G. K. Beale and D. A. Carson, 111–249. Grand Rapids: Baker Academic, 2007.

Wenham, Gordon J. *Genesis 1–15*. WBC 1. Waco: Word, 1987.

Wilken, Robert Louis. "St. Cyril of Alexandria: The Mystery of Christ in the Bible." *ProEccl* 4 (1995): 454–78.

Williamson, H. G. M. *Variations on a Theme: King, Messiah and Servant in the Book of Isaiah*. Carlisle: Paternoster, 1998.

Wise, Michael, Martin Abegg Jr., and Edward Cook. *The Dead Sea Scrolls: A New Translation*. Rev. ed. New York: HarperOne, 2005.

Wolff, Hans Walter. *Hosea: A Commentary on the Book of the Prophet Hosea*. Translated by Gary Stansell. Hermeneia. Philadelphia: Fortress, 1974.

Wright, Christopher J. H. *Deuteronomy*. NIBCOT 5. Peabody, MA: Hendrickson, 1996.

Wright, N. T. *The Climax of the Covenant: Christ and the Law in Pauline Theology*. Minneapolis: Fortress, 1992.

———. *How God Became King: The Forgotten Story of the Gospels*. San Francisco: HarperOne, 2012.

———. *Jesus and the Victory of God*. COQG 2. Minneapolis: Fortress, 1996.

———. *Justification: God's Plan and Paul's Vision*. London: SPCK, 2009.

———. *The New Testament and the People of God*. COQG 1. Minneapolis: Fortress, 1992.

———. *Paul and the Faithfulness of God*. COQG 4. Minneapolis: Fortress, 2013.

———. *The Resurrection of the Son of God*. COQG 3. Minneapolis: Fortress, 2003.

Wright, R. B. "*Psalms of Solomon*." In vol. 2 of *Old Testament Pseudepigrapha*, edited by James H. Charlesworth, 639–70. ABRL. New York: Doubleday, 1985.

Würthwein, Ernst. *The Text of the Old Testament: An Introduction to the Biblia Hebraica*. Translated by Erroll F. Rhodes. 2nd ed. Grand Rapids: Eerdmans, 1995.

Zimmerli, Walther, and Joachim Jeremias. *The Servant of God*. Rev. ed. SBT 20. London: SCM, 1965.

Scripture and Ancient Writings Index

Author Index

Subject Index

as prophet, 3, 5, 108–10, 154–62, 179–83,
    209–10
salvation and union with, 130–33
as Savior, 33, 163, 180n25, 205, 213, 215
transfiguration, 42, 49–50, 102
virgin birth. *See* Jesus Christ: conception and
    birth
John the Baptist, 31, 68–69, 73, 88, 116, 128,
    134, 140n2, 148, 149n33, 155

Korah, 47

Moses, 62–63, 94, 96, 98, 121–22, 126, 167,
    189, 208
Muratorian Fragment, 14n69

Passion narratives, 1–2, 6–7, 12–17, 71, 112,
    114, 134–35, 174
Pharisees, 92, 96, 105–7, 134, 141–42, 172–78,
    215
preaching, 3, 6, 13–14, 72, 103, 107–10, 140n2,
    146, 147n29, 165, 167, 209

regula fidei. See rule of faith
Rome, 147, 196, 207
rule of faith, 21n108, 203–4

Sabbath, 36–37, 44–45, 61, 104–5, 120, 125,
    129, 155, 168, 172, 178n20
Samaria, Samaritans, 127–28, 179–83
Sermon on the Mount, 87, 89–93, 173, 175–76
Solomon, 64, 208, 209n30

temple, 45n101, 64–65, 68, 77, 94n39, 95, 97,
    134, 168, 209n30

virgin birth. *See* Jesus Christ: conception and
    birth

Westminster Confession of Faith and Cate-
    chisms, 61n27, 203n8, 204n18, 206, 212n42,
    212n43, 212n44, 214n51